Toward an Interpretation of the Book of Proverbs

Journal of Theological Interpretation Supplements

MURRAY RAE
University of Otago, New Zealand
Editor-in-Chief

1. Thomas Holsinger-Friesen, *Irenaeus and Genesis: A Study of Competition in Early Christian Hermeneutics*
2. Douglas S. Earl, *Reading Joshua as Christian Scripture*
3. Joshua N. Moon, *Jeremiah's New Covenant: An Augustinian Reading*
4. Csilla Saysell, *"According to the Law": Reading Ezra 9–10 as Christian Scripture*
5. Joshua Marshall Strahan, *The Limits of a Text: Luke 23:34a as a Case Study in Theological Interpretation*
6. Seth B. Tarrer, *Reading with the Faithful: Interpretation of True and False Prophecy in the Book of Jeremiah from Ancient Times to Modern*
7. Zoltán S. Schwáb, *Toward an Interpretation of the Book of Proverbs: Selfishness and Secularity Reconsidered*

Toward an Interpretation of the Book of Proverbs

Selfishness and Secularity Reconsidered

Zoltán S. Schwáb

Winona Lake, Indiana
Eisenbrauns
2013

Copyright © 2013 Eisenbrauns
All rights reserved.

Printed in the United States of America

www.eisenbrauns.com

Library of Congress Cataloging-in-Publication Data

Schwáb, Zoltán S.
　Toward an interpretation of the book of Proverbs : selfishness and secularity reconsidered / by Zoltán S. Schwáb.
　　　page　cm. -- (Journal of theological interpretation supplements ; 7)
　Includes bibliographical references and index.
　ISBN 978-1-57506-707-0 (pbk. : alk. paper)
　1. Bible. O.T. Proverbs—Criticism, interpretation, etc.　I. Title.
　BS1465.52.S39　2013
　223′.706—dc23
　　　　　　　　　　　　　　　　　　　　　　　　　　2013014018

The paper used in this publication meets the minimum requirements of the American National Standard for Information Sciences—Permanence of Paper for Printed Library Materials, ANSI Z39.48-1984.♾™

Table of Contents

Acknowledgements	viii
Abbreviations	x
Introduction	1

PART I
THEOLOGICAL INTERPRETATION OF PROVERBS IN THE LAST TWO HUNDRED YEARS

1 Theological Interpretation of Proverbs between 1800 and 1930		4
1.1	Introduction	4
1.2	Was Proverbs Neglected before the '30s?	5
1.3	An Inventory of Theological Topics	9
1.4	Development or Decline of Israelite Religion?	21
1.5	Conclusions	27
2 Theological Interpretation of Proverbs between 1930 and Today		30
2.1	The Place of Wisdom Theology in the Old Testament	31
2.2	The Definition of Wisdom Theology	43
3 Finding a Way Forward		62
3.1	Order	63
3.2	Creation	64
3.3	What is Distinctive about Wisdom Literature Then?	66
3.4	A Brief Justification of My Questions	67

PART II
METHODOLOGY: A CANONICAL APPROACH

4 A Canonical Approach — 72
    4.1 Introduction: A Preliminary Description — 72
    4.2 My Understanding of 'Canonical Interpretation' — 73
    4.3 Reasons for Applying a Canonical Approach — 75

5 A Canonical Approach and Proverbs — 78
    5.1 The Challenge of Proverbs' Canonical Interpretation — 78
    5.2 The Canonical Significance of Proverbs 1–9 — 82
    5.3 Summary — 85

PART III
DOES PROVERBS PROMOTE SELFISHNESS?

6 A Call for a Thomistic Reading — 88
    6.1 Proverbs: A Selfish Book? — 88
    6.2 Proverbs' Eudaemonism: A Neglected Problem — 91
    6.3 Thomistic Moral Theology — 94

7 Is Proverbs More Self-Interested than the Rest of the Bible? — 100
    7.1 Self-Interest in Proverbs and Deuteronomy — 101
    7.2 Summary — 108

8 Is Proverbs Solely about Material Success? — 110
    8.1 Self-Preservation — 110
    8.2 Honour — 115
    8.3 'Better than Riches' — 117
    8.4 Summary — 126

9 Is God the Highest End in Proverbs? — 128
    9.1 What Does It Mean That God Is the Highest End? — 128
    9.2 Proverbs 2: Its Significance and Translation — 129
    9.3 Does Proverbs 2 Speak about a God-Centred Thinking? — 132
    9.4 Is Proverbs against Serving God for the Benefits of It? — 151
    9.5 Conclusions — 157

PART IV
'THE SECULAR' IN PROVERBS

10 The Meaning of 'Secular' — 162
- 10.1 The Meaning of 'Secular' in General Academic Discourse — 162
- 10.2 The Meaning of 'Secular' in Biblical Scholarship — 164

11 Secular (Universal) vs. National (Particular) I — 175
- 11.1 Proverbs and the Common Language of Humanity — 175
- 11.2 Proverbs 8 as Theological Vision — 177
- 11.3 Summary — 188

12 Secular (Universal) vs. National (Particular) II — 190
- 12.1 The Temple as Theological Vision — 190
- 12.2 Temple, Universe, and Wisdom in the Ancient Near East — 191
- 12.3 Temple, Universe, and Wisdom in the Old Testament — 194
- 12.4 Temple, Universe, and Wisdom in Proverbs — 198
- 12.5 Proverbs' 'Temple-Interpretation' in Canonical Context — 202
- 12.6 Summary: The Solomonic Temple and Proverbs — 208
- 12.7 Conclusions — 209

13 A 'Post-Secular' Interpretation of Proverbs: The Hidden God — 213
- 13.1 Walter Brueggemann's Interpretation of Proverbs — 213
- 13.2 Preliminary Evaluation of Brueggemann's Interpretation — 218
- 13.3 Evaluation of Brueggemann's Interpretation — 220
- 13.4 Wisdom Is Ungraspable in its Fullness — 234
- 13.5 Summary — 239

14 Conclusions — 241
- 14.1 Lessons from the History of Interpretation — 241
- 14.2 Self-Interest and the Secular — 242
- 14.3 A Non-Kantian Reading — 244
- 14.4 Methodological Considerations: A Canonical Reading — 247

Bibliography — 250

Index of Subjects and Authors — 288

Index of Scripture — 306

Acknowledgements

Reading the acknowledgements in the beginning of scholarly works often reminds me that it is the nature of such achievements that, beside the author, many people contribute to them. Yet, it took me writing 'my own' book to recognise the extent of this contribution and how misleading it is to call the book 'my own.'

This manuscript is a revised version of my PhD thesis. Without the generous financial help of some of my friends I would have found it much more difficult to embark on this research. I am also grateful to the Langham Trust for offering me a scholarship and providing academic and spiritual support throughout my PhD studies.

I could not have wished for a better PhD supervisor than Prof. Walter Moberly. I was constantly impressed by the time and attention he paid to my work and by the wisdom with which he provided me freedom to follow my own ideas and at the same time gave me gentle guidance towards becoming a better scholar.

I am also thankful for the encouragement and helpful comments of my PhD examiners, Prof. Robert Hayward and Dr. Katharine Dell.

I was aided by the expertise of many other people at the Theology Department of Durham University. I am especially grateful for the conversations (and friendly debates) with Dr. Stuart Weeks, my secondary supervisor, that always made me even more passionate about biblical wisdom literature. I am also indebted to Dr. Christopher Insole for reading through and commenting on some of my sections on Thomas Aquinas.

This work would be a much poorer writing without the help of my friends. First of all, the support of Dr. Julie Woods included such diverse things as showing me where the vegetable shop is in town and reading through and polishing the English and the logic of an earlier version of this work. She is a model both in friendship and in academic precision. Dr. Charlie Shepherd not only shares my fascination with secret underground tunnels, but I also know few others with whom one could have such exciting conversations in the cafes and badly lit pubs of Durham about Immanuel Kant, hermeneutics, and the absurdity of life. One of those 'few others' is Dr. Andrea Dalton Saner, whose passion for theology is very refreshing and inspirational. I am especially grateful to her for reading through the (almost) final version of this work and saving me from many mistakes by her insightful comments.

I am also thankful to Dr. Murray Rae and Jim Eisenbraun for guiding my manuscript through to actual publication as smoothly as possible.

However, my biggest thanks have to go to my wife, Kati: adviser, proofreader, organiser, emotional and financial supporter, company in good and bad times, and even much more than that. It is a humbling recognition that, although it is my name that is printed on the cover of the book, it was not me who worked the hardest for it or who made the biggest sacrifices for it. Without the help of others this work would look different, but without her help it would not have been written at all.

Abbreviations

Journals, Monograph Series

AB	The Anchor Bible
ACCS/OT	Ancient Christian Commentary on Scripture, Old Testament
AOTC	Abingdon Old Testament Commentaries
ApOTC	Apollos Old Testament Commentary
AT	Arbeiten zur Theologie
ATD	Das Alte Testament Deutsch
ATSAT	Arbeiten zu Text und Sprache im Alten Testament
BETL	Bibliotheca Ephemeridum Theologicarum Lovaniensium
BHT	Beiträge zur Historischen Theologie
BIS	Biblical Interpretation Series
BL	Biblical Limits
BLH	Biblical Languages: Hebrew
BLS	Bible and Literature Series
BN	*Biblische Notizen*
BNTC	Black's New Testament Commentaries
BS	*Bibliotheca Sacra*
BTB	*Biblical Theology Bulletin*
BTCB	Brazos Theological Commentary on the Bible
BWANT	Beihefte zur Wissenschaft vom Alten und Neuen Testament
BZ	*Biblische Zeitschrift*
BZAW	Beihefte zur Zeitschrift für die alttestamentliche Wissenschaft
BZe	Biblische Zeitfragen
CAS	Clarendon Aristotle Series
CBC	The Cambridge Bible Commentary
CBOTS	Coniectanea Biblica Old Testament Series
CBQ	*Catholic Biblical Quarterly*
CBQMS	The Catholic Biblical Quarterly Monograph Series
CEWIK	The Cambridge Edition of the Works of Immanuel Kant

CFTL	Clark's Foreign Theological Library
CRT	*Conversations in Religion & Theology*
CSPR	Cornell Studies in the Philosophy of Religion
EBC	*Expositor's Bible Commentary*
EC	Epworth Commentaries
ET	*Evangelische Theologie*
ETCSL	*The Electronic Text Corpus of Sumerian Literature*
FAT	Forschungen zum Alten Testament
FB	Forschungen zur Bibel
FOTL	The Forms of the Old Testament Literature
FRLANT	Forschungen zur Religion und Literatur des Alten und Neuen Testaments
HAT	Handkommentar zum Alten Testament
HBT	Horizons in Biblical Theology
HCOT	Historical Commentary on the Old Testament
HS	*Hebrew Studies*
HTR	*Harvard Theological Review*
HUCA	*Hebrew Union College Annual*
IB	*The Interpreter's Bible*
ICC	The International Critical Commentary
IRT	Issues in Religion and Theology
ITC	International Theological Commentary
ITL	International Theological Library
JAAR	*Journal of the American Academy of Religion*
JANESCU	*Journal of Ancient Near Eastern Society of Columbia University*
JBL	*Journal of Biblical Literature*
JBR	*Journal of Bible and Religion*
JETS	*Journal of the Evangelical Theological Society*
JQR	*The Jewish Quarterly Review*
JR	*Journal of Religion*
JRS	Journal of Religion Supplement
JRE	*Journal of Religious Ethics*
JSOT	*Journal for the Study of the Old Testament*
JSOTSS	Journal for the Study of the Old Testament Supplement Series
JTS	*Journal of Theological Studies*
KAT	Kommentar zum Alten Testament
KEHAT	Kurzgefastes exegetisches Handbuch zum Alten Testament
KKANT	Kurzgefasster Kommentar zu den heiligen Schriften Alten und Neuen Testaments
LCL	The Loeb Classical Library
LSAWS	Linguistic Studies in Ancient West Semitic
LUÅ	Lunds Universitets Årsskrift
MT	*Modern Theology*

NCBC	New Century Bible Commentary
NFT	New French Thought
NIBC	New International Biblical Commentary
NICNT	The New International Commentary on the New Testament
NICOT	The New International Commentary on the Old Testament
NIDOTTE	New International Dictionary of Old Testament Theology and Exegesis
NIGTC	The New International Greek Testament Commentary
NSBT	New Studies in Biblical Theology
OBO	Orbis Biblicus et Orientalis
OSHT	Oxford Studies in Historical Theology
OTG	Old Testament Guides
OTL	The Old Testament Library
OTS	*The Old Testament Student*
OTSt	Old Testament Studies
RB	*Revue Biblique*
RE	*Review and Expositor*
SB	Stuttgarter Bibelstudien
SBLDS	Society of Biblical Literature Dissertation Series
SBLMS	Society of Biblical Literature Monograph Series
SBLRBS	Society of Biblical Literature Resources for Biblical Study
SBLSS	Society of Biblical Literature Symposium Series
SBT	Studies in Biblical Theology
SEÅ	*Svensk Exegetisk Årsbok*
SH	Scripta Hierosolymitana
SHBC	Smyth & Helwys Bible Commentary
SJT	*Scottish Journal of Theology*
SJSJ	Supplements to the Journal for the Study of Judaism
SOTSM	Society for Old Testament Study Monographs
ST	*Studia Theologica*
STI	Studies in Theological Interpretation
SVSGTR	Sammlung gemeinverständlicher Vorträge und Schriften aus dem Gebiet der Theologie und Religionsgeschichte
SVT	Supplements to Vetus Testamentum
SWBAS	The Social World of Biblical Antiquity Series
TB	*Tyndale Bulletin*
TBC	Torch Bible Commentaries
TBS	Tools for Biblical Study
TDCH	*The Dictionary of Classical Hebrew*
TDOT	*Theological Dictionary of the Old Testament*
THB	Theologisch-homiletisches Bibelwerk
TJ	*Trinity Journal*
TLOT	*Theological Lexicon of the Old Testament*

TOTC	Tyndale Old Testament Commentaries
TS	*Theological Studies*
TT	*Theology Today*
TZ	*Theologische Zeitschrift*
VT	*Vetus Testamentum*
WBC	Word Biblical Commentary
WeBC	Westminster Bible Companion
WEP	*West European Politics*
WMANT	Wissenschaftliche Monographien zum Alten und Neuen Testament
YJS	Yale Judaica Series
ZAW	*Zeitschrift für die Alttestamentliche Wissenschaft*
ZB	Zürcher Bibelkommentare
ZTK	*Zeitschrift für Theologie und Kirche*

Sigla for Textual Witnesses

BHQ	*Biblia Hebraica Quinta*, Jan de Waard, *Proverbs* (Stuttgart: Deutsche Bibelgesellschaft, 2008)
BHS	Elliger and Rudolph (eds.), *Biblia Hebraica Stuttgartensia* (Stuttgart: Deutsche Bibelgesellschaft, 1977)
LXX	Septuagint, as it is found in Alfred Rahlfs, *Septuaginta* (Stuttgart: Deutsche Bibelgesellschaft, 1979)
MT	Masoretic Text, as it is found in *BHS*
Syr.	Syriac Version (Peshitta)
Targ.	Targum
Vulg.	Vulgate
α'	Aquila
ε'	Quinta
θ'	Theodotion
σ'	Symmachus

Bible Translations

ASV	American Standard Version, 1901, Star Bible & Tract Corp.
ESV	English Standard Version, Copyright © 2001, 2007 Crossway Bibles, a division of Good News Publishers
KJV	1769 Blayney Edition of the 1611 King James Version of the English Bible
NAB	New American Bible, Copyright © 1991, 1986, 1970, The Confraternity of Christian Doctrine
NAS	New American Standard Bible, Copyright © 1986, The Lockman Foundation

NJB	New Jerusalem Bible, Copyright © 1985, Darton, Longman & Todd Ltd. and Doubleday
NKJ	The New King James Version, Copyright © 1982, Thomas Nelson
NRSV	New Revised Standard Version, Copyright © 1989, Division of Christian Education of the National Council of the Churches of Christ in the United States of America
TNIV	Today's New International Version, Copyright © 2005, Zondervan

Abbreviations of the Works of Thomas Aquinas

Summa Theologiae

Quotations are always taken from St Thomas Aquinas, *Summa Theologiae, Latin text and English translation, Introductions, Notes, Appendices and Glossaries* (London–New York: Blackfriars, 1963–1981).

When referring to the translator's comments or footnotes to a certain article in Thomas's text, the volume, page number, and the year of publication of the given volume of the aforementioned edition is given in a footnote.

Summa Theologiae is abbreviated as *ST*. When referring to the main text, the parts are given in Roman numerals (so *Prima pars* is 'I'; *Prima Secundae* is 'I–II'; *Secunda Secundae* is 'II–II'; *Tertia pars* is 'III'). The numeral for the part is followed by the question and article in Arabic numerals. Thus, '*ST* I, 63, 1' stands for '*Summa Theologiae, Prima pars*, 63rd question, 1st article.' Reference to an answer of Thomas to a particular objection is in the format of 'ad x' where 'x' is the numeral for the objection in question. Thus, '*ST* I–II, 91, 3, ad 2' stands for '*Summa Theologiae, Prima Secundae*, 91st question, 3rd article, answer to 2nd objection.'

Summa Contra Gentiles

Quotations are always taken from Thomas Aquinas, *The Summa Contra Gentiles*, trans. the English Dominican Fathers (London: Burns Oates & Washbourne Ltd., 1928).

The title is abbreviated as *SCG*; the volume is given in Roman numerals; chapters are given in Arabic numerals. Thus, '*SCG*, III, 37' stands for '*Summa Contra Gentiles*, 3rd book, chapter 37.'

Compendium Theologiae

Quotations are always taken from Thomas Aquinas, *Compendium of Theology*, trans. Cyril Vollert, S.F., S.T.D. (Binghamton: B. Herder, 1947).

The title is abbreviated as *CT*; both the number of the treatise and article are given in Arabic numerals. Thus, '*CT*, 2, 246' stands for *Compendium Theologiae*, 2nd treatise, article 246.

Commentary on Aristotle's Physics

Quotations are always taken from St. Thomas Aquinas, *Commentary on Aristotle's Physics*, trans. Richard J. Blackwell, Richard J. Spath, and W. Edmund Thirlkel (London: Routledge & Kegan Paul, 1963).

The tile is abbreviated as *Com. Physics*; the book is given in Roman numerals; the lecture and paragraph are given in Arabic numerals. Thus, '*Com. Physics* II, 5, 176' stands for *Commentary on Aristotle's Physics*, second book, lecture 5, 176th paragraph.

Introduction

Where does the main inspiration for a biblical interpretation come from? Sometimes this is not easy to determine. Does the text itself furnish the interpretation? Do pre-existing readings hold sway? Or, do scholars bring their personal interests to the task of interpretation? All these factors are given consideration in this particular study.

I made the first decisive step in the direction represented by this work when I was reading nineteenth century interpretations of Proverbs. I saw how much scholars struggled with the ethical problem that Proverbs' motivational system appears to be based on self-interest. The book seems to teach that 'you should behave well *because*, if you do, it will be good *for you*.' I realised that I, too, had had an uneasy feeling about this feature of the book.

Encountering the problem of self-interest in nineteenth century scholarship led me to study more recent interpretations. While investigating how twentieth century scholarship addressed the issue, I realised that it was not considered to be a serious problem anymore. Interpreters seldom spent more than a few lines on the question, if they addressed it at all. They argued that the creation theology of Proverbs simply describes the order of the world, and this order means that if someone's behaviour is right then it will be beneficial for them—but it would be a mistake to call this order-description 'selfishness.' However, as I argue in this work, this twentieth century explanation is not entirely satisfying.

Investigating twentieth century interpretations of Proverbs drew my attention to another topic: 'the secular.' Between the '60s and the '80s in particular, many scholars discussed the secular nature of Proverbs. However, the discussion of the secular theme has also gone out of fashion since then. The category 'secular' was deemed anachronistic and it was said that Proverbs only *appears* to be secular. Although I was basically in agreement with these claims, the apparent secularity of the book prompted a theological question: whether the secular features of the book reflect some kind of secular thinking or whether they are just misleading illusions in the eyes of some modern readers, cannot these (apparent) features of Proverbs be utilised in a theological interpretation for a secular age?

These were the initial reasons why I chose two, once popular but now somewhat neglected problems, for constructing a theology of Proverbs: its apparent selfishness (a nineteenth century question) and its apparent secularity (a twentieth century question).

Although a monograph with a single focus will have a clearer structure than a monograph with two, there are reasons for combining these two subjects. My first reason is the simple recognition that discussing two of the many themes in the book of Proverbs leads to a deeper, more satisfying theological reading than discussing only one. Another reason for discussing both themes within a single study is that, as I hope to demonstrate, they lead to similar theological conclusions. This harmony might not initially be obvious to the reader but it will gradually emerge through the discussion and will ultimately be clarified in the conclusions.

The reader will also notice that the plurality of themes is accompanied by a plurality of disciplinary approaches. Pondering the themes of self-interest and the secular in Proverbs requires detours into contemporary sociology and philosophical theology, which are traditionally not discussed at length in biblical studies. It is recommended that the reader concentrate on the given subject under discussion, be it the medieval *eudaemonistic* theological ethics of Thomas Aquinas, the translation of Proverbs 2, or an evaluation of Brueggemann's interpretation of Proverbs, allowing the threads to be drawn together gradually.

Finally, a few words about the structure of this work are due. The discussion is comprised of four major parts. The main tenets of each part should be understandable even if they are read on their own. However, taken together they provide a more comprehensive theological reading of Proverbs. The first part is a relatively lengthy history of prior research, as the academic study of Proverbs in the last two hundred years has contributed significantly to forming my research questions. Because my methodology was partly a response to previous attempts to interpret Proverbs, I only clarify my (interdisciplinary, canonical) approach to Proverbs in the second part. These two initial parts take up about one third of this work. The remaining two thirds are devoted to the problems of Proverbs' apparent selfishness and its apparent secular nature.

PART I
THEOLOGICAL INTERPRETATION OF PROVERBS IN THE LAST TWO HUNDRED YEARS

1

Theological Interpretation of Proverbs between 1800 and 1930

1.1 Introduction

Critical biblical scholarship of the nineteenth century has often been characterised as neglecting wisdom literature. However, I argue that this in fact applies for a few decades of the twentieth, rather than the nineteenth, century. Before and after these few decades there was a rich scholarly discussion, which is too complex and voluminous to do full justice to it here. One has to be selective. As this work mainly deals with theological questions, the following introduction to the literature focuses on the same issues. Historical questions are discussed only where they have a significant impact on how certain theological problems were handled.

One peculiarity of the following discussion is that as historians speak about a 'long nineteenth century' lasting until the First World War, I speak about an even longer 'nineteenth century' which lasted until the early '30s. This is because, as I argue, a new phase of modern theological interpretation of Proverbs began in the '30s: that is when the idea of creation started to gain prominence.

Not only the 'nineteenth century' itself but also the discussion of it is somewhat longer than is usual in similar articles or chapters. This length is not only justified by the relative neglect of the period in discussions of the history of wisdom writings' interpretation.[1] Scholarship in the nineteenth century recognised by and large the same characteristics of Proverbs which were recognised by later interpreters, but it used somewhat different categories to handle them theologically. As someone learns much about his or her own language by learning

---

1. Two notable exceptions are Smend 1995 and Dell 2013. However, these papers concentrate mainly on historical questions.

a foreign one, it seems to be a valuable exercise to 'learn' these nineteenth century categories, even if some of them have gone out of fashion and been replaced by new ones since then. This will help us to see certain characteristics of our own theological categories more clearly. In fact, in the later sections of this work, a part of my argument is that some categories of the nineteenth century theological interpretations (like 'philosophy') do not do more injustice to the content and nature of Proverbs than those of the twentieth century (like 'creation theology').

1.2 Was Proverbs Neglected before the '30s?

James Crenshaw summarises the history of the research as follows:

> Wisdom literature can be labelled an orphan in the biblical household. Virtually ignored as an entity until the beginning of this century, 'wisdom' suffered the indignity of judgment by alien standards and the embarrassment of physical similarities to non-Israelite parents. In addition, she had a twin (Sirach and Wisdom of Solomon) who was in some circles even excluded from the privileged status of canonical authority, although none could deny her likeness to the more favored sister. . . . The negative assessment of wisdom arose because it was difficult if not impossible to fit her thought into the reigning theological system. The verdict of G. Ernest Wright represents the dominant position for several decades: 'The difficulty of the wisdom movement was that its theological base and interest were too narrowly fixed; and in this respect Proverbs remains near the pagan source of wisdom in which society and the Divine work in history played no real role.' . . . This verdict is substantiated by reference to an absence of (1) a covenant relationship with God, (2) any account of the revelation at Sinai, and (3) a concept of Israel's special election and consequently of Yahweh's saving deeds for his people. Instead, wisdom is said to be directed toward the individual, and consequently to break down all national limits.[2]

Although our immediate interest in this chapter is the interpretation of Proverbs before 1930, it is necessary to quote Crenshaw at length even where he writes about the history of interpretation after that time. What he writes about the more recent history also reveals how he understands earlier interpretation.

First of all, what Crenshaw actually says about the history of Proverbs' interpretation before the '30s needs to be clarified. The very beginning of this long quotation seems to be the most relevant in this respect. The first statement, that wisdom literature was 'virtually ignored' until the beginning of the twentieth century, is straightforward enough. Yet, what is the meaning of the phrase 'suffered the indignity of judgement by alien standards' right after this statement? What does 'alien standards' stand for? The only alien standard explicitly men-

---

2. Crenshaw 1976b: 1–2.

tioned in this text is that they wanted to measure wisdom literature as it relates to the historical acts of God (covenant, Sinai, election), that is, *Heilsgeschichte*, and wisdom literature was found wanting by this standard. However, Crenshaw uses this explicit reference to history only a few lines later, in connection with the middle of the twentieth century, the biblical theology movement, and not with the era before the twentieth century. Can it be that at the middle of the second sentence he suddenly moves on 50 years, in the first half of the sentence writing about the neglect of wisdom literature before the twentieth century, then suddenly introducing the causes for neglect well into the twentieth century? This would certainly be an awkward way of delineating the topic. If, however, the 'alien standards' in the second sentence refers to the nineteenth, and not (only) to the twentieth, century, then not giving the slightest hint of what these alien standards were would also be rather unusual. As a result of these considerations, I tend to believe that Crenshaw sees the lack of historical and national references in wisdom literature as one of the causes for its neglect not only in the twentieth century but also in previous times.

The above quotation is representative of many evaluations of the history of Proverbs' interpretation. It gives only a passing attention to the history before the twentieth century, and lists all the characteristics of Proverbs which are supposed to explain its neglect in the past: no interest in *Heilsgeschichte*, individualism, international character, etc. Murphy, for example, after listing the usual set of characteristics such as Proverbs' international character and its neglect of typical Yahwistic motives (Exodus, Sinai covenant), writes this:

> History bears out the 'benign neglect' of Proverbs.... One gets the impression from certain bench marks that it has served as little more than an 'enforcer' for moral guidance.... The tendency up into modern times has been to relegate the book somewhere behind the Torah as contributing to the ethical ideals of Israel.[3]

To give another example, Whybray, in his brief description of critical discussion before 1923 also seems to suggest that Proverbs was considered problematic in that period:

> An overriding problem for the discussions of the next half-century and more [1850-] was both a literary and a historical one: how the three books Proverbs, Job and Ecclesiastes which constituted the 'Wisdom literature of the Hebrews'... and which differed from the rest of the literature of the Old Testament in their 'philosophical' character and in the total absence of any specific concern with Israel and the Israelites, could be found a place in the history of Israelite thought and religion.[4]

---

3. Murphy 1986: 87-88.
4. Whybray 1995: 1.

However, as we will see, a more thorough look at the nineteenth century reveals a much more complex picture than the one we can find in Crenshaw's, Murphy's, and Whybray's short descriptions.[5]

To start with, it is not entirely clear that Proverbs was neglected. At least the major dictionaries around the turn of the century do not list fewer books and monographs in their bibliography for Proverbs than would be proportionately expected.[6] According to these bibliographies it was certainly not as popular among the scholars of the nineteenth century as Isaiah, Job, or Psalms, not to mention the main interest of critical scholarship, the Pentateuch; but it was by no means a neglected biblical book. Cornill, in his well structured introduction lists 19 works about Proverbs in his bibliography.[7] There are 17 biblical books or book-pairs whose bibliography is shorter, and 11 whose bibliography is longer.[8] However, many of these 11 items have only 20 or 21 books in their bibliography, so practically the same number as Proverbs.[9] The average number of books and articles listed in the *Encyclopedia Biblica*'s articles about biblical books is approximately 28.[10] Proverbs, however, has 58 items listed in its bibliography. Only Deuteronomy, Job, Psalms, and Jeremiah have more. The *Hastings Dictionary* contains 26 works in its bibliography about Proverbs, which almost reaches the average (approx. 29) of similar bibliographies for biblical books in the dictionary, thereby putting Proverbs somewhere in the middle of the range of biblical books in this respect.[11]

Of course, such statistics can be misleading. One bibliography in a dictionary can be more selective than another and the significance of the cited works can vary as well. Nevertheless, it is also telling that I have not come across any works from the nineteenth century that complained about how neglected Proverbs was in research. In fact, as we will see, some scholars were quite enthusiastic about the role Proverbs played in the history of Israelite religion. Thus, at first sight, it seems that Crenshaw's perception about the neglect of the book of Proverbs during the nineteenth century is mistaken.

---

5. More recent evaluations of wisdom literature's position in nineteenth century critical scholarship can be found in Bartholomew and O'Dowd 2011: 22 and Hatton 2008: 22. These are in agreement with the above opinions about its 'neglect.'

6. Cheyne and Black 2003 (the reprint of the 1899–1903 edition); Hastings 1898–1904; Cornill 1907.

7. Cornill 1907.

8. Shorter bibliography: 1–2 Samuel, Chronicles, Ruth, Esther, Ezekiel, Hosea, Joel, Amos, Obadiah, Jonah, Micah, Nahum, Habakkuk, Zephaniah, Haggai, Malachi, Lamentations. Longer bibliography: Judges, 1–2 Kings, Ezra and Nehemiah, Isaiah, Jeremiah, Zechariah, Daniel, Psalms, Job, Ecclesiastes, Song of Songs.

9. I did not count the five books of Moses and Joshua because most of the relevant literature is listed in the chapter about the Pentateuch and refers to some or all of these biblical books, making thereby a comparison with Proverbs complicated.

10. Cheyne and Black 2003.

11. Hastings 1898–1904.

One could, however, argue that although many commentaries and introductions investigated Proverbs from a historical or linguistic point of view, it was not utilised to the measure it could have been in the more theological discussions. Practically all of the major introductions to the Old Testament were interested mainly in questions of date and authorship.[12] Cheyne's *Job and Solomon*, an introduction to the wisdom literature, also focuses on these classical introductory questions and spends only two or three pages on the theological importance of Proverbs.[13] The same is true of the introductory part of commentaries.[14] These works only discuss theological issues briefly, in order to place the book into their alleged history of religion scheme, thereby supporting their theory about the date and authorship of the book.

A similar brevity can be observed in monographs on biblical theology or on the history of Israelite religion. At least this seems to be true for the theologies at the turn of the century and that of the first few decades of the twentieth century. Marti explicitly mentions Proverbs only once in his chapter about the final phase of Israelite religion, the phase where he dates Proverbs in its final form.[15] Similarly, Max Löhr, writing about the religiosity after the exile, refers to Proverbs only occasionally. Rather, he uses Psalms, Ezekiel, Job and other biblical books even when he writes about the topics of individualism, universalism, and divine retribution, for which Proverbs would seem to be an obvious text as these topics were often discussed in contemporary commentaries of Proverbs, as we will see.[16] Davidson mentions Proverbs only on seven pages out of more than 500 pages according to the index of scripture passages in the back of the volume.[17] Kittel writes only a little bit more than two pages on Proverbs in his religion of Israel.[18] Schultz, although he seems to be the most positive about the religious value of Proverbs among the theologians of the turn of the century, only spends eight pages in his two volume theology describing Proverbs' theological value.[19] I have encountered only one exception: the *Biblische Theologie des Alten Testaments* by B. Stade and D. A. Bertholet.[20] However, Stade and Bertholet pay careful attention to every biblical book in its own right. In other words, their work is an exception in its form and not only in its content about Proverbs: it is a combination of a theological introduction to the individual books and a biblical

---

12. For example, Bennett and Adeney 1899: 152–160; Bleek 1869: 252–257; Creelman 1927: 116–122, 283–287; Cornill 1907: 437–447; Driver 1891: 368–383; Gray 1919: 142–148; Sellin 1923: 206–212; Strack 1898: *passim*.
13. Cheyne 1887: 117–178.
14. For example, Delitzsch 1874: 2–51; Strack 1888: 303–311.
15. Marti 1906: 64–80, mentioning Proverbs 8:22 on page 76.
16. Löhr 1906: 128–141.
17. Davidson 1904.
18. Kittel 1925: 206–209.
19. Schultz 1892: 79–86.
20. Proverbs is discussed in the second volume that was written by Bertholet (Bertholet 1911: 83–98). The first volume, by B. Stade, was published six years earlier.

theology. These peculiarities explain why they filled so much of their work with material on Proverbs—they had to, since the layout of the book required them to devote a significant number of pages to every book of the Bible.

Should we conclude then that Proverbs was only interesting for scholars because of its interesting grammatical problems and complex history? Can we say that although it was not neglected in historical and linguistic studies, it was neglected from a theological perspective? Maybe Crenshaw is right after all, at least in this limited sense of 'neglect.' In order to be able to answer this question we have to investigate not only the number of books and pages written about Proverbs but also the content of these scholarly discussions.

1.3 An Inventory of Theological Topics

Describing the history of 130 years' debate about the interpretation of a biblical book and comparing this long story with the present state of the matter is a complicated task, especially if one wants to state it briefly. In order to be able to provide a clear picture, I have chosen to use two different methods in this and the next section respectively.

TABLE 1: Topics in Proverbs' theological interpretation before 1930[21]

Topics discussed in equal measure before and after 1930	• Proverbs' international character • Proverbs' universalistic character • Lack of cult, prayer, Sinai covenant in Proverbs • Proverbs' humanistic character • Proverbs' emphasis on the individual • Proverbs' aim is the education of youth • Proverbs has a practical interest • Figure of Wisdom in Proverbs 8
Topics emphasised somewhat differently before and after 1930	• Proverbs' relationship to the prophets • Proverbs' relationship to the Torah • Proverbs' utilitarianism • Retribution in Proverbs
Characteristic to the era before 1930	• The category of 'philosophy' • An emphasis on monogamy in Proverbs • Recognising the lack of mention of the messiah in Proverbs • Recognising the lack of mention of the life after death in Proverbs • Certain themes were not mentioned at all: feminism, ecology, natural theology, creation theology

---

21. Literary and historical subjects like the etymology and meaning of *mashal* (a favourite topic in the early commentaries; its classic discussion is Eissfeldt 1913 towards the end of our era) or the historical questions of date and authorship are not listed here, though some of them are mentioned in the following discussion where they are directly relevant to our interests.

First, I make an inventory of the main theological topics mentioned in connection with Proverbs in the nineteenth century (see Table 1 above). In this section I will pay attention to historical development and chronological issues only where they are unavoidable. Similarly, I am also avoiding the discussion of the broader intellectual atmosphere in which these topics were debated.

Second, in the following section I give a more chronological, historical description of the development of theological thinking before the '30s, concentrating on the most important theological topics. However, before that, I make some comments about the items in the inventory.

1.3.1 International; Universalistic; Humanistic; Individualistic; Lack of Cult, Prayer, Sinai Covenant

Bernhard Lang gives the following sketch of the history of recognition of Proverbs' international connections: since 1847 the *Instruction of Ptahhotep*, and as such some of the Egyptian literary parallels, has been known. After about 1890 it became widely accepted that the genre of wisdom literature has its origins in Egypt. In 1923 the *Instruction of Amenemope* was discovered, and as a result, many scholars accepted a direct foreign literary influence after this date. According to Lang, although the commentaries often referred to foreign (Indian, Greek, Arabic, etc.) parallels already before 1890, these commentators did not claim that the biblical material was directly derived from or influenced by foreign sources, but rather they only cited those foreign parallels as interesting illustrations for the teaching of Proverbs.[22]

Lang's opinion seems to be correct from a historical-critical point of view. Yet, from a theological point of view it is not relevant that before 1890 scholars used non-Israelite parallels 'only' as illustrative. It is more important that the international nature of Proverbs (if not its foreign literary origins) was fully known throughout the nineteenth century. Already the earliest commentaries and theologies spent considerable effort delineating the similarities between Proverbs and the wisdom of other nations. They did so because even if a direct influence from outside was not considered likely, they nonetheless thought that Israelite wisdom literature represented the same intellectual spirit as non-Israelite wisdom. Wisdom writings as such were considered almost as inescapable results of the maturing of an oriental society, and Israel, rather than being a special case, was seen as a society that followed this general rule, even if many considered Israel's wisdom literature superior to that of other nations. Thus, although direct literary influences were not discussed, the similarities with foreign wisdom were recognised as the results of very similar intellectual developments and as such Israelite and foreign wisdom literature were considered to be intellectu-

---

22. Lang 1972: 19–23.

ally related.²³ A characteristic example from the second half of the century but still from before 1890 is Malan's commentary. He considered it a worthwhile exercise to interpret Proverbs solely through the international parallels to it. In his three-volume commentary, the first part of which appeared in 1889 (according to his foreword the book was based on his old notes assembled in the decades before writing the book), he included many Indian, Greek, Persian and Arabic parallels.²⁴

Whether nineteenth century commentators mentioned foreign parallels or not, the international character of Proverbs was obvious for every interpreter, since the book does not mention Israel at all. The lack of references to the cult in the Jerusalem temple and to definitive national events, the emphasis on individuals and not on the Israelite nation, were not only well-known but often celebrated features of Proverbs throughout the nineteenth and the beginning of the twentieth century.²⁵ What is more, many Christian commentators saw in Proverbs the preliminary step before the New Testament, which with its humanistic, non-nationalistic and individual-focused teaching leads directly to Jesus' message. The following quotations are representative of the appreciation with which these commentators turned to the 'humanistic and universalistic' features of Proverbs:

> It [*Chokma*] was universalistic, or humanistic. Emanating from the fear or the religion of Jahve ..., but seeking to comprehend the spirit in the letter, the essence in the forms of the national life, its effort was directed towards the general truth affecting mankind as such. While prophecy, which is recognised by the *Chokma* as a spiritual power indispensable to a healthful development of a people ..., is of service to the historical process into which divine truth enters to work out its results in Israel, and from thence outward among mankind, the *Chokma* seeks to look into the very essence of this truth through the robe of its historical and national manifestation.... From this aim towards the ideal in the historical, towards ... the human (I intentionally use this word) in the Israelitish, the universal religion in the

---

23. Eichhorn 1824: 67–72; Umbreit 1826: III–XXXII; Vaihinger 1857: 1–6.
24. Malan 1889–1893: *passim*.
25. Bauer 1801: 135; Bertholet 1911: 84, 86; Bewer 1933: 308; Cheyne 1887: 119; Creelman 1927: 117; Gray 1919: 145; Kittel 1925: 208; Löhr 1906: 133; Nowack 1883: XXXVII–XXXVIII (this is a thoroughly updated edition of the earlier KEHAT 7 commentary by Bertheau); Oesterley 1929: LXVII; Pfeiffer 1976: 305–313; Sellin 1923: 206; Toy 1899: XV; Wildeboer 1897: XVII. An exception is Frankenberg, who argued that non-Israelites are not mentioned in Proverbs 1–9 because they, so to speak, did not even exist for the author. Israel and the cult, on the other hand, are not mentioned because they were so strongly presupposed by the author that they did not even need to be mentioned (Frankenberg 1895: 115–116).

Jahve-religion, and the universal morality in the Law, all the peculiarities of the Book of Proverbs are explained.[26]

The teachers of Hebrew proverbial philosophy prepare the way for the Great Teacher of the New Testament. Their teaching is not Jewish but human, or rather perhaps we should say, it is at once Jewish and human.... All that is eternal and immutable in the Law of Moses they acknowledge and build upon; all that is transitory and evanescent they ignore. The substance is retained; the accidents are dispensed with.... In like manner the Divine Author of the Sermon on the Mount, while He declares emphatically that He has 'not come to destroy but to fulfil the law and the prophets,'... yet makes it plain in all His teaching that it is the substance, the spiritual, the eternal, the universal, and not the clothing, the material, the local, the transitory, of which He speaks. He too strips off the garment which conceals and cripples that the form beneath it may come to view and expand.[27]

They [the sages] turned their attention from the rulers and powerful leaders of their race to the individual, to the common man of the street.... Instead of race or class interest, love for mankind became the guiding motives for the work of the later sages.... Narrow racial points of view and interests disappear. It is significant that Israel is not once mentioned in the book of Proverbs. It is to man they speak, and especially to youth, to men and women in the making...
There are many indications that Jesus was a close and appreciative student of the wisdom literature of his race. His interest, like that of the sages, centred not in the nation, nor in certain classes, but in the individual. His aims and those of the Jewish wise men were practically identical.[28]

As a conclusion we can say that it was not a contradiction for nineteenth century interpretation to see Proverbs as a faithful heir of the law and the prophets (see pages 13–15 below) and possessing an international character at the same time. They thought that the sages were successful in finding and emphasising the universal values that were already expressed to a certain extent by the law and the prophets. Proverbs' international character and its 'similarities to non-Israelite parents,' to use Crenshaw's words, were not considered to be an embarrassment but quite the opposite in the pre-1930s literature.[29]

---

26. Delitzsch 1874: 41.
27. Perowne 1899: 28.
28. Kent 1926: 260, 264.
29. In the light of the above, before 1890 they probably would have spoken rather about similarities to non-Israelite brothers and sisters.

1.3.2 Education of Youth; Practical Interest

Some recent commentators emphasise that Proverbs has a practical focus and that it was used particularly in the education of youth.[30] The same notion was important for the pre-1930s commentators, too. It is mentioned in almost all of the books and articles dealing with Proverbs, so the emphasis on the practical and educational role of Proverbs was, if possible, even stronger than in recent times.[31]

1.3.3 Figure of Wisdom in Proverbs 8

The question whether the figure of Wisdom in Proverbs 8 is a person, personification, or hypostasis was hotly debated already before 1930, just like the question whether this figure developed from a foreign deity. Almost all the major opinions we can find in recent scholarship can be found in some form already in nineteenth century scholarship (though the possible *Ma'at* parallels were not yet recognised).[32]

1.3.4 Relationship to Prophets; Relationship to Torah

In contrast to some modern interpreters, before the '30s almost every interpreter emphasised the deeply religious nature of the whole of Proverbs. As Oesterley wrote, 'there was a Godward thought at the back of their [the sages'] minds on all that they wrote, which hallowed what we call worldly wisdom, and which sanctified common sense.'[33]

Although some in the nineteenth century were of the opinion that wisdom was indifferent or hostile to the Torah,[34] the vast majority agreed with Schultz's words: 'This wisdom of Israel ... is based on the revelation of God, especially on that wonderful law which distinguishes Israel above all other nations.'[35]

---

30. Fox 1994: 233–243; Waltke 2004: 94.

31. For example Bertholet 1911: 87; Driver 1891: 369; Kent 1926: 260–261; Kuhn 1931: 2; McCurdy 1889: 327; Oesterley 1929: LX; Reuss 1890: 516; Sellin 1923: 207; Toy 1899: VII, XIX.

32. For extensive bibliography and brief description of the different standpoints, see Davidson 1862: 346–350; Heinisch 1923: 1–62; Hesselgrave 1910: 14–16; Ranston 1930: 77–81; Schencke 1913: 15–25.

33. Oesterley 1929: LVI. See also Cheyne and Black 2003: 118; Cornill 1907: 438; Ewald 1867: 15–17, 57; Perowne 1899: 27–28; Umbreit 1826: XXXV–LVII. There were only a few who considered it important to emphasise the presence of not so religious *'lebensklugheit'* in the book, for example Nöldecke 1868: 157–165. Nöldecke did not pay much attention to how this feature of the book should be utilised in theological thinking.

34. Bruch 1851: 51.

35. Schultz 1892: 84; see also Frankenberg 1898: 6–7 (though we have to note that Frankenberg differentiated between a religious wisdom which depended on the holy scriptures, including prophets and law, and a non-religious one which did not); Hitzig

The special relationship between Proverbs 1–9 and Deuteronomy was especially often recognised.[36]

The relationship with the prophets was mentioned even more often than that with the Torah. Although scholars recognised the differences,[37] they considered the authors and the compilers of Proverbs to be the spiritual heirs of the prophets.[38]

Therefore, although with slightly different nuances, basically almost all biblical scholars before the '30s concluded that the sages were devout followers of the Torah and the prophets—a view which was far from being mainstream throughout much of the twentieth century. According to most pre-1930s scholars, the differences between the sages and the prophets are due to applying the teaching of the prophets to the life of individuals living in different circumstances and religious milieus from the prophets:

> In a sense they were the successors of the prophets, for they coined their teaching into current change. Neither rising to the lofty conceptions of the greatest prophets nor partaking of their glorious enthusiasm, they yet kept the true balance between form and spirit in an age of growing legalism. . . . As pronounced individualists they addressed themselves to individuals . . .[39]

> In dealing with the subject of the religious value of Proverbs one has to remember that the underlying purpose of the Wisdom writers was to apply the religion of the Law and the prophets, so far as this had developed, to the practical, everyday life of the individual.[40]

> Thus they were lay-teachers after the manner of the prophets of old, but in very different times and surroundings. Like the prophets they were independent of the cultus, and like the later of them their concern was rather with individuals than with the mass, but they lacked the prophets' fervour of utterance and their ecstasy of soul. . . . The

---

1858: IX–X; Kuhn 1931: 2; Vaihinger 1857: 31–43; Wildeboer 1897: XVII–XVIII; Zöckler 1867: 1.

36. Some went on to argue for a historical or literary relationship, others just emphasised the similar religious sentiments. Bennett and Adeney 1899: 156; Cheyne 1887: 157; Creelman 1927: 284–285; Driver 1891: 372.

37. Some of these differences were considered to be in favour of the prophets, especially in the second half of the nineteenth, and the beginning of the twentieth, century. In that period the prophets were considered by most scholars to be more enthusiastic, their religion was considered to be more heartfelt and their relationship with God was perceived as more intimate than that of the sages. Cheyne 1887: 176; Löhr 1906: 128; Reuss 1890: 522–523.

38. Bertholet 1911: 84–85; Cheyne 1887: 119; Cornill 1907: 444; Kent 1926: 259; Oesterley 1929: LVII; Perowne 1899: 27; Wildeboer 1897: XVIII; Gunkel is an exception who emphasises strongly the differences between the prophets and the wise: Gunkel 1913: column 1873.

39. Bewer 1933: 308.

40. Oesterley 1929: LIX.

high ethical exaltation of the prophets became proverbial prudence and popular wisdom.[41]

1.3.5 Utilitarianism; Retribution

It seems that by far the greatest ethical problem for the interpreters of Proverbs before the '30s was that it apparently bases its counsels about right behaviour on how profitable that behaviour is for the individual: 'The great motive to wise living is always personal happiness. There is no concern about making others happy. Even when the welfare of others is considered, it is always with reference to oneself.'[42]

Some, like Bewer, simply recognised this feature of Proverbs as a matter of fact, but the majority tried to defend this 'selfish' attitude of the book. There were different explanations available. First, some argued that 'yes, selfishness is there, but there were other, more noble motives, too':

> It is, further, only one side of the truth to say that right-doing is inculcated, and wrong-doing deprecated, solely on utilitarian grounds.... It is impossible to read what is said in Proverbs about God's relationship to men without seeing that so far as the Sages themselves were concerned they implicitly assumed a Godward intention among the motives which should impel men to right-doing or which should restrain them from wrong-doing.[43]

Or, as Cheyne wrote referring to Prov 25:20; 26:23; 27:6, 10, 14, 17, 'we should wrong our "wise men" by treating them as pure *utilitarians*; they are often sympathetic observers of character and circumstance.'[44]

Second, some argued that a certain measure of selfishness is actually practically healthy and, as the self is also an important part of the society, it is also a form of justice to care for the self. Toy was one of those who recognised the practical nature of Proverbs and he was also one who connected this practical interest with the problem of selfishness:

> The motive urged for good living is individualistic utilitarian or eudaemonistic—not the glory of God, or the welfare of men in general, but the well-being of the actor.... It is unnecessary to call attention to the fundamental value of this principle in practical life.[45]

---

41. Kittel 1925: 208; See furthermore Reuss 1890: 513; Wildeboer 1897: XVII.
42. Bewer 1933: 312; see also Bertholet 1911: 94–95; Cheyne 1887: 137; Gramberg 1828: 45–48; Meinhold 1908: 127–128.
43. Oesterley 1929: LVIII.
44. Cheyne 1887: 148; See also Hudal 1914: 230–231.
45. Toy 1899: XIV; Toy also valued Proverbs' regard for the self as a kind of justice (see Toy 1899: XI).

Third, some argued that the main aim was to educate the youth, for which aim referring to selfish benefits is useful, at least at an early stage.[46] It was occasionally emphasised in connection with the third point that referring to self-interest is not only useful for the education of the individual but it is also useful for the education of the people of God. As Perowne wrote, 'it is the Church in her childhood that is here being educated.'[47]

The ethical problem of motivating with selfish reference to rewards and punishment was directly connected to the theological topic of divine retribution. nineteenth century scholarship markedly differed in this from later discussions of Proverbs. As I discuss in more detail in chapter 2, many argued in a major part of the twentieth century that Proverbs simply depicts a world order where benefits quasi-automatically follow good acts.[48] According to this argument the teaching is not about God's retribution, and instead of calling Proverbs 'selfish,' one should rather see the book as a simple description of the good order of the world.

In contrast, before the '30s, divine retribution was considered to be one of the important theological teachings of Proverbs. Especially from about the middle of the nineteenth century, many scholars saw it as the most important theological tenet of the book: 'God is the guarantee of this absolute retribution—this is the real religious content of proverbial wisdom.'[49] Furthermore, it was not only considered important but highly problematic. It was seen as one of the weaknesses of legalistic Judaism that it recognised 'only' the truth of retribution and did not face the fact that retribution does not always work in this world, and that there are more noble divine truths, too.[50]

Although not writing on Proverbs but Judaism, the following quotation by Schleiermacher is representative of much of the nineteenth century. (Let us recognise the recurring motive of childishness in connection with the topic of retribution.)

> Remove everything political . . . by which Judaism is ordinarily characterised. Leave aside the whole experiment of coupling the state not simply to religious institutions but to religion itself. And forget for a moment that Judaism was a regime of sorts, a regime founded upon an ancient tribal history and maintained by priests. Look only at the genuinely religious factors within it. . . . What you find is a consciousness of direct and universal retribution, isn't it? . . . God is constantly

---

46. Oesterley 1929: LX.
47. Perowne 1899: 34; see also Wildeboer 1897: XIX.
48. See Koch 1983: 57–87. The original German article is Koch 1955: 1–42.
49. Bertholet 1911: 98, translations from German sources are always mine unless noted otherwise. See also Cheyne 1887: 121, 163–164; Creelman 1927: 118; Driver 1891: 374; Gressmann 1925: 54–57; Oesterley 1929: LXIII; Wildeboer 1897: XVIII–XIX.
50. A reason why the book of Job was one of the most popular Old Testament books among biblical scholars of the time was precisely that it was considered as the most powerful challenge towards the teaching of retribution in the post-exilic period (Löhr 1906: 137; Marti 1906: 79).

interpreted in terms of this rule, so that the deity is everywhere represented as rewarding, punishing, disciplining particular things in particular persons.... This whole idea is, in fact, extremely childlike.[51]

No wonder, those scholars who connected Proverbs to Judaism (and not to the supposedly cleaner and older 'Hebraism'—see pages 25–27 below) often evaluated Proverbs quite negatively.

Nevertheless, although Proverbs' teaching about retribution was considered clearly inferior to the teaching of Jesus, it was not despised by every theologian of the age but was evaluated by some as an important component of religion, which is restrained but not eliminated by Jesus:

> Although it [teaching of retribution] was all too often externalized in ancient Israel, with the result that Retribution was looked for and found to an undue extent in the outward lot of men, still it remains one of the most important principles of every moral religion and of every higher view of the world—the belief, namely, that the natural and the moral government of the world, however often they seem to be at variance, are not at bottom mutually exclusive; that the course of events in its final purpose serves good and not evil ends; that it is constructive and not destructive; that retribution is a real thing. To be sure, Christianity knows a higher relation between God and man than that of retributive law, but Christianity merely shifts the thought of retribution into the second place—it by no means suspends it. 'Be not deceived: God is not mocked.' Our children understand the message of retribution, for the latter can only be understood when a man has by long and sore experience learned his own impotence, and it is therefore wise to lead our children by the same path that history has trod.[52]

1.3.6 Monogamy; Messiah; Life after Death

There are certain topics which we cannot find in most modern commentaries. Contemporary authors probably think that mentioning the obvious, namely that Proverbs does not contain references to polygamy, the Messiah, or a life after death, is not worth the ink.[53] However, these topics occur again and again in older works.[54]

Almost all of the older critical commentaries agree with the more recent opinion about these issues. The difference is not in the opinion between the older and newer commentaries but the relatively large emphasis with which the

---

51. Schleiermacher 1969: 306–307, the first German edition was published in 1799.
52. Gunkel 1928: 38–39; recognise, again, the connection between retribution and infancy in the quoted discussion.
53. There are occasional exceptions. See, for example, Schmitt's comment on the importance of monogamy in many wisdom writings (Albertz and Schmitt 2012: 396).
54. Bertholet 1911: 88; Bewer 1933: 308; Creelman 1927: 119; Gramberg 1828: 1; Oesterley 1929: LXIV–LXVI; Toy 1899: XV; etc.

older commentaries discuss these topics. However, not everyone followed the mainstream. Löhr, for example, quotes Prov 2:21 as his main example of messianic expectations after the exile.[55] These dissenting voices explain why nineteenth century commentators thought it necessary to mention that we cannot find these topics in Proverbs.

1.3.7 Philosophy

The book's relationship to philosophy is another topic which is surprisingly often discussed in the older commentaries. It seems that the comparison with the Greek philosophers was a pressing issue for Old Testament scholars. They usually agreed that Hebrew wisdom deserves the name 'philosophy,' although some of its characteristics are different from what we normally classify as such. From the frequency that the commentaries discussed this subject one can suspect that the designation 'philosophy' might have counted as an honorary title in the eyes of many. By applying it to Hebrew wisdom, biblical scholars suggested that it is not inferior to the achievements of 'heathen' thinkers.

'Philosophy' also served as a category that could be used by scholars for comparing Proverbs with the prophetic, legal, and historical writings of the Bible. One could say that nineteenth century scholarship recognised the same peculiarity of Proverbs as the twentieth century one: the lack of interest in national history. But instead of emphasising this lack, they used the category of 'philosophy' to name the positive feature of biblical wisdom writings with which they enrich the teaching of the Bible:

> The wise men are not prophets but philosophers; indeed, the Seven Wise Men of Greece arose at precisely the same stage of culture as the Hebrew sages. It is true, the latter never . . . attempted logic and metaphysics.[56]

> We need not hesitate, in view of Col. 2:8, to call the Book of Proverbs a 'philosophical' treatise. . . . When we give the name philosophia to the tendency of mind to which the Book of Proverbs belongs, we do not merely use a current scientific word, but there is an actual internal relation of the Book of Proverbs to that which is the essence of philosophy, which Scripture recognizes (Acts. 17:27; Rom. 1:19f) as existing within the domain of heathendom, and which stamps it as a natural product of the human spirit, which never can be wanting where a human being or a people rises to higher self-consciousness and its operations in their changing relation to the phenomena of the external world. . . . Staudenmaier has done the great service of having worthily estimated the rich and deep fullness of this biblical theologumenon of wisdom [referring to Proverbs 8], and of having point-

---

55. Löhr 1906: 142.
56. Cheyne 1887: 119.

ed out in it the foundation-stone of a sacred metaphysics and a means of protection against pantheism in all its forms.[57]

1.3.8 Feminism, Ecology

Some topics that became prominent in the twentieth century were not discussed during the nineteenth century. The reason for some of these differences between the two eras is rooted in the different cultural environment and sensitivities of the two centuries, as in the cases of feminism and ecology.

1.3.9 Natural Theology

There are some topics, however, that, theoretically, could have been treated more substantially in the nineteenth century as they would have fitted the intellectual milieu of the time. One such topic is natural theology. Natural theology as such was an often-discussed topic throughout the nineteenth century. Yet, I have not found any explicit use of Proverbs in the arguments supporting natural theology either in biblical commentaries and theologies or in classic works on natural theology.[58] In the case of Christian advocates of natural theology this might be because they considered Proverbs as dependent on the teaching of the Law and prophets, that is, on revelation.[59] Other advocates of natural theology were rather hostile to orthodox Christianity and as such to the whole of the Bible, so it is no wonder that they did not use Proverbs in supporting their argument for natural theology.[60]

1.3.10 Creation Theology

Another 'twentieth century theme' that would also have fitted the intellectual milieu of the nineteenth century yet did not receive serious consideration in connection with Proverbs is creation theology. However, the case of creation theology is not as straightforward as the case of natural theology. Whereas the

---

57. Delitzsch 1874: 37, 38, 45; see also Bruch 1851: X–XIV, 49, 60–61, 152–153 (about Bruch's understanding of wisdom as philosophising, see Smend, 1995: 265–266; Dell 2013); Ewald 1867: 57; Perowne 1899: 9–11; Schultz 1892: 83–84; Sellin 1923: 206; Toy 1899: VI, XVII; Zöckler 1867: 3.

58. Of the scholars referred to, Wellhausen came closest to connecting biblical wisdom to natural theology. For Wellhausen, wisdom describes creation as characterised by order and highlights the laws of nature. However, he immediately adds that the same wisdom also emphasises the inscrutable mystery of God's creation and that creation's secrets cannot be completely deciphered but only marvelled at (Wellhausen 1958: 209).

59. E.g., Paley 1860 (originally published in 1802, it was a bestseller for most of the nineteenth century).

60. E.g., Paine 1852 (originally published in three parts in 1794, 1795, and 1807, it was especially popular in the United States).

term 'creation theology,' just like the term 'natural theology,' was never used, the word 'creation' was frequently mentioned.

Most commentators acknowledged that Proverbs describes Yahweh as the creator God. However, a crucial difference from much of the twentieth century is that they did not use 'creation theology' as an important theological category which provides the key for the theological interpretation of the book. They usually only referred to the theme of creation in a passing way. One can only guess the reason for this comparatively brief treatment of the topic throughout the century. It may be that creation is in fact not mentioned explicitly very often in the book of Proverbs. Another reason could be that although nineteenth century scholars recognised the book's peculiarities (e.g., not mentioning history), and also its special contribution to the teaching of the Old Testament, most of them also emphasised the continuities with prophets and the law and did not want to contrast wisdom with the rest of the Bible as many scholars in the twentieth century tried to do. This might be one of the reasons why 'philosophy,' which continues the teaching of the prophets, just on a different level, suited their aims better than the later creation vs. history antithesis.

Nevertheless, there were some scholars who contributed significantly to the discussion of creation in Proverbs. One such scholar was Bernhard Duhm, who emphasised the presence of the theme of creation in Proverbs 1-9. However, in contrast with the authors of many twentieth century works, he did not claim that it was an overarching theological framework for wisdom literature. Neither did he use it for contrasting wisdom with the rest of the Bible; on the contrary, he underlined the similarity between Jeremiah and Proverbs 1–9 in this respect:

> The concept of divine Wisdom in its relation to the creation-story and to the guidance of the people corresponds exactly to what Jeremiah says about the divine creation of nature, about the divine upholding of the natural order, and about the corresponding category, his rule about the world of humans.[61]

Another major contributor to the discussion of the topic was Meinhold, who, in his major work on Israelite wisdom, also emphasised that wisdom described God as the creator. However, discussing the wisdom-teaching about creation, he did not refer to Proverbs.[62] It also needs to be noted that Meinhold claimed that a wisdom layer can be found in almost all parts of the Old Testament (not least in the prophets). So, although he differentiated between a prophetic religion (often with emphasis on national questions) and an original folk-religion (with emphasis on wisdom, creation, and universal interest), he claimed that these two are intermingled in our Bible and form a unity.[63]

---

61. Duhm 1875: 244. Cf. Wellhausen's similar emphasis on wisdom writings' depiction of God as creator (Wellhausen 1958: 209).
62. Meinhold 1908: 33–52.
63. Meinhold 1908: *passim*.

Interestingly enough, the nineteenth century work that appears closest to many twentieth century discussions in its emphasis on the theme of creation in Proverbs can be found at the very beginning of our era. Gerhard Lorenz Bauer contrasted the world-creator God of Proverbs with the national God one can find in the historical books of the Old Testament.[64] As he ponders the tensions between the creator God of Proverbs and the depiction of Solomon's religious activities in 2 Kings and 1 Chronicles, he writes:

> How can these [two pictures of God] be reconciled? How can Solomon in his writings speak about God in such an enlightened and right way.... And here [in the historical books] worship only a national God in Jehovah?
> It is undeniable that the historical books follow more the general principles of popular religion than the concepts that wiser and more talented Israelites acquired through reflection and scholarly education.[65]

Thus, Bauer, just like many in the twentieth century, contrasted the theology of Proverbs with that of the historical parts of the Bible, and he used the depiction of God as creator for this contrast. However, there are important differences between his interpretation of Proverbs and the interpretations of twentieth century scholars. Whereas the main interest of many in the twentieth century was creation theology, and universalism was only considered as one of the many important outworkings of creation thought, Bauer's main interest was in the philosophically sophisticated universalism of Israelite wisdom (as opposed to the narrow-minded particularism of folk-religion) of which world-creation was only one important expression.

As a conclusion we can say that, on the one hand, the twentieth century focus on creation theology is not entirely without forerunners in the previous century. On the other hand, creation theology was usually not regarded as the theological framework for Proverbs and even on the few occasions when creation receives serious consideration in connection with Proverbs, it is from a different angle and with different nuances than in the next century.

1.4 Development or Decline of Israelite Religion?

In the previous section I made an inventory of the major theological ideas that pre-1930 critical scholarship found (or did not find) in the book of Proverbs. This inventory, however, only provides the building blocks they used for constructing Proverbs' theology. The next question to be investigated is how the building itself looked and changed during the century: in other words, how were these notions actually put together to form a coherent theological opinion about Proverbs and how did this opinion changed during our period.

---

64. Bauer 1801: 134–153.
65. Bauer 1801: 152. See also the quotation from Bauer on pages 22–23.

Of course, the theological use of Proverbs was different from author to author. Yet, the principle according to which they ordered the above notions was more or less the same: they tried to reconstruct a history of Israel's religion and find the place of Proverbs in that religious development. Depending on where they positioned Proverbs in this history, they emphasised the (from their perspective) positive features of the book, like its universalism, or the negative ones, like its selfishness, and the doctrine of retribution.

In the beginning of the nineteenth century, mainly under the influence of Kant and Hegel, many scholars were looking for the 'universal world-spirit' in the Scriptures. The more 'Jewish' a text was, the less spiritual it was considered to be by biblical scholars. For Bauer (1801), for example, the historical development of the Jewish religion was equal with the development from particularism to universalism. He found the peak of this development in the wisdom literature, mainly in Job (usually Job and Qohelet, sometimes also some psalms, were the most highly valued books in the whole century, because they were considered the 'least Jewish'), but he valued Proverbs also very highly:

> Concerning religion and ethics, Proverbs of Solomon is one of the most important parts of the whole Old Testament besides the books of Job and Psalms. If the immortality of soul were taught in it and the shades were not descended to a dull netherworld, if ethics were less built on the motive of selfishness, then its ethical and religious understanding would leave nothing to be desired. ...
> God has the name of the national-god Jehovah in it and he appears as the same God who was revealed to the Israelites more specifically; yet he is depicted more as the creator of the whole world, the governor of all events, every people, and human destinies. ...
> That God is the most rational, highest, wise, self-subsistent cause of the world and that humans should understand him as the one who brought forth everything in his omnipotence and arranged everything with the highest and most perfect wisdom as it is now, is repeated and clearly taught [in Proverbs].[66]

As Ollenburger writes about Bauer's work, 'in 1801 Bauer added a supplement (*Beylagen*), which treated the Old Testament books in historical (roughly canonical) order. This allowed him to show the development from particular to universal ideas, a development crowned by Proverbs.'[67] Ollenburger, in fact, is mistaken in claiming that Bauer considered Proverbs to be the 'crown' of the historical development of religion in Israel. Bauer valued the book of Job even

---

66. Bauer 1801: 135.
67. Ollenburger 2004: 5.

higher than Proverbs.[68] Nevertheless, he certainly regarded Proverbs as one of the clearest expressions of the true nature of God, together with Job and Psalms.[69]

Although the simple statement that most critical scholars in the beginning of the nineteenth century envisaged a linear, upward development in Israel's religion is true, it does not cover the full story. We have to make at least four further qualifications to get a more nuanced picture:

1. It was typical of Christian theologians in the nineteenth century to consider the Old Testament inferior to the New Testament. They thought that even the most developed parts of the Old Testament were only preparations for the fuller revelation of the New Testament. This is well illustrated by the fact that the epoch-making lecture of Gabler at the very beginning of the investigated time period and the no-less-emblematic biblical scholar Gunkel, towards the end of it, spoke with one voice about this topic. This doctrine of successive revelation was one of the basic theological claims of nineteenth century critical scholarship:

> Yet all the sacred writers are holy men and are armed with divine authority; but not all attest to the same form of religion; some are doctors of the Old Testament of the same elements that Paul himself designated with the name 'basic elements'; others are of the newer and better Christian Testaments. And so the sacred authors, however much we must cherish them with equal reverence because of the divine authority that has been imprinted on their writings, cannot all be considered in the same category if we are referring to their use in dogmatics.[70]

> Hebrew religion, it is true, is not simply to be identified with the Christian religion. Indeed, in numerous details and in its profoundest thoughts it is much inferior to it; and the type of exposition that is still to be found in many of our schools, an exposition that seeks to obliterate these differences, is open to many objections and involves many dangers. It is just these numerous points where this inferiority of Old Testament religion and morality is most apparent that force the teacher [referring to Sunday school- and other teachers involved in the religious education of the youth], who has not appreciated these differences, either to resort to all sorts of artificial interpretation or to present to children the religion of ancient Israel as a perfect Divine revelation.[71]

---

68. Bauer 1801: 154.
69. Ollenburger might have mainly used the English translation of Bauer's work (Bauer 1838: 80–81). This translation omits significant parts of the original German text, for example the above quoted sentence about Job and Psalms. Ollenburger only quotes sentences in his work which were included in the English translation, although he gives his own translation, so it seems that he consulted the original German, at least for revising the English translation.
70. Gabler 2004: 502.
71. Gunkel 1928: 33.

2. Bauer (and many of his followers) did not claim that chronologically wisdom literature was the last one among the books of the Old Testament. He listed several books as written later than Proverbs and considered many of them as less clear expressions of God's character. Nevertheless, it is true that he considered the value of revelation more or less (!) increasing throughout the historical order of the Old Testament books.[72]
3. We should also add that although the historical–developmental interpretation of Old Testament religion was the most widespread, there were some Old Testament theologies which put less emphasis on the development and which basically understood the different phases of Israelite religion as different versions of the same religion, most of which are not necessarily superior to the other versions.[73]
4. It was a generally accepted reconstruction of religious development that the Judaism Jesus met was a rather degraded type of religion: it was narrow-mindedly nationalistic, relying on the letter and not on the spirit, emphasising (ceremonial) law instead of love. How the gradually evolving Jewish religion ended up with this character by the time of Jesus required explanation. In the first half of the nineteenth century many biblical theologians defined the time of degeneration mainly as the 'inter-testamental' period, possibly detecting the signs of the approaching decline in the very last books of the Old Testament, for example in Chronicles.[74]

Nevertheless, with these qualifications in mind, we can say that the most dominant view in the first half of the nineteenth century was that critical Old Testament theology could successfully reconstruct a fairly straightforward development of Jewish religion at the end of which we find wisdom literature, not least the book of Proverbs. The following quotation from Vatke's influential Old Testament theology expresses in a succinct way the notion that wisdom was the optimal synthesis of everything good in the history of Jewish religion at the end of its development:

> The prophetic exultation and activity lost its historical basis and took the form of reflective wisdom in which the ideal spirit reached its last accomplishment. The former opposition between the outward worship and the freer prophetic teaching was now changed into the careful adherence to the letter of the Levitical Law on the one hand, and on the other into a free reflectiveness, which even got rid of particularism altogether.[75]

---

72. The books he considered later products than Proverbs are Job, Isaiah 40–66, Jonah, Joel, Obadiah, Habakkuk, Zephaniah, Ezekiel, Daniel, Ecclesiastes, Kings, Chronicles, Ezra, Nehemiah, some psalms (Bauer 1801: 154–254).
73. For example Baumgarten-Crusius 1828.
74. Slightly different, but similar expressions of this historical reconstruction can be found in Bauer 1801: 245; Baumgarten-Crusius 1828: 72; Vatke 1835: 578.
75. Vatke 1835: 552.

Noack phrases a similar opinion around the middle of the century:

> While the prophets expressed the universalism of divine world-governance only in its particular reference to Israel, wisdom took a much freer and truer direction. In it the specific relations of divine universal aims to the Jewish nation and outer forms of particularism ... disappear.[76]

However, in the second half of the century a slightly different, less enthusiastic interpretation of Proverbs gained prominence among the majority of theologians. We can detect the roots of this interpretation already in the early years of the century in the influential work of de Wette. He divided the history of Jewish religion into two separate epochs: the so-called Hebraism before the exile and Judaism after the exile. He evaluated the whole of Judaism quite negatively as a legalistic system ruled by the dogma of retribution.[77] This, however, did not affect his evaluation of wisdom literature because he considered it to be part of Hebraism, that is, as a product of the pre-exilic period. He considered the sages, in accordance with the majority of contemporary scholars, as people fighting together with some prophets against the particularism and legalism of some priests. Nevertheless, it has to be added that he mainly wrote about Job and Ecclesiastes in this respect. He thought that, although Proverbs is the product of the 'most beautiful epoch of Hebrew literature,' it is too practical and it does not have too much to offer to a theologian.[78] Yet, what is more interesting for us is that he devalued the whole of Judaism after the exile as a mainly degenerated religion resulting from the trauma of the Jewish nation and some influences from other, non-Jewish (mainly Persian) sources. De Wette had some contemporary followers, but his views about the earlier degeneration of the Jewish religion became even more popular in the second half of the century.[79]

There was another gradual change concerning the evaluation of Proverbs that went side by side with the just delineated development. It concerns the

---

76. Noack 1853: 90–91.

77. De Wette 1831: 53 (the first edition was published in 1813). De Wette's view can be contrasted to that of Vatke and his Hegelianism (see Reventlow 2010: 231–232, 238–239, 242, 262–276, Rogerson 1984: 36–44, 69–78; Smend 2007: 43–56). De Wette was not the first scholar who saw the Exile as the caesura between flourishing and degrading religious and literary activities. Johann David Michaelis had similar views already in the previous century (Legaspi 2010: 102–103). However, de Wette greatly contributed to the dissemination of this view, and he went a step further than Michaelis in stressing the inferior nature of post-exilic literature more strongly.

78. De Wette 1840: 388 (the first edition was published in 1817); see also De Wette 1831: 52.

79. One of the earliest followers was Cölln (Cölln 1836). Of course, not everyone followed de Wette in every detail, not even in the second half of the century. Wellhausen, for example, strongly criticised the widespread and simplistic view that all theologically valuable writings came from before the exile and everything that was written after the exile was theologically useless (Wellhausen 1885: 1–5).

gradual shift of the dating of Proverbs to later periods. It was almost constantly debated throughout the century whether one should consider Proverbs mainly as pre-exilic or post-exilic.[80] Gramberg was the first who suspected a late (end of exile) date for the book.[81] The first influential commentator who clearly judged Proverbs to be post-exilic (5th century) was Vatke.[82] Bertheau's interpretation around the middle of the century exemplified well, how difficult it was for some scholars to contradict the majority of former scholars and opt for a later date. Although he listed several observations that would point towards a post-exilic dating, he was still hesitant to place the final author/redactor of the book after the exile.[83] Smend suspects that this could have been due to his respect for his teacher, Ewald.[84] Yet, though one can hardly speak about a straight, linear development of opinion, the tendency for more and more scholars to date Proverbs to a later period is fairly clear.

Therefore, as the date of (the final form of) Proverbs was pushed later during the nineteenth century, the date of the serious degeneration of the Jewish religion was brought earlier. As a result, the book of Proverbs gradually became a product of a religiously defective age in the eyes of many scholars.

These changes in the general opinion about the dating of Proverbs and the precise reconstruction of Israelite religious history naturally affected the theological evaluation of Proverbs. More precisely, it affected how the commentators balanced the theological notions listed in the previous section against each other. In a somewhat over-simplistic way one could say that for scholars before 1930 the single most positive characteristic of Proverbs was its universalism, whereas its most negative characteristics were its selfishness and focus on effectiveness in this-worldly life. In the first half of the nineteenth century, although the problematic issue of selfishness was recognised,[85] its universalism was very strongly emphasised. However, the emphasis on its selfishness was becoming gradually stronger and by the latter part of the nineteenth century the book was widely regarded as a typical example of the cold retribution-teaching of the degenerated Judaism.[86]

---

80. The arguments pro and contra and the opinions of many nineteenth century scholars are well exposed in Montefiore 1890: 430–453.

81. Gramberg 1829: XXVI; maybe it is not accidental that Gramberg evaluated Proverbs from a theological point of view more negatively in his 1828 commentary than most of his contemporary colleagues. He commented on its *utilitarianism* and *eudaemonism* and criticised those who were too enthusiastic about its religious value (Gramberg 1828: 45–48). About the history of dating Proverbs in the nineteenth century, see Dell 2013; Smend 1995: 259–263.

82. Vatke 1835: 563; see Smend 1995: 259–260; Dell 2013.

83. Bertheau 1847: XXXVII–XLIII.

84. Smend 1995: 263.

85. Bauer 1801: 135; de Wette 1831: 104.

86. Löhr 1906: 137; Marti 1906: 79; Reuss 1890: 522–523.

Nevertheless, Proverbs was seldom if ever evaluated in an exclusively negative way. The old enthusiasm towards Proverbs lived on in some interpreters of the second half of the nineteenth century.[87] Even those who criticised it, recognised its universalism and considered it to be one of the best religious achievements of a degenerate Judaism and as such somewhat of an exception to the low-level literature of late biblical Judaism.[88]

To conclude, the picture one can gain about the change of scholarly opinion concerning the theological value of Proverbs is somewhat blurred by the fact that we can find many competing interpretations side by side during the nineteenth century. The opinions of some major theologians up to the middle of the century could be categorised as follows: Bauer, Vatke, Noack: Proverbs is at the top of the development of the Jewish religion; de Wette, Cölln: Proverbs is good, belongs to the best strata of the Jewish religion, but is too practical to have much theological importance; Baumgarten-Crusius, Umbreit: already the Torah and the prophets were great, Proverbs just continued this line; Gramberg: Proverbs is selfish and in many respects degenerate in its theological views. From the middle of the century such a categorisation becomes increasingly difficult since most interpreters regarded Proverbs as bearing the signs of a religiously inferior/degraded age but still possessing some exceptionally good characteristics. The comparison of such manifold interpretations is not as straightforward as that of the older interpretations. Still, the tendencies are clear enough: we can conclude that in the general opinion of scholars Proverbs lost its fame to some extent. From one of the favourites among the Old Testament books it became one of the favourites among the not so attractive later (Judaic) Old Testament books.

1.5 Conclusions

1.5.1 Was Proverbs Neglected?

I began this chapter with quotations from Crenshaw, Murphy, and Whybray in which they depict early critical scholarship as somewhat neglecting the book of Proverbs. My investigations, however, lead to a distinctly different picture of nineteenth century scholarship:
- Contra Crenshaw, Proverbs was not ignored before 1930. It was praised enthusiastically by many and there was a vibrant scholarly discussion about its theology throughout this period. If in some biblical theologies it was quoted less frequently, this is probably because it was considered 'only' as second-best after Job, Ecclesiastes, and some psalms.

---

87. 'It shows us a fresh religious life in the midst of a benumbing formalism, and points to the hidden springs of the religion of Jesus' (Schultz 1892: 81).
88. Cheyne 1887: 162; Reuss 1890: 522–523; Toy 1899: XVII.

- Contra Crenshaw, I have not found a single hint of the negative evaluation of Proverbs' similarities to Sirach or the Wisdom of Solomon in the pre-1930s scholarly discussion. In fact, especially in the first half of the century, some of the commentators seem to be impressed by the deutero-canonical wisdom books no less than by Proverbs.[89]
- Contra Crenshaw, its similarity to non-Israelite wisdom (which was first considered in the form of literary parallels before it was gradually recognised that direct foreign influence could also be detected in the book) did not cause a theological problem for the early commentators. It was considered a virtue, a sign of the universal spirit rather than an embarrassment.
- It is debatable whether comparing Proverbs to the Law and Prophets is a 'judgment by alien standards' (Crenshaw), but the lack of historical particularities in Proverbs was certainly not an 'indignity' to it; quite the opposite. Many commentators thought that Proverbs actually grasped the spirit of the Law and the Prophets quite well; what is more, many thought that it grasped the eternal spirit even better than the Law or the Prophets.
- It is true that the emphasis on the practical and educational role of Proverbs was stronger before 1930 than after, however, contra Murphy, most interpreters considered Proverbs' theological contribution significant in its teaching about the universal nature of God and his works (including his providence) and its creative application of the teaching of the Law and Prophets to new situations.
- Contra Crenshaw and Whybray, earlier interpreters did not find it problematic to locate Proverbs in the Old Testament. They found Proverbs to be a natural continuation of the Prophets and the Law (either as an improvement or as a degeneration) and were not puzzled by its unusual nature. This seems to be a problem of the middle of the twentieth century and we should not project it into earlier times.

1.5.2 Differences between the Nineteenth and Twentieth Centuries

Although I have detected several differences between how Proverbs was discussed during the (long) nineteenth century and how it has been discussed since then, I think these can be summarised in four main points:
- *Utilitarianism*, selfishness, and the doctrine of retribution were considered the most problematic features of Proverbs before the '30s, but *utilitarianism* and selfishness are hardly discussed at length later.
- Proverbs was considered to be very much in accordance with the Torah and the Prophets, whereas later many scholars understood it in contrast to these or at least as forming a part of an alternative tradition.

---

89. Umbreit 1826: XXXIII–XXXV (it is interesting to note in connection with his appreciation of the deutero-canonical wisdom books that Umbreit was a Protestant scholar).

Theological Interpretation of Proverbs between 1800 and 1930 29

- Certain theological topics that are considered to be important today were lacking from the discussion before the '30s (like creation theology, feminism, etc.).
- Although they recognised many of those peculiarities of Proverbs that have been recognised by more recent scholars, like the lack of historical discussion in it, nineteenth century interpreters used different categories, first of all 'philosophy,' to handle theologically these features of the book.

In order to see the significance of these differences between nineteenth and twentieth century scholarship and to perceive their relevance for our study, we have to turn now to a detailed investigation of the twentieth century interpretation of Proverbs.

2

Theological Interpretation of Proverbs between 1930 and Today

I have argued that most scholars until the '30s had seen Proverbs as a practical outworking of the prophets' teaching. Depending on the interpreter's perspective, it was either seen as a distortion of a former, higher religion (stressing its *utilitarianism* and *eudaemonism*) or quite the opposite, as the high peak of ancient Jewish faith (stressing its universalism). Nonetheless, be it a distortion or an improvement, the majority did not think it represented a different paradigm from the rest of the Old Testament. This, however, started to change from the '30s. As a part of this process of differentiating wisdom from the rest of the Old Testament, some scholars gradually began to interpret it as an expression of the so-called 'creation theology' and to *contrast* it with *Heilsgeschichte*.[1]

I tell the story of post-1930 academic research twice, from two different angles. In the first story I explain how the 'creation theology' of wisdom, starting from a fairly humble position, has become a major player in the theological field. This is a story of wisdom's relationship to the rest of the Old Testament. The second story is about how scholars have been struggling to find the precise definition, kernel, and (contemporary theological) significance of this 'creation theology.' So, to re-apply Crenshaw's metaphor,[2] first I tell the story of how the

---

1. As numerous scholarly discussions are about the theology of wisdom rather than about the theology of Proverbs, I use mainly this broader category in my discussion of the history of interpretation after the '30s. However, I concentrate on those specifics of the scholarly debate which apply to Proverbs and on those scholars who mention Proverbs explicitly in their discussions.

2. Crenshaw 1976b: 1.

'creation theology interpretation' of Proverbs became a beautiful woman from an often-despised little servant girl of Old Testament theology, then I turn to her inner, troublesome search for her own identity.

2.1 The Place of Wisdom Theology in the Old Testament

2.1.1 Creation and Wisdom as Subservient to *Heilsgeschichte*

In an influential essay published in 1936, Gerhard von Rad set the tone for academic discussion about wisdom's place and role in Old Testament theology for the following 30 years.[3] In this essay he connected wisdom with creation theology, a connection which will occupy much of my attention a little later. For my present purposes, however, it is more important to note what value he attributed to this creation/wisdom theology. According to him, the distinctive feature of Israel's faith is her presentation of the *Heilsgeschichte* and the topic of creation only serves this presentation as an introduction, as a stock of metaphors, or as a secondary correction which enriches it. As he wrote,

> We have found a great deal of evidence for the doctrine that Yahweh created the world, but we have not found the doctrine expressed as a religious actuality, standing on its own, forming the main theme of a passage in its own right. It has always been related to something else, and subordinated to the interests and content of the doctrine of redemption.[4]

The very rare passages in which creation appears independently and not only as a theme supporting *Heilsgeschichte* (like Psalms 19 and 104, and the wisdom writings) usually lack a deeply Yahwistic character and they rather have 'an Egyptian outlook passed on to Israel by travelling teachers of wisdom.'[5] This non-Yahwistic nature is the reason why the creation-emphasis of wisdom texts was attached to Israel's testimony about God's saving acts only later:

> The doctrine of redemption had first to be fully safeguarded, in order that the doctrine that nature, too, is a means of divine self-revelation might not encroach upon or distort the doctrine of redemption, but rather broaden and enrich it.[6]

As many have pointed out, von Rad was very probably influenced by Barth. Just like Barth's arguments against natural theology, his article was also polemi-

---

3. English translation: von Rad 1984: 53–64.
4. Von Rad 1984: 59.
5. Von Rad 1984: 62.
6. Von Rad 1984: 63.

cally inspired to discredit the National Socialist ideological use of creation.[7] However, regardless of the possible political motivation behind the writing of the article, von Rad's argument finds its place rather naturally in the contemporary field of Old Testament scholarship. Fichtner, for example, also recognised the connection between wisdom and the Creator God and that this connection gives a foreign, Egyptian–Babylonian, outlook to biblical wisdom.[8] Another, even more influential, forerunner was Walther Eichrodt. Although, contra von Rad, he emphasised the ancient age and theological importance of the doctrine of creation, he agreed with von Rad at two crucial points. First, he also recognised a connection between wisdom and the doctrine of creation. Second, he also argued that the uniqueness of the Israelite version of the creation doctrine was provided only by the context of the covenant and by the integration of the creation-theme into Israelite history.[9] Thus, however important a role von Rad's supposed political motivation played, his article was also a genuine programmatic summary and improvement of the arguments of some influential Old Testament scholars of the early '30s.

That von Rad's article was not purely a political statement gained another confirmation more than 20 years later when von Rad reinforced his view of the secondary nature of creation and wisdom thinking. True enough, by this time there had been some changes in the details of his thought. For example, he did not consider all creation texts as late as in his 1936 essay, and he placed the flourishing of wisdom into a period which he called 'Solomonic Enlightenment,' when the Jerusalem royal court had an international atmosphere and when many of Israel's traditions were de-sacralised.[10] Nevertheless, despite this supposedly venerable history of wisdom, it had still an inferior position in von Rad's thinking. He discussed wisdom at the end of his first volume of *Old Testament The-*

---

7. Brown 1999: 8 n. 32; Brueggemann 1996: 177–190, 178; Miller 1995: 155–168; Rendtorff 1993: 94–96; etc. Susannah Heschel's summary of the argument of some Nazi theologians shows how creation theology was used to justify racism: 'Just as God had created societal orders—marriage, family, Volk, profession, hierarchy, property, and so forth—God had given each Volk a task and place on earth. Believers in racial hierarchy could see it as an extension of the biblical account of God's creation of hierarchical orders within nature, and social orders such as marriage, and Christians were told that racial hierarchies were an extension of the divine order.' (Heschel 2008: 19.)

8. Fichtner 1933: 104–105, 111–113.

9. Eichrodt 1935: 40–50. It is noteworthy that in the 1964 edition of his work Eichrodt refers affirmingly to von Rad's discussion of wisdom in von Rad's Old Testament Theology (Eichrodt 1967: 81 n. 3).

10. Von Rad 1962: 139, 429–431. Von Rad published his thoughts about the so-called 'Solomonic Enlightenment' for the first time in 1944 (von Rad 1966a: 166–204) and he returned to it in several of his later writings. His historical reconstruction of this 'Solomonic enlightenment' was highly influential in the third quarter of the century (see, for example, Kayatz 1966: 135–136). Its importance for the wisdom literature was echoed in the English literature, for example, by Brueggemann 1972 and by Heaton 1974: 101–161.

ology under the section 'Israel's Answer.'¹¹ The core proclamation, to which Israel only answered through its wisdom teaching, was still about the saving acts of God.

There were many who popularised von Rad's views before the late '60s. In the USA, G. Ernest Wright argued that 'the difficulty of the wisdom movement was that its theological base and interest were too narrowly fixed.'¹² B. D. Napier even more than 25 years after the publication of von Rad's original article published a quite thorough English recension of it and argued for its truth:

> Certainly a belief in divine creation was known, and held; but its expression was in this form of cultic recitation [i.e., Deut. 26:5-9] either deliberately avoided, presumably in reaction against what was seen as Canaanite abuse and distortion of that faith, or it was deemed quite unessential in such a terse articulation of the Yahweh faith. For the Yahwist himself, of course, the creation-faith (Gen 2:4b ff.) is essential, it must be articulated; but here too it takes its place in a supporting role, crucial certainly, but secondary.¹³

By this time, however, these views hardly needed a brave defence among biblical scholars. Reventlow lists Anderson, Bauer, Beaucamp, Bernhardt, Boman, Festorazzi, Foerster, de Haes, Hoguth, Humphreys, Lambert, Martin-Achard, Saebø, Vischer, and Zimmerli among others who followed von Rad—and his list is still far from being comprehensive.¹⁴

However, creation theology was about to get a strong advocate who quickly changed this virtually uniform scholarly discussion.

2.1.2 Creation and Wisdom as More Substantial than *Heilsgeschichte*

Although there had been a few dissenting voices already between 1930 and 1965,¹⁵ the real challenge to the scholarly consensus came in the second half of

---

11. Von Rad 1962: 383–457.
12. Wright 1952: 104.
13. Napier 1962: 31.
14. Reventlow 1985: 141; see also Martin's discussion of the neglect of wisdom in the work of some of the here listed scholars in Martin 1995: 92–93.
15. Lütgert thought that the prophets' message is based on a creation-belief and that, though he dismissed the approach of the *Deutschen Christen*, it was a mistake that the *Bekennende Kirche* (including Barth and his followers) downgraded the importance of creation (Lütgert 1984 [reprint of the 1934 first edition]—about the place of creation theology in the theological debates of the German church in the '30s, see Werner Neuer's introduction to the 1984 edition). Lindeskog and Priest both referred to Old Testament creation-doctrine (Priest specifically in connection with wisdom) as a doctrine on equal standing with *Heilsgeschichte* (Lindeskog 1953: 4–6; Priest 1976: 288, originally a paper read at a conference in 1962). Von Rad's placing of wisdom to a theologically secondary place was also criticised by Gerstenberger in 1965 (Gerstenberger 1965b: 118–119). About Gerstenberger's view, see the discussion on page 38.

the '60s and early '70s with the works of Hans Heinrich Schmid.[16] Schmid argued that the ancient Near Eastern thinking in Egypt, Mesopotamia, and Israel was dependent on the notion of world order. This order was created by the supreme god of the pantheon and penetrated the social and the natural worlds alike. According to the ancient peoples, it could be explored and expressed in all spheres of life, namely wisdom, law, nature, warfare, cult, and kingship. This creational world order was not only a key concept of wisdom literature, it was in fact the conceptual frame of the whole Old Testament theology.[17] Thus, according to Schmid, creation theology is not a secondary layer in biblical thinking, quite the opposite, it is the primary layer on which all the other ideas depend:

> The controlling background of OT thought and faith is the view of a comprehensive world order and, hence, a creation faith in the broad sense of the word—a creation faith that Israel in many respects shared with her environment.[18]

The 'order language,' according to Schmid, may be the most obvious in the case of wisdom literature. The wise person 'does *Maat* [the Egyptian expression for world order according to Schmid], speaks *Maat*, creates *Maat*.'[19]

Of course, argued Schmid, besides the substantial similarities, this order-thinking had different nuances and modes of expressions in the different cultures of the ancient Near East. The Israelite parallel to Egyptian *Ma'at* was 'righteousness.' Whenever it is mentioned it refers to the world order:

> The concepts ṣedeq, ṣĕdāqâ, and ṣaddîq—among others—play a dominant role; the emphasis, however, is not upon specific acts of justice but, rather, on aspects of the one, harmonious order of the world.[20]

Since the publication of his works the majority of biblical scholars have accepted Schmid's thoughts about the importance of 'world order' in Old Testament thinking. Some have followed him in considering this order/creation thinking more foundational in one way or the other than anything else in Old Testament theology. Consider, for example, the following statements of Knierim:

> Israel perceived the structure of the world as the ultimate theodicy of Yahweh. If this structure fails, Yahweh fails, and nothing matters any more.... Therefore, creation appears for P as the unshakable realm of God's presence in the world, in contrast to the shaking course of human history including his own history. And it appears as the ulti-

---

16. His two major works were Schmid 1966 and Schmid 1968.
17. Schmid 1974b: 31–63, based on a presentation in Lavaterhause, Zürich, on 10 Sept. 1973.
18. Schmid 1984: 110–111.
19. Schmid 1974a: 67, a paper originally read at the Philosophy department of Bonn University on 16 Nov. 1972.
20. Schmid 1984: 107–108.

mate foundation and criterion from which his conception of Israel's new future will have to be devised.... The 'world-order' explicated what it meant for Israel to say Yahweh.[21]

Or more recently Fretheim:

> God's goal is a new creation, not a new redemption. There must be redemption if creation is to be and become what God intends it to be, but the redemption is not an end in itself; it has finally to do with creation, a new creation.[22]

However, not everyone has followed Schmid the whole way to his conclusion that 'creation is more substantial than history.' Some have stopped at 'halfway' and considered creation and history as equal partners.

2.1.3   Creation and Wisdom as Equal to *Heilsgeschichte*

Around the time of the appearance of Schmid's works there was another important contribution to the question of creation's place in Old Testament theology. Bernhard W. Anderson published an important study in 1967, titled *Creation versus Chaos*. In it, he argued that 'it is quite likely that the period before the monarchy was a time when the creation-faith and the Exodus-faith existed side by side without being harmonized completely,' but, very much in accordance with von Rad's view, 'Israel, in reaction to the prevailing nature religions, *gave* the [creation] belief a secondary place.'[23] Anderson also followed von Rad when he suggested that wisdom found a more favourable setting in the court of the united kingdom. Where he diverted somewhat from von Rad is that in his understanding creation (and creation-based wisdom) played a major role in the Davidic covenant theology of the southern kingdom. Thus, even if creation and wisdom were given a secondary place in general, there was at least one covenantal tradition in which they had an important function. The everlasting Davidic covenant is based on the order established by the creator God:

> Yahweh's power in the creation is related theologically to his covenant with David. Yahweh has established, and he will maintain, order, for 'righteousness and justice' are the foundation of his throne. The Davidic king, standing in this strength, will not be overpowered by any foes.[24]

---

21. Knierim 1981: 76, 81, 86. See also Høgenhaven's critique of von Rad which is mainly based on Schmid's thoughts on order (Høgenhaven 1988: 97–98).

22. Fretheim 2005: 12. We have to add, however, that both Knierim and Fretheim emphasise more than Schmid that they do not want creation and redemption to be collapsed into each other in their theological interpretations of the Old Testament (see Fretheim 2005: 200; Knierim 1981: 83).

23. Anderson 1967: 54, 52–53, original emphasis.

24. Anderson 1967: 67.

This, however, was not true for the history-based northern Mosaic covenant tradition. Thus, according to Anderson, our Bible contains two covenant traditions in one of which creation and wisdom texts play a major role. He argues that the modern reader should pay attention to both traditions: to the contingency of the human history of the Mosaic covenant tradition but also to the stability and grace which can be found in the Davidic, creation-based covenant tradition.[25]

Von Rad published his last book, which happens to be about wisdom, three years after Anderson's *Creation versus Chaos*. In this work von Rad revised his earlier views of wisdom's inferior theological position in the Old Testament. Although there is no sign that he was aware of Anderson's work (at least he never refers to him), there are some similarities between their conclusions. Von Rad did not go into speculations about wisdom's different relationship to different covenants, as (the earlier) Anderson did, but he understood wisdom as an alternative way to covenant in relating to God and the world. According to him there was 'a deep gulf between the intellectual striving of the wise teachers on the one hand and that of the narrators, theologians of history, etc., on the other.'[26] This echoes Anderson's opinion about the two different theological traditions in the Old Testament, but in a way it emphasises wisdom's importance even more as it is not attached to any kind of covenant theology. According to this later von Rad, in other parts of the Bible Yahweh reveals himself through prophets, the cult, and historical events, whereas in wisdom writings it is the world order established by God which turns to people and calls them with the voice of Yahweh:

> In Egypt, the idea of a primitive order, which included both nature and human life, goes back to the earliest period. Can the same not be presupposed in Israel, too? . . .
> It is not Yahweh who is speaking [in Proverbs 8]. This is puzzling, for in these texts we find the form of divine self-revelation. Obviously the situation here is considerably different from what it is in the prophets, who never addressed their readers in the first person. . . . He is much more than the greatest of the prophets, he is, indeed, the mystery inherent in the creation of the world. In the opinion of the teachers, Yahweh had at his service a quite different means, besides

---

25. Anderson 1967: 75–77. Anderson more or less maintains his theory in his later writings (Anderson 1984: 7–8). See Dell's critique of Anderson's historical reconstruction of wisdom's different relationship to the different covenantal traditions in Dell 2007: 63–64. In his recent work, Anderson seems to use more nuanced language, though he still maintains the special relationship between the Jerusalem cult and wisdom: 'Wisdom has influenced all of Israel's covenantal traditions, but it is especially compatible with royal (Davidic) covenant theology.' (Anderson 1999: 260.)

26. Von Rad 1972: 289.

priests and prophets, whereby he could reach men, namely the voice of primeval order, a voice which came from creation.[27]

Von Rad in this, his latest work, was influenced by Schmid, to whose works he referred several times and whose 'order-thinking' he put at the centre of his understanding of wisdom's message. He did not go as far as Schmid, considering order-thinking the most substantial layer of the whole Bible, but he went at least 'half-way,' and, changing his thoughts about the inferior position of wisdom, now he understood it as an alternative to the rest of the Bible on equal footing with it.

My impression is that von Rad managed once more to show the recommended way to many scholars, as many who have tried to clarify the theological importance of creation/wisdom theology in the last 40 years occupy a similar 'middle way.'[28] This tendency can be seen in the works of such influential scholars as Nicholson, who thought that there was an ongoing inner-Israelite controversy between the two 'worldviews' of creation theology and covenant (though he understood the covenant tradition as winning at the end and providing the distinctiveness for Israel's theology); or Brueggemann, who emphasises the different pictures of God's actions in the two theological forms of discourses and tries to hold them on equal status just like the later von Rad.[29]

However, are creation/wisdom and *Heilsgeschichte* two, so neatly differentiable traditions as von Rad or Brueggemann would let us believe? Many have disagreed as we will see shortly.

---

27. Von Rad 1972: 154, 163.
28. Though significant exceptions remain. The clearest example is Preuss who argued that wisdom does not have anything to offer to an Old Testament (and especially Christian) theology, it does not possess anything distinctively Israelite, its view of world order is simply wrong, it only leads to a theological crisis as it is seen in Job and Qohelet and von Rad recommended Israelite wisdom too uncritically in his last book. (Preuss 1989: 165–181; see also his exegetically more detailed article which was written before von Rad's book but in which Preuss occupied the same position as in his later article: Preuss 1970: 393–417.)
29. Nicholson 1986: 193–205; Brueggemann 1997: 333–358. Brueggemann's explicit reference to von Rad as one of the main figures who inspired this understanding is on page 335. It is important to note that when Brueggemann speaks about different theological discourses in tension he refers only to wisdom-thinking and not to all types of creation-thinking; according to him, other strands of creation theology do not necessarily represent an alternative discourse to the narrative/miraculous parts of the Bible. About this question, see also his more recent and more succinct Brueggemann: 2008: 75–193, in which he reiterates much that he wrote in his earlier *Theology of the Old Testament*.

2.1.4 Creation, Wisdom, and *Heilsgeschichte* as a Unity

One could contrast von Rad's and Brueggemann's above-delineated 'two alternative worldviews/forms of discourse' approach with some statements of Roland Murphy:

> [Ancient Israelites] had only one world view, not two, in which the Lord they worshipped was also the God recognized in their experience of each other and the world.[30]

> Nature, as the area in which Yahweh's will and direction ... are also to be found, is not to be separated from history.[31]

Murphy has been emphasising the unity of Israelite thinking and theology consequently from the '70s.[32] His approach has received some encouragement from recent historical research, too.

At the middle of the century, the ruling opinion about the historical origins of wisdom was that, first, wisdom's origin was foreign (mainly Egyptian); second, in Israel it was inculcated by a well-defined, separate group of people, 'the wise'; third, these wise people were connected to the royal court; and fourth, they educated prospering youth in court schools.[33] All of these points would suggest that wisdom-thinking was a well-separated segment in ancient Israel's intellectual life. This view, however, has been challenged from several directions since the late '60s.

In 1965 Gerstenberger argued that a significant part of wisdom (and that of law and cult, too) had its origin in the everyday life of early clans and not in the later royal court.[34] He claimed that this explains the many similarities between law and wisdom.[35]

---

30. Murphy 2000: 198.
31. Murphy 1975: 119.
32. Beside the above listed works, see Murphy 2002: 97–120, 221–222.
33. See, for example, the somewhat different accounts of wisdom's origins by Scott and von Rad, which, despite their differences—von Rad emphasised the Solomonic origin, Scott gave Hezekiah a bigger role—equally were built on these points (Von Rad 1962: 418–453; Scott 1955: 262–279).
34. Gerstenberger 1965b: 62–65, 115–117, 128–129, 141–148; see also Gerstenberger 1965a: 38–51, especially 49–51 and more recently Gerstenberger 2002: 64–65; for a similar recent reconstruction of wisdom's early history, see Albertz 1994: 512 and Albertz and Schmitt 2012: 336–339. Another historical reconstruction which stresses the importance of the sociological background of family for wisdom (though not as exclusively as Gerstenberger and still accepting the existence of a sociologically distinct group of sages) is that of Perdue 1997a: 223–257.
35. Gerstenberger 1965b: 130; see also Blenkinsopp 1995: 80–81, 100; Golka 1993: 70–87.

About ten years later Whybray proposed a different argument with similar effects. Although he was more open to foreign influence,[36] he also denied that wisdom should be specifically connected to the royal court or any other institution. Instead he spoke about a fairly widespread 'intellectual tradition.' According to him, wisdom writings were produced and read by relatively well educated people who

> ... belonged to a variety of circles within Israel rather than that they consciously followed and promoted the continuance of a narrow tradition within a small circle.... These men did not set themselves apart from their fellow-citizens: they were familiar with, and participants in, the other 'traditions' of Israel.... They constituted a separate 'tradition' only in the sense that they concerned themselves more than the majority of their contemporaries in an intellectual way with the problems of human life.[37]

Since these works of Gerstenberger and Whybray, many have argued that the mention of the king in Proverbs and Ecclesiastes does not warrant a royal setting, that the whole proof for a 'Solomonic enlightenment' is very dubious, that there is little evidence for court schools if at all, and that wisdom was more embedded in all layers of Israelite society and life than had been thought earlier.[38]

This understanding of the historical unity between 'wisdom-tradition' and 'other traditions' is also in line with the recognition that many 'non-wisdom' biblical texts possess wisdom features and concerns. The tide has been opened up (again) by von Rad's famous article about the wisdom-influence on the Joseph story, but since then almost all of the biblical books have been recognised by some as influenced by 'wisdom-thinking.'[39] However, not everyone is enthu-

---

36. Whybray 1974: 60. For Whybray's critique of Gerstenberger's theory, see Whybray 1974: 113–116; Whybray 1982: 23.

37. Whybray 1974: 55, 70; about Proverbs relationship to Israel's history, see also Whybray 1968: 65–66.

38. On royal setting, see Dell 1998: 163–186; Golka 1993: 16–35; Kassis 1999: 55–115; Weeks 1994: 41–56; though, see Perdue 2008: 100–107 who still maintains that there is a strong connection with the royal court, and see also the recent defence of the presence of a royal tone in Proverbs by Ansberry 2011. On the 'Solomonic enlightenment,' see Adams 2008: 64; Crenshaw 1976b: 19; Whybray 1982: 13–26; for further bibliography, see Barton 1984: 301 n. 6; Miller 1997: 9–24; Wilson 2004: 33 n. 112. The most positive recent evaluation of von Rad's idea that I am aware of is that of Dell 2004: 256–257 who tentatively argued that though the 'Solomonic Enlightenment' might be an overstatement, one can possibly speak about a 'Solomonic Court.' For a recent argument for the royal court as a possible *Sitz im Leben* for wisdom, see also Saebø 2012: 6–7. On court school, see Crenshaw 1998: 85–113; Golka 1993: 4–15; Jamieson-Drake 1991: *passim*; Weeks 1994: 132–156; for an argument for court (and temple) schools, see Lemaire 1990: 165–181. On wisdom's embeddedness in ancient Israelite life, see Childs 1992: 187–190; Dell 2000: 23–26, 89; Dell 2006: *passim*; Hubbard 1966: 3–33; Kline 1972: 64–67; Sneed 2011: 50–71; etc.

39. Von Rad 1966b: 292–300; Morgan 1981: *passim*.

siastic about this approach. Crenshaw criticised the often careless hunt of many scholars for 'wisdom influence,' and he is certainly right in warning against the methodological pitfalls of identifying 'wisdom influence' everywhere.[40] Sheppard's theory would also deserve some consideration in this respect. He argues that much of this 'wisdom-influence' might be actually fairly late, and, indeed, there might be some truth to his tenet that many wisdom-like texts are the results of a later 'wisdom reinterpretation' of earlier material.[41] Nevertheless, these corrections do not necessarily prove that identifying wisdom-like texts outside the wisdom corpus is irrelevant for understanding wisdom's relationship to the rest of the Bible. Later reinterpretation could hardly account for *every* 'wisdom-like' feature and content of canonical books,[42] and if one speaks about a common worldview rather than 'wisdom influence' then Crenshaw's objections also become more easily avoidable.[43] As Weeks writes,

> Common ground between wisdom and other types of literature can only be explained up to a point by presuming special circumstances in each case. If we find a lot of common ground with a lot of texts, then it becomes more reasonable to explain this in terms of a shared cultural context, and to lower the barriers between different types of author.[44]

If, as these investigations suggest, wisdom/creation, covenant, and cult existed so peacefully in the very same ancient mind, without the ancient person being aware of these 'different traditions,' then the separation of these traditions is only a modern construct, which makes it a less attractive theological option for Murphy and others.[45]

However, if we turn from these historical investigations back to our original question, to the relative importance of creation/wisdom in Old Testament *theology*, then one has to recognise that the picture is not so neat and simple. Even if one suspects that creation and history were not differentiated in ancient minds, even if they did not comprise two separate traditions, one has the right to differentiate between them as two conceptually distinct components of a unified theology. Historical research (either pro or contra a unified creation–history worldview) does not necessarily bind the hands of the Old Testament theologian. In other words, it is important to differentiate between the 'history of Isra-

---

40. Crenshaw 1969: 129–142; see also Weeks 1994: 92–109; for a recent, helpful clarification of the knotty questions of method and terminology, see Wilson 2004: 28–37.
41. Sheppard 1980; see also Clements 1995: 277.
42. Dell 2000: 89–90.
43. Crenshaw 1969: 142 n. 54; Morgan 1981: 22.
44. Weeks 2010: 136.
45. Bartholomew and O'Dowd 2011: 283–288; Dell 2000: 98–99, 167; Murphy 1975: 191–200; Murphy 1978: 35–42; Whybray 1974: 4–5. Sneed helpfully reminds us that although the different genres create their own distinct worlds, this does not necessarily mean that they represent different worldviews (Sneed 2011: 50–71).

elite religion' and the 'theology of biblical text.' One is free to construct an Old Testament theology that goes beyond the theological thinking of any individual author of the Old Testament. Thus, although the above historical arguments do encourage a unified creation–covenant theology, they do not rule out such a construction as that of Brueggemann who sees two separate strands in tension in Old Testament theology.

Nonetheless, quite a few who discuss the relationship between creation and salvation in their presentation of Old Testament theology choose a different route from Brueggemann and rather echo Murphy, who emphasised the unity of creation and history. Lindsay Wilson, for example, suggests that in the Old Testament there is a more comprehensive and fundamental category than either 'creation' or 'salvation,' namely God's active rule, or, in other words, God's sovereignty. Creation (and so wisdom) and salvation are merely two expressions of this one basic biblical tenet, and, whatever the historical background of this phenomenon might be, these two expressions interact and support each other in the Bible, and a canonical interpretation should respect this close interaction.[46]

Others seem to go even further and not only speak about 'interaction' but 'interdependence.' According to Rolf Rendtorff, for example, the Old Testament begins with creation, which shows its substantial role: creation is the presupposition of existence and so the presupposition of history.[47] But the (Noahic) covenant with God is also needed for wisdom to be able to trust in the reliability of creation.[48] Thus, neither creation nor covenant can exist without the other.[49]

A similarly close, interdependent relationship can be seen in Westermann's thought, for whom creation theology (on which wisdom is based) is the theology of blessing. Although he differentiates between blessing (creation) and deliverance (history) in his discussion, he sees these two as interdependent:

> The heart of the Bible in both the Old and the New Testaments is history. But this would not be possible if a one-dimensional salvation

---

46. Wilson 2004: 292–298. Wilson builds on others. He mentions S. Lee, *Creation and Redemption in Isaiah 40–55* (Hong Kong: Alliance Biblical Seminary, 1995); G. V. Smith, 'Is There a Place for Job's Wisdom in Old Testament Theology?' *TJ* 13 (1992) 3–20; R. L. Schultz, 'Unity or Diversity in Wisdom Theology? A Canonical and Covenantal Perspective' *TB* 48 (1997) 271–306; and Boström 1990. One wonders, however, if he could not have mentioned older forerunners, too. Levenson, for example, begins one of his most influential works with the words: 'We can capture the essence of the idea of creation in the Hebrew Bible with the word "mastery."... He reigns in regal repose, "majestic on high," all else subordinate to him. Yehezkel Kaufmann (1889–1963), one of the great Jewish biblical scholars of modern times, went a step further. He considered the concept that I am calling mastery to be more than merely the essence of creation: he deemed it "the basic idea of Israelite religion."' (Levenson 1988: 3.)

47. Rendtorff 2005: 721–724.

48. Rendtorff 1993: 109.

49. A brief summary of this interdependence in Rendtorff's theology can be found in Miller 1995: 161–162.

were involved. If the Bible were only an account of God's salvation and God's judgment, then these two would merely alternate without variation. When the Bible speaks of God's contact with mankind, his blessing is there alongside his deliverance. History comes into being only when both are there together.[50]

> To be sure, the history of the people of Israel begins with a divine act of salvation, ... but ... to this saving is added God's blessing activity, which cannot be simply inserted or subordinated to God's salvation acts. In the structure of the Pentateuch this is demonstrated by the fact that the center (Exodus to Numbers) is determined by God's saving, while the framework (Genesis and Deuteronomy) is predominantly determined by God's blessing.[51]

Therefore, Westermann emphasises that history would not be able to exist without blessing and that, though history is in a sense the centre, blessing is not subordinated. These two strands are differentiated logically, rather for a heuristic reason, but, just like Murphy and others, he emphasises their unity and not the tension between them as Brueggemann does.[52]

Indeed, if one follows Murphy (and Wilson, Rendtorff, Westermann, etc.) and sees wisdom in unity with the rest of the Bible, then not only is the priority of *Heilsgeschichte* not tenable, but the whole question of priority between wisdom and *Heilsgeschichte* might become obsolete.[53]

2.1.5 Summary

Regarding wisdom's place in Old Testament theology, in the last 80 years the whole territory between the extremes of 'theologically inferior' and 'theologically superior' has been traversed.

Von Rad did not follow the judgement of the previous century on the supposedly degenerate Judaism before the time of Jesus, nevertheless his devaluing of wisdom can in a sense be considered as taking further some of the processes that began in the nineteenth century. Just as Proverbs' position was changed during the nineteenth century from being a 'favourite' Old Testament book to being a 'favourite' book among the later, 'degenerate,' Judaistic parts of the Old Testament, beginning in the '30s, due to von Rad's influence, wisdom had to

---

50. Westermann 1978: 4.
51. Westermann 1998: 14, see also his discussion of wisdom in relation to the theology of blessing on pages 99–101.
52. Brueggemann follows Westermann in his general understanding of creation's role and place in Old Testament theology, but in the case of wisdom literature he seems to allow for a much bigger tension between it and the 'core testimony of the Old Testament' than Westermann does. The detailed discussion of Brueggemann's views of wisdom see later.
53. See also Dell 2003: 130.

occupy an even humbler position for a little while. It is one of the ironies of history that as the anti-Judaistic climate of the nineteenth century might have contributed to wisdom losing its once prestigious theological respect, the fight against antisemitic national socialism which legitimised itself by 'creation' might have also contributed to pushing wisdom even further to the margins of theological thinking.

However, whatever social, political, and ideological influences led to the devaluation of biblical wisdom writings, this opinion was not maintained for very long. Since the '60s very few scholars would have agreed with such views. On the contrary, creation/wisdom has increasingly been seen as the most substantial theological layer of the Old Testament (Schmid), or as an alternative theological tradition on equal footing with the other traditions (later von Rad), or as a mode of approach to reality which is so much in harmony with covenantal/historical thinking that it is hardly differentiable from it (Murphy).

So far, however, our focus on the importance of creation/wisdom relative to *Heilsgeschichte* has concealed important nuances of scholars' detailed descriptions of its theology. We shall turn our attention to this question now.

2.2 The Definition of Wisdom Theology

2.2.1 The Debate between the Interpretative Schools of 'Anthropocentric Independence' and 'Cosmic Order' ('30s–'60s)

It was only in 1964 that Walther Zimmerli wrote down his often quoted sentence: 'Wisdom thinks resolutely within the framework of a theology of creation.'[54] However, as we have already seen, the story of contrasting wisdom literature with the rest of the Old Testament and the use of the category of 'creation' for this aim started much earlier. The period between 1930 and 1964 comprised a transitory phase regarding the recognition of creation theology's importance for describing wisdom. At the beginning of this period Baumgartner could still write a brief, but influential work on wisdom, summarising the findings of the previous decades, without referring to creation at all.[55] At the end of it, Zimmerli just stated explicitly what had already been granted by many implicitly.

Already in the '30s many referred to creation as something which provides a distinctive theological vision to wisdom literature.[56] Rankin's discussion is an early representative of this new emphasis on creation, which was soon to become the general trend in Old Testament scholarship. Arguing against Oesterley's view that wisdom was influenced by the prophets, he writes that

---

54. Zimmerli 1964: 148.
55. Baumgartner 1933.
56. Eichrodt 1935: 40–43; Fichtner 1933: 111–113; von Rad 1984: 61–63 (German original published in 1936); Rankin 1936: 9–15.

> Thought, of course, especially in a small nation, can never be confined as in hermetically sealed compartments. Doubtless the wisdom-writers were not uninfluenced by the prophets.... But three things appear to belong to the 'wise' and to their teaching, as possessions under their own title-deed and right, namely, the individualism..., the idea of reward... as the motive of good or social conduct, and above all the application of the creation-idea.[57]

But what did 'creation theology' mean for these scholars? Zimmerli himself contributed to the debate over the precise nature of this creation theology by one of his early essays, published in 1933.[58] Although in that essay he did not use the expression 'creation theology,' it was there implicitly. In his emblematic 1964 article he basically repeated the main claims of his 30-years-earlier essay, identifying its reconstruction of wisdom-thinking with 'creation theology.' Furthermore, many who have been struggling with the meaning of wisdom- and creation-thinking since the '30s, explicitly or implicitly keep referring to the statements of that 1933 article. Therefore, Zimmerli's 1933 essay seems to be a good starting point for our story of the scholarly definitions of creation/wisdom theology.

Zimmerli's main claim in 1933 was that Old Testament wisdom had an 'anthropocentric–eudämonistic' point of departure.[59] Wisdom describes humans as autonomous agents, free to make their own decisions:

> It is autonomous man—not apprehended nor enslaved by any prior order—who wants to organize freely from himself outwards and to assess the world....
> Wisdom admonition lacks authoritative character.... Authority rules categorically. Counsel is debatable.[60]

Thus, instead of focusing on God, wisdom literature is mainly interested in the happiness of humans, and the chief motivation to follow the counsels of the wise is God's reward:

> One could multiply the examples which show that in exactly those places where we most expect some reference to a fixed order and authority by reference to Yahweh as the justification to an admonition, we do not find the creative, ordering God, but rather the God who rewards in the consequence of man's upright conduct (conversely, punishing the fools and the godless).[61]

---

57. Rankin 1936: 14.
58. English translation: Zimmerli 1976a: 177–204.
59. Zimmerli 1976a: 197.
60. Zimmerli 1976a: 177, 183.
61. Zimmerli 1976a: 185.

It was Hartmut Gese who, in 1958, challenged Zimmerli's claims most forcefully.[62] Contrary to Zimmerli, argued Gese, the focus of wisdom is not on human beings but on the order of the world. In Egypt, explained Gese, the divine order of the world was called *Ma'at* and even the gods had to obey the rules of this order.[63] Israelite wisdom was searching for a similar order. This order and wisdom's interest in it is most explicitly expressed by the so-called *Tun–Ergehen Zusammenhang* (act–consequence connection).[64] Here Gese was referring to the theory of Klaus Koch, who had claimed that the Old Testament does not teach that God rewards and punishes humans for their deeds but that the reward and punishment are already incorporated into the acts themselves.[65] Yahweh, like a midwife, might care for the birth of consequences and occasionally might speed up the process, but he does not inflict a punishment or reward from outside of the deed itself.[66] Koch's claim was almost immediately heavily contested by many, especially his more general claim about the whole Old Testament,[67] but most scholars working on Old Testament wisdom literature accepted his argument in the limited case of wisdom.[68] So did Gese, too.[69]

Therefore, Gese argued, one cannot claim that the ideal of a wise person in Proverbs is the 'autonomous person':

> We cannot say, that the wise is 'the autonomous man—not apprehended nor enslaved by any prior order—who wants to organize freely from himself outwards and to assess the world.' It is in fact the task of the wise to 'listen' to the order; he cannot organize the world from himself, only in submission to the established order.[70]

---

62. Gese 1958; Gese's opinion was adumbrated by earlier interpreters, for example by Eichrodt and Fichtner who had discussed order in relation with creation and wisdom already in the '30s: Eichrodt 1935: 40–43; Fichtner 1933: 111–113.
63. Gese 1976: 11–21.
64. Gese 1976: 42–45.
65. Koch 1983: 57–87.
66. Koch 1983: 73.
67. For a thorough bibliography for Koch's thesis and its reception, see Krašovec 1999: 152 n. 85–86. It might be worthwhile to note that many of his followers and attackers used stronger, less nuanced language than Koch himself. They spoke about a relation between act and consequence 'effected automatically' (Schmid 1984: 106), about a 'mechanical correspondence' between deeds and their results (Murphy 1987: 450), or about an 'automatic or built in retribution' (Barton 1979: 11).
68. See, for example, Reventlow's article, which criticises Koch's theory in general but accepts it for the early wisdom (Reventlow 1960: 311–327, especially 315 and 325–326). Crenshaw 1976a: 293, somewhat misleadingly, refers to Reventlow's article as a complete refutation of Koch's arguments—this is true indeed about most parts of the Old Testament, but not about sentence-wisdom where Reventlow accepted Koch's views.
69. Gese 1958: *passim*, especially 42–45.
70. Gese 1958: 35, quoting Zimmerli 1976a: 177.

Furthermore, wisdom is not *eudaemonistic* as it is not primarily interested in one's happiness but in finding the world order. The *eudaemonistic* outlook, argued Gese, is only a misleading appearance, resulting from the ancient's 'synthetic life understanding,' that is, from that peculiarity of their worldview that they did not differentiate between deeds and their results.[71]

The most influential follower of Gese was Hans Heinrich Schmid.[72] They disagreed in some details; for example Gese thought that the speciality of Israelite religion was that many proverbs affirmed Yahweh's freedom from the world order, whereas Schmid did not see a difference here between Israelite and foreign thinking.[73] However, their understanding of 'order' was basically the same.

As we have seen in the previous section about the place of creation/wisdom in Old Testament theology, Schmid went even a step further than Gese and suggested that the world order is not only the key concept of Egyptian and Israelite wisdom, but that it was in fact a most important theological category in the whole ancient Near East, and it is the most substantial idea of the whole Bible, not only wisdom literature. Not everyone was able to follow Schmid in this, but the vast majority accepted that the world order is the key concept of at least Old Testament wisdom. It basically became a *terminus technicus* for the theology of wisdom and creation for many. As Crenshaw wrote in 1976, 'It is no longer necessary to justify the claim that the concept of order lies at the heart of wisdom thinking.'[74]

However, Zimmerli's original ideas about the anthropocentric nature of wisdom were not completely defeated. Just as Gese's book (1958) was at least partially an answer to Zimmerli's 1933 article, we can understand Zimmerli's 1964 article as an answer to Gese. In it he accepted that wisdom is interested in the order of the world and, therefore, one cannot call it *eudaemonistic*. Thus, in these issues Zimmerli had changed his mind, no doubt partly because of Gese's

---

71. Gese 1958: 43.

72. Another important work which closely follows the direction set by Gese is that of Kayatz, who argues that the figure of Wisdom in Proverbs 1 and 8 is parallel with the Egyptian goddess *Ma'at* (Kayatz 1966: *passim*).

73. Schmid did not think that Yahweh interrupted the deed–consequence relationship in Proverbs. Sometimes he did cause one to do a deed, but if someone has already done a deed than Yahweh was bound by the order. If this is freedom, then all the other gods in the ancient Near East were free, too, argued Schmid (Schmid 1966: 147–148). For Gese's view, see Gese 1958: 45–50; many have followed Gese in this opinion, for example Humphreys 1978: 187; a similar opinion is also echoed by Zimmerli himself (Zimmerli 1976b: 48–49).

74. Crenshaw 1976b: 27; scholars who speak about order as the key concept of wisdom included, without the slightest intention of comprehensiveness, Baumann 1998: 63, 70; Blenkinsopp 1995: 19; Fox 1968: 55–69; Hermisson 1978: 43–44; Jenks 1985: 44; Knierim 1981: *passim*, for example 74–75, 87, 91; Kugel 1997: 9–32; Perdue 1977: *passim*; see, for example, 135–137; Williams 1981: 17ff; Whybray 1965b: 61–63.

arguments.[75] However, according to Zimmerli, it is questionable whether this world order was wisdom's *main* interst. He argued that Proverbs teaches about world order only to enable humans to act as responsible, autonomous persons:

> Egyptian Wisdom shows that Wisdom lives in the sphere of a comprehensive faith of an order that can be characterised by the conception of divine *ma'at* (truth). But having secured this insight we must ask what is a more precise understanding of the Wisdom structure. Is Wisdom to be described simply as the preaching of the worship of *ma'at*? Does Wisdom intend some kind of service of God—the God behind *ma'at*? If we accept this understanding, do we not alter the central aim of both Egyptian and Israelite wisdom? Do we not confuse Wisdom's honouring of the sphere of *ma'at*, in which Wisdom lives without doubt, with the real intention of Wisdom?...
> Wisdom shows man as a being who goes out, who apprehends through his knowledge, who establishes, who orders his world.... Israel's faith must understand the creation of man by God as an event in which God bestows on man a great gift... in giving His gift to man God empowers him with a striking independence.[76]

We can conclude that between 1930–1964, besides 'creation theology' gradually gaining the status of the main theological interpretative framework for wisdom literature, there was an ongoing debate among those who connected wisdom with creation. Some saw wisdom's creation theology as a humble, pious search for God's creation order (Gese), others described it as an emphasis on human autonomy (Zimmerli).

2.2.2. 'Secular' Interpretation (late '60s, early '70s)

Zimmerli's later article proved that it is possible to combine the above mentioned two understandings of creation theology, though one has to decide whether world order or humans provide the main focus of the text. Zimmerli's own solution was that world order provides the general background for wisdom-thought but the latter is mainly interested in human possibilities in this order.

The interpretations which stress the notion of 'secular' can be seen as variations on Zimmerli's theme. 'Secular' was one of those words which seldom received a clear definition and could refer to a number of things like human-centredness; this-worldliness; lack of interest in cult, God, and sacred history;

---

75. Already three years before publishing his article, in 1961, he admitted in a small symposion that by then he would '... wholeheartedly drop ... his view of a eudaemonistic objective of Proverbs, and declared that today he would formulate many of the statements of his former, youthful article more cautiously, although he would stick to his view of the anthropological design of wisdom and thence an element of aiming at success and prosperity.' (Gemser 1976: 208–219.)

76. Zimmerli 1964: 148, 150–151.

building on experience rather than revelation; etc. But whatever its often unspoken definition was, just like 'creation theology,' it was suitable to set wisdom-thought in contrast with the rest of the Bible.

Gunkel might have been the first one who used the concept 'secular' in an emphatic way to characterise wisdom. Ever since then the word has often been used, but the heyday of the 'secular' interpretation was the late '60s and early '70s. Then historical and theological interests in 'secular wisdom' went hand in hand.

Concerning theological approaches, it was first of all von Rad (1970) and Brueggemann (1972) who emphasised the 'secular' in wisdom. Von Rad contrasted the 'pan-sacralism' of pre-monarchic Israel with the 'secular,' 'enlightened' Solomonic early wisdom:

> Since the objects of this search for knowledge were of a secular kind, questions about man's daily life, systematic reflection on them was held to be a secular occupation.... [This] intellectual curiosity of old wisdom... stands in considerable contrast to the spirituality of the pre-monarchic period... which we can describe, in a felicitous expression of M. Buber's, as 'pan-sacralism'.[77]

According to von Rad, 1 Samuel 13–14 is a good example of this earlier, 'pan-sacral' thinking:

> If one follows the fairly complicated course of events, it becomes immediately clear that the narrator brings every decisive event, military advantages and setbacks as well as all human conflicts, into association with the world of the sacral and the ritual.... Every event was encompassed by rites and sacral ordinances.... [However,] in the understanding of reality, in the whole sphere of comprehension in which men's lives operated, some decisive changes must have taken place, particularly with Solomon.... To the obvious question as to the way in which this new conception finds characteristically theological expression, one must unhesitatingly reply that it does so in the recognition of a relative determinism inherent in events and also in the recognition of a relative value inherent in worldly things (life, property, honour, etc.).[78]

However, adds von Rad, we have to recognise that even in the old wisdom these secular sentences which refer to the inherent value and causality of worldly events are mixed with more obviously religious statements. The mixing of the two groups of sayings which speak about the 'experience of the world' and the 'experience of Yahweh' expresses on the one hand that 'Yahweh and the world

---

77. Von Rad 1972: 57–58.
78. Von Rad 1972: 58–59.

Theological Interpretation of Proverbs between 1930 and Today 49

were certainly not identical,' and, on the other hand, that 'Yahweh encountered man in the world.'[79]

Walter Brueggemann, combining Zimmerli's emphasis on anthropocentrism and von Rad's emphasis on secular vs. pan-sacral thinking, built his 'secular' interpretation of wisdom around the ideas of human freedom, responsibility, and Yahweh's 'non-intrusive' relationship to the world:

> Both Cox and Van Leeuwen find in the central biblical symbols of Torah, creation, exodus, and Sinai the handles by which we may understand secularization and which in part have been an impetus to it. But it is equally clear that these symbols (with that of creation excepted) really belong themselves to a sacral view of reality in which the *intrusion* and authority of the holy in the realm of human affairs causes the decisive turn....
> I believe it is much more plausible to suggest that in the wisdom tradition of Israel we have a visible expression of secularization as it has been characterised in the current discussions. Wisdom teaching is profoundly secular in that it presents life and history as a human enterprise.... Wisdom is concerned with enabling potential leaders to *manage* responsibly, effectively, and successfully. It consistently places stress on human freedom, accountability, the importance of making decisions.[80]

The theological interest in the 'secular' understanding of God and the world represented by von Rad, Brueggemann, and others,[81] was accompanied by a historical-critical interest. When Gunkel wrote about the question he did not claim that the final form of wisdom literature could be described as 'secular,' but maintained that the *oldest* wisdom was 'secular' and only 'yahwehised' later.[82] The search for the precise steps and nature of this 'yahwehisation' occupied much of the historical-critical scholarship in the twentieth century.[83] The most influential model of this 'theologisation' process was that of McKane. In his commentary, published in 1970 (the year von Rad's book about wisdom was published in Germany), he even discussed the text of Proverbs not in the order of the canonical sequence of verses but in the presumed chronological order of his hypothetical three layers (individual-focused, community-focused, God-focused verses).[84] Whybray also published a number of studies in the '60s and '70s in which he (often very tentatively) argued for a complex process of 'theo-

---

79. Von Rad 1972: 63.
80. Brueggemann 1972: 81–82, original emphases.
81. For a discussion of further literature, see Towner 1977: 132–147.
82. Gunkel 1913: column 1873.
83. Crenshaw 1976b: 24–25; Doll 1985: 42–48, 79; Eichrodt 1951: 23; Fichtner 1933: *passim*; Fox 1968: *passim*; Rylaarsdam 1946: *passim*; etc.
84. McKane 1970.

logical reinterpretation,' during which most of the Yahweh-sayings were inserted into the text of Proverbs.[85]

However, the arguments against a developmental theory which depended on an original 'secular' text and later religious re-interpretations have received significant critique in the last few decades. As the critics of such a theory usually refer only to a few of their favourite arguments, it might be worthwhile to try to collect very succinctly all of the different factors that militate against this 'from secular to religious' developmental scheme:

- The existence of a 'Solomonic enlightenment' has lost its credibility.[86]
- A large number of (otherwise seemingly old) proverbs refer to God.[87] Indeed, in some of the (probably) later sections of Proverbs (like Proverbs 25–29), there are fewer mentions of Yahweh than in some of the (probably) earlier ones (like Prov 10:1–22:16). This makes a gradual 'yahwehisation' less likely.[88]
- In many sayings it is obvious that there is a religious element involved even when Yahweh is not explicitly mentioned (like in Prov 28:9 where 'abomination' is mentioned but not Yahweh).[89]
- The explicit mention or non-mention of Yahweh can be understood simply as 'one of the variables that one can see in Proverbs (other variables being, for example, the mention or non-mention of the king, different types of parallelism, and the presence or absence of various kinds of metaphor).'[90]
- There are some passages where it is far from clear what logic would have led a redactor when he or she inserted the Yahweh sayings as they do not really relate to the context, or they relate to it in a way which even Whybray found difficult to explain by his theory of later Yahwistic insertions (like Prov 3:1-12; 19:18-23; end of chapter 21 and beginning of chapter 22).[91]
- The criteria for deciding what is early and what is late is often based on the presence or the lack of a religious flavour in the verse, which makes the whole argument suspiciously circular.[92]
- Some features of the style and structure of sayings in the different saying-collections of Proverbs differ from each other. The Yahweh sayings usually follow closely the stylistic and structural characteristics of the say-

---

85. Whybray 1965b: 72–104; Whybray 1979: 153–165.
86. Adams 2008: 64; Barton 1984: 301 n. 6; Crenshaw 1976b: 19; Wilson 2004: 33 n. 112.
87. Fox 1995: 39.
88. Dell 2006: 121–122.
89. Rendtorff 2005: 366; Dell 2004: 262.
90. Garrett 2008: 573.
91. Dell 2006: 92, 114–115.
92. Camp 1985: 45, 152; Weeks 1994: 59–60.

Theological Interpretation of Proverbs between 1930 and Today   51

ings in those sections of Proverbs in which they appear, which makes it unlikely that they are later insertions.[93]
- If there was a shift from the secular to religious in other ancient Near Eastern literature (which is debated), such a shift happened well before biblical wisdom literature was written. In the light of this cultural milieu it is unlikely that biblical wisdom began with a secular phase.[94]
- Even the supposedly early layers express a keen interest in 'order,' so it is unlikely that they were less religious and did not refer to Yahweh—Schmid in fact argued that there was rather a development in the other direction: from a more theological wisdom into a more human-centred one.[95]
- It is only the literary convention of sentence-literature (i.e., that they are without context) that makes them sound secular.[96] Ignoring the context, one could find numerous 'secular looking' verses even in Ben Sira, although no one would suspect that there was an original, secular proto-Ben Sira.[97]
- In the case of certain saying-pairs it is just as plausible to conjecture that one of them presupposes the other as it is to suspect that one of them is a later insertion (like Prov 12:2 and Prov 12:3).[98] The religious elements often do not seem to be only an 'afterthought.'[99]
- The views of McKane, Whybray and others might have been too influenced by an insufficiently self-critical evolutionary/developmental thinking of the twentieth century.[100]
- Theories of a more organic relationship between wisdom and non-wisdom have gained credibility. If a separation from prophets and priests is not likely then why do we not find a 'secular' layer in their works, too?[101]
- The 'wisdom-influence' in other parts of the Bible suggests that the topic of 'the interrelationship between the human and the divine was there from the beginning,' and the stress on the human side is not the privilege of only one age.[102]
- Some, seemingly non-religious sayings might in fact be deeply religious in the light of an ancient Near Eastern worldview. For example, the king in some sayings can be understood as God's representative.[103]

---

93. Weeks 1994: 64.
94. Adams 2008: 78–79; Priest 1976: 284; Weeks 1994: 66–69.
95. Dell 2000: 29; Schmid 1966: 144–168.
96. See Camp 1985: 165–166.
97. Priest 1976: 284; Waltke 1979: 307.
98. Gese 1958: 37–38, see also page 32 about the impossibility of dating ancient Near Eastern texts based on their religiosity.
99. Hubbard 1966: 18.
100. Adams 2008: 78–79; Dell 2000: 31; Hubbard 1966: 19; see also Weeks 1994: 62–63.
101. See, for example, Dell 2006: 15.
102. Dell 2000: 171–172; Morgan 1981: 153.
103. See Dell 1998: 176, 182, 185.

- Yahweh and wisdom often seem to be interchangeable in certain parts of Proverbs, which also gives a flavour of religiosity even without using religious vocabulary.[104]
- If the role of Yahweh is stressed more in later texts, it often simply makes more explicit what was already implicitly there in the earlier texts.[105]
- The divide between secular and religious is anachronistic when applied to the ancient Near East, and the lack of clarity regarding the definition of 'secular' makes the whole theory less credible.[106]
- The expression 'fear of God' occurs in older biblical texts just as well as it occurs throughout the ancient Near East (though probably not as often as in biblical texts), which makes it unlikely that one could designate a text as 'later' based on the occurrence of this expression in it.[107]
- Both wisdom and Yahweh are such key concepts in the book of Proverbs that it is hard to imagine that one of them is there primarily as a result of later redaction.[108]

Not all of the above points are equally persuasive; nevertheless, because of the cumulative force of so many possible counter-arguments, the theory of a clear process of theologising gradually lost its popularity.[109]

In parallel with the loss in confidence in finding an older 'secular' layer in the book, the term 'secular' became less popular among those, who tried to fit wisdom into their (biblical) theologies.[110] Maybe this is a side effect of the historical refutation of the existence of an earlier, 'secular' layer in wisdom literature. Maybe the term lost its attractiveness for theological interpretation of wisdom because as the cultural revolution of the '60s faded away, interest in secular world-interpretations went with it. Whatever the reason was, the concept of the 'secular' ceased occupying such a prominent role in the theological utilisations of wisdom as in that of the later von Rad or the earlier Brueggemann.

2.2.3 The Proliferation of Interpretative Categories and Interests (from the '70s)

So far I have described the post-1930s history of 'creation theology interpretations' of wisdom by referring only to three main concepts: anthropocen-

---

104. Dell 2004: 261–262; Dell 2006: 125.
105. Crenshaw 2010: 82–83; Dell 2006: 58.
106. Baumann 1996: 275–276; Murphy 1978: 40.
107. See Dell 2006: 95.
108. See Dell 2006: 105.
109. Apparently not everyone is persuaded. Davies 2010: 204–215 still follows McKane's interpretation of Proverbs, without substantial interaction with the counter-arguments listed here.
110. Though it is occasionally mentioned, like in Fretheim 2005: 202–203, who uses the term while speaking about the 'autonomy' of the world.

trism, order, secularity. Even if scholars discussed other ideas of the text, the major focus of the debates was the validity and usefulness of these three categories. However, the story becomes much more colourful from the '70s onwards. Creation theology still remains *the* theology of biblical wisdom for most interpreters; anthropocentrism and order still define for many what creation theology is; the word 'secular' is still used occasionally—but numerous other interpretative categories gain special significance. Some of these are brand new; others are old, but now reinvigorated. It is technically true for many interpreters that these new themes often just define the old categories of creation, order, and anthropocentrism more precisely or bring out their significance for today. Practically, however, they represent the major interests of the given interpreter, and the old, broader categories are mentioned often only in passing. In the following I am going to provide a brief inventory of these new themes.

2.2.3.1 Theodicy, Divine Justice

James Crenshaw is one of the few who argues that creation theology is not *the* theology of wisdom. According to him, the main interest of wisdom is the justice of God (or the failure of that justice) and creation theology is only an aspect of this question: 'The function of creation theology, in my view, is to undergird the belief in divine justice.'[111]

2.2.3.2 Liberation

Some have argued that wisdom literature stabilised the social status quo through its teaching about order.[112] However, many have emphasised that it is not inherently against liberation. People can legitimate their wish for *another* order by it, and it gives a broader scope for liberation: it involves the nations, the rich as well as the poor, and it also emphasises that the creator God supports liberation by his creation power.[113]

2.2.3.3 Feminism

The female figure of Wisdom in the book of Proverbs has attracted many feminist interpreters, though they reach opposing conclusions about wisdom literature. Some stress the feminine metaphors for the divine (in general, femi-

---

111. Crenshaw 1976b: 34; See also Crenshaw 1976a: 289–304.
112. Brueggemann 1990: 117–132; Ruether 2005: 91 argues, based on Perdue's reconstruction of the *Sitz im Leben* of Proverbs 1–9 in the Persian period (Perdue 1997b: 78–101), that Proverbs aims to stabilise the ruling orders of Yehud after the return from the exile. Rogerson 2009: 63 also contends that reading Prov 8:22-32, if unaccompanied by other Old Testament texts, encourages the reader to accept and affirm the present world order.
113. Landes 1984: 135–151; Middleton 1994: 257–277; not referring to 'liberation theology' explicitly, John J. Collins also highlights that wisdom literature can undermine structures and contains 'the seeds of a debunking tendency' no less than the other parts of the Bible (Collins 1980: 1–17).

nist interpreters are more willing to identify Lady Wisdom with the divine than others) and the intrinsic value of everyday life;[114] others criticise the lack of call for breaking down hierarchical systems and the typical male image of women as potentially dangerous.[115] Some try to describe both the supposed positive and the negative sides of wisdom;[116] others, while recognising the patriarchal setting of the book, seek to interpret it in a way that empowers women.[117]

2.2.3.4 Ecological Interpretation

Ecological interpretation emphasises nature's potential to describe the divine and the complex interrelatedness of humans, nature, and God in wisdom texts. It also stresses the human responsibility in maintaining the divine order which comprises both the natural and the social spheres.[118]

2.2.3.5 Ecofeminism

The last two interests are often combined. Ecofeminism 'claims that all forms of oppression are connected,' and one cannot fight only one of them without fighting all of them, the whole 'model of hierarchy.'[119]

2.2.3.6 Unification of Different Modes of Biblical Theologies

Terrien argues that there are two different theological modes in the Old Testament. One is based on listening, integrating the themes of obedience, ethics, divine name, and social justice. The other concentrates on seeing, including glory, ritual, and cult. Terrien sees wisdom as the bridge between the two. Wisdom emphasises listening, but the image of Wisdom playing in the presence of Yahweh (Proverbs 8) also 'summons a mental concreteness of visibility. The call to ethical obedience is articulated with a feminine personification of wisdom, mediatrix of communion with the transcendent Creator.'[120]

2.2.3.7 Blessing

Westermann suggested the category of blessing for describing creation–wisdom thinking: 'Deliverance is experienced in events that represent God's intervention. Blessing is a continuing activity of God. . . . It cannot be experienced in an event any more than can growth or motivation or a decline of strength.'[121]

---

114. Baumann 1996; Camp 1985; Camp 1997: 100–101; Schroer 2000; Yee 1992: 85–96. Brueggemann discusses the topic of everyday life in connection with feminist interests in Brueggemann 1996: 188.
115. Newsom 1989: 142–160; Ruether 2005: 96–97.
116. Habel 2001: 23–34; Wurst 2001: 48–64.
117. Camp 1988: 14–36; Camp 1997: 85–112.
118. Dell 2010: 56–69; Dell 1994: 423–451; Johnston 1987: 66–82; Yee 1992.
119. Hobgood-Oster 2001: 37. See also Ruether 1983: 85.
120. Terrien 1981: 137.
121. Westermann 1978: 4.

2.2.3.8 Hiddenness

Brueggemann, building on the picture of the non-intrusive God emphasised by Westermann, suggests that wisdom literature speaks about the God who is hidden from human beings. Similarly Terrien: 'Between the Mosaic theophany and the final epiphany, the God of Israel does not manifest himself in history. Through wisdom, however, the *deus absconditus* still remains the *deus praesens*.'[122]

2.2.3.9 Bridge to Other Religions

Westermann also suggested that, because of its international character, biblical wisdom literature could be utilised today as a bridge to other religions. (In fact, Hubbard's suggestions were very similar already in 1966.)[123]

2.2.3.10 Natural Law, Natural Theology

Some argue that wisdom literature is a good example of natural law. Depending on the precise definition of 'natural law,' it either teaches that 'ethical principles are somehow "found written in the hearts or consciences of men"' or that ethical judgements can be 'obtained by reflecting on man's ordinary experience,' without relying on revelation.[124] Not unrelated to this topic, interpreters also speak about 'natural theology' which claims that 'there is disclosure of God, God's will, and God's nature' in the natural processes of life.[125]

2.2.3.11 Natural Rights

Following others who worked on other segments of biblical literature, Claus Westermann and Peter Doll differentiated between two creation-traditions in wisdom literature: world-creation (Proverbs 1–9) and creation of humans (Proverbs 10–31). Doll argued that the creation of humans tradition (Prov 14:31; 17:5; 22:2; etc.) is a valuable source for contemporary discussions about international human rights.[126]

2.2.3.12 God's Relationship to the World; Immanence/Transcendence

Though seldom referred to in titles of articles or books about biblical wisdom,[127] this topic has come up again and again in many interpretations of biblical wisdom. In a sense this question is one of the sources, and also a descendant,

---

122. Terrien 1981: 137; cf. Brueggemann 1997: 333–358.
123. Westermann 1995: 132–133; Hubbard 1966: 30.
124. Barr 1993; Barr 1999: 468–497; Barton 1979: 1–14; Clements 1992: 177–179; Collins 1977: 25–67; Fretheim 2005: 137, 143, 199, 202, 209; Rodd 2001: 52–64, especially 54–59. Quotations are from Barton's discussion of the definition of natural law in Barton 1979: 1–2.
125. Brueggemann 1996: 178.
126. Doll 1985: 85; Westermann 1998: 86–87.
127. The only exception known to me is Crenshaw 1977: 353–369. Another notable exception could be Eckart Otto's article on creation in the Old Testament (Otto 1983: 53–68). However, he exegetes only some psalms and Genesis 1 but does not deal with wisdom texts.

of the above-discussed 'secular interpretation,' but it is also related to the themes of natural theology and blessing. As Murphy writes, 'from a biblical point of view, the action of YHWH penetrates all things' and one of the important functions of wisdom-thinking is 'finding God in experience, a wrestling with what we would call the "secular."'[128]

2.2.3.13 An Attitude

Not wisdom's teaching itself but the attitude behind it, that is, an openness to the world in front of God, is what is most important, argues Murphy:

> Wisdom ... is not to be reduced to a teaching. ... It is as much an attitude, a dialogue with the created world, as it is a set of admonitions or insights concerning various types of conduct. ... The approach of the sage turns out to be a model for living, a style of operation that aimed at life, the gift of the Lord.[129]

2.2.3.14 Beauty, Metaphor, Imagination

Beauty, metaphor, artistry do not only provide a nice ornament in the case of wisdom literature, but they are inherently connected to the core of its message, argues Perdue: 'Sapiential imagination, ... the metaphors for God, humanity, and the world ... do not simply enhance the elegance of linguistic expression, but ... stimulate the imagination by creating a world of beauty, justice, and meaning.'[130]

2.2.3.15 Material Interests

A recurring topic in interpretations of wisdom is that an obvious and important ramification of creation theology is the importance of the material aspects of life: faith is not 'removed from human birth, suffering, and dying—bodily and communal processes in which the mystery of human life is lodged.'[131]

2.2.3.16 Worship, Meaning-Providing Affirmation

Some have emphasised wisdom literature's worshipful, joyous affirmation of the order of the universe and that the certainty about this order, that every little part has its own function, provides meaning to individual lives: 'Creation theology, as here expressed, is a glad affirmation that "the thing works!"'[132]

2.2.3.17 Moral Formation

William P. Brown emphasised 'character-formation' as a major topic in wisdom literature. This is more than simple education as it is aimed not only at

---

128. Murphy 2000: 196; Murphy 1975: 124.
129. Murphy 1985: 6–7; see also Clements 1995: 280.
130. Perdue 1994: 48.
131. Brueggemann 1996: 178; see also Westermann 1984: 92.
132. Brueggemann 1997: 337; see also Hermisson 1978: *passim* but especially pages 44 and 48.

knowledge but at human virtues.¹³³ Others also argued that Proverbs seems to be one of the few Old Testament texts which offer a vision directly comparable to that of virtue-ethics.¹³⁴

As I have noted above, the majority of these directions can be seen as practical outworkings of classic categories like 'order,' 'creation,' or 'anthropocentrism.' In 1994 Perdue organised the opinions of different scholars into four categories. Those focusing on 1. anthropocentrism (like Zimmerli); 2. cosmology (i.e., world order, like Gese); 3. theodicy (like Crenshaw); 4. the tension between anthropology and cosmology (like von Rad or Perdue himself).¹³⁵ Indeed, most, if not all of the aforementioned interpretations could be placed into one of Perdue's groups.

However, the quest for wisdom theology has become more complicated recently. Some of the most basic categories which used to be held as crucial for understanding wisdom theology, namely 'world order' and 'creation,' have been questioned as well.

2.2.4 'Creation' and 'Order' as Interpretative Categories Questioned (from the '90s)

'Order' was never without its critics. Doll thought that it unhelpfully covers the differences between the theologies in wisdom.¹³⁶ Murphy denied that recognising regularities could be described as a search for world order.¹³⁷ He was also suspicious of the idea that the wisdom writers believed in a 'buffer zone of order [that] comes between the sage and the Lord.'¹³⁸ As we have seen, Crenshaw thought that creation is only one of the many important topics in wisdom. Nevertheless, the concepts of 'order' and 'creation' were applied to wisdom literature by the vast majority of interpreters.

In 1990, however, Lennart Boström published an important study about Proverbs' concept of God (*The God of the Sages*), in which he challenges many of the majority opinions.¹³⁹ He joins Crenshaw in warning against an overemphasis on creation; joins Murphy in arguing against the usefulness of the category of 'order'; and joins those who considered Koch's *Tun–Ergehen*

---

133. Brown 1996; see also Brown 1999; Clements 1995: 281, 284–286; Estes 1997: 68–70; Treier 2011b.
134. See Briggs 2010: 28–33; Lyu 2012.
135. Perdue 1994: 34–48.
136. Like world-creation vs. human-creation or secular theology vs. religious reinterpretation (Doll 1985: 7–13, 39, 78, 83–84).
137. Murphy 1975: 121; Murphy 1985: 9; for a thorough investigation of the (somewhat changing) thought of Murphy on the subject, see Crenshaw 1995: 344–354.
138. Murphy 1987: 451; for a similar warning, see von Rad 1972: 106–107, though von Rad accepted and built on the category of order.
139. Boström 1990.

Zusammenhang, one of the pillars of an order-based interpretation, untenable. In all three areas there have been others after him who have gone even further.

2.2.4.1 Tun–Ergehen Zusammenhang

Koch's theory about the intrinsic connection between deed and consequence has never been unanimously accepted even among scholars writing about wisdom.[140] Beginning in the '90s, however, it has received an especially strong critique. Boström argued that Proverbs does occasionally express the Lord's direct role in retribution (e.g., Prov 23:10-11; 24:11-12; 29:26).[141] Freuling in his precise study of the question also lists many verses (like 10:22; 15:9-11; 20:22; 24:17-18; 25:21-22; etc.) that seem to assign a much more active role to Yahweh than Koch would have acknowledged.[142] Hatton also claims that the selection of verses mentioned by Koch provides a misleading picture.[143] Van Leeuwen drew attention to proverbial verses which actually claim or presuppose that right behaviour does not always lead to desirable results.[144] Others, partly following Van Leeuwen, also claims that the *Tun–Ergehen Zusammenhang* language has a rhetorical function (like creating the right value-system in the reader), which actually allows many exceptions and which presupposes Yahweh's active participation.[145] Some have pointed out that the verses which do not mention who the punisher or reward-giver is only emphasise the certainty of the event, and from this silence, one should not draw the conclusion that the verse speaks about an impersonal process.[146] Janowski emphasises that some proverbs (like 24:11-12) and also other passages outside of Proverbs (like Psalm 18) show that (the passive use of) שלם and שוב are not *termini technici* for impersonal processes as Koch suggested.[147] He also emphasises the social aspect of retribution, that is, that punishment is a result of reciprocal interaction between the actor and the whole society and/or God.[148] As Schmid argued that a similar *Tun–Ergehen Zusammenhang* worldview existed in Egypt in the New Kingdom

---

140. See Westermann 1995: 78; Barton 1979: 10–12; and Murphy 1978: 36 for a careful evaluation of the serious limits of the *Tun–Ergehen Zusammenhang* understanding. In relation to the prophetic literature, see Miller 1982: 121–139.

141. Boström 1990: 136.

142. Freuling 2004: *passim*, for a succinct summary of main critiques of Koch's theory in relation with Proverbs, see pp. 107–108. See also Lucas 2008: 907–908.

143. Hatton 2008: 83–116; Hatton 2011: 375–384.

144. Van Leeuwen 1992: 25–36.

145. Bartholomew and O'Dowd 2011: 270–275; Sandoval 2006: 61–66; for all of the points mentioned so far, see also Hausmann 1995: 231–247.

146. Adams 2008: *passim*, for example, pp. 3–4, 17, 79, 84, 92; Murphy 1998: 266–277.

147. Janowski 1994: 247–271, especially 261–270.

148. Janowski 1994: 256–257.

period, it is also relevant that Assmann has shown that Koch's argument is not valid for Egyptian literature of any time, either.[149]

2.2.4.2 World Order

Though the idea of world order is not necessarily connected to an 'automatic' *Tun–Ergehen Zusammenhang*, it can very easily have this connotation, as Boström warns:

> The problem with using the term 'order' ... lies in the connotations: ... it designates a particular world-view ... in which 'order' is regarded as an impersonal principle governing all things ... rendering God's continued involvement redundant. However, it should be noted that one could hardly find a view which was more contrary to what we know of the mindset of the sages or the textual material.... There is reason to be hesitant in applying to the material a term which is not represented in wisdom's own vocabulary and which usually is understood as signifying an independent entity which acts on its own.[150]

Gese and Schmid based their arguments for world order on Egyptian parallels. However, more recent Egyptologists, most notably Jan Assmann, have refuted the earlier view of the existence of an impersonal world order in ancient Egyptian thinking. Assmann argues that the basic meaning of *Ma'at* is not 'order' but 'righteousness.'[151] He claims that Egyptian thinking always counted on the gods' involvement in worldly affairs, and that it was somewhere between the Greek notion of Cosmos, which was indeed an independent, timeless world order (à la Schmid) which even the gods obeyed, and the Israelite worldview in which God was able to confront the world from outside if he so wished. According to Assmann, Egyptians imaged gods who wanted to maintain the world and had the power to do so (contrary to Greeks), but who could not want otherwise as, in a sense, they were the world (contrary to the Israelites's understanding).[152]

Michael V. Fox focusses more specifically on biblical wisdom literature and its supposed allusions to Egyptian 'order-thinking.' Quoting numerous Egyptian texts he also argues that Egyptians never believed in a mechanistic world order, for the order always required gods and humans to create and maintain it.[153] World order was not a cause but a result of other processes.[154] Though Fox does not refer to Schmid but to Egyptian literature when he states that 'one cannot really "speak" world order or "do" world order or "make world order great,"' this sentence nicely contrasts Schmid's statement that the wise person

---

149. Schmid 1966: 69–71; Assmann 1995: 66–67; see also Adams 2008: 29–30; Fox 1995: 43.
150. Boström 1990: 137.
151. Assmann 1995: 33.
152. Assmann 1995: 32–35.
153. Fox 1995: 43.
154. Fox 1995: 40–41.

'does *Maat*, speaks *Maat*, creates *Maat*.'[155] About Schmid's theory Fox writes that his 'analogy [between צדקה and *Ma'at*] is weakened by the vagueness and generality of the similarities it rests on and in any case cannot explain the particular character of Wisdom literature.'[156] According to him, it would be a mistake to see a 'search for world order' in proverbial sentences that count on causality or predictability since 'one could hardly imagine a didactic literature *without* the assumption of predictability.'[157]

More recently Weeks has argued against the concept of world order as a key to wisdom literature. According to him, concepts of divine-, human-, and natural causations might have peacefully lived together in the minds of wisdom writers and 'it is hard to see how we are dealing with a concept more powerful or integrated than most commonplace human expectations about causation.'[158]

2.2.4.3 Creation

Boström joined Crenshaw in warning that, though they might be significant, passages about creation are actually few in Proverbs: 'Creation is referred to in two poems in chapters 1–9.... In Proverbs 10–31 God is referred to around seventy times. One tenth of these references are linked to the idea of creation.'[159] It is Stuart Weeks (again), who goes a step further and expresses a stronger critique against seeing creation theology as the framework or main message of biblical wisdom. He observes that the theme of creation expresses different things in different segments of wisdom literature, so one can hardly speak of a unified 'creation theology' or a systematic thinking that could have been intended to be in contrast with the theology of the rest of the Bible in any way.[160] Passages mentioning creation are often in fact 'just employing illustrative anecdotes rather than formulating general conclusions.'[161] The reason why the few, not always obviously significant, creation-texts gained such a prominent place in scholarly investigations is only the result of the lack of topics like law, covenant, salvation-history, which, in turn, can be the result of a focus on the individual and an inclination to think through issues on a more abstract, non-national level.[162]

The arguments of Boström, Assmann, Fox, Adams, Weeks and others do not mean that there is now a new scholarly consensus. There are still some who straightforwardly presuppose a *Tun–Ergehen Zusammenhang*,[163] many (the

---

155. Fox 1995: 41; Schmid 1974a: 67.
156. Fox 1995: 39.
157. Fox 1995: 40, 47–48; on the mistaken nature of the *Ma'at*–Wisdom parallel, see also Steiert's opinion in Whybray 1995: 130.
158. Weeks 2010: 112–113.
159. Boström 1990: 80.
160. Weeks 2010: 111–112.
161. Weeks 2010: 114.
162. Weeks 2010: 110; Weeks 2010: 122. See also Weeks 2005: 298–299.
163. For example Brueggemann 2008: 158–159; Rendtorff 2005: 367.

majority?) affirm the usefulness of 'order' for interpreting wisdom,[164] and most scholars continue to see 'creation' as the theological basis for wisdom-thinking.[165] But we can no longer speak about a *communis opinio* in these issues, as Assmann could in 1990 or as Perdue could in 1991 when he stated that 'no one today would take issue with Zimmerli's claim' that wisdom was grounded theologically in creation.[166]

---

164. Anderson 1999: 264; Brueggemann 2008: 158, 172; Ceresko, 2002: 23–46; Dell 2010: 58; Yee 1992: 93–94; etc.
165. Anderson 1999: 265; Bartholomew and O'Dowd 2011: *passim*; Dell 2007: 3; etc.
166. Perdue 1991: 13; Assmann 1995: 32 (second edition).

3

Finding a Way Forward

As we have seen, despite the claims of some more recent scholars, nineteenth century scholarship did not show the signs of uncertainty or lack of interpretative categories when facing the peculiarities of Proverbs. Yet, twentieth century scholarship claimed that it found a theological category that fitted Proverbs even better than those applied by earlier scholarship: creation theology. Although this was programmatically expressed only in 1964 by Zimmerli, a wisdom–creation connection had already been recognised by many scholars since the '30s.

I have attempted to show how this creation/wisdom thinking gradually gained more significance in Old Testament theologies, then I have followed the story of its precise definition. I have tried to demonstrate that, between the '30s and the '60s, some scholars emphasised the anthropocentrism of wisdom; others the more pious order-thinking. In the late '60s and '70s, major biblical theologians struggled with the idea of the 'secular' in connection with wisdom. Since the '70s, though virtually everyone has agreed that creation theology comprised the horizon of wisdom, theological utilisations of this 'creation theology' and the descriptions of its theological kernel have become more diverse and numerous. Then, beginning in the '90s, the scholarly consensus has been shaken again even in the few points on which scholars had agreed before, as the ideas of 'order' and 'creation' have been questioned forcefully by some.

It is time to evaluate some of the arguments, and to clarify briefly the direction from which the rest of this work will attempt to contribute to scholarly discussion.

3.1 Order

On the one hand, I have been persuaded by Boström, Murphy, Assmann, Fox, Weeks, etc. that it is better to avoid the category of 'order' in one's interpretation of Proverbs. This is so not only because the connotation of 'order' can falsely give the impression that a 'buffer zone . . . comes between the sage and the Lord,'[1] but also because it can become a concept that stands between the text and the interpreter. What I mean is that one can deduce the idea of an abstract order from the text, and then, instead of interacting with the actual biblical text itself, one can start speculating about the theological utilisations of the idea of this deduced concept of world order—without recognising that they are not engaged with the text anymore but only with their reconstruction of the text's teaching. For example, some argue that 1. Proverbs teaches that there is a world order, and 2. order validates natural law, so 3. Proverbs teaches natural law. This kind of argument can be seen in Barr's work:

> Brunner's plea for a new natural theology included an emphasis on the *orders* . . . of creation, and Barth was correspondingly dismissive towards these structures. But to modern Old Testament scholarship there can be no question that the idea of a world *order* is extremely central. It is evident especially in the Wisdom literature.[2]

However, this argument misses the point that Proverbs actually mainly encourages the reader to listen to instruction rather than to explore reality with an open mind;[3] that, besides listening to the fathers' teaching, the key of wisdom is the fear of the Lord and not a search for natural regularities;[4] that many proverbs teach 'that human perception of a situation may be false unless it is informed by prior instruction, and that bad things may very easily seem good';[5] and that teaching in Proverbs is rarely, if ever, based on experience.[6]

To do justice to Barr, he actually recognised some of these features of Proverbs. Yet, he found the argument from the presence of a world order for the presence of natural theology in the Bible so strong, that he did not draw the conclusion from his observations that perhaps there is no natural theology in the Bible (or that the modern understanding of 'natural theology' should be changed in order to adjust it to a biblical understanding of natural theology). Instead he concluded that though the Bible advocates natural theology, it actually cultivates it rather badly sometimes:

---

1. Murphy 1987: 451.
2. Barr 1993: 173, original emphases.
3. Fox 1989: 98.
4. Nel 1982: 101, 126.
5. Weeks 2010: 115.
6. Fox 2007; Fox 2009: 963–967; cf. Bartholomew and O'Dowd 2011: 275–283.

> Though I think there is much use of natural theology in the Bible, I am not sure that its natural theology is always right. It does not seem to me to be definitely or necessarily true. First, ... it is not proved by the warrants that are offered in order to prove it; secondly, it is poorly informed about some of the realities of the world; thirdly, it is not really 'autonomous' natural theology, but is itself derived from previous religion and is dependent on previous religion.[7]

However, if one does not press the idea of 'order' which is not often expressed explicitly in the Bible anyway, then the basis for finding the equivalents of modern natural theology in the Bible is significantly weakened.

To give another example, one can argue that 1. Proverbs teaches that there is a world order, 2. a world order makes it possible for human beings to make decisions freely, so 3. Proverbs is about human autonomy.[8] But this interpretation does not consider the numerous proverbs which actually emphasise human dependence on God (see Prov 3:5-6; 9:10; 14:12; 16:1-9; 28:5; etc.). So, again, the interpretation is mainly based on the idea of a world order which is (rightly or wrongly) deduced from the text. The idea of 'world order' became a concept that stands between the text and its interpreter, and this might lead to an interpretation which pays attention to the text only selectively.

On the other hand, I accept much of what scholars have described with the idea of 'order.' For example, I accept that there was no such demarcation between the natural world and the social world in ancient Israelite thinking as in the modern one and that social rules and cosmological rules were paralleled;[9] that wisdom described a predictable world; that to simply call it 'anthropocentric' is a misleading simplification; that God can be experienced in the world (order); and that the ordered world teaches one to trust in God.[10] However, in such cases the term 'world order' can be easily substituted with 'God' or 'belief in God' or 'world' and, I believe, that wording would be even more in harmony with the text of Proverbs and potentially less misleading.

3.2 Creation

Similarly, I am going to avoid referring to 'creation' as *the* key theological concept of Proverbs in the following discussion—even though, similarly to the

---

7. Barr 1993: 147.
8. As Zimmerli (see discussion on pages 44–48) and Brueggemann (see discussion on pages 213–240) seem to argue in some of their works.
9. Baumann 1996: 299; Brown 1999: 1–2; Clifford 1985: 509; Clifford 1988: 155–156; Levenson 1988: 12, 69; Schmid 1984: 103–104; this is why the existence of separate world-creation and human-creation traditions—suggested by Albertz, Westermann, Doll, and others—seem to be unlikely to me. For a critique of the separate traditions opinion, see Clifford and Collins 1992: 7–9.
10. Knierim 1981: 88; Von Rad 1972: 64–65, 298.

case of 'order,' I do agree with many statements of those who rely heavily on this concept in their interpretation.

'Creation' has become an umbrella expression, which can signify many things to many people from liberation through ecology to material interests or moral formation. However, one can speak about such concepts without referring to the 'umbrella term.' This would also help one avoid creating a concept that unnecessarily stands between the text and the interpreter, a danger I referred to in relation to the concept of 'order.'

To use such an 'umbrella term' to describe wisdom may be attractive because it helps to unify conceptually the seemingly very diverse teachings of Old Testament wisdom and, at the same time, it also helps one to contrast it with, and differentiate it from, the rest of the Old Testament. However, one has to be careful here. Dell writes that 'for too long wisdom had been a casualty of the long-running quest for a theological centre in the Old Testament.'[11] I wonder if wisdom scholars make a similar mistake when they search for the theological centre of wisdom literature. It does not necessarily have such a centre.

I agree that creation is probably presupposed everywhere in wisdom, but I am not sure that this is different in other biblical books.[12] 'Creation faith' is part of an ancient Near Eastern worldview.[13] As Westermann writes, it is often not mentioned precisely because it is so substantial:

> Why is it that in the Old Testament the words 'creator' and 'creation' are never used in the context of believing? . . . [Because] the Old Testament notion of belief presumes the possibility of an alternative. . . . In the Old Testament an alternative to belief in Creation or Creator is quite unthinkable. The creation of the world is not an object of belief, but a presupposition for thought.[14]

To use Barton's words, we are speaking about 'a paradigm or set—in effect, a conceptual apparatus through which the world is perceived, which cannot itself become the object of conscious attention so long as one remains in the culture to which it belongs.'[15]

Barton might go a bit too far claiming that 'it cannot itself become the object of conscious attention.' Elements of worldviews do become the objects of conscious attention occasionally, even on the part of their adherents. They can sometimes emerge out of the status of unrecognised presuppositions and become explicit teachings or consciously recognised vehicles of ideas. This is what probably happens in Proverbs 8 or in Genesis 1–3 with the topic of creation. However, this does not mean that the theology of Proverbs is a 'creation theolo-

---

11. Dell 2006: 10; similarly Clements 1995: 269–270.
12. Similarly Weeks 1999: 29.
13. See Estes 2008: 856–858.
14. Westermann 1974: 113–114.
15. Barton 1984: 313.

gy,' however important creation occasionally becomes for the authors. Creation might be always in the background, but to take it as the centre of Proverbs' theology runs the danger of mistaking presuppositions with explicit teaching, worldview with theology, form with content; and actually goes against the observation that it is not often mentioned explicitly in the text.

Keeping these caveats in mind, I, in fact, do not necessarily have a problem with the use of the term 'creation theology.' However, this usage should not oppose wisdom literature with the rest of the Bible, or wisdom thinking with cult and history; it should not suggest the existence of an independent world order; it should not give the impression that creation is explicitly mentioned in many parts of Proverbs; and it should not silence the plurality of theological themes offered by Proverbs besides creation. Yet, as the term has been used by many to suggest these things, I consider it better to avoid speaking about Proverbs' 'creation theology.'

3.3 What is Distinctive about Wisdom Literature Then?

Even if there is no obvious theological centre, there may be a common style and a common angle of discussion. It is an old observation that Proverbs is explicitly written from the perspective of the individual and concentrates on everyday life, and these differentiates it from much of the biblical literature.[16]

There might be also some truth in the opinion that, for whatever reason, wisdom writers were interested in certain questions on a more abstract, theoretical level than national history. As Weeks argues, speaking about God as the god of the whole world was a tool which enabled the wisdom writers

> ... to speak about very general issues and concepts without reference to specific national and historical relationships. ... It is fair to suppose that they, like their foreign counterparts, are motivated by a desire to engage with the questions at this level, rather than by an ideological rejection, as such, of theological ideas rooted in more local or national concerns.... We cannot really speak of wisdom thought here then, so much as of common ground occupied by the wisdom writers, or of a mode of discourse that they share.[17]

Speaking about a 'mode of discourse' which is on a more 'theoretical level' is actually not far away from the nineteenth century category of 'philosophy.' Though, again, it is probably a term best avoided because of its potentially mis-

---

16. Just to name a few scholars from the last two hundred years who made this observation: Anderson 1999: 263; Baumgartner 1933: 4; Gramberg 1828: 45–48; Hubbard 1966: 5, 21; Kline 1972: 64–67; Priest 1976: 281–282, 288; Toombs 1955: 193–196; Westermann 1995: 78.

17. Weeks 201: 122; see also Whybray's 'intellectual tradition' approach in Whybray 1974: *passim*.

leading connotations of Greek thinking. Nevertheless, it seems to me more accurate to emphasise the authors' special interest in this 'abstract level of discussion' and the individual, and understand the lack of clear historical references as simply a side effect of these interests, rather than presupposing a 'wisdom tradition' that taught something radically different than the rest of the Bible. Wisdom is more an alternative 'mode of discourse' than an alternative teaching.

However, whether it is the content of their teaching, or, as I tend to think, it is their special 'mode of discourse' that makes biblical wisdom texts special, it is obvious that they do differ from the rest of the Bible. But do they differ from the rest of the ancient Near Eastern wisdom literature? One has to admit that there is not much in the information offered by Proverbs that we could not find in, say, Egyptian or Babylonian literature. As I see it, the main difference is not *in* the book but *around* the book. It is its embeddedness in Old Testament literature, its allusions to and echoes of typical biblical topics and thoughts which make it characteristically different from other ancient Near Eastern literature. Of course, these features of the book can only be recognised and utilised theologically to their full potential if the book is consciously read in its canonical context.

The situation is somewhat parallel to that of the currently popular notion of 'spirituality.' Spirituality is not about unique propositions. Spiritual practices can be very similar, even identical, in different traditions. The focusing of attention, or breathing techniques, or settings of silence, or sentences about personal contentment can appear to be the same in the case of a Catholic and a Buddhist monk. Yet, the seemingly identical spirituality can be experienced very differently, and it can express different things as it is embedded in different contexts.

3.4 A Brief Justification of My Questions

If creation theology and order do not provide the key to Proverbs then how shall we approach it? I am not persuaded that there is an ultimate answer to this question; so, more modestly, I am only going to provide *one* possible theological reading and not *the* theology of the book of Proverbs.

I am going to interpret it through the problems of the 'secular' and 'selfishness.' The importance of the former topic is suggested by the fact that the relationship between the (human) world and God is mentioned in the secondary literature very often. Virtually everyone, whether accepting the categories of 'creation' and 'order' or not, whether considering wisdom theologically as 'subordinate' to the rest of the Bible or not, spares a few words for this relationship. Let us consider, for example, the following quotations from a very diverse group of scholars:

> Wisdom literature attempts to deal with one of the major paradoxes... inherent in the experience of the holy God in the world: God's transcendence and God's immanence.[18]
>
> In all of Israel's religious literature, it is the wisdom tradition that most clearly discloses... a meeting place of the divine and the human.[19]
>
> Tension between the human and divine is at the centre of an understanding of wisdom.... Human experience is not divorced from the realm of God who stands behind it as the orderer and creator, nor is God divorced from humanity in that he reveals himself in all human experience and in the created world.[20]
>
> By living in accord with the rules of the universe established at creation, one obtains God's presence. In addition, God comes to meet his creatures in Dame Wisdom. Human discovery and divine disclosure stand in a complementary relationship.[21]
>
> The world-order revealed goodness, wisdom, glory, and righteousness, it also revealed Yahweh's presence in the world in an ultimate way, and more directly than human history could reveal it.[22]
>
> Wisdom literature makes yet another contribution to the roundness and wholeness of the biblical revelation by helping to bring a balance between the elements of transcendence and immanence.[23]
>
> Personified wisdom is immanent to creation, while distinct from the 'works' of God; she speaks in the name of Yahweh.[24]
>
> Much of the literature seeks also to understand the relationship between the human and the divine.[25]
>
> One might profitably think of Proverbs in its eclectic 'collage' state as part of the Jewish critique of idealism. One's face is rubbed in *the near*, as Leo Baeck has put it—the nearness of the divine, the nearness of the world, the nearness of the uncanny fusion of world and divinity.[26]

The list of quotations could be continued. This unanimity of opinion makes it tempting to think that finally we have found the central interest of wisdom literature. However, the divine–human or divine–world relationship is such a broad topic that one could probably successfully argue for its centrality in the

---

18. Anderson 1999: 273.
19. Camp 1988: 32.
20. Dell 2000: 6, 30.
21. Crenshaw 1977: 365.
22. Knierim 1981: 88.
23. Hubbard 1966: 21–22.
24. Murphy 1978: 38–39.
25. Weeks 2010: 117.
26. Shapiro 1987: 320, original emphasis.

case of most biblical, indeed most ancient, writings. It could also be a matter of debate if this topic is more central in Proverbs than, let us say, education, character formation, success, trust, choice, or life. Nevertheless, it might be worthwhile to take a closer look at the issue especially if it can be formed into a slightly more concrete question.

In order to make the question somewhat more focused I am going to reinvestigate the possibilities of an interpretation focusing on the problematic of the 'secular.' The question of 'secular' is not only a trendy topic in contemporary thinking, but it is also not unrelated to the broad question of world–divine relationship. The term has been used and discussed less frequently in connection with Proverbs since its heyday in the '70s, but this is probably mainly because of the concerns about a reconstruction of a 'secular to religious' developmental scheme in its history. Yet, the book's concentration on the everyday life of the individual prompts the question of what we can say about the 'secular' life from a theological point of view in the light of Proverbs, regardless of the historical problem of whether a 'more secular' wisdom ever existed.

As for the question of 'selfishness,' this was maybe *the* main problem of pre-1930 interpretation but since then it has faded away from the horizon of interpreters. If it receives attention at all it is usually dealt with in a brief comment, claiming that wisdom simply describes the act–consequence order of the universe and this cannot be called selfishness.[27] However, the question might deserve some further investigation, not only because the concepts of an 'order' or the *Tun–Ergehen Zusammenhang* are questionable, but also because it is not clear that they would solve the problem even if they were granted. (See the more detailed exposition of the problem in chapter 6.)

'Selfishness' and 'secularity' are not as distinct as they might appear at first sight. Proverbs motivates good behaviour through the self-interest of the reader, and, at the same time, this motivation apparently concentrates on this-worldly, material, if you like 'secular,' gains and not on 'spiritual' rewards. Thus, 'selfishness' and 'secularity' comprise two problematic sides of Proverbs' motivational system. Discussing both of these topics will, I hope, enable us to achieve a richer, more complex theological reading of Proverbs.

However, before turning to these issues, it is necessary to clarify the methodology applied to the investigation of Proverbs in the rest of this work.

---

27. Crenshaw 1976b: 4–5; Crenshaw 1998: 72, 178; Gese 1958: 7–11.

PART II
METHODOLOGY: A CANONICAL APPROACH

4

A Canonical Approach

4.1 Introduction: A Preliminary Description

Reading about the different attempts to grasp Proverbs' theological message and significance, one can observe that many of them are primarily concerned with the meaning of the texts in their world of origins, regardless of later understanding and uses. Besides the obvious exceptions of the different liberation approaches (feminist, ecological, etc.), there is little interest in the hermeneutics of recontextualisation, reception, appropriation, and their possible implications for understanding and use today. Yet equally it is apparent that at least some of the divergences in interpretation are the result of contemporary theological concerns being brought to bear (as it is the case not only in von Rad's contrast with *Heilsgeschichte*, but in the different utilisations of categories like 'creation,' 'secular,' 'natural theology').

The particular approach taken in this work differs somewhat from this general scholarly tendency to focus primarily on the origins of the text and not on the later contexts of its reading. My approach can be characterised by the following list of catchphrases:

- **The book as a whole**—reading the book of Proverbs as one book and not as a collection of independent writings;
- **Literary framework**—paying a special attention to the literary framework of the book, mainly chapters 1–9, and to how it influences the interpretation of the rest of the book;
- **Synchronic reading**—concentrating on the received form of a text and not on the history of its 'evolution';

- **Intertextual reading**—paying attention to possible resonances with other biblical texts;
- **Church tradition**(s)—consciously interacting with the theological traditions of religious groups that read Proverbs as Scripture;
- **Interdisciplinary**—freely interacting with other disciplines like philosophical theology, historical theology, sociology, etc. whenever this interaction can enrich the interpretation.

This approach, or at least most of its elements, is probably best described as 'canonical.'

4.2 My Understanding of 'Canonical Interpretation'

As the term 'canonical' is contested and used in many ways, it calls for some explanation. However, it should be emphasised that the aim of this chapter is not to compare and evaluate the different understandings of the term, and neither is it to present a thoroughgoing analysis of the complex thought of Brevard Childs, the main figure who probably comes to the mind of most Old Testament scholars hearing the word 'canonical.' The aim, more modestly, is simply to clarify how the term 'canonical' is used in this work.

Three interdependent reading strategies should be highlighted as a clarification to my canonical approach:
1. Canonical interpretation focuses on the canonical form, that is, on the received form of the book of Proverbs.
2. Canonical interpretation focuses on the canonical context, that is, on intertextual allusions to other canonical texts.
3. Canonical interpretation builds on the interpreter's church tradition.

There is, however, a deep theological and at the same time practical question which can be asked about all three points: Which canonical form? Which canonical context? Which church tradition?

It has to be recognised that we actually have more than one final form of the book. The LXX, for example, differs significantly from the MT.[1] This fact, however, does not necessarily present a serious theoretical difficulty. I can easily accept the idea that a canonical work has more than one canonical (final, accepted by the church) form. Be that as it may, this question will be largely avoided for pragmatic reasons. In an ideal world all of the received forms of a book would require a thorough investigation, but due to space and time restrictions I am going to focus on the MT and will not discuss other forms of the book on their own right; I will only use them occasionally to inform my reading of the MT.

---

1. Consider the major re-organisation of the second half of the text (the order in the LXX is: 22:17–24:22; 30:1-14; 24:23-34; 30:15–31:9; 25:1–29:27; 31:10-31) and the many smaller differences, some of which will be discussed later (Cook 1997: 1).

As for the canonical context, the same problem arises even more acutely: which canon are we speaking about? Are we speaking about the Jewish, the Protestant, the Catholic, or an Orthodox canon? Although Proverbs is not contested and is in all of these canons, the question is not completely without significance for a canonical interpretation, since a decision will determine in what corpus one searches for canonical resonances for Proverbs. The issue of the canon becomes even more complicated if one considers the pertinent debate about whether the canon should be understood as a set list of books, or as a 'rule of faith,' 'the true teaching of Christ' as it seems to have been understood in the second century CE, or whether it is possible to bridge these two meanings somehow.[2] In order to cut through the Gordian knot of these problems I do not see any other option than to switch to a more personal tone for a moment and to reveal the particular tradition in the context of which the present interpreter is reading the text: I personally have a Protestant background so when I hear the word 'canon' it is mainly a list of 66 (39+27) biblical books which comes to my mind. However, I am sympathetic to the understanding of canon as a rule of faith expressed through a textual corpus that has somewhat blurred borders, which means that I am open to texts that are outside of the Protestant canon but part of the wider Christian tradition.

However, the question of 'which canonical context' is probably less significant in the case of the particular canonical reading of Proverbs offered by this work than it might appear at first sight. Although some brief references will be made to texts outside of the Protestant canon, all of the main texts that are investigated in the following discussion happen to be part of all of the above listed 'canons.' At the same time I am not aware of any texts in the Catholic or other canons the detailed discussion of which would significantly change my arguments.

The struggle with the second issue ('which canon') leads on to the third issue ('which church tradition'). This question also has to be answered on a personal level. Despite being a Protestant, I have found the thought of some Orthodox and many Catholic theologians most stimulating for my theological reflection on Proverbs. My main theological conversation partners are Catholics. Thus, most of what is said could probably be easily adapted to many communities of faith even if my Protestant angle is occasionally undeniable. Furthermore, although Christian categories are used in the following nterpretation, I do not intend to offer a Christological, or Trinitarian reading of Proverbs. The reason for this is purely practical: even though some of the observations could be easily developed into that direction, a substantial interaction with these parts of Christian doctrine would require a much longer discussion. The result of this avoid-

---

2. For a succinct introduction to the different understandings of canon, see Driver 2010: 21–29.

ance of detailed interaction with Christological and Trinitarian doctrines is that, I believe, most of my reading is compatible with Jewish religious persuasions, too.

Finally, another feature of my canonical approach has to be noted: it is an interdisciplinary approach. I consider this interdisciplinarity to be directly connected to the aforementioned 'which church tradition' question. The previous paragraph highlights that through the act of canonical reading the reader is drawn to a reflexion on the traditions of his or her reading community and on the traditions of other communities that also take the same text as canonical. This encourages the reader to be involved in interdisciplinary research which, besides biblical studies, can incorporate philosophical and historical theology, sociology, anthropology, etc.

4.3 Reasons for Applying a Canonical Approach

I can see six main reasons for applying this canonical interpretation to Proverbs. Most of these reasons are mentioned in one way or another in the following quotation from Childs:

> The final canonical literature reflects a long history of development in which the received tradition was selected, transmitted and shaped by *hundreds of decisions*.... However, the various elements have been so fused as to *resist easy diachronic reconstructions* which fracture the witness of the whole.... The canonical approach to Old Testament theology rejects a method which is *unaware of its own time-conditioned quality and which is confident in its ability to stand outside*, above and over against the received tradition in adjudicating the truth or lack of truth of the biblical material according to its own criteria.... To suggest that the task of theological reflection takes place from within a canonical context assumes not only a received tradition, but a *faithful disposition* by hearers who await the illumination of God's Spirit.[3]

My first reason for a canonical reading is a practical one: due to wisdom literature's lack of concrete historical references and its flourishing throughout thousands of years, dating and establishing the order of influence between different texts is even harder than in the case of other texts. This material really 'resists easy diachronic reconstructions.' There are some questions in which a near consensus exists among scholars. Most interpreters, for example, regard chapters 1–9 as later than 10:1–22:16. Nevertheless, many of the historical debates provide only sand on which it would be unwise to build a house of interpretation. It would be quite risky to base too much on reconstructed theological and chronological layers in the sentence literature, or on a supposed direction of relationship between 1 Kings 1–11 and Proverbs 1–9; or between Isaiah 11 and Proverbs 8, etc.

---

3. Childs 1986: 11–12, my emphases.

My second reason is that the whole is (often) more than the sum of the parts. Understanding a text does not equal understanding its (alleged) strata on their own. The received tradition mirrors 'hundreds of decisions,' and this can not only mean distortions but also an accumulation of richness.

The third reason is that interpreting a text in a canonical frame of reference is a self-revealing theological statement in itself. It expresses that the interpreter counts him- or herself as belonging to the tradition formed by and responsible for the canon, and as such it expresses that the interpreter tends to identify with the 'faithful disposition' of that particular tradition. This openness about one's own stance encourages a thoroughgoing theological reflection on the text, one which is sometimes lacking from serious academic biblical interpretation.

Fourthly, this openness about the particular frame of reference in which the interpreter does his or her interpretation can also encourage the interpreter towards constant self-reflection. The interpreter who works in a twenty-first century context *and* a canonical context at the same time is constantly confronted by the time- and space-conditioned particularity of the text, his or her religious tradition and his or her (post)modern culture. He or she is forced to make conscious choices or reconciliations between these particular viewpoints. It is no longer possible to hide his or her subjective judgements under the disguise of a neutral or universal perspective. Being 'unaware of one's own time-conditioned nature' and avoiding questions like 'do I really agree with every element of the tradition represented by the canon?' or 'does the canon faithfully represent my tradition and vice versa?' becomes difficult for one who tries to do justice to his or her canonical tradition and twenty-first century context simultaneously.

My last two reasons for a canonical reading are not mentioned in the above quotation by Childs. One is that the interpretation of a given proverb depends on its context. Many scholars try to recover the 'original' *Sitz im Leben*, the situation in which the particular proverb might have been born. However, proverbs can be re-used indefinitely in many different contexts and, accordingly, they can gain many different meanings. The exercise in recovering a supposed 'original' *Sitz im Leben* might serve better some purposes (like some historical reconstructions), but for other purposes, considering the meaning and significance of the proverb in a 'different' context can be even more revealing. At any rate, why should we neglect the context of the canonical form of the book and its wider literary (canonical) context in our interpretation of a given proverb?

Finally, the irrefutable justification for the approach: for whatever reason, this is what happens to interest the interpreter. It is perfectly legitimate to approach the text with historical interests. Why should it be illegitimate to approach it with (literary and/or theological) canonical interests?

A concrete example might help in elucidating these points. William McKane writes in his commentary on Proverbs:

> It [the strata representing Yahwistic piety and 'moralism'] has the extreme tidiness, the sterility and the disengagement from reality....

> Instruction and sentence ... are employed to give expression to a precious piety which left no questions open, no ends untied and which secured its mathematical precision by detaching itself from the messiness and confusion of men's lives in the world and by shutting its ears to the still, sad music of humanity.[4]

From a canonical point of view one could criticise McKane's confidence with which he identifies the different strata (see my first point above) and the little attention he pays to the received form of the text in his commentary (second point). His evaluation of the different strata is also noteworthy. He likes the former ones and does not like the latest because they have lost touch with reality. Of course, this is a subjective evaluation since it depends on what McKane himself thinks the reality is like—a rather obvious point he does not emphasise very much (see point four). A canonical reader, in the light of point three, would rather try to listen humbly to the text (a characteristic not alien from the teaching of Proverbs itself) and give the chance to it to form his or her perception of reality.

At this point it might be necessary to add that, despite this humble listening, a canonical approach does not mean necessary acceptance of everything in the canonical text. My approach here is similar to that of Ellen F. Davis:

> If we disagree with a certain text on a given point, then it must be in obedience to what we, in community with other Christians, discern to be the larger or more fundamental message of the Scriptures. In other words, disagreement represents a critical judgment.... Therefore,... members of the church, or the church as a whole, should come to such a judgment slowly and to a degree reluctantly—with the reluctance any of us might feel, as we begin to realize that on a given point we cannot accept the view of a revered elder, a parent, or a beloved mentor. Further, in this matter, self-suspicion is a sign of spiritual maturity.[5]

Finally, a canonical approach does not mean a dogmatic rejection of diachronic interpretation or investigating allusions outside the canon, either. These are necessary not only because without them a meaningful conversation would be difficult in the modern scholarly community. Even if certainty about the history of a text is seldom achievable, intelligent guesses about this history can enrich our understanding of the texts' final form. The term 'canonical' simply speaks about the focus and the aim of the investigation not about what the interpreter is 'not allowed' to do.

---

4. McKane 1970: 19; very similarly Westermann 1995: 67, 70.
5. Davis 2007: 39.

5

A Canonical Approach and Proverbs

5.1 The Challenge of Proverbs' Canonical Interpretation

In Proverbs' case there is a special reason for interpreting it in a canonical way, namely that this approach has been somewhat neglected. I can see two main reasons for this neglect. First, the style of Proverbs is so international that reading it in a (Jewish or Christian) canonical context might seem a distorting, rather than an illuminating, way of interpretation. Second, although the scepticism of the canonical approach towards reconstructing the different historic layers of the book with certainty is well applicable to the attempts of dividing the book into, say, religious and secular layers, or concrete and speculative layers, nevertheless, some parts of the book are clearly differentiated from others. No one could miss the dissimilarity of chapters 1–9 from 10:1–22:16. The headings found in the book make it even more obvious that it is a collection of more than one work. Thus, it appears to be a reasonable exercise to study those works on their own. In the following pages I look at these arguments in more detail.

5.1.1 International Style

As a response to the first objection against a canonical reading, we have to realise that 'distortion' is a value-laden word. Providing a different context for a text and thereby changing the atmosphere, connotation, or even the meaning of the text produces a *different* text. Whether it is a distortion or an improvement depends on the criteria of evaluation.

Furthermore, it should also be noticed that even if one prefers a diachronic reading and understands every deviation from the original intention of the author as 'misuse,' the distorted nature of our text is far from certain. It is not obvious that the authors were 'humanists' who were less imbedded in Jewish culture and religion than the authors of other biblical books and who wanted to express a universal, 'non-Jewish' teaching. Many scholars, who are interested more in diachronic readings than in canonical ones, argue that the internationality of 'wisdom styles' (e.g., the forms of proverbs and instructions, typical phrases, topics, etc.) can be misleading. As Stuart Weeks helpfully observes:

> Their [instructions'] cultural underpinnings are not always clear in individual works, especially those most interested in daily life: for every Amenemope, with its frequent, explicit references to Egyptian deities and ideas, there is an Any, which more often presumes them quietly. However universal an instruction may seem, in fact, we are unlikely to understand its original purpose if we neglect its original context.... To take a loose analogy, if we were to try to read Proverbs 1–9 solely in the light of the foreign instructions, rather than the Jewish context in which it was composed, this would be like reading the Aeneid solely on the basis of the Greek epic tradition while ignoring its context in Roman literature and thought.[1]

Weeks, later in his book, identifies many conceptual and verbal parallels between Proverbs 1–9 and Deuteronomy and shows that the wisdom of this first part of Proverbs can be very easily understood as the internalised Law.[2]

Katharine Dell also realises the close affinity between wisdom and Deuteronomy.[3] Furthermore, investigating the sections of Proverbs one by one, she concludes that the conceptual framework we find in Proverbs is not dissimilar to that of other biblical literature. Even if some concepts are missing, they can be presupposed. Unless we start with a dogmatic belief that 'Proverbs is different,' nothing warrants us to give different meanings to key terms (like חסד ואמת) than we find in other biblical books.[4]

5.1.2 Collection of Separate Works

Mentioning Weeks and Dell leads us to the second concern mentioned above. Although, as it has just become clear, these two scholars realise the importance of the Israelite setting (contra the first concern), both of them are

---

1. Weeks 2007: 32, 37; similar opinion was expressed earlier by Crenshaw 1976b: 4–5 and Perdue 1977: 227. Even Scott realised that a religious attitude can be presupposed behind 'secular' sayings though he did not utilise this insight too much in his writings. See Scott 1972: 154.
2. Weeks 2007: 102–113.
3. Dell 2006: 168–169.
4. Dell 2006: 117, 175.

somewhat reluctant to focus too much on the book as a whole. This reluctance is understandable if we consider the strong academic tradition of equating understanding with knowing the social and historical background of a work. According to this paradigm, as Proverbs is a collection of many works stemming, presumably, from somewhat different social backgrounds, it follows that we have to analyse the different parts of it separately. As Samuel L. Adams puts it, 'Theological assertions are always made from a specific context, and it is incumbent upon the modern interpreter of sapiential literature to locate the material as precisely as possible.'[5]

Indeed, theological assertions are made from a specific context, but does it necessarily follow that we can only understand them if we understand their particular social context? Trying to figure out the social background of a text is certainly a valuable exercise. However, we have to be precise about what it is useful for and what it is not. To explicate these questions a bit more I provide three brief examples by C. V. Camp, C. Westermann, and K. Dell.

Claudia V. Camp writes: 'The attempt to understand the meaning of female Wisdom within a socio-historical setting is important because it reminds us that all theology is done contextually.'[6] It should be recognised that the word 'understanding' is used rather loosely in this quotation. Camp seems to mean 'understanding the sociological and theological motivations of the author.' She writes in her book that 'Wisdom is the mediator between God and humankind as it is clear from the chiastic structure of 8:30b-31.'[7] Then, on the following pages, she explains that the ancient writer felt it necessary to introduce wisdom as a mediator not only because in the Persian time God felt distant but also because they could not count on the king to be the mediator anymore. This is interesting and illuminating indeed (if true), but surely, her claim is that she understands the mediatory role of Wisdom *from the text*. The historical background only helps one to understand the *motivations* of the authors and not the text itself. Maybe knowing the social background can specify, clarify, and enrich the meaning (e.g., 'Wisdom mediates *like* the king used to') but it is not the case that without knowing the social background we could not understand the 'Wisdom as mediator' idea at all.

Westermann explains that

> Wisdom literature emerged as a result of both these processes: the collecting and then recording of proverbs previously handed down orally, and their being joined together with didactic poems.... One can neither understand nor explain the book of Proverbs, originating as it did in this way, without reviewing this process.[8]

---

5. Adams 2008: 12.
6. Camp 1985: 17.
7. Camp 1985: 272.
8. Westermann 1995: 3.

Again, the main question is what he means by 'understanding.' Westermann also seems to be too general claiming that without knowing the history of the text the book of Proverbs remains inexplicable. What he really seems to mean, however, is that the surprising difference between the style of chapters 1–9 and 10–31 would remain inexplicable, which is a much more modest claim.

Similarly to Westermann, Dell proposes that 'The book of Proverbs is best understood when divided into different sections.... Whybray argues that one should not try to posit just one social context for the whole book of Proverbs, because each of the sections has a different character.'[9] Do I disagree with Dell and Whybray when they say that we should not posit just one social context for the whole book? Certainly not! But I am arguing that however helpful it is, positing the different contexts does not equate to *understanding* the book. A book can have a coherent meaning even if it is a composite of multiple books stemming from different social contexts. True enough, some layers of the meaning of one or all of the works might have changed when they began to be read together with each other, but this is not the point here. We should not forget either that if the final composition is the work of an editor/artist/theologian, then, in a sense, his or her social context becomes the social context of the whole work—even if we have no chance to decipher what that social context might have been.[10]

Thus, it seems to me that knowing the social background can enrich our interpretations in many ways, and it can also contribute significantly to the understanding of a text when it clarifies some obscure, culture-specific concepts or expressions, but equating it with understanding a text is an exaggeration.

The warning of Jeremy Black is helpful here:

> It [modern research] treats 'literary texts' exactly as any other form of historical 'text', discarding as too subjective and unscientific any attempt to account for precisely those distinctive qualities that make literature 'literary': the meaning and effect of the experience of reading. The result has been that literary works have been trawled for evidence of social conditions or historical facts, as sources for the history of

---

9. Dell 2006: 15; see also her discussion of the unity and diversity of the book in Dell 2004: 259.

10. In this respect my approach is not dissimilar to Rosenzweig's and Buber's approach to the Pentateuch: 'We ... translate the Torah as one book. For us ... it is the work of a single mind. We do not know who this mind was; we cannot believe that it was Moses. We name that mind among ourselves by the abbreviation with which the Higher Criticism of the Bible indicates its presumed final redactor of the text: R. We, however, take this R to stand not for redactor but for *rabbenu*. For whoever he was, and whatever text lay before him, he is our teacher, and his theology is our teaching.' (Rosenzweig 1994: 22–26, 23, original emphasis.) An important difference is, however, that I would not equate the teaching of Proverbs' final redactor(s) with 'our teaching' as his/her/their teaching can be enriched, nuanced, even modified by its (Christian) canonical context. See von Rad's similar comments on Rosenzweig's thoughts in von Rad 1961: 41–42.

thought or religion, or for the history of literature itself: the history of genres, the tracing of influences and the development of traditions.[11]

Black writes about the literary analysis of Sumerian poetry, but his remarks are applicable to the theological interpretation of the Old Testament, too. However valid and helpful the historical and sociological analyses are, we should not forget that historical understanding, which focuses more on the motivations, aims, and circumstances of the authors, cannot be equated completely with the understanding of a biblical text.[12]

5.2 The Canonical Significance of Proverbs 1–9

Let us focus now more closely on our specific problem. Should Proverbs 1–9 be read as a preface for the whole book? If so, what significance does this have for our interpretation?

Many scholars mention that, in a sense, these nine chapters form the preface for the whole book.[13] Weeks, however, seems to be less enthusiastic about this possibility:

> [That Proverbs 1–9 functions as a prologue] is an attractive [idea], and it offers an explanation both for the lack of correspondence to the subsequent superscriptions and to the notoriously mysterious 'seven pillars' of 9:1 (taking those to be the seven sections of the book). If Proverbs 1–9 does currently serve as a prologue, however, I think that this is an editorial rather than a compositional matter. While some links exist with material in the other sections, the number of these is small, and the direction of influence unclear; it would be difficult to maintain that Proverbs 1–9 presupposes the presence of the other sections. At most, therefore, it is not so much a prologue as a free-standing, introductory essay, but I think it is more likely to have enjoyed an independent existence when first written.[14]

Dell, similarly, recognises the 'preface quality' of Proverbs 1–9 but warns against 'overstating' it:

> Proverbs 1–9 is often regarded as a preface to the rest of the book of Proverbs. . . . The opening verses of ch. 1 certainly have that character, but it may be overstating the introductory quality of the chapters

---

11. Black 1998: 7.
12. For the mistake of understanding texts purely as historical sources and how this not only flattens our understanding of them but can even lead to misusing them as historical sources, see Sommer 2011.
13. Bartholomew and O'Dowd 2011: 82; Baumann 1998: 44–78; Clifford 2009: 242–253; Fox 2000: 6, 48; Fuhs 2001: 15; Longman 2006: 58–61; Murphy 1998: xix–xx; Saebø 2012: 33; Zabán 2012: *passim*; etc.
14. Weeks 2007: 40 n. 15.

to apply this role to the whole section. In fact, we find two major genres of material in Prov 1–9 that do not appear extensively elsewhere in the book and that give the section a distinctive character of its own.[15]

If I understand them well, Weeks's and Dell's concerns are that even if Proverbs 1–9 serves as a preface today, this was not the intention of the original author(s) and, besides being significantly different from the rest of Proverbs, these chapters make perfect sense on their own. This might be so and the investigation of chapters 1–9 on their own is certainly an interesting historical task and also a valuable task for the interpretation of the whole book.[16] But why should the interpretation of the received text—that is, chapters 1–9 as part of the whole book and as a frame of reference for understanding and appropriating the sentence literature—be seen as an 'overstatement'?

As Van Leeuwen argued, over-emphasis on the separateness of these chapters can actually lead to missing some important parallels between them and the following chapters.[17] Furthermore, even if Proverbs 1–9 does not 'presuppose' chapters 10–31 (which, if I understand it correctly, means that Proverbs 1–9 makes sense on its own), some 'oddities' of it become more explicable in the light of Proverbs 10–31. For example, both Dell and Weeks realise that 6:1-19 seems to be a collection of topics from Proverbs 10–31, as if someone inserted those verses there to show the introductory nature of Proverbs 1–9.[18] Another feature of chapters 1–9 which might make better sense as introduction, rather than as an independent work, is the present form of chapter 9. It does not end in a summary or conclusion. Quite the contrary, the tension is not resolved but if possible heightens at the end of the chapter (in contrast to chapter 31). Proverbs 9 is about the 'competition' between woman Wisdom (חכמות) and woman Folly (אשת כסילות) to attract young men. It finishes with the words of woman Folly, with her proverb about the pleasures of secret food and drink (9:17), and an observation by the narrator of her and her followers who go to Sheol (9:18). All of these motives are nicely matched by the tension between the wise son (בן חכם) and the foolish son (בן כסיל) of 10:1 and by verse 10:2, which teaches that evil treasures do not help (cf. 9:17) but righteousness saves from death (cf. 9:18). One can even suspect that the somewhat awkward structure of chapter 9 (not ending with a real conclusion but with the figure of woman Folly; some 'more

---

15. Dell 2009: 229. See also Dell 2006: 53.
16. Snell's data about repeated verses and half-verses can be understood as supporting the original independence of Proverbs 1–9 (Snell 1993: 79).
17. Van Leeuwen 2007: 78–79, writing about the parallels between 3:19-20 and 24:34 and between 9:1 and 14:1.
18. Dell 2006: 43–44; Weeks 2007: 50; for a discussion of this and other (though not always equally persuasive) parallels between Proverbs 1–9 and the rest of Proverbs, see Hatton 2008: 68–81.

summary-like' verses between the speeches of woman Wisdom and woman Folly) might be (partly) the result of making it into an introduction to 10:1 onwards.[19]

My conclusion is that modern academic scholars should not be ashamed of interpreting Proverbs 1–9 as the preface for the whole book. It does make sense on its own, so, in this sense, it is true that it does not presuppose the following chapters. However, there are parts of it which clearly point toward the following chapters if they are read together, and there are oddities in it which might be read more naturally in the light of the following chapters. These might be the results of editorial activity indeed, but this is irrelevant for the question whether we should read it as an introduction to the whole of Proverbs. It certainly does not make less sense in this role than in the role of an independent essay, and this is how it is part of the received text, mirroring the 'hundreds of decisions' of the faith communities responsible for its shaping.

But how does taking Proverbs 1–9 as introduction inform our understanding of the book? Claudia V. Camp famously argued that Proverbs 1–9 provides context for the proverbs of 10–31.[20] She referred to Mieder's often quoted maxim that a proverb is dead without a context and that it only becomes alive if there is a framework in which we can understand it.[21]

In fact, I would rather say that in a sense proverbs are too alive without a context. They can have many meanings, connotations, nuances. Many of them can be approached from a theological perspective, or from a psychological one, or from a historical one, etc., as the reader wishes, basically without restrictions.

My contention is that whatever the original context of the proverbs of Proverbs 10–31 were, Proverbs 1–9 provides a *theological* context, which invites the reader to a religious interpretation of Proverbs 10–31.[22] The book of Proverbs (in its received form) is not a mere listing of proverbs compiled by an anthropologist without the slightest intention of providing a context—the sort of collection Mieder was speaking about and criticising.[23] It offers a clear frame of reference for the interpretation of its proverbs.

Does this mean that the presence of Proverbs 1–9 changes the meaning of the proverbs of chapters 10–31? Or might it be that Proverbs 1–9 restricts the meaning of the individual proverbs? Neither of these possibilities reflect precise-

---

19. For the textual problems in the second half of Proverbs 9, see Clifford 1999: 106; Fox 2000: 306–307; Fritsch and Schloerb 1955: 836; Gemser 1937: 40; Goldingay 1977: 80–93; McKane 1970: 368–369; Meinhold 1991a: 150–158; Murphy 1998: 58; Plöger 1984: 105–106; Toy 1899: 192–193; Waltke 2004: 438–439, Weeks 2007: 222–223, 228.

20. Camp 1985: 176–177.

21. Camp 1985: 165–166. See also Clifford 2009: 243; Fontaine 1982: 55–56; Heim 2001: 22–23; Longman 2006: 41.

22. Here my emphasis slightly differs from that of Camp, who stressed less the theological nature of the introduction of the first nine chapters; she rather developed their literary aspects.

23. Mieder 1974: 892.

ly my own view. Proverbs 1–9 does not really restrict or change the meaning of most individual proverbs. A proverb's warning against false witness (Prov 12:17; 14:5, 25; 19:5, 9, 28; 21:28; 24:28; 25:1) is not changed in meaning because of chapters 1–9. Instead, the first 9 chapters control and change the relationship between the reader and individual proverbs. In other words, they provide a vision, in the light of which the meaning of individual proverbs gains new significance for the interpreter. The reader brings the vivid picture of Lady Wisdom from chapter 8 (and other chapters) with him or her to the later chapters. As Roland Murphy puts it,

> In the book of Proverbs she [Wisdom] proclaims her birth from God, her (active?) presence before and during creation, and her delight to be with human beings. She appears to be the link between the practical, down-to-earth realities of daily living and life with God (Prov. viii 35). This gives a decidedly religious hue to the entire book, so different from the common verdicts of 'worldly' and 'profane' that past and recent scholarship has favoured.[24]

After the vision of Lady Wisdom in Proverbs 1–9, listening to individual proverbs will inevitably be understood as listening to this Wisdom, who is so closely associated with Yahweh. As a result—as I argue in the second half of this work—reading the book of Proverbs, including its individual proverbs, will be understood in the context of the reader's relationship to Yahweh.

5.3 Summary

Clarifying my 'canonical approach' I have described it as concentrating on a synchronic reading of the received form of the book (though not hostile to historical interests), paying special attention to the framework of the book (especially the first 9 chapters) and focusing also on possible intertextual resonances. I have also argued that this canonical approach can lead to increased cultural and theological self-awareness of the reader and can help to form and articulate theological and various interdisciplinary reflections on the text.

Of course, the ultimate test of an approach is its application, so now it is time to turn to Proverbs itself and to address our specific questions delineated in Part I, namely Proverbs' relationship to 'selfishness' and its 'secular' nature. Part III investigates the problem of 'selfishness,' leaving the question of 'secular' to Part IV.

---

24. Murphy 1995: 231; similarly Fox 2009: 358; Murphy 2002: 28, 234.

PART III
DOES PROVERBS PROMOTE SELFISHNESS?

6

A Call for a Thomistic Reading

6.1 Proverbs: A Selfish Book?

Pippa Norris and Ronald Inglehart, two well known sociologists, proposed a new theory in 2004 for why religious practices are declining in the north Atlantic region and Australia.[1] They claim that the data in the World Values Survey show a strong negative correlation between the existential security that a society provides for its members (i.e., social networks, education, life expectancy, personal income, etc.), and the popularity of religion: the higher existential security is in a country, the less religious the people are.[2]

It is beyond the scope of this book to interact with the Norris–Inglehart theory of secularisation, but a look at some theological responses to their views will be relevant for our subject. José Casanova, for example, criticised the Norris–Inglehart theory in a public debate as follows:

> It is too simplistic a theory in terms of what religion is supposed to do. My response would be, first, that these scholars assume that people have religion precisely because they have existential insecurity, that religion is a response to material deprivation.... My response is: Look at all the world religions.... The great religions—Islam, Buddhism, Christianity—never appealed simply to the satisfaction of material needs. They have a completely different orientation. True, they

---

1. Norris and Inglehart 2004.
2. The data of the survey is available on-line: http://www.worldvaluessurvey.org/.

are immersed in relatively poor, traditional agrarian societies, where only the elite, the literati, can practice a higher form of religion.[3]

Casanova speaks here about a 'higher form of religion' which goes beyond a simple 'satisfaction of material needs.' This, of course, presupposes that there is a lower form of religion, too.

Charles Taylor, although not writing directly on the Norris–Inglehart theory, expresses a similar critique of some theories of secularisation. He does not think that religious motives are only tied to the 'misery, suffering, and despair of the human condition.'[4] He claims that although earlier religion often focused on human flourishing, after the axial period (mid-first millennium BCE), that is, after the activities of Confucius, Gautama, Socrates, and the Hebrew prophets, higher forms of religion appeared, which focused on higher goals, leading to a transformation of the believer,[5]

> ... a transformation of human beings which takes them beyond or outside of whatever is normally understood as human flourishing, even in a context of reasonable mutuality (that is, where we work for each other's flourishing). In the Christian case, this means our participating in the love (agape) of God for human beings.[6]

If religion is shrinking because of the higher level of existential security then this can only be true for the 'lower' type of religion, suggests Taylor.[7]

Casanova's and Taylor's views of 'higher' religion are similar to those of Nicholas Lash, who sees (higher) religions as schools whose purpose is to purify human desire, mainly to purify love from egoism and to participate in the divine love.[8]

Now, this differentiation between 'higher' and 'lower' religion poses a serious question to the theological interpreter of Proverbs: if we follow those who argue that the true essence of (higher) religion is that it points beyond existential security and human flourishing, then how are we to account for the heavy emphasis of Proverbs precisely on these 'lower' issues?

One of Proverbs' main aims is to encourage right behaviour. The first nine chapters contain very little practical advice; rather, they contain many and long exhortations.[9] In chapters 10–29 there are at least 171 sayings (a few of them comprising more than one verse) which speak about the bad or good results that follow bad or good behaviour, and they often do so without specifying the be-

---

3. Casanova and Steinfels 2007.
4. Taylor 2007: 434–435.
5. Taylor 2007: 150–151; for the recent discussion of the definition and significance of the 'axial age,' see the works of Robert Bellah: Bellah 2011 and Bellah 2012.
6. Taylor 2007: 430.
7. See Taylor 2007: 261.
8. Lash 1996: 35–38.
9. Most famously Proverbs 8. Almost the whole chapter is a long exhortation, which aims to motivate the reader (Fox 2000: 267).

haviour (like 'what the wicked fears, that comes upon him, and the desire of the just will be granted' Prov 10:24).[10] These verses aim to motivate the reader to behave well, thereby making motivation proportionately by far the most significant function of these chapters.[11] The last two chapters do not contain any practical advice which cannot be found in the previous chapters, and they put a similarly strong emphasis on motivation, especially if we understand the last chapter as an allegory of wisdom.[12] This means that, throughout Proverbs, the emphasis is at least as much, if not more, on the motivation for good behaviour than on actual practical advice.

Of course, this heavy emphasis on motivation should not be a problem in itself. The problematic feature of the motivation is *how* these verses motivate the reader. At least one's first impression might be that it is not that 'if you are wise then you will be able to love God and your neighbour better,' but 'if you are wise then it will be good for you.' Is this not an argument which is built on egoism—precisely that kind of egoism which is supposed to be cured by higher religion? It is not just that Proverbs puts a heavy emphasis on human flourishing. More than that, it seems to use it as the *basis* of its motivational system.

In the light of the thoughts of Inglehart and Norris, can Proverbs still be relevant to a western believer in the twenty-first century, who lives in a materially secure society? In the light of the thoughts of Casanova, Taylor, and Lash, is it wise to read this book today in our self-interested, success-oriented society? Would it not strengthen the 'lower religion' and the materialistic features of our society?

---

10. Biblical quotations are always my translations unless noted otherwise. See also 10:2, 3, 6, 7, 8, 9, 10, 17, 21, 22, 24, 25, 27, 28, 29, 30, 31; 11:2, 3, 4, 5, 6, 8, 9, 17, 19, 21, 23, 27, 28, 29, 30, 31; 12:3, 6, 7, 12, 13, 14, 20, 21, 24, 26, 28; 13:2, 3, 4, 6, 9, 13, 14, 15, 17, 18, 21, 22, 25; 14:1, 3, 11, 14, 19, 22, 26, 27, 32, 35; 15:6, 10, 19, 24, 25, 27, 31, 32; 16:5, 14, 17, 18, 20, 22, 31; 17:2, 5, 11, 13, 19, 20; 18:6, 7, 10, 12, 20, 21; 19:2, 3, 5, 8, 9, 15, 16, 17, 23, 27, 29; 20:4, 5, 7, 13, 17, 20, 21, 26; 21:5, 6, 7, 16, 17, 18, 20, 21, 22, 23, 25, 28; 22:3, 4, 5, 8, 9, 11, 12, 16, 22-23, 24-25; 23:10-11, 20-21, 29-35; 24:3-4, 5-6, 11-12, 13-14, 15-16, 19-20, 21-22, 30-34; 25:21-22; 26:17, 24-26, 27; 27:12; 28:2, 5, 8, 10, 14, 16, 18, 20, 22, 25, 26, 27; 29:1, 6, 14, 16, 24, 25. My estimate of 171 is still very moderate. One should probably add those verses which speak about the people who praise or curse the good/bad people (10:6; 11:10, 26; 12:8, 9; 13:15, 18; 14:17, 20; 16:21; 18:13; 24:8-9, 24, 25; 25:10; 27:2; 29:27); or verses about Yahweh, who watches, hates, or loves good/bad persons (11:20; 15:3, 8, 9, 11, 26, 29; 16:2, 5, 11; 17:3, 15; 21:2, 3; 22:12; 24:11-12).

11. However, not all of these sentences are formally motivational. Nel counted 103 formal motive clauses in connection with admonitions (that is, not counting the wisdom sayings) in the whole of Proverbs (Nel 1982: 65–67). Even this more moderate number is relatively high compared to other parts of the Old Testament. Deuteronomy, for example, which contains a high number of motive clauses compared to other legal materials in the Old Testament, contains only 60–70 motive clauses (depending on how one counts some debatable cases; see Gemser 1953: 51).

12. McCreesh 1985: 25–46.

6.2 Proverbs' *Eudaemonism*: A Neglected Problem

These questions, of course, are not new to Proverbs' interpreters. As we have seen, many scholars argued, especially in the nineteenth century, that Proverbs presents an individualistic *eudaemonism*, that is, it contains a moral teaching which considers happiness or personal well-being the chief good for the individual human being,[13] a teaching which has seemed to be too selfish to at least some Christian interpreters.

Immanuel Kant had a devastating opinion of *eudaemonism* as a moral theory and, by and large, his opinion was the most influential one during the nineteenth century. Fergus Kerr summarises Kant's opinion like this:

> Kant... was deeply opposed to what he dismissively called 'happiness theory' (*Glückseligkeitslehre*): the focus on happiness, rather than on duty, could only lead to 'egoism', placing the determining principle of action in the satisfaction of the individual's desire. The last thing worthy of Christians was to want to be happy.[14]

It is no wonder that this supposed *eudaemonism* was a stumbling block for nineteenth century commentators on Proverbs. To summarise (and to simplify) my earlier discussion of nineteenth century approaches to the problem, they dealt with it in two major ways: they either condemned Proverbs for it; or claimed that Proverbs is a product of a less developed stage of religious maturation (and as such useful only for people at a certain phase of their own religious/ethical maturation), which is superseded by other, less self-centred parts of the Bible—an argument in line with the above mentioned division between 'higher' and 'lower' religions, except that, here, both categories are within the boundaries of the Bible.

However, in some philosophical–theological circles, partly because of the resurgence of Aristotelian–Thomistic moral theory, *eudaemonism* is not considered so negatively anymore.[15] Yet, there is little sign of this more favourable understanding of *eudaemonism* in biblical scholarship. Some scholars occasionally use the word '*eudaemonistic*' as a neutral description of Proverbs without attaching any value judgement to it,[16] but the word still seems to retain its negative connotations for the majority.[17] Most of these scholars argue, however, that Proverbs cannot be described as *eudaemonistic*. According to them, the *appearance* of Proverbs as *eudaemonistic* is due to a misunderstanding of its creation theology. In fact the problem of Proverbs' *eudaemonism* has retreated into the background in more recent biblical scholarship, and if the ethically problematic

---

13. My definition here echoes that of the Encyclopaedia Britannica (Safra 2010: 591).
14. Kerr 2002: 130–131.
15. See the Thomistic theological works referenced in the following discussion.
16. For example Barton 2003: 70.
17. Nel 1982: 89; Waltke 2004: 53; for further examples, see following footnotes.

nature of the 'apparent' *eudaemonism* of the book is dealt with at all, it is usually done briefly, as scholars claim that a proper understanding of creation theology solves the problem. As James Crenshaw writes,

> It is no longer possible to describe wisdom as eudaemonistic.... In truth, wisdom does ask what is good for man, and envisions the good as health, honour, wealth, and length of days. But this pragmatism which sought to secure the good life must be understood in terms of the concept of order ordained by God and entrusted to man's discovery and safe-keeping.[18]

According to this argument, as we have seen in the discussion of the history of research, wisdom literature teaches that the creation is ordered in a way that good deeds automatically lead to beneficial effects for the doer. By acting ethically, people recognise (and, as Crenshaw adds, safe-guard) this order. Thus, beneath its happiness-centred message Proverbs has a deeper concern: the order of creation. Proverbs' apparent selfishness simply mirrors this creation order.[19]

However, this 'world order explanation' of Proverbs' 'apparent' *eudaemonism* requires more careful nuancing, mainly for three reasons. First, the existence of a systematic creation theology and a teaching about world order as the background of wisdom literature is far from obvious in the light of recent scholarship, as I have argued in my discussion of the history of research. Second, I do not think that the force of the problem of Proverbs' 'selfishness' is recognised in its fullness in contemporary scholarship. For, once one considers that the book not only *recognises* that right behaviour is beneficial for the actor but it actually *motivates* right behaviour through the appeal to the reader's self-interest, a brief reference to the order of creation should not satisfy the Christian interpreter—even if one accepts the creation theology interpretation of wisdom literature. The third reason for reconsidering the problem of selfishness is that, interestingly enough, though the word '*eudaemonism*' is often used, biblical commentators have paid little attention to the so-called *eudaemonistic* moral tradition which is customarily connected to Aristotle, but which also has influential Christian versions, most notably, Thomas Aquinas' moral teaching with its contemporary appropriations.

I am aware of four major exceptions to my last statement about the lack of comparison between Proverbs and *eudaemonistic* thinkers. A notable exception is Michael V. Fox, who, in his major commentary on Proverbs, devotes an essay to comparing the ethics of Proverbs with Socratic ethics.[20] Many of his claims

---

18. Crenshaw 1976b: 4–5.
19. Crenshaw 1998: 72, 178; Gese 1958: 7–11; Nel 1982: 83–92; Zimmerli 1964: 152; Schmid 1968: 96–97.
20. Fox 2009: 934–945 (see also some comments of his earlier article: Fox 2007; and the similar approach of his student: Lyu 2012). The idea that virtue seems to be identified with knowledge in Proverbs was recognised by some earlier commentators, too, though not discussed in the systematic way Fox does in his commentary. See Toy 1899: XVI.

about the similarities between the two ethics are in line with the following discussion. However, he only notes the similarity between the worldviews of Proverbs and the Socratic tradition without providing a more detailed theological interpretation of Proverbs in the light of this similarity, which is my concern. Also, he does not address the specific questions of *eudaemonism* and self-interest directly.

Another exception is the recent theological interpretation of Proverbs by Daniel J. Treier.[21] He uses an (almost entirely Thomistic) system of virtues and vices to order and discuss the instructions of Proverbs 10-29. Again, much of Treier's book is in line with the following discussion, but he does not address the problem of the self-interested nature of Proverbs' motivational system.

A third exception is the short essay by Carol A. Newsom: 'Positive Psychology and Ancient Israelite Wisdom.'[22] In this essay Newsom does not understand *eudaemonism* in a negative way and recognises that Proverbs, in some respects, can be compared to the *eudaemonism* of Aristotle and other ancient authors. However, as the title of her essay shows, she rather focuses on a comparison with the positive psychology movement (which is, of course, not unrelated to ancient *eudaemonistic* predecessors). Just like Fox and Treier, she does not discuss explicitly the problem of 'selfishness' in Proverbs.

Finally, a fourth exception might be the much earlier work of Harry Ranston who probably comes closest to my approach among the biblical scholars of whom I am aware.[23] He states that *eudaemonism* is not necessarily a bad thing and, in fact, 'even Christianity may be termed eudaemonistic.'[24] However, he develops this point in only a few pages without going into much detail, barely discussing the structure of *eudaemonistic* thinking or mentioning important *eudaemonistic* philosophers and theologians like Aristotle or Aquinas.

Consequently, a closer look at Proverbs in the light of Thomistic moral theology has not received much attention, at least not in terms of explaining Proverbs' 'selfishness.' This is even more surprising given that *eudaemonism* is a key concept for Thomas, and as such his thought might provide some potentially helpful directions and theological categories for understanding Proverbs' 'selfishness.' In the rest of Part III, I provide a short summary of Thomistic moral theology first, then give a more detailed exegetical investigation of self-interest (and related topics) in Proverbs, with a special emphasis on the similarities and dissimilarities to the Thomistic system.

---

21. Treier 2011b
22. Newsom 2012: 117–135.
23. Ranston 1930: 93–97.
24. Ranston 1930: 95.

6.3 Thomistic Moral Theology

First of all, an important clarification is in order. The main aim of this discussion is not the interpretation of Thomas Aquinas but to use his system heuristically for the interpretation of Proverbs. This means that I cannot enter the (many) debate(s) about Thomas's thought here. The following interpretation of virtues, self-interest, hierarchy of human ends, and natural law in Thomas draws upon one strand of Thomas-studies: it is mainly influenced by the interpretation offered by Jean Porter. Besides that of Jean Porter I have found the works of Romanus Cessario and especially the writings of Fergus Kerr, Russell Hittinger, and (though he disagrees on many points with Kerr and Hittinger) Denys Turner most helpful for a theological interpretation of Thomas's thoughts.[25] Even if the experts whom I am following misunderstood Thomas, one can say that this 'misunderstood theory' is used here to help to sharpen a theological understanding of Proverbs—so the potential misrepresentation of Thomas is not that problematic as long as the misrepresentation provides a coherent, sophisticated theory in its own right that can be contrasted with Proverbs.

It should also be noted that the comparison between Thomas and Proverbs will be very limited. Thomas's moral theology, his whole theological-philosophical system, and his way of handling Scripture will be discussed only to the extent that they serve a comparison in the specific question of 'selfishness.' Nevertheless, a very brief overview of Thomas's *Summa Theologiae* might help us to see Thomas's thoughts in their broader context. The *Summa Theologiae* has three major parts. The first (*Prima pars*) deals with God, the second (*Secunda pars*) with ethics, that is, with 'the journey to God of reasoning creatures.'[26] This second part, in its two sub-sections (*Prima Secundae* and *Secunda Secundae*), clarifies notions like 'happiness,' 'habit,' 'virtue,' etc., and discusses the individual virtues. The third part (*Tertia pars*) discusses 'Christ, who, as man, is our road to God.'[27] So, a simplified structure of the *Summa* would look like this:

I. God
II. Ethics (the journey to God)
III. Christ (the way to God)

From this brief structural analysis it should be clear that Thomas's ethics, which is often discussed in isolation, is embedded in, and, for Thomas, probably undividable from his theology. The topics of *imago dei* and *imitatio Christi* sur-

---

25. Porter 1994; Porter 2005; Cessario 2002; Kerr 2002; Hittinger 1997: 1–30; Turner 2004; see also Weinandy 2000. As an introduction to Thomas's thoughts on prudence, self-interest, and moral theology I also found useful Pieper 1959 and King 1999: 101–132. Concerning the so-called 'new natural theory' perspective I learned the most from Finnis 1998. For the works of some other scholars and some other works of these scholars, see the footnotes for the particular issues discussed later.
26. Thomas's own words from the preface before *ST* I, 2, 1.
27. Thomas's own words from the preface before *ST* I, 2, 1.

round and explain his thoughts on ethics.[28] As most issues directly relevant for our interests are in the *Secunda pars*, it is especially important to bear in mind their theological centrality as we are discussing them. To these issues we now turn.

6.3.1 Human Ends

According to Thomas Aquinas, the principles of moral life are similar to the axioms of theoretical thinking: it is not appropriate to seek logical proof for these axioms as they are to be grasped by the rational human being through observation and insight (*ST* I–II, 91, 3; *ST* II–II, 47, 6).[29]

These principles follow from the main ends for which human beings strive. The most basic such principle is that every being wants to preserve its life, self-preservation being the most basic end (*ST* I–II, 94, 2). This is not something to be condemned, this is simply how God intended human (and other) beings to function. This principle is subordinated to the higher ends like living in community and knowing God (*ST* I–II, 90, 2; *ST* II–II, 26, 4). When these ends seem to be in conflict in a particular situation then the higher end is to be chosen. However, this subordination does not mean in Thomas's thinking that the higher end makes the lower (and often more immediate) end wrong (*ST* II–II, 47, 11).[30] The higher ends influence the way in which someone strives for the lower ends but do not demolish them.[31] The higher ends are achieved through striving for the lower ones and striving for the higher ones is the well-spring for the striving for the lower ones. Thus, self-interest—as long as we understand 'self-preservation' as 'self-interest'—plays a crucial and positive role in Thomas's moral theology.[32]

6.3.2 Virtues

The question arises, however: how is one able to comprehend the right hierarchy of ends? Furthermore, how is one able to recognise in every given situation what act would bring a person closer to those ends? Finally, what enables one to perform those acts? Thomas's answer is: the virtues.

Virtue, in Thomas's thinking, is a quality that makes its possessor good and renders his or her acts good (*ST* II–II, 47, 4). It is a 'perfect power' which directs the human being's 'particular choices in such a way that she acts in accordance

---

28. Kerr 2002: 114–133.
29. For the role and nature of 'insight,' or more precisely 'intellect,' see Turner 2004: 75–88.
30. See Aquinas 1963–1981, vol. XXXVI (1974), 38 note f. (For the system of referring to footnotes in the translation of Thomas's works, see the section on 'Abbreviations of the works of Thomas Aquinas' in the Abbreviations section.) See furthermore *ST* II–II, 17, 6 and *ST* II–II, 25, 4.
31. See, for example, how the love of God relates to the love of self in *ST* I–II, 109, 3.
32. Davenport 2001: 291–292.

with her own good and the wider goods that she seeks (*ST* I–II, 56, 5; *ST* I–II, 60, 3).'[33] 'The virtues are precisely those qualities the possession of which will enable an individual to achieve *eudaimonia* and the lack of which will frustrate his movement toward that *telos*.'[34] According to Thomas's terminology these virtues are 'habits,' but they are not

> ... unthinking habits of action of the sort that could be produced by mindlessly drilling children in certain patterns of behaviour. To say they are concerned with 'choice' (*prohairesis*) means they involve not a tendency to some noncognitive urge or brute impulse but rather a stable disposition to act in the relevant way when appropriate because one thinks and feels in the right way about the situation.[35]

Thomas groups the virtues into three main categories. The first two categories are the intellectual virtues (wisdom, science, understanding, *ST* I–II, 57, 2) and the moral virtues (the four cardinal virtues: prudence, justice, courage, temperance, *ST* I–II, 61, 3). The third category, the theological virtues (faith, hope, charity, *ST* I–II, 62, 3), comprise a special group, they are entirely 'infused' by God, that is, they are unavailable for the natural person on his or her own. They are necessary for reaching the highest end, which is contemplation of God and partaking in the divine nature (*ST* I–II, 62, 1). This is perfect happiness. However, an incomplete happiness is theoretically attainable by everyone through the rest of the virtues which, to a certain extent, can be acquired without supernatural infusion (*ST* I–II, 4, 5–7; *ST* I–II, 5, 5–7; *ST* I–II, 62, 1; *ST* I–II, 65, 3).

TABLE 2: The Thomistic system of virtues; gifts; beatitudes; sins; fruits[36]

The seven main non-intellectual virtues	Charity, justice, courage, temperance, faith, hope, prudence
The seven gifts of the Holy Spirit	wisdom, courage, piety, fear, understanding, science, counsel
The seven beatitudes	peacemaker, hungry and thirsty after justice, meek, poor in spirit, mourner, pure in heart, merciful
The seven capital sins	wrath, sloth, gluttony, lust, pride, envy, avarice[37]
Twelve fruits of the Holy Spirit	joy, peace, faith, charity, patience, long-suffering, meekness, moderation, continence, chastity, goodness, benevolence

---

33. Porter 1994: 103.
34. MacIntyre 1984: 148.
35. Davenport 2001: 276; see *ST* I–II, 55, 1–4; *ST* I–II, 63, 1–2.
36. As charity and prudence will be discussed shortly, the gifts, sins, etc. corresponding to these two virtues are underlined. The table was reconstructed on the basis of the following places: *ST* I–II, 70, 3; *ST* I–II, 72, 3; *ST* II–II, 24, 12; *ST* II–II, 28, 4; *ST* II–II, 29, 4; *ST* II–II, 52, 1–4; *ST* II–II, 53, 6; *ST* II–II, 55, 8; *ST* II–II, 45, 1–6.
37. All of the sins oppose charity (*ST* II–II, 24, 12). The ones which oppose prudence, too, are underlined with a bold line.

The virtues comprise the most important part of a complex system. In this system every virtue can be perfected by a particular divine gift, correspond to a beatitude, be opposed by some sins, and be expressed in fruits. Table 2 lists the theological and cardinal virtues and the other, non-virtue elements of the system.

6.3.3 Self-Interest is Accepted

I have already noted that self-preservation is the most basic human end in Thomas's system of ends, and it is perfectly natural and good for a human being to strive for that end. However, Thomas goes even further than emphasising the natural inclination for self-preservation. To see this positive presentation of self-interest more clearly, it will be useful to take a closer look at two of the above listed virtues.

Let us begin with charity, the most important theological virtue in Thomas's system (*ST* II-II, 23, 6). As the primary object of charity is God, one could expect it to divert a person's attention away from him or herself completely. The picture is, however, more complex than this. Thomas not only refers to self-love in a positive light (*ST* II–II, 123, 12; *ST* II–II, 126, 1), but claims that even one who loves with (divine) charity, loves him or herself the foremost except God. This is so not because the self is necessarily more precious than one's neighbour, but because the one who loves from charity loves God in everything and God is more directly present in the self than in the neighbour (*ST* II–II, 26, 4; *ST* II-II, 25, 4).

Charity is also relevant for our investigations because in Thomas's system it is connected to wisdom. However, we have to recognise that it is not the (intellectual) *virtue* of wisdom that it is connected to, but the *gift* of wisdom. The two are related but are not to be confused. The (intellectual) virtue of wisdom enables a person to know the deepest causes of the phenomena *of the world* and so helps in ordering them (*ST* I–II, 37, 2). The gift of wisdom, however, enables one to know the highest and deepest cause without qualification, that is, God (*ST* II–II, 45, 1), and this gift enables one to love God properly in everything.

However, there is another virtue which is even more promising than charity, if one tries to find parallels to the practical admonitions of Proverbs in Thomas's thinking. It is the virtue of prudence. If charity is one of the least self-oriented virtues, prudence is one of the most self-oriented. It is basically the virtue of putting the moral theory into proper action here and now, in the actual, messy reality of the world. Prudence, in Thomas's thinking, is nothing else than practical wisdom in human affairs (*ST* II–II, 47, 2).[38] As we have seen, he defines wisdom as an intellectual virtue which helps one to perceive the deepest causes of worldly phenomena and helps one to order those phenomena appropriately (*ST* I–II, 37, 2). Similarly, prudence puts the different interests and contradicting

---

38. See Aquinas 1963–1981, vol. XXXVI (1974), 10 note j.

desires of the manifold everyday life into proper order and enables one to achieve the human end, that is, happiness. This happiness ensues when ill is banished and desires are fulfilled (*ST* I–II, 5, 3). As I have noted above, this happiness has an incomplete form (relative security, living harmoniously in a community) and a complete form (security, community, and partaking in God). To reach either of them one has to have the appropriate desires and has to use the appropriate means to fulfil them. This is where prudence helps.

6.3.4 Not Every Kind of Self-Interest is Accepted

In summary, we can say that self-interest and self-love recur often in Thomas's moral theory and play a crucial role in it: self-preservation is accepted as a legitimate human end; the one who loves God with charity also loves the self in a particular way because that is where God is the closest; and one of prudence's main roles is that it helps the prudent person to achieve happiness.

At the same time, the natural inclination for self-preservation and the priority of self-love does not mean selfishness in this system.[39] I can see three main factors in Thomas's thinking that differentiate proper self-interest from selfishness:

- The higher human ends should govern (but not cancel) the lower ones. The highest good for a human is to live and know God in a God-fearing community, so proper self-love means love of the community, and proper love of a community also involves and supports a proper love of the self.[40] This hierarchy of ends is what differentiates Thomas's moral theology from most *utilitarian* systems. As Insole writes, 'Aquinas stands ready to invoke the criterion of "great usefulness or necessity" (*ST* I–II, 97, 3) when considering the rightness of actions, precisely because there is always a higher end to which human things are to be measured and used.'[41]
- The virtue of justice is the cardinal virtue which is completely other-oriented, but this virtue is in accordance with prudence, which is self-oriented, precisely because the communal goods and individual goods are in harmony (*ST* I–II, 60, 3).[42] Thus, justice complements prudence. It is not possible to have one of these virtues and lack the other (*ST* I–II, 65, 1).
- The spiritual self, not the physical self, is to be loved the foremost.[43] E.g., the neighbour is to be loved more than one's own body (*ST* II–II, 26, 5), but one's soul is to be loved more than the neighbour.[44]

---

39. Cessario 2002: 121.
40. Finnis 1998: 111–117, 120–121; MacIntyre 2009: 315–316; Porter 1994: 48–51.
41. Insole 2008: 474.
42. See also Porter 1994: 48–51, 124–127.
43. About the body/soul relationship in general, see *ST* I–II, 2, 5.
44. See also Cessario 2002: 78, 85. About the body/soul dichotomy in relation to prudence, see *ST* II–II, 55, 1.

In other words, Thomas not only accepts self-interest as a crucial part of his system, but very carefully describes what that self-interest should look like. According to this, the main question is not 'how much' a person is self-interested but 'how' he or she is self-interested.[45] Though Thomas does not say this explicitly, I would suggest that a correct paraphrase of Thomas's teaching is that prudence is the ability to love oneself properly.[46] Prudence is the *right sort* of (practical) self-love, that is, the self-love which is beneficial for the individual, the human community, and also for the relationship of humans with God.

Is this the self-love and self-interest we can see in Proverbs? Do we find the same checks on self-interest there as in Thomas's moral theology? In the following pages I investigate Proverbs' 'selfishness' with regular attempts to relate my exegetical investigations to these questions.

---

45. Cf. Chapman 2000: 93.
46. See his description of deliberate sin as something harmful for the actor and stemming from a disordered love (*ST* I–II, 78, 1).

7

Is Proverbs More Self-Interested than the Rest of the Bible?

Is the assertion that Proverbs' apparent selfishness is different from the rest of the Bible true at all? If it is true, then what is the nature of its special selfishness? Does it speak more about human needs and less about Yahweh than other parts of the Bible—thereby neglecting the 'highest human end,' which is an important Thomistic check on self-interest? Is it more individualistic than other biblical books—thereby failing to be in harmony with love for the community, which is another important Thomistic check?

A comparison with the whole Bible would be too big a task for the present. However, a comparison with Deuteronomy will serve our purposes well. Though Deuteronomy is not entirely dissimilar to Proverbs,[1] it is different in its way of presentation (i.e., written in a story- and homiletic-form), and it possesses all of those characteristics which are often listed as non-sapiential but characteristic for most books of the Bible: it emphasises the role of Yahweh in history, the importance of the Law, the nation of Israel, and its covenant relationship with Yahweh. Thus, if Proverbs has a special selfishness then we would expect to find something else in Deuteronomy that represents the 'normal' mode of biblical utterance.[2] This contrast might help us to clarify the nature of Proverbs' self-interest.

---

1. Daube 2010: 3–55; Dell 2006: 167–178; Weinfeld 1972.
2. See Zimmerli, who emphasised the difference between the work of the deuteronomistic writer and the works of the sages (Zimmerli 1964: 147).

7.1 Self-Interest in Proverbs and Deuteronomy

7.1.1 Is Proverbs More Self-Interested than Deuteronomy?

Cyril S. Rodd contrasts the ethics of Proverbs with the ethics of the Old Testament Law. Whereas the latter is comprised by commandments, the former, says Rodd, is 'humanistic.'

> This is confirmed by the kinds of motives for obeying this teaching.... Unlike the motive clauses in the law, these are similar to those in non-biblical wisdom writing. McKane comments that their function in the Instruction of Ptah-hotep and the Instruction of Merika-re is to recommend the advice by showing that it is reasonable and effective.... This might equally be said of Proverbs. Even where Yahweh is mentioned in the motive clauses, instead of referring back to his salvation in the past, the sages declare that he watches the actions of men and women (e.g., Prov. 5.21; 24.17-18). He protects those who 'walk in integrity' and 'keep sound wisdom' (e.g., Prov. 2.7-8; 3.21, 26). He pleads the cause of the poor and 'despoils of life' those who despoil them (Prov. 22.23). Wisdom declares that those who find her obtain favour from Yahweh (Prov. 8.35). The upright are admitted into the divine council (Prov. 3.32). For the most part, however, the motive clauses speak of the happy consequences which follow doing right.... The motive clauses may be analysed under six heads:
> (1) to follow the teaching of wisdom or the sages will give pleasure (e.g., Prov. 2.10; 3.13-18; 8.33-34);
> (2) various happy consequences will follow, such as a long and happy life (e.g., Prov. 3.2, 18; 4.10, 13, 22, 23; 8.35), or great prosperity (Prov. 3.10; 8.18-21);
> (3) wisdom will protect those who seek her (Prov. 2.11-12; 3.23; 4.6);
> (4) disaster will come to those who do not follow the teacher's advice (Prov. 5.9-11; 6.11, 26, 32-35; 23.3, 5, 8, 9, 21, 27-35), and 'death' will be the fate of the wicked (Prov. 1.32; 2.18-19; 5.4-6, 22-23; 7.26-27; 8.36; 9.18);
> (5) sometimes this reward or punishment is ascribed to God's intervention (e.g., Prov. 2.6-8; 3.12, 26; 5.21; 23.11; 24.12); and
> (6) more often the retribution is the natural consequence of some actions and follows automatically without any direct action by God (e.g., Prov. 1.26-27; 2.21-22; 6.15, 27-29; 22.25; 23.21; 24.16, 20).[3]

However, if we make a similar analysis of the motive clauses in Deuteronomy, we find that the difference between the motivational system of Proverbs

---

3. Rodd 2001: 57. I have changed the layout of the analysis of the motive clauses by printing every heading as a new paragraph, in order to make it easily comprehensible.

and that of the Law is not as significant as it might first appear.[4] In the following table I give the analysis in the left column. In the right column I provide a few explanatory comments relating to the concrete points of the analysis.

TABLE 3: The motive clauses of Deuteronomy

Motive clauses in Deuteronomy	Comments about how Proverbs compares with Deuteronomy
You shall follow the teaching of this book because then . . . (2) Happy consequences will follow (long and happy life, prosperity): 4:1, 40; 5:16, 29, 33; 6:2, 3, 18, 24; 7:12-15; 8:1; 10:13; 11:8-9, 13-17, 22-25; 12:25, 28; 13:17-18; 14:29; 15:4-5, 10, 18; 16:15, 19-20; 19:13; 22:7; 23:19-20; 24:19; 25:15; 28:1-14; 29:8; 30:5-6, 9, 15-16, 19-20; 32:47. (4) Disaster and death will come to those who do not follow Deuteronomy's teaching: 4:24ff; 5:9, 11; 6:15; 7:4, 10, 26; 8:19-20; 27:14-26; 28:15-68; 29:20; 30:17-18. (5) Usually the reward and retribution is ascribed to God's intervention: for example 4:24ff; 5:9-10, 11; 6:15; 7:4, 12-15; 11:13-17, 22-25; 15:10; 32:20-26. (6) Sometimes the text does not mention God, so the reward/retribution seems to follow automatically: for example 4:1, 40; 5:15, 29-33; 6:2, 3; 8:1; 10:13; 19:13; 22:7; 29:8.	Most of Deuteronomy's motive clauses can be ordered under Rodd's headings. Though there are a few 'happy consequences' that do not feature in Proverbs (like occupying the country [Deut 4:1; 16:20; 19:9] or a special emphasis on long life *in the land* [Deut 4:40; 25:15; 30:20; 32:47; etc.]), Deuteronomy, just like Proverbs, speaks mainly about long life and material prosperity and security. There are only two of Rodd's categories that are missing from Deuteronomy. The giving of pleasure (number 1) and protection (number 3). As for the former, I am not convinced that it is a fortunate category even in the case of Proverbs. The Hebrew word נעם, from which Rodd seems to derive the special category of 'pleasure,' might indeed be etymologically connected to physical pleasure, but it has a very broad meaning and diverse connotation,[5] especially in the wisdom literature, where it simply means 'lovely, good.' It might have been used partly because it does have the connotation of the taste of a sweet food, but this hint at physical pleasantness only expresses that, for example, the right words are as sweet and pleasant as honey (Prov 16:24) but this hardly motivates by promising physical pleasure directly. So, for example, the 'so that it might go well' phrase in Deuteronomy (5:29; 6:18; 12:25, 28; 22:7), however general it is, provides a good parallel

---

4. Gemser provided a classic analysis of the motive clause in Old Testament law (for further literature, see Chirichigno 1981: 303–313). His four headings are: explanatory, ethical, religious, historico-religious (Gemser 1953: 56–61). My aim is not to define the main categories of motive clauses in Deuteronomy, and so not to compete with Gemser's categories, but to concentrate on the more specific question of self-interest in them (which was not discussed in Gemser's analysis) and to compare Deuteronomy with Rodd's analysis of Proverbs. Thus, however useful his headings are for a broader categorisation of motive clauses in Deuteronomy, I will work with more categories than Gemser did and where possible I will follow Rodd's categories.

5. Kronholm 1998: 467–474, Clines 2001: 705–706.

Motive clauses in Deuteronomy	Comments about how Proverbs compares with Deuteronomy
	to the נעם motivational clauses in Proverbs. As for number 3 in Rodd's list, the explicit mention of (physical) protection is indeed lacking in the motivational clauses of Deuteronomy, though it must not be alien to Deuteronomy's thinking as it is logically included in the promise of long life and prosperity which, as it can be seen in the left column, features quite often in the book.
Beneath this line are listed all the motivational clauses in Deuteronomy which do not have a direct parallel among the motivational sentences of Proverbs as listed in Rodd.	
You shall follow the teaching of this book because . . . Doing what is opposite to it is hateful/abhorrent to the Lord: 12:31; 16:22; 17:1; 18:9-12; 20:16-18; 21:22-23; 22:5; 23:18; 24:4; doing what is in accordance with it is right in the eyes of the Lord: 12:23-25.	Rodd has not listed all of the motivational sentences of Proverbs in his analysis. A prime example is the 'do not do this because that is abhorrent to the Lord' type which features in Proverbs as it does in Deuteronomy: Prov 3:32 (see also 6:16; 12:22; 15:8; 20:10, which are not motivational formally but are clearly so semantically).[6]
The judgement is God's: 1:17.	Though not in formally motivational clauses, but the idea does occur in Proverbs (e.g., Prov 16:33; 29:26).
Then the king's descendants might reign for a long time in Israel: 17:20.	Though not an exact parallel, especially because <u>Israel is not specifically mentioned</u>, Proverbs mirrors the same idea when it speaks about how the throne is established if one rules according to the principles of righteousness and wisdom (for example Prov 8:15-16; 16:12).[7]
Then the Lord will be with you (so do not be afraid); you can trust him as he was with you in the past: 1:30-31; 2:7; 3:22; 7:9; 8:1-5; 31:3-8.	<u>Validation of the Lord's trustworthiness by referring to salvific events in the past is indeed missing</u> from Proverbs. However, the importance of trust in God with its behaviour-modifying effects are a major topic in Proverbs, too (Prov 3:5; 16:20; 22:19; 23:17-18; 28:25-26; 29:25).
Then you will learn to fear the Lord: 6:2; 14:23; 17:19.	Again, the idea is significant in Proverbs, too. These sentences might not be formally motivational, but there is no doubt that they are semantically (especially Prov 2:5; but also 1:7; 9:10; 15:33; etc. For the

---

6. I regard as 'formally motivational' those clauses that motivate the reader to do something by giving a reason why he or she should act that way, and which are also introduced by a word grammatically signalling this function (like כי or למען). Of course, there are plenty of sentences that might have a motivational purpose and/or motivational effect on the reader, yet they do not express explicitly that they are motivational. These I take as 'semantically motivational.'

7. The underlined comments show where Proverbs lacks a parallel to Deuteronomy.

Motive clauses in Deuteronomy	Comments about how Proverbs compares with Deuteronomy
	connection between long life and fear of the Lord, which we can see in Deut 6:2, see Prov 10:27; 14:27; 19:23).
Caring for other people will be regarded as a righteous act in the sight of the Lord: 24:13.	Although there is no direct parallel in Proverbs, the ideas of caring for others, righteousness, and that the Lord pays attention to these issues are certainly present (cf. Prov 2:9; 12:10; 16:2; 21:3).
Caring for the safety and honour of the oppressed, innocent, weak and poor, and providing everyone with what he or she deserves is ethical: 5:14; 15:11; 20:5-8; 20:19; 21:14, 17; 23:15-16; 24:6; 25:3.	Caring for the weak, poor, oppressed is a major topic in Proverbs, too. Usually this behaviour is motivated by promising rewards for the carer (as in Deuteronomy); even if close, verbal parallels are missing, the topic can be found in Proverbs (Prov 29:7; 30:14; 31:5, 8-9).
Otherwise you might incur guilt (חטא): 15:9; 23:21-22; 24:15.	Again, though not in a formally motivational clause, it is also stated by Proverbs that socially irresponsible behaviour makes one a sinner (חוטא; Prov 14:21).
The temptation is only a test from the Lord: 13:2-3.	As far as I am aware, Proverbs does not describe a temptation as coming explicitly and unambiguously from the Lord. However, the idea that God has power over temptations and he can use bad, tempting events for character formation is not alien to Proverbs (see Prov 17:3; maybe 16:4 can be read this way, too).[8]
Not following the book's teaching would defile the land: 21:23; 24:4.	The 'defilement of the land' as a motivation for right behaviour is lacking in Proverbs.
The Lord will (or will not) give success in occupying a land: 2:5, 9, 19, 31.	The 'occupation of the land' as a motivation for right behaviour is lacking in Proverbs.
You can remember (that you were a slave yourself, that the Lord spoke to you and was with you): 4:31-38; 5:15; 7:18-19; 10:19; 11:1; 15:15; 16:1, 3, 12; 17:16; 23:3-6; 24:8-9, 17-18, 21-22.	Historical memory as a motivation for right behaviour is lacking in Proverbs.
You must be holy so that he might not turn from you, for you are the Lord's: 7:6; 14:1-2, 21; 23:14; 27:9-10.	The holiness of the nation Israel as a motivation for right behaviour is lacking in Proverbs.

---

8. See Ehrlich 1968: 89.

On the one hand, we find exactly that difference between Deuteronomy and Proverbs that we expect to find there, as it is shown by the last few items in the above table. That is, national history, covenant with Yahweh, the holiness of the nation, and the holiness of the national land, which have a place in the motivational system of Deuteronomy, are absent in Proverbs. At the same time, self-interest does not play a less significant role in the motivational system of Deuteronomy than in Proverbs.

Deuteronomy has fewer motive clauses than Proverbs (see footnote 11 on page 90) and as a result its reader might find the presence of self-interest less overwhelming than in Proverbs. However, when motive clauses occur, self-interest does not play a less significant role than in Proverbs.[9] Deuteronomy is full of sentences like 'So that you, your children and your children's children may fear the Lord your God all the days of your life and keep all his ordinances and commandments that I am commanding you so that your days may be long' (6:2b), or 'However, there will be no poor people among you because the Lord will surely bless you in the land that the Lord, your God, is giving to you as a possession to occupy, but only if you listen obediently to the voice of the Lord your God' (15:4-5), or 'Keep the words of this covenant and do them so that you may prosper in all your deeds' (29:8).

Similarly, the various curses and blessings in chapters 27–33 are all about material issues and appeal to self-interest. They speak about long life, military success, prosperity, fertility, etc. Though most of these sentences might not contain formal motivational clauses, their rhetorical function is presumably to have a strong motivational effect on the reader.

Although Rodd is right when he says that it is a peculiarity of Proverbs that it does not refer to Yahweh's salvation in the past, Deuteronomy refers to that salvation only in a minority of the motive clauses and even when it does, it usually refers to the effectiveness of the right behaviour in the same sentence. The vast majority of the motive clauses in Deuteronomy are about effectiveness and long life. Therefore, when Rodd writes that 'McKane comments that their function in the Instruction of Ptah-hotep and the Instruction of Meri-ka-re is to recommend the advice by showing that it is reasonable and effective.... This might equally be said of Proverbs,' then one could add, 'and regardless of the differences between Proverbs and Deuteronomy, this might equally be said of Deuteronomy, too.'[10]

---

9. A similar understanding of Deuteronomy's motive clauses is presented by Blenkinsopp 1995: 45. See also Daube 2010: 23–24.

10. In one of his articles Gammie recognised the importance of anthropocentric self-interest in Deuteronomy's teaching about retribution, but he claimed that Deuteronomy, in its final form, 'move[d] on to theocentricity' (Gammie 1970: 9). Even if one grants Gammie's reconstruction of religion-history, self-interest appears in his 'later, more developed, theocentric' sections, too (like 8:1-9:6; 10:12-13). So, regardless of the truth

7.1.2 Is Proverbs Less Yahwistic than Deuteronomy?

However, even if the role of self-interest is just as central in Deuteronomy as in Proverbs, is not Rodd still right in claiming that there is something special in the nature of Proverbs' self-interest? After all, it is true that Proverbs does not refer to Yahweh in most of its motive clauses.

I have to admit, I cheated a little in the above table when I listed motive clauses from Deuteronomy which do not mention Yahweh. In fact, in most of the cases it is clear from *the context* that they do not speak of an independent world order but a world which is constantly ordered by Yahweh. Even if those verses only state, 'do this, and then you will prosper' (like 29:8), the context almost always emphasises Yahweh's role in that prosperity (like 29:16-28). However, this difference between Proverbs and Deuteronomy (and many of the non-sapiential works of the Bible) is probably only apparent and comes from the different nature of the two genres: namely, that there is a narrative context in Deuteronomy that is lacking in Proverbs. If the reader disregards the narrative context then he or she can find sentences in Deuteronomy that do not seem less 'humanistic' than many of the context-less sentences in Proverbs. Of course, there is no compelling reason for disregarding the narrative context of Deuteronomy when one is reading the book.[11] Similarly, if one takes Proverbs 1–9 as the context of Proverbs' sentence-literature, then it is no less Yahwistic than Deuteronomy.

7.1.3 Is Proverbs 'Individualistic'?

If it is not the non-Yahwistic nature of Proverbs' motivation which makes it special, then can it be its focus on the individual? After all, compared to Deuteronomy, it does have an individualistic flavour, as it does not mention the nation and the holy land. Does not this 'individualism' make Proverbs' self-interest distinctively selfish? No, it does not, the different foci of the two books are just that: different foci. For, while there is a real difference here between the two

---

in Gammie's argument, it does not invalidate my claims about the crucial role of self-interest in Deuteronomy's motivation system.

11. When someone wants to decipher the composition-history of the book it is legitimate to suppose and argue that the narrative context is a later layer. (There are numerous reconstructions for the composition-history. More recent ones include theories like Crüsemann 1996: 201–215; 265–275 and Rofé 2002: 4–9.) However, if one wishes to understand the book as a whole then paying attention to all of its parts and their interactions is advisable and possible (see, for example, Christensen 2001: LXVIII–LXX; McConville 2002: 38–40). Deuteronomy is an excellent example of the literary and theological importance of the narrative framework in a book. Note, for example, the dominant role of Moses in Deuteronomy, even though his name never appears in Deuteronomy 6–26. (I am grateful to Prof. Walter Moberly for drawing my attention to this feature of Deuteronomy.)

works, it does not necessarily reflect two fundamentally different worldviews, anthropology, or religious thinking.

The narrative context in Deuteronomy makes an emphasis on the communal, national side of life almost inevitable. Moses addresses the nation just before occupying the national land and urges them to obey the law in order that the nation can live long and prosper in the land. Nevertheless, it is obvious that it is the individual who has to keep the law. It is an individual who finds the ox of a neighbour and not the nation (Deut 22:1), an individual who must have right, honest weights (Deut 25:15), an individual man and not a nation who engages a woman (Deut 28:30), and it is not only the nation but the individual, too, who will gain a long life through responsible behaviour in such situations and will enjoy the fruits of his or her deeds (Deut 22:7). Therefore, although Deuteronomy looks at the issues from a national perspective, it also counts on the responsibilities, aims, and rewards of the individual.

Similarly, though Proverbs is written from the perspective of individuals, it is hardly 'individualistic' in the sense of being blind to corporate issues. Indeed, wisdom as such already presupposes a community, as many of its functions relate to relationships with others.[12] Just as Solomon asked for wisdom in order to be able to govern Yahweh's chosen nation (1 Kgs 3:9) so we read in Proverbs that kings and rulers rule through wisdom (8:15-16) and kings uphold the justice and well-being of the whole community (16:10; 20:8, 26; 29:4). What is more, it is a major role of righteousness and wisdom to enable not only kings but also commoners to build their community.[13]

What might be somewhat misleading is that besides the numerous references to the benefits of wisdom for the whole community, Proverbs contains many verses that do not refer explicitly to society. However, even in these individual-focused verses, the vocabulary does not let the reader forget about the corporate side of wisdom. Take, for example, one of the key categories of Proverbs, the 'righteous' person.[14] I suggest that the implied reader of the text is supposed to remember every time he[15] reads about the 'righteous' that righteousness is intrinsically connected to the well-being of the whole society. He is supposed to remember this simply because it is mentioned so often in other verses. The wise and the righteous provide knowledge, healing, and life to oth-

---

12. The 'community' implied by the Solomonic title of the received form of the book is the whole of Israel, but, of course, the actual reader (as differentiated from the implied reader) might also think of the particular community of which he or she is a part, be it the Persian province of Yehud or the Christian community.

13. In most ancient Near Eastern societies the king represented the god(s) by mediating his/their justice and righteousness. About the democratisation of this idea in Israel, see Levenson 1988: 114–117.

14. In a linguistic study of appellations in Proverbs, Heim argued persuasively that חכם and צדיק are usually co-referential (Heim 2001: 77–103).

15. The usual 'my son' address and other features of the text suggest that the implied reader is male.

ers (Prov 10:21; 12:18; 15:2, 7), they care for the needs of others (12:10; 14:21), they provide wise guidance for the whole nation (11:4), and promote impartiality in judgement. For this community-building behaviour they are praised by the whole nation (24:23-24; 28:21). It is no wonder that the whole city rejoices when it goes well for the righteous (11:10).

If we search all of those verses of the whole Bible that contain either צדק, צדקה or צדיק, we find that the three most common words mentioned together with righteous people and righteousness are יהוה, רשע, and משפט. These terms define the place and function of the צדיק in society. רשע is the opposite of a צדיק (some proverbial examples are Prov 10:2, 3, 6, 7, 11, 16, 20, 24, 25, 28, 30; 11:5, 8, 10, 18, 23, 31; 12:3, 7, 10, 12, etc.); יהוה loves the צדיק and protects him (Prov 3:33; 10:3; 15:9, 29; 18:10); and משפט, (right) judgement, seems to be one of the main activities of a צדיק (Prov 1:3; 2:9; 8:20; 12:5; 16:8; 21:3, 5). משפט incorporates caring for the well-being of the poor, the neighbour, and anyone who has a just cause against someone else. This close connection between משפט and righteousness shows, again, the corporate function of a צדיק. Thus, the frequent use of terms like צדיק and משפט keeps the social significance of wisdom constantly in the reader's attention, even where the corporate aspects of wisdom are not explicitly mentioned.

William P. Brown has reached a similar conclusion. He writes, 'To welcome wisdom necessarily involves becoming a responsible and productive citizen of a community whose character is formed by justice and equity by those who have gone before, laying a foundation for those to come.'[16]

Consequently, Deuteronomy and Proverbs should probably be understood as speaking about two sides of the same coin. The two books simply construct different implied readers: one is a nation at the border of the land to be occupied; the other is an individual member of that nation who already lives in the land. But the difference in implied readers, and therefore the emphases of the two books, does not necessarily mean that one is 'individualistic' and the other is 'communal.'

7.2 Summary

We have seen that if Proverbs' 'selfishness' seems special compared to Deuteronomy's then it is:

- because there are a few (but only a few), typically Israelite religious motivational sentences in Deuteronomy;
- because most proverbial sayings lack a Yahwistic context (but the literary framework of Proverbs can provide such a context);
- because the emphasis is on the individual (though this does not make Proverbs 'individualistic').

---

16. Brown 1996: 34, see also p. 35 about the communal significance of Prov 3:27-31; see also Treier 2006: 43.

We can draw three main conclusions from these observations. First, compared to Deuteronomy, the special nature of Proverbs' 'selfishness' is more apparent than real. Second, this does not mean that Proverbs' motivational system is as 'selfless' as that of Deuteronomy. In fact, quite the opposite: Deuteronomy's appeal to self-interest seems to be as undeniable as that of Proverbs. This means that the problem of self-interest is not a special problem of Proverbs, but a more general one, probably relevant for much of the Bible. If Proverbs is more suitable for investigating this problem than many other biblical books then it is so because the aforementioned three characteristics make self-interest more palpable for the modern reader in it but not because it is more real there. Third, the most significant difference between the two books seems to be a difference in perspective. Namely, the implied reader of Proverbs is the individual and not the community as in Deuteronomy. However, the individual perspective of Proverbs does not rule out, but presupposes, communal aims.

If these thoughts about the relationship between the individual and communal interests in Proverbs are right, then Proverbs' teaching is not dissimilar to the thinking of Thomas Aquinas in these matters. After all, Thomas also emphasised the complementarity of individual and communal interests. He also taught that the individual, by acting according to his or her true interest, builds up the community, and that the other-oriented justice has to accompany the self-interested prudence.

However, the acknowledgement of self-interest and its combination with other-oriented justice and communal interests are only two, though crucial, agreements between Proverbs and Thomistic thinking. Thomas goes further than this. He can accept self-interest as a motivation because it does not focus solely on material issues and because it is subordinated to higher aims. Can we find parallels to these aspects of Thomistic thinking in Proverbs, too? Let us have a look first at the former issue: is Proverbs solely about material gains?

8

Is Proverbs Solely about Material Success?

As we have seen, Thomas differentiates between the spiritual self and the material self in his system. The body is something to be cared for, but it is the soul and not the body that is to be loved more than anything else except God. The material body, in fact, is to be loved less than other people. Such a differentiation between soul and body mirrors ancient Greek and medieval thinking, and one looks for its equivalent in the Hebrew Bible in vain.[1] However, the lack of a clear borderline between body and soul obviously does not have to mean that Proverbs is only interested in material success and lacks any interest in spiritual gains. So, what kind of gains exactly does Proverbs promise to those who follow its teaching?

8.1 Self-Preservation

It seems that the most important feature of wisdom is that it protects the wise. Scholarly discussions often define wisdom as the 'know-how' of living, as something that is integral to 'living life well,' or as the 'knowledge and art of living.'[2] These definitions are faithful to the text in broad terms, yet they disguise what is the most significant feature of wisdom in the book of Proverbs, namely, that it is a tool to *survive*. Proverbs sees the world as a fundamentally dangerous place. Whybray notes in connection with chapters 10:1–22:16 and

---

1. Wolff 1974a: 7–9.
2. Weeks 2007: 106–107; Moberly 1999: 16; Barth 1960: 433–439.

Is Proverbs Solely about Material Success?

25–29 that it is dominated by the language of disaster. No less than 103 verses (out of 513) are about different possibilities of personal disasters.[3] And the references to different snares of life seem to be no less common in other parts of Proverbs, either. One can be trapped in debt slavery (6:1-5; 22:26) or drunkenness (23:29-35), one's unguarded speech (before equal peers, kings, or God) can cause big losses (4:24; 6:2, 12), and loose women try to entice the student of wisdom (7:1-27; 23:27-28; 30:3).

As the following table about the benefits mentioned together with the חכם word group shows, the topic of protection and (long) life forms quantitatively the most significant benefit of wisdom:

TABLE 4: The benefits of being wise[4]

verse	Hebrew for wise/wisdom	result/effect of wisdom
1:2	חָכְמָה	
1:5	חָכָם	
1:6	חָכָם	understanding proverbs, parables and riddles
1:7	חָכְמָה	
1:20	חָכְמוֹת	living in safety, without fear of harm (verse 33)
2:2	חָכְמָה	understanding the fear of the Lord, finding knowledge of God (verse 5)
2:6	חָכְמָה	protection (verses 7-8)
2:10	חָכְמָה	protection (verse 11)
3:7	חָכָם	health (verse 8)
3:13	חָכְמָה	long life, riches, honour (כָּבוֹד) (verse 16)
3:19	חָכְמָה	establishing the world plus(?) life (verse 22) and security (verses 23-26)
3:35	חָכָם	honour (כָּבוֹד)
4:5	חָכְמָה	protection (verse 6)
4:7	חָכְמָה	honour (כבד, verse 8)
4:11	חָכְמָה	protection, security (verse 12), life (verses 10 and 13)
5:1	חָכְמָה	life through avoiding the 'strange woman' (verses 2-6)
6:6	חכם	sustenance, food (verse 8)
7:4	חָכְמָה	protection from the 'strange woman' (verse 5)
8:1	חָכְמָה	
8:11	חָכְמָה	

---

3. Whybray 1990: 23.
4. In order to make the overview of the table easier, I use the following code in it: protection; life; speech; honour, shame, appreciation by others; and riches. I have left the right column blank where it is not clear what precise results the given verse or its context suggest.

verse	Hebrew for wise/wisdom	result/effect of wisdom
8:12	חָכְמָה	riches, honour (בָּבוֹד, verse 18)
8:33	חכם	life (verses 35-36)
9:1	חָכְמוֹת	life, understanding (verse 6)
9:8	חָכָם	
9:9	חָכָם	more wisdom
9:10	חָכְמָה	
9:12	חכם	reward
10:1	חָכָם	the father's joy (and mother's)
10:8	חָכָם	protection (see 10:8b)
10:13	חָכְמָה	
10:14	חָכָם	help in (keeping back) speech
10:23	חָכְמָה	
10:31	חָכְמָה	
11:2	חָכְמָה	
11:29	חָכָם	the fool will be the servant of the wise
11:30	חָכָם	life for others (?)
12:15	חָכָם	
12:18	חָכָם	the speech of the wise heals
13:1	חָכָם	
13:10	חָכְמָה	
13:14	חָכָם	life, protection from death
13:20	חָכָם	more wisdom
14:1	חָכָם	builds house (metaphor for life?)
14:3	חָכָם	wise speech (which protects the speaker)
14:6	חָכְמָה	
14:8	חָכְמָה	guard against (self)deception
14:16	חָכָם	avoidance of evil
14:24	חָכָם	riches (?)
14:33	חָכְמָה	
15:2	חָכָם	knowledgeable speech
15:7	חָכָם	helps in teaching
15:12	חָכָם	
15:20	חָכָם	the father's joy (and mother's)
15:31	חָכָם	
15:33	חָכְמָה	honour (?)
16:14	חָכָם	appeasing the king's deathly wrath
16:16	חָכְמָה	

Is Proverbs Solely about Material Success?

verse	Hebrew for wise/wisdom	result/effect of wisdom
16:21	חָכָם	appreciation by others
16:23	חָכָם	makes wise the mouth
17:16	חָכְמָה	
17:24	חָכְמָה	
17:28	חָכָם	
18:4	חָכְמָה	
18:15	חָכָם	seeks knowledge
19:20	חכם	
20:1	חכם	modesty in drinking
20:26	חָכָם	helps the king to recognise and defeat the wicked
21:11	חָכָם	makes one teachable
21:20	חָכָם	provides riches
21:22	חָכָם	success in attacking strongholds (metaphorical?)
21:30	חָכְמָה	
22:17	חָכָם	
23:15	חכם	the father's joy
23:19	חכם	
23:23	חָכְמָה	
23:24	חָכָם	the father's delight
24:3	חָכְמָה	builds house (metaphor for life?)
24:5	חָכָם	strength
24:7	חָכְמוֹת	
24:14	חָכְמָה	future, hope
24:23	חָכָם	
25:12	חָכָם	precious rebuke
26:5	חָכָם	
26:12	חָכָם	
26:16	חָכָם	
27:11	חכם	the father's joy (and honour)
28:11	חָכָם	
28:26	חָכְמָה	escape
29:3	חָכְמָה	the father's joy (since the son does not squander his wealth)
29:8	חָכָם	turning away anger
29:9	חָכָם	
29:11	חָכָם	controls his (or others'?) anger
29:15	חָכְמָה	does not bring shame on his mother
30:3	חָכְמָה	

verse	Hebrew for wise/wisdom	result/effect of wisdom
30:24	חָכָם	gives food, <u>protection,</u> efficiency (verses 25-28)
31:26	חָכְמָה	<u>speech</u>

Protection features 15 times in the immediate context of the חכם word group, but we should also add to these 15 occurrences verses which speak about turning away the anger of someone, since, for example, the anger of the king is a potential source of danger (29:8). We can also add at least some of the verses that simply speak about '(long) life,' since a long life presupposes that one has successfully avoided the snares of death (8:33; 9:1). Many of those verses that speak about wisdom's help in speaking well should also be connected with the topic of protection, since one of the main sources of danger in Proverbs is unguarded speech (10:14; 14:3; etc.). Thus, protection is overwhelmingly the most significant effect of wisdom.

The tenet that survival in a dangerous world is a most significant topic in Proverbs is also confirmed by the high number of words referring to protecting and guarding people. נצר appears 19 times,[5] which makes the book second (but proportionately the first) after Psalms in terms of using this word. שמר is also often used; after Psalms and Deuteronomy Proverbs uses it most often in the whole Old Testament.

Therefore, the special emphasis of wisdom is on long life and the ability to avoid dangerous situations. This emphasis is too little recognised in scholarly discussions,[6] maybe because of wisdom's special connection with the wise and fabulously rich Solomon, and maybe also because of the sociological context of many modern western interpreters, who are probably more interested in prosperity than in survival. As a relatively recent empirical sociological investigation states,

> The transition from industrial society to post-industrial societies... brings a polarization between Survival and Self-expression values. The unprecedented wealth that has accumulated in advanced societies during the past generation means that an increasing share of the population has grown up taking survival for granted. Thus, priorities have shifted from an overwhelming emphasis on economic and physical security toward an increasing emphasis on subjective well-being, self-expression and quality of life.[7]

---

5. Not counting the Qere in 23:26 where the Ketiv has רצן instead of נצר.

6. However, it is recognised occasionally. See, for example, Gerstenberger's comment about 'family religion,' which he connects with wisdom sayings: 'in fact, when we speak of family religion, this is primarily a theology of the elementary needs of life' (Gerstenberger 2002: 27).

7. Inglehart 2011.

This shift in the priorities of modern western interpreters, however, should not distort their perception, and they should recognise that it is precisely the 'survival values' which are mirrored in the book of Proverbs.

Therefore, even if one is troubled by the fact that self-interest seems to be the most decisive factor in Proverbs' motivational system, and that this is predominantly expressed in material terms, one has to recognise that this self-interest is accentuated in an important way. It does include prosperity, but the emphasis is on self-preservation. This in itself might not be enough to 'tame' the self-interested nature of Proverbs, but it at least calls to mind what Aquinas said about self-preservation as an undeniable and acceptable basic good of human beings.

However, Aquinas wrote about a hierarchical system of human ends, in which self-preservation is only the most basic one. Can we detect other human ends in the book of Proverbs, ends which we could call more 'spiritual'?

8.2 Honour

Some verses suggest that we can summarise the results of a wise life by grouping the benefits of wisdom into three main categories: honour, riches, and long life. These are the three rewards offered to Solomon, the paradigmatic wise king in 1 Kgs 3:13-14: 'And also, what you did not ask, I give to you: both riches and honour, so that there will be no equal to you among kings in your lifetime. And if you walk in my ways and keep my statutes and commands just like David your father did, I will lengthen your days.' We should probably recognise that the triplet of benefits is divided into riches and honour on the one hand and long life on the other. The latter is conditional upon a special and constant obedience to God's ordinances.[8] These three rewards are also listed together in Proverbs 3:16 ('length of days in her right hand, in her left hand riches and honour') where length of days is again separated from riches and honour. They are also mentioned in 22:4: 'the wage for humility—the fear-of-the-Lord sort—is riches, honour, and life.'[9]

The occasional separation of 'length of days' may signal its special importance as we have just seen. Nevertheless, even if the main emphasis is on a long and secure life, honour and riches must be significant, too. These two benefits of wisdom are mentioned several times in different forms throughout the whole book of Proverbs. Wisdom helps one to acquire (or preserve) riches (3:16; 8:18; 14:24; 21:20; 28:20; 31:11; etc.). Honour (כבוד) and shame (מביש,[10] חרפה, and קלון) are also often discussed (3:35; 6:33; 9:7; 10:5; 12:16; 13:18; 15:33; 18:3, 12; 20:3; 22:4; 25:2, 27; 26:1; 29:15; etc.). We can probably also

---

8. Though the condition might apply to all three gifts (Briggs 2010: 78).
9. I follow Waltke's translation here (Waltke 2005: 193).
10. Proverbs always uses the participle form of בוש.

take at least some of those verses that discuss the wise son as a source of joy to the father and the mother as references to the topic of honour and shame since certain verses connect the joy of parents with these benefits (27:11; 29:15).

Have we found a non-material, spiritual gain offered by Proverbs by identifying one of its main promises as 'honour'? On the one hand, the answer seems to be 'no.' Of course, 'honour' is clearly non-material, but it still would not satisfy a Thomist thinker who searches for spiritual gains. Honour, i.e., one's reputation in the society, is still something external to one's 'soul' (so Thomas in *ST* II–II, 103, 1 and *ST* I–II, 2, 2); it speaks more about a person's success than about his or her spiritual formation—or so it might seem at first sight. The fact that it is sometimes emphatically mentioned in parallel with riches also does not help one to recognise it as the spiritual benefit offered by Proverbs. For one might have the impression that honour and riches speak rather about the 'career-development' of someone, to use a modern category, and not about one's spiritual formation.

On the other hand, one could argue that this is an anachronistic understanding of 'honour' which does not count on the fact that in ancient thinking, or at least in some important versions of ancient thinking, honour was more intrinsically connected to personal qualities than in modern thought.[11] Alasdair MacIntyre describes this kind of thinking as follows:

> Excellence and winning, it is scarcely necessary to repeat, are not the same. But it is in fact to winning, and only to excellence on the occasions when it does in fact produce victory, that a certain kind of reward is attached, a reward by which, ostensibly at least, excellence is to be honoured. Rewards of this kind—let us call them external rewards—are such goods as those of riches, power, status, and prestige, goods which can be and are objects of desire by human beings prior to and independently of any desire for excellence. In societies and cultures, such as that represented in the Homeric poems, in which the pursuit of these latter goods and that of excellence are to some large degree linked together within the dominant social institutions, any incompatibilities between the human qualities required for the pursuit of such goods and the qualities required for the pursuit of excellence are apt to remain latent and unacknowledged.[12]

Though MacIntyre writes about the Homeric world, this kind of thinking probably comprises a part of what some Old Testament scholars mean by 'creation theology.' It affirms the order of the universe in the sense that, at the end, it is the honourable people who get the honour, and the 'external' reward is inseparable from the 'internal' value of a deed or person.[13] Although earlier I have

---

11. See Treier's complaint that people in our culture are much more interested in the opinion of others than in excellence (Treier 2011b: 97–98).
12. MacIntyre 1988: 31–32.
13. Gese 1958: 10.

expressed reservations about superimposing a 'Greek-style' autonomous world order on Hebrew thinking, these reservations do not have to prevent us from following MacIntyre in our interpretation of Proverbs. It does not really matter if it is an independent world order that connects honour with character, or a God, who guarantees that honourable people get the honour (in other words keeps up a 'non-independent world order'). The main point is that honour and character are closely related in the thinking of ancient people. If this is so, then, when Proverbs mentions 'honour,' it also means 'honourable character,' which is already a more clearly non-material gain.

However, though this explanation is suggestive and can be part of a solution, it is far from irrefutable and it does not answer certain questions. Even if Israelites perceived a closer relationship between honour and character than moderns do, it is questionable whether the reader can simply replace one of these concepts with the other on every occasion that it appears in the text. And even if this could be granted, it would be strange if Proverbs never referred to unambiguously internal gains that a modern reader would also recognise as such. Even if ancient people had a more 'holistic' worldview and did not differentiate between 'external' and 'internal,' 'material' and 'spiritual' goods so neatly (or artificially) as modern people, they did not lack the vocabulary to name those qualities that moderns would call 'internal' or 'spiritual.' If Proverbs never mentions internal gains unambiguously, then one starts to wonder if this modern scholarly talk about the holistic worldview of the ancients and about world order is only a romantic justification of a way of thinking, which is after all focused on the material needs, and only on the material needs, of people. So, do we have *explicit* references in Proverbs to what modern readers would also recognise as internal and spiritual gains?

8.3 'Better than Riches'

One of the clearest indications of the importance of the non-material sides of wisdom's gains are the so-called 'better than' sayings, which can be found in the three longest sections of Proverbs (1–9; 10:1–22:16; 25–29), and which repeatedly remind the reader that wisdom is better than riches. Before a short analysis of these sayings, let me provide a list of them together with some textual and basic interpretative notes, and also with a list of those qualities that these sayings promote (in opposition to riches).

TABLE 5: The 'better than' sayings[14]

Hebrew verse	Translation	Paraphrase	Qualities Recommended
3:14 כי טוב סחרה מסחר כסף ומחרוץ תבואתה	For her profit is better than the profit of silver and her income better than gold.	Wisdom is more valuable than riches.	Wisdom
8:11 כי טובה חכמה מפנינים וכל חפצים לא ישוו בה	For wisdom is better than rubies, no treasure compares with her.	Wisdom is more valuable than riches.	Wisdom
8:19 טוב פריי מחרוץ ומפז ותבואתי מכסף נבחר	My fruit is better than gold, even fine gold, and my income than choice silver.	Wisdom is more valuable than riches.	Wisdom
12:9 טוב נקלה ועבד לו ממתכבד וחסר לחם	Better a lowly one who is a servant to himself than one who glorifies himself and lacks food.[15]	Depending on the translation it either means: • Humble, hard-working attitude is better than proud pretentiousness. • (Basic) material gains are better than (false) self-esteem with hunger.	Humility, self-preservation, (maybe) hard-working attitude

---

14. The list of 'qualities recommended' in the right column is almost identical with the list reconstructed by Perry 1993: 42: 'work, fear of God, love, righteousness, lowliness of spirit, slowness to anger, quiet (peace), integrity, openness, nearness, and wisdom.'

15. The translation is problematic. If one repoints עֶבֶד as עֹבֵד with the LXX, Syr., and Vulg. then it says: 'Better a lowly one who serves (works) for himself . . . ' Some have suggested עבד be emended to עבר (Fox 2009: 550): 'Better a lowly one who has (agricultural) produce . . . ' The usual translation of the MT (NAS, NJB, NKJ, NRSV, TNIV, KJV, ESV, etc.) is 'better a lowly one who has a servant.' In my translation I follow Ehrlich 1968: 61–62, who keeps the MT without emendation but suggests that it can have the meaning: better is a lowly one who is willing to do the work that a servant is supposed to do than one who glorifies himself and behaves as if he had a servant and rather hungers instead of doing the 'dirty' work. This interpretation understands the verse as recommending a humble, hardworking attitude, as does Fox's and the ancient translations, which follow a different Hebrew from the MT.

Is Proverbs Solely about Material Success?

Hebrew verse	Translation	Paraphrase	Qualities Recommended
15:16 טוב מעט ביראת יהוה מאוצר רב ומהומה בו	Better a little with the fear of the Lord than a full storehouse with turmoil.	Peace[16] (based on the trust in the Lord) is more valuable than riches.	Fear of the Lord
15:17 טוב ארחת ירק ואהבה שם משור אבוס ושנאה בו	Better is a meal of vegetables but with love than a fattened ox but with hatred.	Loving peace is more valuable than riches.	Love
16:8 טוב מעט בצדקה מרב תבואות בלא משפט	Better a little with righteousness than a large income without justice.	Righteousness is more valuable than riches.	Righteousness
16:16 קנה חכמה מה טוב מחרוץ וקנות בינה נבחר מכסף	To acquire[17] wisdom, how much better than gold, and acquiring understanding is preferable to silver.	Wisdom is more valuable than riches.	Wisdom
16:19 טוב שפל רוח את (עניים) [עניים] מחלק שלל את גאים	Better to be humble in spirit and to be with the lowly than to divide spoil with the proud.	Humility is more valuable than riches.	Humility
16:32 טוב ארך אפים מגבור ומשל ברוחו מלכד עיר	Better the one who is slow to anger than the mighty, and who rules his temper than one who captures a city.	Self-control is a better achievement than controlling others.	Self-control (slow to anger)
17:1 טוב פת חרבה ושלוה בה מבית מלא זבחי ריב	Better a dry morsel and peace with it than a house full of feasting with strife.[18]	Peace is more valuable than riches.	Peace(fullness)

---

16. See my interpretation on page 124.

17. The MSS and ancient translations are divided in their pointing. Some read קְנֵה (participle), while others read קְנֵה (Qal imperative) instead of קְנֹה (a rare inf. construct). However, these variants do not alter the meaning of the proverb. For the LXX translation, which reads קִנּוֹת (nests), see Fox 2009: 1012.

18. Literally 'sacrifices of strife,' which probably means that those who offer the sacrifice and eat the sacrificial meal together are not at peace with each other (Fox 2009: 623–624; Waltke 2005: 35). The parallel between 17:1a and 17:1b suggests that it is not the sacrificial nature of the meal that is significant but its richness. It is also possible that the Hebrew does not necessarily have the connotation of a sacrifice at all.

Hebrew verse	Translation	Paraphrase	Qualities Recommended
19:1 טוב רש הולך בתמו מעקש שפתיו והוא כסיל	Better a poor man walking in his integrity than one of crooked lips who is rich.[19]	Integrity is more valuable than riches.	Integrity
19:22 תאות אדם חסדו וטוב רש מאיש כזב	... better a poor man than a liar.[20]	Honesty (or truthfulness, or fidelity) is more valuable than riches.[21]	Honesty, or truthfulness, or fidelity
21:9 טוב לשבת על פנת גג מאשת מדינים ובית חבר	Better to live on the corner of the roof than in a house shared with a quarrelsome wife.[22]	Peace is more valuable than physical comfort.	Peace

---

19. The MT reads כסיל (fool) instead of עשיר (rich). The almost identical 28:6 has עשיר just like the Syr. of 19:1. Some scholars have suggested that this might be the original reading, and maybe a scribe who was accustomed to the frequent condemnations of fools unintentionally altered the text to כסיל (Clifford 1999: 175; Ehrlich 1968: 107; Fox 2009: 647–648). I accept the emendation because it fits the structure of the 'complex better than' sayings better (see discussion later) and because it sounds banal to declare that a person of integrity is better than a fool.

20. The translation of 19:22a and its connection to 19:22b is contested. The main options are: 'What people desire in a human being is his unfailing kindness' (Waltke 2005: 115–116); 'One's desire, one's disgrace' (Murphy 1998: 140–141, 145); 'What is desired of a person is his fidelity' (Clifford 1999: 175, 178); 'A man's kindness is his fruit' (Fox 2009: 658–659); and 'A man's desire should be [to show] kindness' (Ramaq, Radaq, Hame'iri, in Fox 2009: 659). It is unlikely that we should follow Gemser in emending כזב at the end of the verse to אכזר on the basis of Prov 11:17 since the MT makes sense as it is and the LXX also follows the MT (McKane 1970: 532).

21. At least if the verse is supplemented by the reader with the logical word pairs: poor (but honest) vs. (rich) but liar; or if 19:22a is connected to 19:22b and חסד is understood as the opposite of being a liar. If the verse is not supplemented or if 19:22b has to be understood on its own (cf. Wehrle 1993: 171–172), then the major emphasis is on the negative characteristic as if it said 'anything is better than being deceitful.'

22. The meaning of בית חבר is uncertain. Some emend it to בית רחב (Ehrlich 1968: 122–123), others have suggested different translations, e.g., a busy household (as compared to the solitude of living on the roof), alehouse, granary, etc., based on Akkadian and Ugaritic parallels. For a list of suggestions, see Fox 2009: 683; Lyu 2012: 86 n. 24; Waltke 2005: 175 n. 72; Wehrle 1993: 121–122. Though some of these translations would fit the 'complex better than' pattern better, it is far from certain that the saying fits into that pattern (see discussion later). Here I follow the translation of Waltke 2005: 1161, ESV, NAS, NJB, NKJ, NRS, TNIV, because it seems to be more in accordance with 21:19, though other possibilities cannot be ruled out.

Hebrew verse	Translation	Paraphrase	Qualities Recommended
21:19 טוב שבת בארץ מדבר מאשת (מדונים) [מדינים] וכעס	Better to live in a desert land than with a quarrelsome and angry wife.	Peace is more valuable than physical comfort.	Peace
22:1 נבחר שם מעשר רב מכסף ומזהב חן טוב	An (honourable) name is to be chosen rather than great riches and favour is better than silver and gold.	Good reputation is more valuable than riches.	Good reputation
25:7 כי טוב אמר לך עלה הנה מהשפילך לפני נדיב אשר ראו עיניך	For it is better for him to say 'come up here' than that he humiliate you before a nobleman (whom your eyes have seen).[23]	Trying to exalt oneself might be embarrassing in the end.	Humility
25:24 טוב שבת על פנת גג מאשת (מדונים) [מדינים] ובית חבר	Better to live on the corner of the roof than in a house shared with a quarrelsome wife.	Peace is more valuable than physical comfort.[24]	Peace
27:5 טובה תוכחת מגלה מאהבה מסתרת	Better open rebuke than hidden love.	Hidden love is useless and not pleasant.	Honesty/active love[25]

---

23. The function and meaning of 25:7c is not clear in this sentence. Most commentators join it to the next sentence. Clifford 1999: 220, 223; Gemser 1937: 70–71; Longman 2006: 447, 452; McKane 1970: 250, 580–581; Murphy 1998: 187–188, 191; Plöger 1984: 294, 296; Ringgren and Zimmerli 1962: 100, 102; Saebø 2012: 315, 319; Scott 1965: 153, 155; Toy 1899: 458–461; Waltke 2005: 303, 316–317. However, some disagree (e.g., Wehrle 1993: 164–165).

24. If the verse is read together with the previous verse, 'North wind produces rain, and a secretive tongue (produces) an angry face,' then the idea of living on the roof might connote being exposed to uncomfortable weather (Van Leeuwen 1988: 85).

25. Bühlmann, partly on the basis of Sir 19:13-17, speculates that the situation behind the saying might be that when one is offended by his/her friend, instead of withdrawing ('hidden love') he or she should openly rebuke the offender, thereby providing opportunity for clarification and reconciliation (Bühlmann 1976: 114–116). This is a possible conjecture though it might be a bit too specific for such an open-ended proverb. Nevertheless, read together with the following verse, 'Faithful are the wounds by a friend (אוהב) and profuse the kisses of an enemy (שונא),' our verse seems to recommend some kind of honesty.

Hebrew verse	Translation	Paraphrase	Qualities Recommended
27:10c רעך ורעה אביך אל תעזב ובית אחיך אל תבוא ביום אידך טוב שכן קרוב מאח רחוק	Do not forsake your friend and your father's friend and go not into your brother's house on the day of your hardship.²⁶ Better a neighbour nearby than a brother far away.	A distant relative is not useful. A close neighbour is useful.	Love (?),²⁷ friendship²⁸
28:6 טוב רש הולך בתמו מעקש דרכים והוא עשיר	Better a poor man walking in his integrity than one of crooked ways who is rich.	Integrity is more valuable than riches.	Integrity

Michael V. Fox helpfully notes that there are two basic types of 'better than' sayings. He calls them 'simple better than sayings' (3:14; 8:11, 19; 16:16, 32; 19:22b; 22:1; 25:7; 27:10c) and 'complex better than sayings' (12:9; 15:16, 17; 16:8, 19; 17:1; 19:1; 21:19; 25:24; 27:5; 28:6). A simple 'better than' saying simply states that X is better than Y. The complex one states that A with B is better than A' with B'. 'The point is that B is so good that it outweighs something everyone desires, even when combined with something less desirable. The logic requires that A be less desirable than A', and B much more desirable than B'.'²⁹ like 'Better a little (A) with the fear of the Lord (B) than a full storehouse (A') with turmoil (B')' (15:16).

First of all, let me make two comments on Fox's system. The first is that, although usually it is obvious which saying belongs to which category, this is not always so. For example, Fox takes 27:5 ('Better open rebuke than hidden love') as complex (openness + rebuke > hiddenness + love), but he takes 27:10c ('Better a neighbour nearby than a brother far away') as simple. I do not see a significant difference between the structure of the two sentences. On the one

---

26. Some suggest to omit אל or to translate it as 'surely' as in Ugaritic. However, there is no textual support for emendation here and the usual translation of the verse makes sense as it is. See Davies 2010: 140.

27. 'Nearness' is not necessarily spatial, it can be metaphorical, too (Lev 21:3; Ruth 2:20; Ps 148:14; see Fox 2009: 808; Waltke 2005: 379).

28. The relationship between 27:10ab and 27:10c is contested. See, for example, the different opinions of Clifford 1999: 238 and Fox 2009: 808, the former taking the three parts of the verse as closely connected, the latter interpreting 27:10c as a separate proverb. If we connect them to each other than the whole verse could be interpreted as speaking about the value of friendship as opposed to kinship.

29. Fox 2009: 597.

hand, 27:5, just like 27:10c, lacks the usual preposition (ב, with) of the complex sayings, while on the other hand, 27:10c can be construed as a complex saying just as easily as 27:5 (i.e., closeness + neighbour > distance + brother). Both 27:5 and 27:10c lie somewhere on the borderline of simple and complex 'better than' sayings.

Similarly, the sayings about the troublesome wife (21:9, 19; 25:24) do not fit neatly the 'complex better than' category that Fox puts them in. In 21:9 (and 25:24), for example, B is missing (Better to live on the corner of the roof [A] than in a house [A'] shared with a quarrelsome wife [B']). 21:19 looks like a simple 'better than' saying with only two elements: 'Better to live in a desert land [X] than with a quarrelsome and angry wife [Y].' Interestingly, when Fox discusses the difference between the simple and complex 'better than' saying, he lists 21:19 as a complex saying, but right in the next paragraph he quotes it as an example of the simple sayings without any explanation for the apparent contradiction.[30] The explanation can be found one hundred pages later in his commentary on 21:19, where he writes that it has a simple 'better than' structure but a complex 'better than' 'deep structure,' and the missing elements are presupposed by the text. He reconstructs this deep structure as 'Better to dwell in a desert land (without a contentious woman) than (in a decent house) with a contentious woman.'[31] However, as it is possible to reconstruct a complex deep structure in the case of most if not all of the simple sayings,[32] it is still not clear why Fox lists 21:19 among the complex sayings. Be it as it may, the 'quarrelsome wife' sayings might comprise a category on their own that is somewhere in between the simple and the complex sayings.

My other observation is that, although Fox only states that 'A be less desirable than A', and B much more desirable than B',' we can actually be more specific about the relationships between A vs. A' and B vs. B' in the 'complex better than' sayings. They are usually opposites. Table 6 shows that in the clear majority of cases A–A' and B–B' are opposites. There are 18 clear opposites and 8 not so clear or non-opposites. The majority of the not so clear or at least not clearly and explicitly stated opposites are in 21:9, 19; 25:24; 27:5, 10c but, as we have just seen, all of these verses are examples of 'imprecise complex better than' sayings, which might not be rightfully categorised as 'complex better than' sayings at all. If we do not count these verses then we have 13 clear opposites and 3 not clear ones. In 12:9[33] the precise meaning of the verse is opaque, so we should not draw a conclusion from the fact that we cannot be sure how B and B' oppose each other if they do at all. In 16:19,[34] though A and A'

---

30. Fox 2009: 597.
31. Fox 2009: 688.
32. Fox 2009: 598.
33. 'Better a lowly one who is a servant to himself (?) than one who glorifies himself and lacks food.'
34. 'Better to be humble in spirit than to divide spoil with the poor.'

are not clear opposites, they have opposing connotations: humble in spirit (contrite, powerless, fragile, poor, see Isa 57:15) vs. dividers of spoil (powerful, arrogant, in control, rich, see Prov 1:13-14). The only unclear case left is the pair fear of the Lord–turmoil in 15:16.[35] I would suggest that, based on the opposing relationships in other cases, we should let 'turmoil' clarify the meaning of 'fear of the Lord' in this case and understand it as some kind of peaceful state, or a complex state that at least includes some kind of peacefulness and feeling of security.[36]

TABLE 6: Logical relations in the 'complex better than' sayings[37]

	A vs. A'	B vs. B'
12:9	lowly ↔ glorifies himself	servant to himself(?) ? lacks food
15:16	little ↔ full storehouse	fear of the Lord ? turmoil
15:17	vegetable ↔ ox	love ↔ hatred
16:8	little ↔ large income	righteousness ↔ without justice
16:19	humble in spirit ? divide spoil	with the lowly ↔ with the proud
17:1	dry morsel ↔ feasting	peace ↔ strife
19:1	poor ↔ rich	integrity ↔ crooked lips
21:9	corner of the roof ↔ house	(peacefulness[?]) ? troublesome wife
21:19	desert land ? (peacefulness[?])	quarrelsome ? angry wife
25:24	corner of the roof ↔ house	(peacefulness[?]) ? quarrelsome wife
27:5	openness ↔ hiddenness	rebuke ? love
27:10c	neighbour ? brother	nearby ↔ far away
28:6	poor ↔ rich	integrity ↔ crooked ways

After these clarifying notes, it is time to turn back to our original quest for non-materialistic gains in Proverbs. Are these 'better than' sayings a good place to search for them? It seems so. The majority of these sayings recommend a good character comprised by virtues like wisdom, honesty, integrity, humility, love, self-control, righteousness. They also clearly state that such human qualities are much better than material riches.[38]

However, the issue might be a bit more complicated than it appears at first sight. Why precisely are these qualities better? Fox, commenting on 19:1, answers the question as follows:

---

35. 'Better a little with the fear of the Lord than a full storehouse with turmoil.'

36. Fear of the Lord is associated with trusting the Lord and his protection in Prov 3:5-8 and 14:26. Trust in the Lord is considered the major protection against trouble and the source of a secure life and peaceful mind (Prov 3:21-26; 28:25-26).

37. The question marks in the table signal uncertainty in translation or interpretation. Many of them have been discussed at Table 5. The oppositions (signalled by ↔) are not always perfect. For example, 'crooked lips' in 19:1 is not the perfect opposite of 'integrity' because they are on different levels: Integrity vs. *an example* of being corrupt. Yet, the opposition between the concepts is clear.

38. Cf. Lyu 2012:83–93.

The reasons why an innocent poor man is better than a dishonest rich one are not stated here, but other proverbs give them: The innocent man lives in confidence, the wicked one in anxiety (28:1). The innocent man is delivered from disaster, and the wicked one takes his place (11:8). The innocent man is remembered after death, while the wicked one sinks into oblivion (10:7). The list goes on and on. All the benefits ascribed to righteousness easily outweigh the benefits of wealth.[39]

Yet, I suspect, most items on this 'ongoing list' can easily be grouped under the three headings I suggested above: protection (long life), honour, and riches. Wisdom repeatedly claims about herself that she provides riches, so, though it is not stated explicitly, one can logically deduce that wisdom is better than riches because wisdom can provide riches, whereas riches do not lead to wisdom. Furthermore, the context of some of the 'better than' sayings suggest that this virtuous character is useful for survival and protection. For example, between 16:16 and 16:19, two 'better than' sayings recommending wisdom and humility, there are two sayings about how carelessness and pride can lead to disaster. Thus, 16:16-19 read together might lead the reader's thoughts towards the conclusion that a humble, wise character is better than riches because it provides better protection.[40] Or, humility, which is recommended in the 'better than' sayings of 12:9; 16:19; 25:7, is so often and so emphatically connected to honour in Proverbs (15:33; 18:12; 22:4; 29:23) that a reader might be expected to connect humility and honour and think, 'Of course humility is better than riches, as it leads more surely to honour.' Therefore, at least part of the answer to the question regarding why good human character is more valuable than riches is that which I have stated above: because it leads to protection, honour, and riches.

Nevertheless, these 'better than' sayings might also point to something else besides these three, not clearly spiritual benefits. Some of these sayings acknowledge the fact that it is possible that someone is virtuous, yet poor (like 16:8; 17:1; 19:1; 28:6). Yet, they clearly state that even if integrity does not lead to wealth, it is better than wealth. Of course, one possible explanation, as we have just seen, is that it is better because it leads to long life and honour. However, as we have also seen, this is not often stated explicitly in these sentences, rather, it is conjectured by the reader from the context of some of them. Would not we expect more explicit praise of protection and honour in these sentences if their provision is the only reason for a good character's superiority to riches? There is an intrinsic openness of formulation in these verses that invites more than one interpretation. 'Better' may not always mean 'more useful for gaining "external" gains' but, instead, 'more useful for fulfilling one's role in society,' or 'more rewarding in itself than the "external" rewards of riches and honour

---

39. Fox 2009: 648.
40. Indeed, this is how Knut Heim interprets this section (Heim 2001: 219–220).

and long life,' or, in other words, 'more worthwhile than riches, honour, and long life.'

This latter possibility is strengthened by the fact that these sentences seem to refer to a fourth desirable gain besides honour, riches, and protection, one which might be even more highly valued than these: (inner and outer) peace and contentment.[41] Regardless of the uncertainties in the interpretation of 12:9,[42] the verse arguably promotes acceptance of one's situation and warns against reaching beyond it. As I have just noted, fear of the Lord might also have a 'peaceful' connotation in 15:16. Proverbs 15:17[43] is also about the value of a peaceful social life. The context of 16:8 (namely 16:7)[44] also suggests that the reward of righteousness might be a peaceful, strife-free life. Proverbs 17:1[45] explicitly values peace above riches. The troublesome wife sayings (21:9, 19; 25:24) definitely emphasise the value of trouble-free life.

Based on these sentences, the reward of a virtuous life in Proverbs could be described as 'happiness,' even if that is a vague term.[46] The notion of happiness can be comprised by the material benefits, like long life and riches, the social benefits, like honour, but it also expresses something of the peaceful, content mindset that is mirrored in many of these verses. This is, finally, something which, though not necessarily unrelated to material needs, goes beyond them, and satisfies even a reader who searches for non-material, 'spiritual' gains.

8.4 Summary

We have seen that the word 'success' is not precise enough as a description of what is promised by Proverbs, as the book has a prime emphasis on self-preservation. Yet, it talks about success too, and the paradigmatic gains it offers besides a long, secure life are riches and honour. Although honour is not an unambiguously spiritual gain, it might not be an exclusively 'external' one either, as it is probably intrinsically connected to virtuous character. Indeed, there are explicit and very emphatic references to virtues and their importance in the 'better than' sayings. These sentences also emphasise that peaceful contentment is at least as important as the other, more 'material,' gains. Therefore, I have proposed that we could summarise all the goods that one can obtain by

---

41. Compare with Thomas's thought in which peace is one of the fruits of charity, which is, in his system, accompanied by the gift of wisdom (*ST* II–II, 29, 4; Stump 1999: 62).

42. 'Better a lowly one who is a servant to himself (?) than one who glorifies himself and lacks food.'

43. 'Better is a meal of vegetables but with love than a fattened ox but with hatred.'

44. 16:7-8: 'When the Lord likes someone's way he makes even his enemies peaceful towards him. Better is a little with righteousness than a large income without justice.'

45. 'Better a dry morsel and peace with it than a house full of feasting with strife.'

46. Similarly Lyu 2012: 56–59.

acquiring wisdom and integrity as 'happiness,' which seems to me to be a fair description of a contented, peaceful, protected life furnished with necessary material resources.

There is much in this description that echoes Thomas's moral theology. He also emphasised that the ultimate end of human life is happiness, acknowledged that some basic human needs (like self-preservation) are indispensable for that end, and claimed that living a virtuous life is the way towards that happiness.

One significant difference is that Thomas acknowledged the value of riches and honour more cautiously than Proverbs. He acknowledged that honour is a natural reward for honourable deeds, and as such a reward to be sought (*ST* II–II, 129, 1–2); that it can be an assurance to one that he or she walks in the right way (*ST* I–II, 2, 2); that it can be an encouragement for good acts (*ST* II–II, 131, 1); and that it, together with riches, can be a tool for performing magnificent and magnanimous virtuous acts (*ST* I–II, 4, 7; *ST* II–II, 134, 3). However, he also emphasised that one should not be too preoccupied with honour and riches (*ST* II–II, 129, 2; *ST* II–II, 131, 1–2) because too much desire for them can lead one astray (*ST* II–II, 131, 1; *ST* II–II, 132, 2–3). Also he warned that they are external rewards (*ST* I–II, 2, 2; *ST* II–II, 103, 1) and, as such, too connected to the material body and not to the soul's happiness (*ST* I–II, 2, 5; *ST* I–II, 2, 1; *ST* II–II, 131, 1), and that they can be misleading since the 'right' persons do not always get them (*ST* I–II, 2, 3). Thus, he acknowledged them as rewards which can be enjoyed with moderation, but they are definitely not the right ends which provide happiness to the soul.

One can argue, of course, that Thomas's cautious recognition of honour and riches as good rewards and rejection of them as potential sources of real happiness (and, as such, human ends) stem at least partly from his differentiation between body and soul. If one takes into consideration that Proverbs does not make this differentiation and also that the 'better than' sayings emphasise a contented, inward happiness, then Proverbs' view of human ends appears to be much closer to the system of Aquinas than it might initially appear after a cursory comparison between what Proverbs and Thomas say about honour and riches.

Nevertheless, even if the common points are emphasised, this Proverbial thinking is still different from that of Thomas in one crucial respect. Namely, Thomas would recognise this happiness as only partial since it is not connected to the most important factor for Thomas: the highest human end, that is, God. As I have mentioned earlier, Thomas considers that 'The highest good for a human is to live and know God in a God-fearing community.' Thus, in a Thomistic system, the lower human goods find their meaning in the highest one. Is Proverbs writing only about 'incomplete' happiness, available to the 'natural' human being, without reference to God as the 'highest end'?

9

Is God the Highest End in Proverbs?

9.1 What Does It Mean That God Is the Highest End?

As we have seen, Thomas taught that self-interest can be good as long as it is subordinated to higher ends. However, what does it precisely mean that God is the highest end and how is one supposed to subordinate the other ends to this one? The answer to these questions can be deduced from Thomas's explanation of a section of the Sermon on the Mount (Matt 6:19-34). There he lists four factors which make self-interest 'inordinate':[1]

1. Serving God for the sake of benefits ('We should not ... serve God for the sake of the necessities of food and clothing').
2. Not hoping in God ('We should not so concern ourselves about temporal things as to lose hope in divine help').
3. Relying on one's own powers ('We should not think that we are able to procure all the necessities of life by our own concern without divine help').
4. Obsessive anticipation of the problems of the future ('Concern is inordinate when a man anticipates the time of it, by being concerned now about something which is a matter of care for the future, not for the present').

Points 2 and 3 are closely related: one should hope in God (2) and not in oneself (3). Point 4 is somewhat different, but it is not unrelated to trusting in God and therefore to points 2 and 3. Separating these points was probably suggested only by the text of the Gospel, which Thomas wanted to follow closely. However, if we take into account the overlap between the four points and focus

---

1. *ST* I–II, 108, 3, ad. 5; see also *ST* I–II, 77, 4.

on the broader issues behind them, then we can say that, according to Thomas, having God as the final end requires two crucial things:

A. Not serving God because of the benefits of that service (1).
B. Having God-centred thinking, hope, and trust (2–3–4).

9.2 Proverbs 2: Its Significance and Translation

Are these two criteria true to Proverbs? The answer will be given mainly on the basis of Proverbs 2. The choice of Proverbs 2 as a starting point for my investigations is justified by two factors.

First, as Weeks comments, Proverbs 2 'comes as close as anything to epitomizing Proverbs 1–9 as a whole.'[2] Called the *Lehrprogramm* for Proverbs 1–9 by Meinhold, it introduces the major motifs of the later chapters (like the foreign woman and the path metaphor), and therefore it is one of the most significant introductory chapters for the whole book.[3]

Second, and even more significantly, the chapter concerns the 'knowledge of God' (Prov 2:5; variations of this expression also occur in Prov 9:10 and 30:3), which happens to be Thomas's typical phrase referring to the highest end of human existence.[4] Thus, if anywhere, here one can expect to find some parallels with Thomas. However, caution is recommended. This lexical parallel does not necessarily mean that the meaning, role, and significance of the 'knowledge of God' are the same in Thomas and Proverbs. These issues require a thoroughgoing investigation.

Before attempting to clarify the meaning of Proverbs 2 and to decide whether the aforementioned two Thomistic criteria of having God as the final end can be found in it, a translation of the chapter is provided. Some exegetical observations are made in the footnotes.

[1] My son, if you take in my words and hide my commands with(in) you,	בני אם תקח אמרי ומצותי תצפן אתך
[2] [then], turning your ear to wisdom,[5] you will direct your heart to understanding.[6]	להקשיב לחכמה אזנך תטה לבך לתבונה

---

2. Weeks 2007: 62.
3. See Meinhold 1991a: 43.
4. *ST* I–II, 3, 4; *ST* I, 12, 1–13 (especially *ST* I, 12, 13); *ST* III, 9, 1–4; *SCG*, III, 37–63.
5. I take להקשיב as a gerundive ל + inf. which specifies the manner or method in which the finite verb of the previous clause is executed (Merwe, Naudé, and Kroeze 1999: 155; Waltke 2004: 213 n. 1).
6. Imperfect forms can express *apodosis* (Waltke and O'Connor 1990: 510–513). My translation somewhat separates the first 2 verses, as an introductory section, from the rest of the chapter. It roughly follows the translation of Waltke (Waltke 2004: 213) and parallels the LXX, which also takes verse 2 as the *apodosis* of verse 1 (see Cook 1997: 114, 118).

³ Indeed, if to insight you call out, to understanding you raise your voice,
⁴ If you seek it like silver, and like treasure you search for it,
⁵ Then you will understand the fear of the Lord and the knowledge of God you will find,
⁶ Because it is the Lord himself who gives wisdom, and from his mouth [come]⁷ knowledge and understanding.
⁷ He hides⁸ prudence⁹ for the upright—(he is)¹⁰ a shield for those who walk in integrity,
⁸ Guarding the paths of justice he safeguards the way of his faithful ones.¹¹

כי אם לבינה תקרא לתבונה תתן קולך
אם תבקשנה ככסף וכמטמונים תחפשנה
אז תבין יראת יהוה ודעת אלהים תמצא
כי יהוה יתן חכמה מפיו דעת ותבונה
(וצפן) [יצפן] לישרים תושיה מגן להלכי תם
לנצר ארחות משפט ודרך (חסידו) [חסידיו] ישמר

---

7. The 'come' is presupposed by the preposition מן. The Targ., α', σ', θ', and ε' has 'and from his face' (ומפניו).

8. I translate the Qere (יצפן), which is supported by Targ. and Vulg. Ketiv (וצפן) is supported by the LXX and Syr. The textual difference does not have theological significance. I chose 'hide' and not the more usual 'store up' (Clifford 1999: 44; Fox 2000: 114; McKane 1970: 213; Murphy 1998: 13; Waltke 2004: 214; NRSV, etc.) as a translation of צפן because I see a hiding–seeking–finding motif running through Prov 1:10–2:5 (2:1, 5; cf. 1:11, 13, 18, 28).

9. The LXX apparently translates תושיה (σωτηρία, salvation) but this does not necessarily presuppose a different *Vorlage*. It could simply be a misreading of the Hebrew or an interpretation of it (Cook 1997: 120). Some translate תושיה as 'success' (Murphy 1998: 13; Waltke 2004: 214), some as 'resourcefulness' (Clifford 1999: 44; Fox 2000: 114), others argue that its basic meaning is probably close to that of חכמה (Weeks 2007: 197). Job 5:12 suggests that one can do תושיה with his/her hands, which would suggest 'success' and not 'resourcefulness.' The concept of 'wisdom' is also a possible candidate as it can also refer to practical skill and תושיה often occurs simply as a general parallel to wisdom or counsel, which would make a more restricted meaning unlikely (Job 11:6; 26:3; Prov 8:14—though in this verse it can be taken as parallel to גבורה (strength); Isa 28:29). So, based on these observations, 'wisdom' seems to be the best translation. However, 'success' or 'resourcefulness' might be more appropriate for Job 6:13, though the precise meaning of the verse is not clear. Other appealing solutions would be 'competence,' suggested by McKane 1970: 282, or 'sound judgement' by Waltke 2004: 225. I (tentatively) chose 'prudence' because it captures well its close relationship to wisdom and also its connotations with resourcefulness, success, sound judgement and competence.

10. Grammatically 'shield' can be in apposition both to Yahweh and also to prudence. As 'shield' is a common Old Testament metaphor for the Lord (cf. Prov 30:5; Deut 33:29; Ps 3:4) and it is clear that the Lord is the subject of 2:7a and 2:8b, to suppose that the Lord is the subject throughout verses 7-8 seems to me the most natural reading. However, the ambiguity might also be intentional, or at least it can be utilised in an interpretation that is in harmony with the context. See later discussion.

11. It cannot be ruled out that there is a more complicated textual history behind the text than what is suggested by the simple ketiv/qere variation in the MT. This is the only occurrence of the word חסיד in Proverbs. The Syr. translates חסה, which also occurs in 14:32 and 30:5. The LXX also seems to translate חסה, when it renders the Hebrew as

⁹ Then you will understand righteousness and justice and equity,¹² every good track,
¹⁰ Because¹³ wisdom will come into your heart and knowledge will be pleasant to your soul.
¹¹ Shrewdness will safeguard you, understanding will guard you:
¹² Saving you from the way of the evil one,¹⁴ from the man who speaks perversions,
¹³ Those who abandon straight paths to walk in ways of darkness,
¹⁴ Those who delight in doing evil, who rejoice in evil perversions,
¹⁵ Whose paths are twisted and who are crooked in their tracks;
¹⁶ Saving you [also] from a strange woman, from an outsider who has polished her words,
¹⁷ Who abandons the companion of her youth, and forgets the covenant of her God.
¹⁸ For her path descends to death and her tracks to the realm of the dead:¹⁵
¹⁹ None who go to her return or regain the paths of life.
²⁰ Thus you will walk in the way of the good and keep to the paths of the righteous.

אז תבין צדק ומשפט ומישרים כל מעגל טוב

כי תבוא חכמה בלבך ודעת לנפשך ינעם

מזמה תשמר עליך תבונה תנצרכה

להצילך מדרך רע מאיש מדבר תהפכות

העזבים ארחות ישר ללכת בדרכי חשך

השמחים לעשות רע יגילו בתהפכות רע

אשר ארחתיהם עקשים ונלוזים במעגלותם

להצילך מאשה זרה מנכריה אמריה החליקה

העזבת אלוף נעוריה ואת ברית אלהיה שכחה

כי שחה אל מות ביתה ואל רפאים מעגלתיה

כל באיה לא ישובון ולא ישיגו ארחות חיים

למען תלך בדרך טובים וארחות צדיקים תשמר

εὐλαβουμένων (those who respect [him]), as in 30:5. Cook suggests that the LXX translator (or redactor) might have been influenced by 30:5 (Cook 1997: 121–122).

12. Masoretic accents suggest that the list of objects overflows into the second colon. At first sight it appears as if the LXX understood the second colon as a separate sentence with its own predicate. However, κατορθώσεις is not necessarily a verbal form ('you will make straight,' from κατορθόω), but it can also be taken as a noun (from κατόρθωσις; see *BHQ*, p. 32, the commentary on the critical apparatus). At any rate, the parallel with Prov 1:3 makes an emendation unnecessary here.

13. From this point on the LXX is different from the MT. It takes 2:10 as a *protasis* and verses 11-12 as the *apodosis* and does not mention the 'foreign woman' in verses 16-18. For a brief overview of LXX's understanding of the section and scholarly opinions about its interpretation, see Fox 2000: 374–376.

14. Or from 'evil way.' Here I follow Fox who, on the basis of the parallel with 2:12b and 2:16, argues that רע is not an adjective but a noun (Fox 2000: 117). This uncertainty of translation does not affect my argument.

15. The text is full of lexical and grammatical problems. Is שחה to be derived from שחה (bow down, lay on the floor) or שוח (sink down, walk)? Or should we emend it to שוחה (pit)? The בית is masculine, whereas the verb is feminine. Should we emend ביתה to נתיבתה (my translation follows this suggestion)? What is the precise meaning of רפאים? Regardless of these difficulties, the general meaning of the verse seems to be clear and these lexical problems do not affect my interpretation. For these and further suggestions, see Clifford 1999: 45; Fox 2000: 121–122; Fuhs 2001: 59; Longman 2006: 116–117; McKane 1970: 287–288; Murphy 1998: 14; Toy 1899: 48–49; Waltke 2004: 215–216; Weeks 2007: 201.

²¹ Surely the upright will inhabit the land and those with integrity will be left in it,
²² But the wicked will be cut off from the land, and the treacherous will be torn from it.

כי ישרים ישכנו ארץ ותמימים יותרו בה

ורשעים מארץ יכרתו ובוגדים יסחו ממנה

9.3 Does Proverbs 2 Speak about a God-Centred Thinking?

9.3.1 Wisdom: Seeing the Divine Providence

9.3.1.1 The Structure of Proverbs 2

As we will see shortly, the structure of Proverbs 2 makes it likely that the answer to this question is 'yes.'

TABLE 7: The structure of Proverbs 2

> A. *If* you listen to me (v. 1)
>   B. *then* your heart will turn to wisdom (v. 2).
> C. *If* you seek wisdom (i.e., listen to me) (vv. 3-4)
>   D. *then* you will know God (v. 5),
>   1. *because* it is **God** who gives wisdom (v.6),
>   2. and protects you (vv. 7-8)
>   E. *then* you will know righteousness (v. 9)
>   3. *because* **wisdom** will come into your heart (v. 10),
>   4. and she will protect you (v. 11)
>   F. 5. from wicked men (vv. 12-15) and
>   6. from wicked women (vv. 16-19),
>   G. so that you will walk on the right path (v. 20),
>   H. which is the salvation of the righteous one (vv. 21-22).

My structural analysis is basically identical with that of Michael Fox.[16] There is only one minor divergence between Fox's analysis and mine: I take the first two verses of the poem as an introductory sentence. Fox understands the first 4 verses as one long *protasis*. I tentatively choose to separate the first two verses, recognising that the translation of Fox and others is also possible, even if, in my opinion, it provides a less smooth reading.

From the modern commentaries and monographs that discuss the Hebrew of Proverbs 2 extensively, Pardee's is the only one that diverges somewhat from this structural analysis.[17] He reconstructs three grammatically independent conditions in the first half of the chapter: verses 1-5; 6-9; 10-11. His analysis is,

---

16. Fox 1994: 235; it is in broad agreement with Clements 2003: 440; Clifford 1999: 45–46; Estes 1997: 119; Farmer 1991: 31; Fontaine 1988: 452; Fuhs 2001: 59–67; McCreesh 1990: 456; McKane 1970: 213–214; Meinhold 1991a: 63; Murphy 1998: 14–15; Oesterley 1929: 13–14; Plöger 1984: 24; Ringgren and Zimmerli 1962: 17; Saebø 2012: 53–60; Waltke 2004: 216–219; Weeks 2007: 61.

17. Pardee 1988: 69–71.

however, not followed by most scholars, and I also find it slightly less persuasive. Nonetheless, much of what I am going to argue for could be adjusted to his structure, as well.

The structure shows sophisticated symmetries in the chapter. The first 11 verses (A to E in Table 7) comprise three, 4–4–3 verse long strophes (A-B-C; D; E). The second half of the chapter also has a 4–4–3 verse long strophe structure (F5; F6; G-H). This 'tightly knit structure,' as Fox describes it, makes theories of redactional intrusions somewhat speculative.[18] But even if there is a redactional history behind the text, the received form of it 'forms a meaningful, well-structured literary and conceptual unity.'[19]

The first half of the chapter contains a long conditional sentence, verses 3-4 being the *protasis* which is picked up by two *apodoses* (verses 5 and 9). The parallel between the two *apodoses* (verses 5-8 and 9-11) is the structural feature which is immediately relevant for us. In verses 10-11 *wisdom* is the subject whereas in verses 6-8 it is *Yahweh*. (Verses 5 and 9 will be discussed later.) In verse 10 *wisdom* comes into the heart of the student though in verse 6 *Yahweh* gives wisdom to the student. In verse 11 *wisdom* defends the student, but in verses 7-8 *Yahweh* defends him. It appears as if verses 6-8 tell the same story as verses 10-11, but from a different angle. It is as if verses 6-8 provide important background information that is not necessarily visible to the observer who sees only the reality of verses 10-11. This background information is that it is Yahweh who is behind wisdom.

This message is beautifully expressed by the—maybe only accidental—ambiguity of verse 7 as well. It is not entirely obvious there whether 'shield' describes prudence or Yahweh. Grammatically, both are viable options. The broader context, however, makes it clear that the real actor is Yahweh. Those who see the broader context of the verse (and also of life) can see Yahweh behind wisdom's protection.

To conclude, we can say that the structural parallel between wisdom and Yahweh exemplifies and recommends a God-centred thinking.

9.3.1.2   The Logical Order of Some Key Concepts in Prov 2:5-6

The teaching that divine providence lies behind human security provided by wisdom is not only expressed by the structure of the chapter. It is also conveyed by other literary tools.

God is introduced into the thought-world of the chapter by a powerful rhetorical tool: one would expect that if someone is looking for wisdom as eagerly as it is recommended in verses 1-4, then she or he will find wisdom. Instead of finding wisdom, however, verse 5 promises finding the knowledge of God and understanding the fear of him. That this surprising turn is a deliberate rhetorical

---

18. For such theories, see Michel 1992: 233–243; Murphy 2002: 236–237; Whybray 1966: 486–492.
19. Fox 2000: 127–128. See also Saebø 2012: 53–60; Schäfer 1999: 66–74.

tool is signaled by the following verse, which gives an explanation for it: for it is *Yahweh* and no one else who gives wisdom. The author is apparently well aware that the message of verse 5 takes the reader by surprise and requires some clarification. He applies preposing in verse 6,[20] that is, יהוה is placed before the verb. Though preposing is not always used to give extra emphasis to the first element of the sentence, especially not in a poetic text, it probably is here, after the surprising statement of the previous verse.[21] A comparison with the parallel verse 10 makes this even more obvious, as there we can find an unmarked word order:

[10] כי תָבוֹא חָכְמָה בלבך ודעת לנפשך ינעם   [6] כי יְהוָה יִתֵּן חכמה מפיו דעת ותבונה

Yet, a careful reading of the chapter reveals that however emphatic the role of Yahweh is, verse 5 speaks about wisdom, too. As we will see shortly, verse 5, when read together with its wider context, suggests that seeing Yahweh's importance is precisely what wisdom is.

The sequence of happenings in the first six verses in order of appearance is: seeking (verses 1-4); finding God (verse 5); and getting wisdom (verse 6). It could be argued that this is not only a literary but also a temporal order, i.e., finding God precedes finding wisdom. However, this is unlikely in the light of the parallel between verses 5-8 and 9-11. In verses 9-10 it is the arrival of wisdom (verse 10) which explains the student's understanding of righteousness (verse 9), so the action of verse 10 logically precedes verse 9. It seems to be a natural reading of verses 5-6 if one sees the same logical order there, namely, that the action of Yahweh in verse 6 (i.e., providing wisdom) is a presupposition of the student's understanding in verse 5. This leaves open two possibilities: First, that one gets wisdom from God (verse 6) and *after that* understands God (verse 5). In this case the logical order of the verses represents a temporal order of the actions mentioned by the verses.[22] Or, second, that one gets wisdom from God (verse 6) and at the same time understands God (verse 5), that is, being wise is (manifested in) understanding God. In this case the text speaks only about a logical order but this does not represent a temporal sequence. The latter option seems to be more likely for several reasons:

1. In the parallel statements of verses 9-10, where ethical behaviour flows from gaining wisdom, we can hardly think of a stage when someone is already wise but still non-ethical. So, verses 9-10 seem to speak about a logical and not about a temporal relationship.
2. תבין in verse 5 can remind the reader of בינה, which is one of the synonyms of wisdom (1:2; 8:14; 9:10; etc.), and דעת in the second half of the

---

20. I am adopting the terminology from Moshavi 2010.
21. 'Emphasis' is an imprecise word for the effect of preposing. However, it describes well the complex role preposing plays in this particular text. Using the terminology of recent linguistic approaches, it signifies both 'focusing' and 'topicalisation.' For the intricate question of the function of preposing, see Moshavi 2010: 18–47, 90–103.
22. See Fox 1994: 238.

verse can also call to mind wisdom, as it is one of its synonyms, too (1:4, 7; 8:12; etc.). These associations can give the impression that, although not mentioned explicitly, already verse 5 is about wisdom.

3. Prov 9:10b states that 'the knowledge of the Holy One is understanding.'[23] Here it seems that understanding, which is parallel with the wisdom of 9:10a, is identical with the knowledge of the Holy One. Thus, if one reads 2:5 together with 9:10 (which would be quite natural as they are similar and both of them are at structurally key positions in Proverbs 1–9)[24] then an obvious reading of 2:5 would be to take wisdom and knowledge of Yahweh as simultaneous, quasi-identical phenomena.

Therefore, it seems that the reader's expectation to find wisdom after the search for it in verses 1-4 is satisfied, after all. Verse 5 does not use the actual word 'wisdom' only because it wants to emphasise the most important element of wisdom's content: the knowledge of God and understanding the fear of the Lord.

To summarise my interpretation so far, verse 5 emphasises Yahweh's central role in giving wisdom and also that knowing God is actually the most important part of wisdom. The verse expresses these ideas by its position in the whole chapter and also by its word order. In the following section I argue that verse 5 uses a third literary tool, too, by which it similarly suggests that the main part of wisdom is the perception of Yahweh's central role in life. This tool is the careful selection of words with theologically rich connotations.

9.3.1.3 *The Meaning and Connotations of* בין

'Then you will understand the fear of the Lord' (Prov 2:5a). תבין, to begin with the first verb of the verse, seems to be a surprising word choice. Does the 'fear of the Lord' require cognitive apprehension? One would rather expect verse 5 to say 'then you will *start* to fear the Lord.' The appearance of the same word in the parallel verse 9 just makes the expression even more peculiar: can it really mean there that the student was not familiar with the concepts of justice and righteousness and that he had to learn what they are? Would not 'then you will *become* righteous, just, etc.' read more naturally in 2:9?

Explaining Prov 2:5, Fox writes: 'when the object of *hēbîn* is a mental state (such as fear of God) or a cognitive faculty, the verb means to *acquire* the desig-

---

23. דעת קדשים בינה; I take דעת קדשים as referring to God. This is in agreement with the majority of modern commentators (Clifford 1999: 107; Ehrlich 1968: 45; Fritsch and Schloerb 1955: 837; Fox 2000: 308; Kidner 1964: 83; McKane 1970: 368; Murphy 1998: 60; Ross 2008: 105; Toy 1899: 194; Waltke 2004: 441; Whybray 1972: 53). It cannot be completely ruled out that it refers to the heavenly court as an expression of the divine realm (Ringgren and Zimmerli 1962: 41; Weeks 2007: 223) but that would not make much difference to my argument.

24. 'Fear of the Lord' (a key term both in 2:5 and 9:10) and its significance will be discussed later.

nated object in an insightful, cognitive way.'[25] There are important factors that make Fox's suggestion persuasive: the second half of 2:5 uses מצא in relation with the 'knowledge of God,' and this parallel would make a similar meaning for תבין natural;[26] Prov 1:3 promises that the reader of the book will acquire (לקח) precisely the three characteristics mentioned in 2:9.

On the other hand, though 'acquiring a mental state in a cognitive way' seems to be a feasible explanation of the term in some contexts, we will see a little later that it is a matter of question how much 'fear of the Lord' can be equated with a 'mental state.' Furthermore, the phrase 'acquire in a cognitive way' describes a consequence of understanding something truly—but I wonder if there are other consequences that are also included in the connotations of בין and to which one should pay attention.

The semantic field of the verb בין is wide. Besides 'understanding' the dictionaries list possible meanings like 'discern,' 'recognise,' 'acknowledge,' 'apply understanding,' 'experience,' 'give heed to,' 'have regard.' It regularly occurs in parallel with verbs of perception (ראה, שמע, האזין).[27] It is worth quoting some characteristic examples from other biblical books.

Isaiah 6:9-10 famously says:

> And He said, Go and tell this people, 'listen carefully but do not understand (תבינו), see carefully but do not know.' Make the mind of this people dull, make their ears hard of hearing, close their eyes. So that they would not see with their eyes, hear with their ears, understand (יבין) with their minds, and turn and be healed.

Then in Isa 32:3-4a we read, 'Then the eyes of the seers will not be blind, and the ears of the listeners will hear, the mind of the rash will understand well (יבין לדעת).' In these verses the word means something like *true* perception which goes beyond mere knowledge of the facts; it involves perceiving the existential importance of the prophet's words, a perception that leads to action (i.e., repentance).

In other places we meet the word in contexts that recall wisdom literature. In Deut 32:29, after reading about God's harsh dealings with a rebellious Israel, we read 'If only they were wise and would understand this and would perceive (יבינו) what their end will be' (see also Jer 9:12). In Ps 73:17 and 92:6-7 it is about understanding the end of the wicked. Thus, in these verses the word refers to an understanding of where wicked deeds lead, to an understanding of the connection between behaviour and fate, to a true understanding of cause and effect.

In the light of these biblical passages I find Ehrlich's suggestion for the meaning of the word in Prov 2:5 and 2:9 especially attractive. He suggested that

---

25. Fox 2000: 110.
26. Though, see Ceresko 1982 who argues that מצא can mean 'understand' in certain contexts, for example in Prov 2:5.
27. See Ringgren 1977: 99–107; Schmid 1997: 230–232; Clines 1995: 142–146.

we should understand it as 'appreciating, valuing' (*Würdigung*) the already known facts.[28] It is clearly close to how it is used in the aforementioned Isaian texts where it refers to the right appreciation of seen and heard things. It is also in accordance with the idea of seeing clearly where things will lead and the correct evaluation of certain factors (like wicked behaviour) in the chain of causation (cf. the just discussed Deut 32:29; Ps 73:17; 92:6-7).

These connotations would be very much at home in the context of Proverbs, where the student is encouraged to see that wicked behaviour leads to destruction (cf. 1:10-33) and that right behaviour (2:9) and 'fear of the Lord' (2:5) both have the opposite effect. Therefore, besides 'understand,' probable shades of meaning of תבין in verses 5 and 9 are 'appreciate,' 'evaluate rightly,' 'see where it leads.'

If this understanding of תבין is correct, then it is very much in line with the aforementioned message of the whole section: wisdom is a right vision of reality, the perception of the crucial role Yahweh plays in protecting people. If one has this right vision, then he or she will also see the value of fearing Yahweh.

9.3.1.4 The Connotations of דעת אלהים

'And the knowledge of God you will find' (Prov 1:5b). The same message is conveyed by the expression 'knowledge of God.' The *locus classicus* for deciphering the meaning of 'knowledge of God' is the book of Hosea, since the word ידע, with the objects of יהוה, אלהים, and God's deeds, occurs there especially frequently (Hosea 2:10, 22; 4:1, 6; 5:4; 6:3, 6; 8:2; 10:12 (LXX); 11:3; 13:4).[29] In fact, outside Proverbs the exact phrase דעת אלהים appears only in Hosea (Hos 4:1; 6:6).[30]

Before H. W. Wolff's influential article ('"Wissen um Gott" bei Hosea als Urform von Theologie') it was customary to understand דעת אלהים in the light of Hosea 1–3, and stress its sexual, marital, and intimate connotations.[31] Wolff, however, argued for the primacy of a covenantal context.[32] Though one probably should not contrast marriage with covenant, since marriage is sometimes

---

28. Ehrlich 1968: 8, 16.

29. I am not going to engage with the ongoing debate about the redaction-history of the book of Hosea or about the relationship between the deuteronomic movement and (the book of) Hosea (see Andersen and Freedman 1980: 52–57; Emmerson 1984; Rudnig-Zelt 2006; Yee 1985). My conclusions can be adjusted to fit with all of the currently available historical reconstructions.

30. Certain verses in Jeremiah (e.g., Jer 22:16) could be compared to Hosea. Deuteronomy also contains sections that are often similar to passages in Hosea (Deut 4:39 cf. Hos 13:4; Deut 7:9 cf. Hos 4:1, 6; 6:6; 8:1-2; Deut 8:5-10 cf. Hos 2:10; 11:1-4; 13:4-8; Deut 9:3-6 cf. Hos 2:10; 8:1-6; 11:1-4). Furthermore, Isa 5:12-13 and the appearance in the Prophets of the so-called 'recognition formula' ('and you [they] will know that I am Yahweh') are relevant (see Daniels 1990: 112–114). These texts seem to use the expression and/or the idea of 'knowledge of God' in a similar way to the Hosean usage.

31. Wolff 1953: 533–554.

32. See also Wolff 1974b: 53.

conceived covenantally (see Mal 2:13-16), and one should not ignore completely the metaphorical power of intimate family relationship,[33] I find Wolff's argument persuasive. For, in Hosea, knowing God is mentioned together with חסד and אמת (Hos 4:1; 6:6), with the word 'covenant' (6:6-7; 8:1-3),[34] with the deliverance from Egypt, the giving of the land, the living in the land (Hos 4:1; 11:1-11; 13:4), and idolatry (Hos 8:2). Thus, the covenantal context is hardly deniable.

According to Wolff, and many of his followers, there are two important components of this covenantal understanding of דעת אלהים in Hosea: history and law.[35] I concentrate on law a little later. As for history, Hosea wanted the Israelites to know about God's historical acts: that he led the nation out of Egypt; gave the land to Israel; and provided everything for them (Hos 2:10; 10:12; 11:3; 13:4; etc.).

Though Proverbs 2, as typical wisdom literature, is devoid of any references to the national history of Israel, it has an obvious parallel with Hosea. The Hosean emphasis is not purely on knowing the historical facts but also on perceiving that it was the Lord who was behind those historical events: 'She did not know that it was I who gave her the grain, the wine, the oil' (Hos 2:10a), 'it was I who taught Ephraim to walk, I took them up in my arms, but they did not know that I healed them' (11:3). All this is in line with Prov 2:6-8, which, just after mentioning the 'knowledge of God,' teaches that it is Yahweh and Yahweh alone who provides wisdom and protection.

9.3.1.5 Summary

As a summary of the discussion so far we can say that Proverbs 2 provides the same God-centred vision as Hosea by means of several literary tools. The literary structure of the chapter (i.e., parallel between verses 5-8 and 9-11), the logical structure of verses 5-6 (i.e., that knowing God is wisdom) and the careful choice of vocabulary (תבין, דעת אלהים) all aim to teach the reader to perceive God behind wisdom, justice, protection, and success. All of these literary tools depict a God-centred worldview and place God at the centre of the wisdom quest. This

---

33. Achtemeier 1996: 28–29, 35; Birch 1997: 47–48; Macintosh 1997: 84–85; Mowley 1991: 116–117; Perry 2008: 117–118; Waltke 2004: 222–223. Some scholars still emphasise the marital intimacy more than the covenant: McKeating 1971: 88; Simundson 2005: 45. Morris stresses the importance of the introductory role of Hosea 1–3, nevertheless, he also takes the covenantal context as primary (Morris 1996: 113). The majority follows Wolff in his emphasis of the covenantal context: Andersen and Freedman 1980: 336; Daniels 1990: 111–116; Davies 1992: 88; Davies 1993: 22–26; Hubbard 1989: 88–89; Limburg 1988: 16–17; Naumann 1991: 70; Rudnig-Zelt 2006: 81, 194–197; Stuart 1987: 75.

34. Covenant is mentioned only in these two places in Hosea (Birch 1997: 48; Limburg 1988: 17).

35. Daniels 1990: 111–116; Davies 1992: 22–26. Rudnig-Zelt argues that 'knowledge of God' originally referred mainly to history, and it referred to legal material only in a later redaction of the book (Rudnig-Zelt 2006: 81, 194–197).

is very much in harmony not only with Hosea's God-centred vision but also with what Thomas said about having God as the final end. Thomas taught that this means having God-centred thinking, and it is just such thinking that is encouraged by Proverbs 2.

The element of Thomas's statement that we have not mentioned yet in connection with Proverbs is that Thomas not only spoke about God-centred thinking but also about God-centred trust. There is, however, hardly any difference in this between Proverbs 2 and Thomas. Though Proverbs 2 does not use the word 'trust,' the idea is there as it speaks about divine providence. In fact, the reader does not have to wait long for an explicit mention of trust. The next chapter, continuing the theme of knowledge of God and the way-metaphor, both introduced in Proverbs 2, connects 'knowing him in all your ways' (3:6) with trusting in him and not relying on one's own wisdom (3:5).

Teaching the reader how to trust in God and nothing else is certainly an important topic in Proverbs (see 3:21-26; 22:19). The security that Proverbs offers to the reader is not a cheap security. It does not say 'do not worry, you are secure.' It says, 'Trust not in your wisdom (3:5; 28:26), trust not in unethical means promising success (1:10-19; 9:17), but trust in the Lord and *then* you will be secure.'

Thus, one of the two Thomistic criteria of having God as the final human end, that is, having God-centred thinking, hope, and trust, is satisfied by Proverbs 2. Before going on, however, to investigate the other Thomistic criterion, namely that one must not serve God because of the benefits of that service, we should discuss another feature of Proverbs 2's God-centred worldview, which provides some interesting further parallels with Thomistic thinking.

9.3.2 Wisdom: Not only Seeing but Participating in Divine Providence

In this section I argue that behaviour is just as crucial as knowledge. 'Having God-centred thinking and trust' includes physical, not only mental activity.

Whereas the vocabulary of Prov 2:9 conveys the connotation of physical activity since 'righteousness,' 'justice,' and 'equity' are at least as much behavioural as cognitive patterns, the words of Prov 2:5 seem to depict mainly cognitive processes: 'understanding,' 'fear (of God),' 'knowledge (of God).' It would be a mistake, however, to make such a distinction between the two verses. Whereas the connotations of the words of 2:5 might seem predominantly cognitive for the modern reader, they present a strong emphasis on activity, especially if they are read in a canonical context.

9.3.2.1. דעת אלהים *and Behaviour*

As for the 'knowledge of God,' we have seen that most commentators understand it in Hosea in a covenantal framework in which it refers both to history and law. We have also seen that in the case of history it means more than simply being aware of the historical facts; it also means knowing that it is Yahweh who is behind those historical facts. It very probably also means more than simply being aware of some legal precepts, in the case of law. Knowledge is not enough: true knowledge is expressed by action.[36] In Hosea 4:1-2 we read that there is no knowledge of God in Israel; instead there is 'swearing, and deceit, and murder, and stealing, and adultery.'[37] In Hos 6:1-3 the people think that the 'knowledge of God' is like a few days' long devotion in the temple, which they can easily accomplish, but in 6:4-6 God reminds them that it is rather steadfast love (חסד) expressed continuously in everyday life.

This 'behavioural understanding' of the 'knowledge of God' is also in line with Jer 22:15-16 which offers a 'quasi-definition' of knowing God, equating it with משפט and צדקה,[38] two terms that occur in Prov 2:9, the parallel verse to Prov 2:5.[39] This behavioural aspect is further emphasised by the 'way' metaphor in the verses following 2:5 (להלכי תם [verse 7], ארחות and דרך [verse 8], כל מעגל טוב [verse 9]), which is 'used by most of the biblical writers to refer to human behaviour.'[40]

9.3.2.2 יראת יהוה *and Behaviour*

Defining the meaning and connotation of the other key expression of Prov 2:5, 'fear of the Lord,' is more complicated than the case of the 'knowledge of God.' Is it primarily an emotion and attitude,[41] or does it rather refer to obeying God's rules without reference to emotions?[42] Is it the 'Hebrew equivalent to "faith" in Christian parlance,'[43] or is it fear from (the punishment of) God?[44] The complexity of the problem is well exemplified by Fox's explanation of the phrase in Prov 2:5. He argues that one can construct two types of 'fear of the Lord' lying behind the single biblical expression: 'Fear of God motivates the search for wisdom, which develops into a more sophisticated fear of God, one in which a moral conscience is fused with knowledge of his will.'[45] A few pages later he seems to imply that the first fear is a fear from external calamity whereas the 'more sophisticated fear' is a sort of internalised fear, which becomes an intrinsic part of the student's character.[46]

---

36. Fohrer 1955: 169 n. 16; Rudolph 1966: 100.
37. Whether this list is dependent on (some form of) the Decalogue or not is debated (Naumann 1991: 20 n. 11).
38. Moberly 2006: 66–70.
39. Though, to be precise, Prov 2:9 uses צדק and not צדקה.
40. Weeks 2007: 61. Concerning the possible Deuteronomic, legal connotations, see Weeks 2007: 150–154.
41. Fox 2000: 112.
42. Clifford 1999: 35; see also von Rad 1952: 206.
43. Moberly 2000: 79.
44. Clines 2003: 57–92.
45. Fox 2000: 113.
46. Fox 2000: 133–134.

I will return to Fox's explanation a little later. Now I will simply argue that despite the difficulties in pinpointing the meaning of the term, one can be certain of its strong practical connotations, which are probably even more apparent than in the case of 'knowledge of God.'

One major source of difficulty is that we are speaking about an 'open ended' term which occurs in many contexts with many different connotations.[47] As Moberly writes, '"fear of God/YHWH" is such a fundamental term within the Old Testament that it risks being as difficult to elucidate as terms such as "religion" or "morality"; any single or simple definition is likely to be partial and more or less inadequate to the range of textual data.'[48] The most common solution to this problem in standard twentieth century discussions was to construct a 'semantic development,' that is, to attribute distinct meanings to the occurrence of the phrase in texts written in different ages or in texts belonging to different genres.[49] However, besides the notorious problem of dating texts, it seems unlikely that different traditions could exist in isolation without influencing each other. On a hermeneutical level it is also questionable whether someone reading a text in a canonical context should ignore resonances created by the textual corpus even if some authors were not necessarily aware of all of those resonances. Thus, for historical and hermeneutical reasons, I tend to agree with Dell, who, after listing possible numinous, cultic, legal, covenantal, and ethical connotations of the phrase, writes:

> While different contexts may indicate nuances of meaning, the question is raised whether one needs to posit a whole different set of meanings for the use of such terms in wisdom literature, or whether in fact one should bring to the wisdom context the wider overtones of meaning contained in the concepts as used elsewhere. I propose the latter path.[50]

However, even if one allows for the possibility that the phrase retains the richness and deepness of its meaning created by its diverse connotations in other biblical texts, it is nevertheless pertinent to try to ascertain which connotations best fit the text in hand. I would like to draw attention to three such connotations, all of which refer at least as much to behavioural patterns as to cognitive ones: ethical behaviour, serving God, and imitating God.

First, 'fear of God' is closely related to ethical behaviour throughout Proverbs.[51] As 14:2a writes, 'the one who walks in his uprightness fears the Lord' (see also 8:13; 16:6; 23:17). In our text, 2:5's parallel with 2:9 underlies this ethical connotation: there the student is supposed to 'understand' (תבין) right-

---

47. Moberly 2000: 80.
48. Moberly 2000: 88.
49. E.g., Becker 1965; Plath 1962.
50. Dell 2006: 175.
51. Cox 1982: 83–90; Murphy 1998: 93; Frydrych 2002: 171–172.

eousness and justice and equity just as he is supposed to 'understand' (תבין) 'fear of the Lord' in 2:5.

Second, 'fear of the Lord' probably has the general connotation of serving God. Stuart Weeks makes a brief comment in relation to 'fear of the Lord' in Proverbs 1–9, saying that 'the fear of YHWH should probably be understood to imply a relationship of loyal, obedient respect: Mal 1:6 suggests that fear is something owed to a master, just as honour is something owed to a father.'[52] As a matter of fact, 'honour' is due to both father and master according to Mal 1:6 and not only to a father, but this does not refute Weeks' observation. Just as Weeks suggests, the servant is supposed to honour his master *fearfully* in Mal 1:6: 'A son honours [his] father, and a servant his lord. If I am a father, where is the honour due to me; and if I am the Lord, where is the fear (מוראי) due to me?—says the Lord of hosts to you—The priests despise (בוזי) my name. But you ask: in what have we despised (בזינו) your name?'[53]

Weeks, in a footnote, refers to Deut 6:13 as a verse which strengthens this servanthood connotation of 'fear of the Lord.' In fact, however, the themes of being God's servant and fearing him are mentioned together several times besides Mal 6:13 and Deut 6:13 (Deut 10:12, 20; 13:5 [English 13:4]; Josh 24:14; 1 Sam 12:14, 24; Neh 1:11; Job 1:8; 2:3; Ps 119:38).

Proverbs itself does not mention 'serving' explicitly in connection with 'fear of the Lord.' Nevertheless, it does connect 'fear of the Lord' with a character trait which is typical for servants: obedient listening. In Proverbs we find three variations of the statement 'the fear of the Lord is the beginning of wisdom.' The first is in a programmatic sentence to the whole book (1:7), the second at the end of the first section (9:10), and the third towards the middle of the whole book (15:33). At these structurally significant places the sentence is placed next to verses which speak about paying attention to instruction. Proverbs 1:7 is followed by two verses motivating the student to listen to his father's and mother's instruction (מוסר). Proverbs 9:10 is preceded by three verses discussing the different reactions of scoffers and wise people to others correcting (יסר) them. Proverbs 15:33 is preceded by two verses that speak about the positive and negative reactions given to instruction (מוסר).[54]

A similar connection can be observed in Prov 1:20-33, where listening to wisdom's instruction (1:20-25, 33) surrounds the mention of the 'fear of the Lord'

---

52. Weeks 2007: 113.

53. It is the first half of the verse that is especially relevant here. However, it is noteworthy that in the second half of the verse the opposite of fearing is despising (בזה), just like in Prov 1:7 and 14:2.

54. The precise relationship of these three verses to their immediate contexts would deserve a much longer discussion than the restriction of space allows here. In all cases it is possible that these verses (i.e. 1:7; 9:10; 15:33) are later insertions. Nevertheless, even if this is so, it is telling that the person(s) who inserted them found those contexts that speak about listening obediently to instruction particularly suitable to accommodate them.

(1:29). The topic is carried over into chapter two, which begins with an encouragement to listen to the words of the father (Prov 2:1-2). In fact, this encouragement in 2:1-2 follows the encouragement to listen to wisdom in 1:33 so swiftly that an inattentive reader might even miss the change of speaker. The swift change creates an effect that gives the father a special authority and that makes the impression that listening to him is like listening to (divine) wisdom.[55]

Therefore, although there is no explicit mention of servanthood in Proverbs, the context does not disallow such a connotation of the 'fear of the Lord,' and the emphasis on listening to instruction might even activate it.

A canonical reading which views Proverbs 2 in the light of Deuteronomy also suggests that the servanthood connotation of 'fear of the Lord' is accommodated well by that chapter. Proverbs 2 contains numerous deuteronomic elements: living in the land (Prov 2:21-22, cf. Deut 4:10; 5:16, 33; 6:18; 11:9; 15:4-5; 16:20; 17:20; 22:7; 25:15; 32:47); the idea of knowledge of God (Deut 7:9); path metaphor (Deut 11:28; 13:6 [English 13:5]); and warning against foreign women (Deut 7:4).[56] Such a canonical reading would strengthen the servanthood connotation of 'fear of the Lord' because, as we have already seen, the ideas of servanthood and 'fear of the Lord' occur in close proximity several times in Deuteronomy (6:13; 10:12, 20; 13:5 [English 13:4]).

The servant metaphor is actually very useful for grasping the complex and elusive concept of the 'fear of the Lord.' When describing such an open-ended idea then it might be a wise tactic to use an image that is equally open to many connotations instead of a fixed definition. A servant can obey his master automatically, out of fear of retribution, or out of love. The emphasis can be on his actions, his feelings, his thinking, or his humble status, depending on the context. Thus, the image of the relationship between a servant and his lord is as similarly open-ended as the concept of 'fear of the Lord,' but maybe more suggestive to the modern reader. The picture of a servant also underlies how indivisible 'fear of the Lord' is from action. Being a good servant is always expressed in action, not only in thought.

The servant metaphor leads us to our third point about the possible connotations of 'fear of the Lord,' which is the connection between 'fear of the Lord' and *imitatio dei*.[57] Israel, as a servant of God, was expected to mirror God's actions, as seen in Deut 10:12-20, in which the themes of fearing God, serving God, and imitating God are intermingled:

---

55. We have already seen some parallels between wisdom's and God's actions. The parallels between wisdom and God are discussed further in Part IV.

56. For a recent discussion of the deuteronomistic language of Proverbs 1–9 and possible historical connections between Deuteronomy and Proverbs 1–9, see Weeks 2007: 150–152, 169–179.

57. For succinct, general discussions of the *imitatio dei* theme in the Hebrew Bible, see Barton 2003: 50–54; Buber 1997: 66–75.

And now, Israel, ... *fear the Lord your God*, walk in all his ways, love him, and *serve the Lord your God* ... because the Lord your God is God of gods and Lord of lords, the great God, mighty and awesome, who is not partial and takes no bribe, does the justice of the orphan and the widow, and *loves the alien*, giving him food and clothing. *You shall [also] love the alien. ... The Lord your God you shall fear, him you shall serve.*[58]

The theme of *imitatio dei* is clearly connected to 'fear of the Lord' in Psalms 111–112, too. Taken as one unit, as it is often done, 'fear of the Lord' is at the centre of these twin psalms (111:10; 112:1).[59] There are 11 words or phrases that are used in both psalms.[60] Many of those which describe the God-fearer in Psalm 112 are used to describe God in Psalm 111:[61]

TABLE 8: *Imitatio Dei* in Psalms 111–112

Yahweh	God-fearers/righteous
His righteousness continues forever (צדקתו עמדת לעד) (111:3)	Their righteousness continues forever (צדקתו עמדת לעד) (112:3, 9)
He is merciful and affectionate (חנון ורחום) (111:4)	They are merciful and affectionate (חנון ורחום) (112:4)
The works of his hands are just (משפט) (111:7)	They conduct their affairs in justice (משפט) (112:5)
His wonderful deeds (or he himself?) are remembered (זכר) (111:4)	They will be remembered (זכר) (112:6)
His deeds are firm (סמוך)(111:8)	Their hearts are steady (סמוך)(112:8)
He gives (נתן) food to those who fear him (111:5)	They give (נתן) to the poor (112:9)

This *imitatio dei* theme also fits the context of Proverbs 2. We have seen that the deeds of wisdom and that of Yahweh are parallel in verses 6-8 and 10-11, so one can suppose that the God-fearing, wise person also follows the divine pattern of behaviour. In this respect we should note how Prov 2:9 is related to the previous verses. In Prov 2:8 we read that God guards justice (משפט). Maybe it is significant that the text does not say 'just people' but 'justice.' The concept itself is dear to God, not only certain people. In the next verse (2:9) the student begins to 'appreciate' (בין) precisely the justice that is so important for Yahweh.

---

58. My emphases.
59. It is somewhat debated whether these psalms are the products of one author or whether the author of Psalm 112 reflected on the earlier Psalm 111. For a further discussion of these issues, see Allen 2002: 128–130; Anderson 1972: 776; Clifford 2003: 184; Curtis 2004: 220–221; Day 1990: 54–55; Gerstenberger 2001: 274; Mays 1994: 359; Mowinckel 1962: 111–112; Rogerson and McKay 1977: 71; Terrien 2003: 760–761; Whybray 1996: 68.
60. Allen 2002: 128.
61. Allen 2002: 128; Mays 1994: 359; Whybray 1996: 69.

In a (limited) way, the student becomes similar to God, just like the God-fearer of Psalm 112 is similar to the God of Psalm 111.[62]

9.3.2.3 Knowledge, Action, Participation in the Divine: Thomas and Proverbs 2

We have seen that both 'knowledge of God' and 'fear of the Lord' have strong behavioural connotations in Prov 2:5. They describe knowledge and a servant attitude that are expressed through action. The student not only knows about divine providence but also acts according to this knowledge.

This 'behavioural' understanding of knowledge is not far from how Thomas understood it. He also thought that happiness, which is the knowledge of God, was connected to virtuous behaviour just as much as to perceiving God's providence (*ST* II–II, 180, 4). Not only does contemplating virtuous behaviour lead to a knowledge of God but this knowledge of God, claimed Thomas, leads to a virtuous behaviour, too:

> Now, granting that wisdom is the knowledge of divine things, our notion of it is one thing and that of pure philosophers, another. For us, life is directed towards the eventual possession of God and its principal orientations are those deriving from our participation in the divine nature by way of grace, with the result that we do not look upon wisdom as merely yielding knowledge about God (as do the philosophers), but even as directing human life.[63]

However, there is an important dissimilarity between Proverbs 2 and Thomas. Thomas differentiated between an imperfect contemplation, which was only 'through a glass' and 'in a dark manner' (*ST* II–II, 180, 4), and a perfect one. Perfect contemplation, for Aquinas, was only attainable in the heavenly bliss, and it is a direct vision of God not 'disturbed' by actions. As he wrote, 'the more our mind is raised to the contemplation of spiritual things, the more is it withdrawn from sensible things.'[64] He thought that virtuous behaviour is imitation of God only in a limited, metaphorical sense:

> The last end of all is to become like God. . . . Now this is not in regard to moral actions, since suchlike actions cannot be ascribed to

---

62. See Prov 3:3 and 16:6 where it is difficult to decide whether חסד refers to a human or to a divine characteristic. For differing views, see Clifford 1999: 158; Ehrlich 1968: 89; Fox 2000: 144; Fox 2009: 612; Fritsch and Schloerb 1955: 873; Heim 2001: 210; Longman 2006: 330; McKane 1970: 498; Meinhold 1987: 473; Meinhold 1991b: 267; Murphy 1998: 121; Oesterley 1929: 128–129; Perdue 2000: 180; Plöger 1984: 190–191; Ringgren and Zimmerli 1962: 68; Ross 2008: 146; Toy 1899: 322; Van Leeuwen 1997: 158–159; Waltke 2004: 241; Waltke 2005: 13–14; Whybray 1972: 94. In a similar fashion, Christopher Wright has argued that the virtues mentioned throughout Proverbs imitate the characteristics of God (Wright 2004: 369–371). See also Estes 2010: 164 about Proverbs 1–9 and the imitation of God.

63. *ST* II–II, 19, 7.

64. *SCG*, III, 47.

God, except metaphorically ... therefore man's ultimate happiness, which is his last end, does not consist in moral actions.[65]

According to Thomas, moral actions are useful here on earth; they enable one to contemplate God, but they only lead to an end without significantly taking part in that end.[66]

This differentiation between the earthly contemplation that is connected to action and the heavenly one that is not connected to practical life goes well beyond the text of Proverbs, which does not know about a 'perfect,' heavenly knowledge of God unaided by action.

Nevertheless, the earthly, imperfect knowledge of God was crucial for Thomas's moral theology, and, as we have just seen, very much in line with Proverbs' understanding of the knowledge of God: both include a certain worldview, an understanding of God's providential actions, and also a life accompanied by actions that are in accordance with this worldview. In this respect we should also note that for Thomas, just as for Proverbs, this (earthly) knowledge of God is connected to the theme of *imitatio dei*.

Some of Thomas's modern interpreters explain even Thomas's most debated and most influential concept, the natural law, in a way that is very much in line with the *imitatio dei* understanding of right human actions and the teaching of Proverbs 2.

Thomas differentiates between four types of law:
- eternal law: it is in God's mind and occasionally identified with God himself;[67]
- divine law (divided into Old and New law): it can be found in the Bible;
- human law: the regulations of society;
- natural law: it is in (human) nature.

Now Thomas, in *Summa Theologiae*, devotes only one question to discussing natural law (*ST*, I–II, 94) and eighteen others to discussing the other laws (*ST*, I–II, 90–93; 95–108). If quantity is a sign of interest then Thomas's interests were somewhere other than where later scholarly interpretations of his thought imply, for they focus much more on his thoughts about natural law.

Hittinger suggests that, by utilising the concept of natural law, one of Thomas's major interests was to provide a theological framework for right human action.[68] This framework sees appropriately self-interested human behaviour as a conversation with God, even as participation in divine providence. According to this interpretation of natural law it is important to understand that natural law is explicitly defined in the context of eternal law. As Thomas writes in *ST* I–II, 91, 2:

---

65. SCG, III, 34.
66. SCG, III, 34; see also *ST* I–II, 3, 5.
67. Kerr 2002: 107.
68. Hittinger 1997: 1–30. See also Kerr 2002: 101–121.

> Intelligent creatures are ranked under divine Providence the more nobly because they take part in Providence by their own providing for themselves and others. Thus they join in and make their own the Eternal Reason through which they have their natural aptitudes for their due activity and purpose. Now this sharing in the Eternal Law by intelligent creatures is what we call 'natural law'.

In other words, God provides for his creatures, and when rational creatures provide for themselves (and others) then they imitate God, that is, participate in his eternal law.[69] Following the principles of natural law, in other words caring for one's own material, social, and spiritual needs, is nothing else than taking part in God's providence; at least if someone conducts this self-care wisely, making the right choices that lead to appropriate human ends.[70] Thomas basically describes prudence as an imitation of divine providence. It is not only an accident, he claims, that the very name of prudence is taken from providence (*ST* II–II, 49, 6, ad. 1; see also *ST* I, 22, 1). This Thomistic vision is in accordance with Proverbs 2, in which wisdom is expressed in actions that are in parallel with God's providential activity.

In this sense, of course, one can participate in divine providence without being aware of this participation. But for Thomas and for Proverbs 2, human happiness contains awareness. Knowing that God provides and acting in a God-imitating way (i.e., providing for oneself and for others) goes hand-in-hand in both Proverbs and Thomas.

9.3.3 Summary

According to Thomas's ethics, a non-selfish person is supposed to consider God as the highest end. Such a person has a God-centred thinking, hope, and trust. Does Proverbs lead its reader towards this kind of thinking and attitude? The answer I have given to this question is affirming. In Proverbs 2 the focus on God is expressed by

- A God-centred **worldview** (parallels between wisdom [Prov 2:9-11] and Yahweh [Prov 2:5-8], knowing [that] God [is behind protection] [Prov 2:5-8], and valuing the fear of the Lord [Prov 2:5]).
- **Trust** in God (presupposed by Proverbs 2, explicitly taught later by Prov 3:5).
- God-imitating **action** (Prov 2:9, connotations of 'fear of the Lord' and 'knowledge of God' in Prov 2:5).

---

69. DeYoung, McCluskey, and Van Dyke 2009: 161; Hittinger 1997: *passim*; Kerr 2002: 101–121. Not everyone stresses the *imitatio dei* aspect, but many emphasise that, according to Thomas, natural law is participation in eternal law. See the very different essays by May and Long, who, nevertheless, agree on this point: Long 2004: 166, 188, 191; May 2004: 119, 122. See also Porter 1999: 160–164.

70. See Porter 1999: 157.

Before going on to Thomas's other criterion for having God as the final end (i.e., not serving God for its benefits), I will address these three points again in relation to some theological issues. I will also underline some further similarities between the thought of Thomas and Proverbs.

9.3.3.1   Worldview

As one of Thomas's interpreters puts it, for Thomas 'wisdom ... is a matter of having a certain understanding of reality.'[71] The teaching of Proverbs 2 is similar. It stresses that one has to understand reality correctly in order to be able to make wise decisions. In other words, values and criteria for wisdom are not created by individual humans, not even by human society, but they are based on this reality. As Jonathan Sacks puts it,

> Religious faith suggests that ... the moral rules and virtues which constrain and enlarge our aspirations are not mere subjective devices and desires. They are 'out there' as well as 'in here'. They represent objective truths about the human situation.[72]

Speaking about 'reality' and moral rules being 'out there' might call to mind one of the key expressions of modern biblical Proverbs interpretations: world order. However, I have already expressed my sympathy with the opinion of some scholars who claim that it is dubious whether the category 'world order' is a useful one for describing Proverbs' teaching. Can these seemingly different views be reconciled?

Proverbs 2 undeniably describes reality in a certain way, and, if one wants, one can call this reality an 'order.' However, a simple statement like this can be misleading. First of all, one has to recognise that speaking about this order does not necessarily mean that it can be deciphered purely by human rationality. In Proverbs 2 the whole learning process begins by listening to the teaching of the father and not by careful investigation of the world. There is not a single admonition for such an investigation in Proverbs 2. If Thomas maintained that one can get to know God and the order of reality by using his or her rational abilities, then his teaching is not supported by Proverbs 2.[73]

---

71. Stump 1999: 30.
72. Sacks 1995: 6.
73. The tentativeness of this sentence is deliberate. It is debated to what extent Thomas (and the medieval scholastics in general) thought rational human beings could decipher the order of reality, especially when reality includes God. See Goyette, Latkovic, and Myers 2004; Kerr 2002: 35–51, 97–113; Porter 1999: 173–177; Porter 2005: 74; Porter 2009: 53–95; Turner 2004. Regardless of the scholarly debate, we can at least say that Thomas was very cautious about making statements about the power of human mind. At the beginning of his *Summa Theologiae* he says that, though humans could figure out some things about God, this knowledge 'would only be known by a few, and that after a long time, and with the admixture of many errors' (*ST* I, 1, 1; see also *ST* II–II, 2, 4). He wrote elsewhere about divine providence—which is the subject of Prov 2:6–

Furthermore, Proverbs 2 does not teach that the 'world order' is independent from Yahweh. On the contrary, the order of reality is that wisdom, and therefore justice and protection, proceed from Yahweh. The teaching is not about Yahweh *and* the world order but about Yahweh's mind *as* the world order. If one longs for understanding the world properly, then he or she has to understand God first, as he is the order of the world. God is the reality. As Prov 9:10 puts it, 'the knowledge of the Holy One is understanding' (דעת קדשים בינה). That is, knowing God means understanding reality properly. It is noteworthy that this equation, at least in 9:10, works only one way, from God to the world. It does not claim that knowing the world means knowing God. The 'knowledge of the Holy One' is a definite noun phrase and as such more determined than the indefinite 'understanding,' consequently it is the subject and 'understanding' is the predicate of this nominal sentence.[74]

Therefore, though Proverbs 2 can be understood as recommending that the reader know the 'world order' properly, this knowledge is somewhat different from what the connotation of the expression 'world order' might suggest at first sight. It is knowing a person, namely Yahweh, and this knowledge is expressed by a humble, trustful, servant-like relationship to him.

9.3.3.2 Trust

However, one might still ask why the God-centred worldview of Proverbs 2 makes self-interest 'ordinate.' Can one not use his or her knowledge of God-centred reality, even his or her trustful relationship to Yahweh, for achieving selfish aims? Although this seems to be a viable option, the nature of trust will not allow it.

Trusting despite the temptation of easy, though unethical, success is not convenient. Trusting in the face of imminent danger is hard, hence the need for frequent promises of security in Proverbs and the often emphatic encouragement to trust in God (3:5, 21-26; 16:20; 22:19; 23:17-18; 28:25-26; 29:25). It is not an accident that Thomas connected trust and hope with the virtue of courage (*ST* II–II, 129, 6; *ST* I–II, 23, 3; *ST* I–II, 45, 1–2; *ST* I–II, 40, 4). Or, as a scholar of the Hebrew Bible, Levenson writes:

> Though the persistence of evil seems to undermine the magisterial claims of the creator-God, it is through submission to exactly those claims that the good order that is creation comes into being. Like all other faith, creation-faith carries with it enormous risk. Only as

---

8—that it is only visible to faith and not to human intellect: 'Even though we prove by reason that God is one, the fact that He governs all things directly or that He wishes to be worshipped in some particular way, is a matter relating to faith' (*CT, 2, 246*). Nevertheless, though recognising Thomas's complex thought and its debated interpretation, since I am not an expert on Thomas, I refrain from arriving at a verdict on this issue.

74. For the differentiation between subject and predicate in Hebrew nominal sentences, see Dyk and Talstra 1999: 133–185.

the enormity of the risk is acknowledged can the grandeur of the faith be appreciated.[75]

To use the philosophical terminology of Charles Taylor, being wise and trusting in the Lord is a 'strong evaluation' that restricts 'preferences' that involve direct personal satisfaction.[76] So, though in a sense being wise (i.e., trustful) for the sake of security is a self-interested act, in concrete cases it might involve courageously giving up one's control over one's situation. The way to security might lead through seeming insecurity.

The opposite of trust in God in Proverbs is not so much 'doubt' in God (which is seldom mentioned if at all, at least not explicitly) but trust in oneself (cf. 3:5 vs 3:7; 28:25-26.) No wonder the reader of Proverbs is so often reminded about the dangers of pride. In the case of pride we can see similar dynamics to what we have just seen in connection with trust: one has to give up something to attain it. In order to acquire honour, one has to give up control over it, e.g., by avoiding boasting, that is, actively and explicitly trying to acquire honour. Human control (i.e., boasting) is less effective, yet it requires integrity and trust in God to avoid it. Thus, the theoretically shrewd calculation of not boasting in order to get honour is, in practical terms, a very hard lesson in character formation. We can say that, in a paradoxical way, appropriate self-interest is nothing else than giving up the self.

It is noteworthy in connection with pride and the lack of trust in God that Thomas maintains that 'it amounts to the same thing whether pride or self-love be called the beginning of all sin' (*ST* I–II, 84, 2, ad. 3). Both pride and inordinate self-love represent a self-centred way of thinking instead of a God-centred one. This means that both pride and inordinate self-love are expressed in contempt for God, in lack of willingness to submit or listen to him.[77] The similarity between the thinking of Thomas and Proverbs is shown by Proverbs' frequent condemnations of the same behavioural pattern, namely mocking, pride, not listening to divine and human correction, feeling contempt for the Lord and (divine) wisdom (Prov 1:22; 3:34; 8:13; 9:7-8; 13:1; 14:2, 6; 15:12; 16:5, 18-19; 18:12; 19:29; 21:24; etc.) and also by the connection between humble listening and fear of the Lord, which we have observed above (pages 142–143).

9.3.3.3   Action

Understanding God-centred reality and trusting in God is also expressed in action. In connection with this point I have argued that the theological interpreta-

---

75. Levenson 1988: 156.
76. C. Taylor, 'What is Human Agency?' in T. Mischel (ed.), *The Self* (Oxford: Blackwell, 1977) 103–135; C. Taylor, *Human Agency and Language* (Cambridge: Cambridge University Press, 1985); C. Taylor, *Philosophy and the Human Sciences* (Cambridge: Cambridge University Press, 1985); all of these works are referred to in Chapman 2000: 94.
77. See *ST* I–II, 84, 2. See also Stump 2003: 438–439, 441.

tion of the idea of natural law, which places the emphasis not on its independence from divine revelation but on its identity with God's mind, is very much in line with the *imitatio dei* theme in Proverbs 2. According to this interpretation of Thomas and the teaching of Proverbs 2, acting in harmony with reality (i.e., behaving wisely) is crucial precisely because it connects one to God through imitating him and participating in his providence.

The vision of wisely 'self-interested' actions that connect one to God opens up the possibility of seeking wisdom not primarily because it provides security—and, only as a by-product, connects to God. On the contrary, it might encourage one to seek wisdom primarily because it connects to God—and, only as a by-product, provides security. The investigation of this possibility belongs to Thomas's second criterion for considering God as the highest end.

9.4 Is Proverbs against Serving God for the Benefits of It?

Aquinas's tenet of not serving God for its benefits seems straightforward at first sight. Similarly, in the light of my earlier discussion it also seems clear that Proverbs does build on those benefits in its motivational system. Therefore, Thomas and Proverbs are apparently in disagreement about this point. In this section I argue that both statements about the thought of Thomas and Proverbs are oversimplifications and that it is possible to read Proverbs in a Thomistic frame of reference though not necessarily the way Thomas himself read it.

Thomas recognised that the Bible itself often gives the impression that a proper relationship with God could be motivated by its benefits. To handle the issue he utilised Aristotle's complex theory of causation.[78] In order to understand Aquinas's thinking at this point it is necessary to quote him at length:

> Is God to be loved because of himself? . . . The term, *because of*, signifies some kind of causal relationship. Now there are four kinds of cause: final, formal, efficient, and material, the last including material dispositions also, which are not causes simply speaking in a qualified sense. It is in terms of these then that we say that a thing is loved because of something else: thus, medicine because of health—final cause; a man because of virtue—formal cause, for it is virtue that makes him formally good and consequently lovable; others because they are the children of some particular father—efficient cause. But in terms of a disposition, which for our purposes comes to the same as a material cause, we talk about loving something because of what disposes us to love it, as for example favours received; and this holds after we have already begun to love, even though then it is not because of such favours that we love a friend, but because of his worth.

---

78. Charlton 1970: 28–31 (*Physics* II, 3, 194^{b}16-195^{b}30). A succinct summary of Aristotle's theory can be found in Falcon 2011, or in Grant 1952: 29–33, or in Adams 2010: 8.

> As to the first three ways, then, it must be said that we do not love God because of anything else, but because of himself alone. For, being himself the last end of all things, there is no other end to which he is subordinate; nor does he need any other form to make him good, since his very substance is his goodness and the exemplar of all other goods; nor does his goodness derive from another, rather is he the source of whatever goodness there is in everything else. But if we consider the fourth way, then God can be loved because of something else; for we are disposed by other things to advance in loving him, for example by favours already received, by the rewards we hope for, or by the punishments which, by his help, we purpose to avoid.[79]

As it can be seen in this lengthy quotation, Aristotle's concept of causation, which Thomas follows, is very different from the modern understanding. Today the word 'cause' usually refers to an event that precedes its effect. In Aristotle's and Thomas's thought it has a wider meaning. According to them, a system of causes answers all of the possible 'why questions.'[80] The Aristotalian-Thomistic 'cause' could be rendered in contemporary English as 'reasons for the being of X' or 'the thing which is in any way responsible for X.'[81]

According to Aristotle, all aspects of the existence and nature of a being can be explained through four factors (causes). For example, a particular statue exists because it has material (material cause), because it has a distinct form (formal cause), because the sculptor made it (efficient cause), and for the purpose of decoration (final cause).

There is much in Aristotle's (and Thomas's) theory of causation that would require elucidation, but for our limited purposes it suffices if we concentrate on the material cause. According to Aristotle's theory, without a material cause nothing exists, as everything has some kind of matter.[82] Thomas would not agree completely with Aristotle in this as, according to him, angels, for example, are non-material beings. Nevertheless, Aristotle's observation applies to our love of God, says Thomas, as it is made of something. Thomas argues that, in a sense, the only real explanation for our love of God is God himself, since God is the formal, efficient, and final cause of our love for him. However, besides these three, most important causes, our love towards God also has a 'material cause,' even if this 'cause' does not play a comparable role to the other three causes in explaining our love.

According to Thomas, the material from which this love is made is our disposition to love God because of the possible rewards. But if this is so, then how can Thomas say that in the most decisive sense the love of God is not because of

---

79. *ST* II–II, 27, 3.
80. 'We do not think that we know anything unless we grasp the "why", which is to grasp the cause.' *Com. Physics* II, 5, 176.
81. Derksen 2011; Charlton 1970: 98.
82. Grant 1952: 30.

rewards? It seems to me that Thomas's answer to this question can be found at the end of the first paragraph of the above quoted section, where he says that 'we talk about loving something because of what disposes us to love it, as for example favours received; and this holds after we have already begun to love, even though then it is not because of such favours that we love a friend.' Here he says that the disposition of loving for favour precedes 'real' love, which does not think of favours any more—yet, that 'real' love is still caused by the original, 'selfish' disposition in a certain sense, even when the disposition has already changed.

But then in what sense is this disposition still the material of the later, mature love if its 'selfish' nature is not present anymore? At this point a statement of Thomas from one of his other works might shed some light on the problem. In his commentary on Aristotle's *Physics*, while discussing the nature of the material cause, he uses the example of flour. He argues that though we say that flour is the material of bread, the flour in the bread looks rather different from what it used to look like before baking. By receiving a new form, the nature of flour changes, yet, it is still the flour from which the bread is made.[83] Maybe the same picture could also be used here to explain our quotation: just like the flour in the bread is in a changed form, so the original 'selfish' disposition of love of God gains a new form in the final, mature love: it does not look at rewards any more, yet, there is a continuum between that later disposition and the former one—just like the flour in the bread, though dissimilar, is still the same flour that the bread has originally been made from.

Whatever explanation we provide for the not always clear logic of the above quotation, its general gist seems to be clear enough: having the material of the love of God (i.e., the disposition of loving him for rewards) does not equal the *proper* love of God, but it is an essential prerequisite for it.

This idea fits the wider context of Thomas's thought. Happiness, for Thomas, meant contemplating God and becoming like God as much as possible (*ST* II–II, 19, 7). For reaching perfection in this, one needs God's grace, for God has to implant into one certain virtues (faith, hope, love). However, this does not mean complete passivity on the human's part. Humans can acquire certain dispositions (a broad category that includes virtues, see *ST* I-II, 49, 1-4), in other words acquire the matter that can receive the perfect form provided by God (that is, perfect, unselfish love of God). This acquisition of 'matter' means forming our dispositions and in this formation reward and punishment can play an important role.[84]

Put simply, Aquinas talks about perfect and imperfect love, and he presupposes a learning process during which human beings first have to develop vir-

---

83. 'Flour is called the matter of bread, but not insofar as it stands under the form of flour.' *Com. Physics* II, 5, 184. See also Aquinas 1963–1981, vol. XXII (1964), 124–125, Appendix 8.
84. Besides *ST* II–II, 27, 3, see also *ST* II–II, 17, 8.

tues (learn the imperfect love) in order that they can receive the gift of the perfect love from God. During this learning process they are motivated by reward and punishment.

Therefore, for Thomas, interpreting Proverbs did not pose a serious problem. He eventually explained the whole Bible according to this theory, claiming that the Old Testament contains many references to rewards because it is written mainly for the formation of largely 'unformed' people. However, he notes that there were a few rather virtuous people already in the time of the Old Testament and in order to provide them with 'spiritual food,' not all of the Old Testament passages are full of earthly motivations. Similarly, there were people during the New Testament times who were still quite 'unformed,' which is why we occasionally find New Testament passages that motivate by reward and punishment (*ST* I–II, 107, 1; *ST* I–II, 91, 5).[85]

Thomas also understood the Bible's teaching about the fear of the Lord in the same educational context. He stated that fear of God is the beginning of wisdom in two senses (*ST* II–II, 19, 7). First, a person fears punishment, and this fear motivates him or her to behave well, and, consequently, a good character begins to be formed in that person. As he or she becomes receptive through this process, God provides the gift of wisdom to him or her. This wisdom will produce a fear that is not a fear of punishment anymore but a fear of getting separated from God. The first fear was a fear of a slave who was afraid of punishment, the second is a fear of a son who loves his father and longs to be with him (*ST* II–II, 19, 4; *ST* II–II, 19, 10). This way, the first fear is the beginning of wisdom in the sense that it leads to wisdom; the second fear is the beginning of wisdom in the sense that it is the first effect of it (*ST* II–II, 19, 7).[86]

Even if one accepts Thomas's general theory of the role of reward and punishment, some of its specific points seem to be questionable. Concerning the fear of the Lord, there is no textual indication that there are two distinct types of it. This, of course, does not necessarily mean that one cannot interpret the phrase along these lines. (Indeed, it is striking how similar Thomas's understanding of the two types of fear of the Lord is to Fox's interpretation of Prov 2:5).[87] It only means that the support for this interpretation is in a frame of reference which is

---

85. This, however, does not mean that the scholastics neglected the Old Testament completely. See Porter's insightful account of the scholastics' respectful handling of the Old Testament (which, however, might to some extent downplay the developmental scheme of the Old Testament—New Testament relationship explained above): Porter 2002: 226–243.

86. How much the first, servile fear is only a preparation and how much it is already an effect of charity is not always clear in Thomas's discussion. However, a detailed discussion of this question belongs to the field of Thomistic studies and as such goes beyond the scope of this work. Thomas's differentiation between two different fears follows an old tradition of interpretation of the fear of God. See Bede's interpretation in Wright 2005: 7.

87. See discussion on pages 140–141.

outside of the text. Nevertheless, I would prefer to keep the unified but open-ended notion of 'fear of the Lord' instead of dividing it into filial fear and servile fear. This is why I used the image of a servant, something that is beyond the text of Proverbs though explicitly used in other biblical texts and indirectly supported by Proverbs, too. This image is capable of drawing out many implications of the text while at the same time keeping the phrase's unity and ambiguity.[88] This way, the particular connotations of the phrase are always dependent on the immediate context. This raises the question of whether there are two different types of contexts. In other words, is Thomas right in his differentiation between the more reward-focused (mainly) Old Testament texts and the more God-focused (mainly) New Testament texts?

Thomas's understanding of the Old Testament as suitable for 'less formed' people is not dissimilar to the theological framework in which some nineteenth century scholars tried to make sense of the book of Proverbs. One wonders, however, if it is a presupposition rather than a conclusion. Of course, one could argue that the New Testament puts a stronger emphasis on *heavenly* rewards, but it is not clear that there are significantly fewer New Testament passages referring to rewards than Old Testament passages. It is enough to read through the Sermon on the Mount, one of Thomas's texts from which he deduces what counts as inordinate self-interest, to see how often the New Testament refers to rewards and punishment (Matt 5:4, 5, 6, 7, 19, 25, 46; 6:1, 4, 6, 14-15, 18, 33; 7:1-2).[89]

Instead of following Thomas in dividing biblical texts (and fear of the Lord) into two groups, I would rather suggest that biblical texts (and fear of the Lord) can be often interpreted in two ways. The Sermon on the Mount teaches, first, that one should seek the righteousness of God and his kingdom, and, second, that God will then provide. On the one hand, this can easily be read as saying that one should take God as the final end of one's life. On the other hand it is not impossible that one would be attracted to this God-seeking lifestyle through the texts's promise of security.

Similarly, many other biblical texts can be read on these two levels. To take a New Testament example first, Philippians 2 (in combination with Philippians 3

---

88. Referring to the fear of the Lord in a biblical context as the attitude of a servant does not necessarily mean an inferior, servile fear, in the Thomistic sense—see Philippians 2 in which Christ became the servant thereby providing the pattern one should follow. עבד יהוה is also an honorific term in the Old Testament (cf. Deut 34:5; Judg 2:8; Ps 18:1; Isa 5:17).

89. Many verses that speak about 'entering the Kingdom of God' or receiving an undefined reward from God are not listed above (e.g., 5:3, 10, 12, 22, 29-30; 7:7-12, 21) as they could more readily be interpreted by Thomas as referring to union with God (though modern NT exegesis would probably question this interpretation in many of these cases). For a similar evaluation of the New Testament's motivational system, see Lewis 1941: 263.

where Paul's 'personal testimony' represents his appropriation of Philippians 2)[90] encourages the reader to leave behind his or her status and empty him- or herself in order to imitate Christ and become a true servant of God. However, at the end, it promises exaltation if one does so (Phil 2:9-11; 3:21). When turning to the Old Testament, we find that Abraham, a paradigmatic God-fearer of the Bible (Gen 22:12), is indeed willing to give God everything—but because of this willingness, God promises him blessing in the end (Gen 22:16-18). Job, another God-fearer, was tested to see whether he feared God for the sake of benefits coming from God (Job 1:1. 9).[91] But again, in the epilogue to the book, we read about the rich blessings Job gains from God for enduring the test (42:12-17). Solomon did not ask for riches and honour but for wisdom—however, God gave him riches and honour because he did not ask for them (1 Kgs 3:10-14). These texts suggest that Christ, Abraham, Job, and Solomon did not fear God for his blessings. The mention of the gains usually comes at the very end, sometimes (as in Job) rather as an afterthought and not as the main message of the text. However, the reader of (the final form) of their stories *can* argue that knowing the whole picture, it is worth serving God because it pays, eventually.

Thus, in a sense, many 'higher texts,'[92] which are supposedly written for the virtuous people, are more ambiguous than Thomas would like to admit. But one should also recognise that this ambiguity is equally true for texts supposedly written for 'beginners.' These texts might appear as detailed outworkings of the 'afterthought' in the story of Job. Proverbs, for example, clearly stresses the '. . . and God will provide' part. Yet, I have argued that the 'seek his righteousness and kingdom' is not missing either. Proverbs 2, besides highlighting the benefits of knowing God and being righteous, offers a vision of being similar to God and serving him by partaking in his providence. As it is possible that the reader of Philippians 2–3, Genesis 22, Job, or 1 Kings is motivated by the benefits and not by the interest-free communion with God, so it is possible that the reader of Proverbs 2 is mainly influenced by this vision of imitating God and not by the benefits themselves. In other words, just to refer back to the introductory thoughts of Part III, Proverbs is not only attractive to those who live in low existential security (as described by Pippa Norris and Ronald Inglehart), but it can also provide satisfying spiritual food for the members of a 'higher religion' (as described by Casanova, Taylor, and Lash).[93]

---

90. Moberly 2006: 175.
91. Moberly 2000: 84–88.
92. Or texts representing 'higher forms of religion,' to refer back to the discussion of Inglehart, Taylor, Casanova, and Lash in the Introduction to Part III.
93. See discussion on pages 88–90.

9.5 Conclusions

We have seen that self-interest plays a crucial role in Proverbs. The book motivates the reader towards good behaviour by promising (mainly) material and/or external goods for it. The beneficial effects of wise behaviour are not only recognised but they are at the focus of the book's argument. This is why it is problematic to overcome the problem by simple reference to the order of the creation.

We have also seen that Thomas Aquinas had a lot to say about self-interest. However, he differentiated between good self-interest and inordinate selfishness. According to Thomas, self-interest is legitimate as long as

- it is aimed at self-preservation;
- justice, as a community-oriented virtue, complements self-interested prudence;
- the spiritual self is loved more than the material self;
- there is a hierarchy of ends: higher human ends (community and God) modify the lower ones (self-preservation)

As Proverbs used to be 'accused' of being *eudaemonistic* because of its 'selfishness,' and Thomistic moral theology is an *eudaemonistic* system (that is, it claims that 'happiness' is the appropriate human end), a comparison of the two might shed some light on Proverbs. Is it possible to interpret Proverbs in a Thomistic frame of reference? Can we find the same or at least similar qualifying factors in Proverbs' teaching about self-interest as in Thomas's moral theology? The answer to these questions seems to be a qualified 'yes.'

There are significant differences between the thought of Thomas and Proverbs: there is no sign of a heavenly reward in the book of Proverbs; there is also no clear sign of Thomas's two types of fear of God in it; Proverbs does not know about a differentiation between a perfect, heavenly and an imperfect, earthly knowledge of God; Proverbs does not teach that the moral order can be discovered purely through rational investigation (though it is questionable how much Thomas teaches this).

On the other hand, there are also many similarities: wisdom means having a certain worldview; having the right worldview is expressed by right action; being prudent means participation in providence, imitating God; speaking about reality means speaking about God's mind. These and other similarities provide ground for a 'Thomistic' interpretation of Proverbs. So, in the light of all these, how does Proverbs comply with the four Thomistic checks on self-interest?

9.5.1 Does Proverbs Focus on Self-Preservation?

Yes, but only partly. We have seen that there is a very strong emphasis on 'survival' which is, however, sometimes overshadowed in commentaries by an emphasis on 'success.' Nonetheless, it is undeniable that Proverbs puts stronger emphasis on material/external success (i.e., riches, honour) than Thomas does.

9.5.2 Does Justice Complement and Regulate Self-Interest?

Yes, it does. 'Justice' and 'righteousness' are key notions in Proverbs that characterise God, the king, and the wise person equally.

9.5.3 Is the Spiritual Self More Loved than the Material Self?

No, it is not. Physical well-being is not so neatly divided from spiritual well-being in Old Testament thinking as it is in Thomistic thinking. This seems to be the main difference between Thomas and Proverbs. However, a partial parallel even to this Thomistic division might be found, for the 'better than' sayings reveal the non-material side (mainly peace) of happiness.

9.5.4 Does Proverbs Speak about a Hierarchy of Ends?

Yes, but the parallel between Thomas and Proverbs is only partial. Thomas's moral theology is a well developed system, Proverbs is not. Proverbs does not offer an explicit, systematic hierarchy of ends. However, it does provide a plurality of ends. Furthermore, even if these ends are not ordered clearly and explicitly into a strict hierarchy, there are certain hints in the text that point in the direction of such a hierarchy, or at least make it easy for the interpreter to read Proverbs in harmony with a Thomistic hierarchy. For example, as I have just mentioned, though there might be a stronger emphasis on material interests in Proverbs than in Thomas's writings, the 'better than' sayings teach that 'happiness' is the main aim and this does not necessarily involve financial well-being. Furthermore, though Proverbs might be written for and about individuals, it is not 'individualistic.' The community plays an important role in it, as is clear from the emphasis on righteousness and justice. Thus, the end of self-preservation is accompanied and regulated by the ends of spiritual well-being and communal well-being.

With regard to the highest end, can we say that Proverbs requires the reader to see God as the final end of his/her life? Thomas offers two criteria for deciding if this is so. One of them teaches that one should have a God-centred thinking, hope, and trust. Proverbs satisfies this criterion, as it clearly presents a God-centred worldview. It also speaks about a trust in God that involves a rejection of using unethical, though seemingly effective tools. Therefore, although the book promises security, the way to it is through wrestling with (apparent) insecurity. This underlies the emphasis on the relationship with God as opposed to simple emphasis on self-preservation.

Thomas's other criterion for seeing God as the highest end, namely that one should not pursue God because of its benefits, is a trickier one. Thomas has suggested that there are two types of biblical texts: one that clearly teaches this criterion; and one that motivates through offering rewards in order to form the character of the reader. Instead of this division between biblical texts, I have suggested that most (if not all) biblical texts can be read in two ways. Indeed, this is what one, who thinks in the paradigm of Thomas's *eudaemonism*, would expect. After all, according to this paradigm, what is good is also beneficial. If a text is true to reality, it must describe both sides of this relationship, and the reader can stress one or the other in his or her reading. Consequently, Proverbs can be read in two ways. It can be understood as teaching that a person should be with God because it will serve the other ends, but it does not have to be read like this. The vision of being in the presence of God and imitating him is there, and it can motivate the reader by itself.

If one decides to interpret Proverbs in a Thomistic framework, then her/his interpretation will inevitably emphasise the 'serving God' and the 'imitation of God' themes in the book. Such an approach will give a slightly larger prominence to the theme of the God–human relationship than is usual in many interpretations of Proverbs. This emphasis raises again the second issue that was highlighted at the end of Part I: the issue of secularity. How is a Thomistic emphasis on God as the final end able to handle those parts of Proverbs that are mainly interested in mundane everyday life? I address this question, among many others, in the next part.

PART IV
'THE SECULAR' IN PROVERBS

10

The Meaning of 'Secular'

10.1 The Meaning of 'Secular' in General Academic Discourse

Let us consider the following three examples of the usage of the word 'secular' in connection with wisdom literature:

> That wisdom, a secular concept, should become a component of both Testaments of the Bible is due to the fact that it is inherent in creation—more specifically, human creation.[1]

> Proverbs presents a special challenge to anyone who raises questions about theology. It is often dismissed as being 'secular,' and it may be inferred, not really theological.[2]

> Are they [the Yahweh sayings] to be seen as moral formation in a religious manner, or as religious education, or are they simply chance references in a substantially secular set of proverbs of a generally ethical nature?[3]

What I would like to direct our attention to is not so much the content of these statements but the relative ease with which they use the word 'secular.' None of the quoted works provide a thorough definition of the term, and this represents the general trend in commentaries of biblical wisdom literature with only a few exceptions. This unreflected use of the word by biblical scholars is

---

1. Westermann 1995: 1.
2. Murphy 2001: 5.
3. Dell 2006: 106.

remarkable given that philosophers, sociologists, and philosophical theologians fill hundreds of pages in their works with clarifying its meaning. Therefore, if someone wants to analyse the issues concerning Proverbs' supposed secularity, the first task is to find out what exactly biblical scholars mean when they use the word 'secular.'

However, before that, it will be useful to have a look at how the word is used in the broader academic discourse. The word 'secular' comes from Latin *saeculum* which originally meant 'time' or 'age.' In the Middle Ages it was often used in opposition to *regular* (religious). The *regular* clergy belonged to a monastic order, that is, lived 'closer' to eternity, whereas the *secular* clergy lived in 'this time.' Thus, 'secular' means 'our time,' 'this worldly time' as opposed to eternity.[4]

This basic meaning of the word which opposes 'temporal' and 'eternal' or 'worldly' and 'heavenly' is nuanced further in the academic discourse of the last one hundred years, mainly due to sociological investigations of the so-called 'secularisation' of western societies. In order to make the topic searchable and the results quantifiable sociologists had to come up with more refined definitions of 'secular' than simply 'this worldly.' If they wanted to measure 'worldliness' they had to clarify precisely what they were measuring. 'Secularisation' and consequently 'secular' came to be defined according to one or a combination of the following three factors:

A. **The decline of reference to the divine in public space**, as expressed in the careful separation of religious and non-religious institutions like the church and the state.
B. **The decline of attention to the divine in private life**, as shown by the drop of church attendance or the time spent on prayer by individuals.
C. **The decline of 'mythical,' 'enchanted,' 'sacral' human thinking**, defined as rationalisation which resulted in the 'disenchantment' of the world. 'Properly secularised' modern people are not supposed to count on unpredictable, supernatural forces in their practical planning or scientific thinking, even if they are religious people otherwise.[5]

At first sight all of these definitions seem to be anachronistic in connection with ancient Near Eastern societies and their literary products. State and church were not separated as they are in post-enlightenment countries, and it is also hard to imagine that devotion of some kind and counting on supernatural forces

---

4. Taylor 2007: 54–55; see also Boer 2010: 1.
5. I am following Charles Taylor's classification of the definitions of 'secular'; he mentions the first two definitions. I am adding the third one which, for me, does not seem to be included in the first two but has also been playing a significant role in defining the 'secular' since the appearance of Max Weber's works. Weber made the 'disenchantment' of the world (or, to translate the German *Entzauberung* more precisely, 'the losing of its magic') a major topic in the works about secularisation. See Aldridge 2000; Sherry 2000: 66–67; Weber 1976: 105; Weber 1989: 3–31.

164   Toward an Interpretation of the Book of Proverbs

did not play a significant role in the everyday life and thinking of ancient Near Eastern people.[6] Nevertheless, as we will see shortly, these definitions are not without parallels in some biblical scholars' understanding of the 'secular' in the book of Proverbs.

10.2 The Meaning of 'Secular' in Biblical Scholarship

As most biblical scholars do not give a succinct definition of 'secular,' one has to decipher their understanding of the term from the context in which they are using it. Given the vast amount of literature and the limits of this work, a comprehensive investigation is impossible. This also means that my selection of texts is somewhat subjective. It is important to note that I do not even claim that my results are always representative of the whole work of the scholar I am quoting below as many scholars use the word 'secular' with various meanings throughout their works. I concentrate only on the concrete quotations themselves. Nevertheless, the excerpts in Table 9 are taken from a diverse collection of contributors to scholarly discussion, who often represent contradictory views on the subject, so, even if the range of quotations is far from being comprehensive, they cover, I hope, most typical usages of the word 'secular.'

All of the quotations in Table 9 are taken from works written on Proverbs (or on biblical wisdom literature but referring to Proverbs). The words most relevant for our purposes are printed in bold. The right column does not summarise the meaning of the quotations but tries to capture the meaning and/or the connotations of the word 'secular' in the quotation regardless of whether the particular author thinks that the word describes Proverbs properly or not.

TABLE 9: The use of the word 'secular' by biblical wisdom scholars

Author	Text	Meaning and Connotations of 'Secular'
Bossman, D. M.	Although the modern age did not invent secularity, it did enable secularity to flourish. In turn, **moderns were freed, by secularity, from non-rational bonds that had too long restrained human endeavors through lack of accurate knowledge and the imposition of substitute fictions.** The Bible's own brand of secularity may be a distinguishing characteristic of some of the **Wisdom Literature that has frequently discom-**	Rationalisation, no fictions

---

6. Of course, even using the modern terms 'state' and 'church' in connection with ancient Near Eastern societies is anachronistic as neither of these existed as such.

Author	Text	Meaning and Connotations of 'Secular'
	forted some religionists for its this-world realism.[7]	This-world realism
Brueggemann, W.	Both Cox and van Leeuwen find in the central biblical symbols of Torah, creation, exodus, and Sinai the handles by which we may understand secularization and which in part have been an impetus to it. But it is equally clear that these symbols (with that of creation excepted) really **belong themselves to a sacral view of reality in which the *intrusion* and authority of the holy in the realm of human affairs causes the decisive turn.** . . . I believe it is much more plausible to suggest that in the wisdom tradition of Israel we have a visible expression of secularization as it has been characterised in the current discussions. **Wisdom teaching is profoundly secular in that it presents life and history as a human enterprise.** . . . Thus, wisdom is concerned with enabling potential leaders to *manage* responsibly, effectively, and successfully. It **consistently places stress on human freedom, accountability, the importance of making decisions**, and using power prudently and intelligently.[8]	No sacral view of reality Presents life as human enterprise Stress on human freedom and responsibility
	While expressed in mythological form **it [creation faith] is secular because it is concerned with the primacy and dominance of man over his world.** Though this tradition is cast in the form of myth, its drive and intent are linked to wisdom: **it is concerned with the freedom, power, and responsibility of man** to manage his world.[9]	Concerned with the freedom, power, and responsibility of man
Clements, R. E.	**Wisdom's concepts and images of the physical world accord with a broader, more secular, and more universal**	Universal

---

7. Bossman 2001: 2.
8. Brueggemann 1972: 81–82.
9. Brueggemann 1972: 83.

Author	Text	Meaning and Connotations of 'Secular'
	portrayal of it than that which the cultus offered.... For the cultus, Israel's existence as a nation, its occupation of a specific territory, and its ability to ward off the threatening powers of darkness and uncleanness, all formed part of one single continuum. **This belonged within a comprehensive mythological world-view which was focused on the institutions and rituals of the cultus.**[10]	No cultic worldview No mythological worldview
	So **wisdom has begun a process of systematizing ideas on the themes of virtue and well being which had not previously formed part of any system. On the contrary, ideas of uncleanness, abomination, evil, violence and disease had all belonged to a very confused and ill-defined world of what threatened danger and harm to the unprincipled or unwary....** The very fact that such notions subsume and greatly modify earlier notions which were directly related to cultic activity fully bears out our main contention that **wisdom had begun a process of 'de-sanctifying' and 'de-mystifying' a number of basic areas of human understanding.** These had previously largely been the province of the priesthood and cultus. **In the urgent necessity to cater for the daily life of Jews** which could no longer rely on immediate and direct access to the sanctuary of the temple and the ministry of its priests a process of **'secularising' and isolating from cultic activity** had been set in train.[11]	No confused and ill-defined worldview No cultic activity De-sanctifying and de-mystifying Catering for daily life
Crenshaw J. L.	Thus Hartmut Gese writes: 'It is well known that the wisdom literature constitutes an alien body in the world of the Old Testament.' This verdict is substantiated by reference to **an absence of (1) a**	No covenant relationship with God

10. Clements 1992: 57.
11. Clements 1992: 83–84.

Author	Text	Meaning and Connotations of 'Secular'
	covenant relationship with God, (2) any account of the revelation at Sinai, and (3) a concept of Israel's special election and consequently of Yahweh's saving deeds for his people. Instead, wisdom is said to be directed toward the individual, and consequently to break down all national limits. Gese concludes that 'from the point of view of Yahwism wisdom can only appear as wholly secular.'[12]	No Sinai revelations No salvation history Focus on individuals, no national limits
	Much early wisdom appears to have been remarkably 'secular' in mood and content; its fundamental purpose was to encapsulate **precious observations about reality for the benefit of posterity. The subject matter is largely domestic; agrarian interests and natural phenomena abound.**[13]	Focus on domestic, agrarian, natural reality
Dell, K. J.	I would argue, therefore, that **the [Yahweh] sayings already existed independently in an oral context before they were placed in their present context. This was not in the service of a Yahwehization process of otherwise 'secular' or even 'foreign' material;** rather, they were placed where they were to reinforce the messages of other Proverbs within a religious context and to give structure to the material as it was formed into literature.[14]	Not mentioning Yahweh Parallel with 'foreign'
	While wisdom, at its roots, springs from an attempt to understand human experience of life, **much of its concern is with relationship with the divine, and there are serious questions whether the word 'secular' is at all appropriate** when	No relationship with the divine

---

12. Crenshaw 1976b: 2; Gese actually does not use the word 'secular' but uses 'Profanität' (profane) (Gese 1958: 2). However, the two words do seem to be interchangeable in the context of his discussion, but even if they are not, the quotation represents how Crenshaw has understood the word 'secular.'
13. Crenshaw 1976b: 24.
14. Dell 2006: 117.

Author	Text	Meaning and Connotations of 'Secular'
	referring to wisdom literature, which is grounded in experience of God and the created world.[15]	
Perdue, L.	**Efforts to view the early wise as secularistic humanists who functioned within an international setting devoid of doctrinaire theologies** fail to take into consideration the fact that the concepts of order as justice, God as creator, and God as the overseer of the principle of retribution point to a religious, theological foundation to wisdom thinking, and that **the wise of the major cultures of the ancient Near East, at least with respect to cult, do engage in certain cultic ideas and practices which are unique to their own cultures.**[16]	International No doctrinaire theology No cultic activity
von Rad, G.	Thus, since **the objects of this search for knowledge were of a secular kind, questions about man's daily life,** systematic reflection on them was held to be a secular occupation. . . . **If one reads over these and other sentences, one sees at once that wisdom and the acquiring of it is here a human activity which is open to everyone.** . . . The intellectual curiosity of old wisdom, its cultural impetus and the zeal with which **it studied the corresponding cultural achievements of other nations** stands in considerable contrast to the spirituality of the pre-monarchical period, even of the period of Saul. Whether we speak of **a process of secularization starting fairly suddenly, of the discovering of man, that is of a humanization,** or of the beginning of a rational search for knowledge, at any rate this strong, intellectual movement must have been preceded by **an inner decline, the disintegration of** an understanding of reality	Focus on daily life Open to everyone, to other cultures, too Humanisation

---

15. Dell 2006: 127–128.
16. Perdue 1977: 227 n. 7.

Author	Text	Meaning and Connotations of 'Secular'
	which we can describe, in a felicitous expression of M. Buber's, as **'pan-sacralism.'** . . . There are . . . narratives which stand wholly on the earlier side of this great intellectual upheaval. We are afforded interesting insights by the comprehensive narrative which depicts one stage of Saul's military involvement with the Philistines (I Sam. 13f.). If one follows the fairly complicated course of events, it becomes immediately clear that the narrator **brings every decisive event, military advantages and setbacks as well as all human conflicts, into association with the world of the sacral and the ritual.**[17]	Decline of 'pan-sacralism' No focus on the sacral and the ritual
Westermann, C.	[Writing about the supposedly older sayings of Proverbs.] **The Creator** has entrusted his creature, the human, with this gift [the book of Proverbs] because he **reckons him capable of finding his way through the world, using the special endowment given to him of understanding his own humanness. Proverbs ascribe the importance to the human intellect that it is due. They express an autonomy that is rooted in creatureliness**, in contradistinction to a conception that places too great an emphasis on education and instruction. . . . 27:20: 'As Hades and the abyss are never satisfied, neither are the eyes of man.' . . . One initially marvels that such a 'worldly' appearing statement is found in the Bible. . . . We can only conclude that these people thought and spoke in a much worldlier fashion than it appears to the interpreters and readers of the Old Testament. It is a bold comparison that is being ventured here—'Hades and the abyss'—truly insatiable when we consider the huge number of those who are	Human autonomy

---

17. Von Rad 1972: 57–58.

Author	Text	Meaning and Connotations of 'Secular'
	deceased! ... Even more conspicuous ... is **the seeming absence of any indication of condemnation that might appear in the Christian ethic of many; rather, this phenomenon is viewed as something that is inherently human, whether one perceives it as good or not**. Such an observation applies to all the proverbial statements, especially those about humanity. **They intend to express, not condemn, the nature of being human.**[18]	No ethical condemnation of human nature Pure, human-centred observation
	None of the important dates of this history is mentioned—**neither the flight from Egypt nor the revelation at Sinai nor the covenant; neither the migration into the land nor the law. Very little is spoken of worship to God, while priests and the sanctuary are never mentioned.** Perhaps even more important is that **God never speaks in the proverbs.... Furthermore, nothing is ever spoken to God** (a prayer appears only in a later supplement, 30:7-9).... The reason for this can only be that **the proverbs employ a language of the workaday world, the context of which is to be found only in people relating to one another** ... **The proverbs as such have a universal character**. Proverbs can surface anywhere among humankind, just like accounts of creation or the flood.... [Proverbs mentioning God] have no specifically theological function in an explicitly theological context. Rather, **they speak of God in such a manner as would any person without stepping outside of everyday, secular discourse.**[19]	No salvation history No cultus God never speaks Humans do not speak to God Focus on human relationships Universal Focus on everyday

---

18. The word 'secular' is not used in this quotation, but Westermann uses the word 'worldly.' Westermann 1995: 8–9.

19. Westermann 1995: 129–130.

Author	Text	Meaning and Connotations of 'Secular'
	Wisdom has no place within this basic framework of an Old Testament theology, since **it originally and in reality does not have as its object an occurrence between God and man; in its earlier stages wisdom is overwhelmingly secular**. A theological wisdom develops at a later stage. . . . The theological home of wisdom can be found within the context of human creation; **the creator gives humanity the ability to understand its world and to become oriented within it**.[20]	Not about the relationship between God and humanity Human independence, ability to comprehend the world
Zimmerli, W.	**Differentiation of the purely secular rule of utility,** the moral rule and the religious rule does not depend upon the essence of wisdom; rather, what is significant for it is that it sets all three groups of rules equal and only quantitatively establishes gradations among them.[21]	Measures everything on the basis of utility

For the sake of clarity I list the keywords from the right column of the above table (for the key for underlining, see next page):

Bossman, D. M.   rationalisation, no fictions
                 this-world realism
Brueggemann, W. no sacral view of reality
                 presents life as human enterprise
                 stress on human freedom and responsibility
                 concerned with the freedom, power, and responsibility of man
Clements, R. E. universal
                 no cultic worldview
                 no mythological worldview
                 no confused and ill-defined worldview
                 no cultic activity
                 de-sanctifying and de-mystifying
                 catering for daily life
Crenshaw J. L.   no covenant relationship with God
                 no Sinai revelations
                 no salvation history

---

20. Westermann 1998: 11.
21. Zimmerli 1976a: 204 n. 27.

	focus on individuals, no national limits
	focus on domestic, agrarian, natural reality
Dell, K. J.	not mentioning Yahweh
	parallel with 'foreign'
	no relationship with the divine
Perdue, L.	International
	no doctrinaire theology
	no cultic activity
von Rad, G.	focus on daily life
	open to everyone, to other cultures, too
	humanisation
	decline of 'pan-sacralism'
	no focus on the sacral and the ritual
Westermann, C.	human autonomy
	no ethical condemnation of human nature
	pure, human-centred observation
	no salvation history
	no cultus
	God never speaks
	humans do not speak to God
	focus on human relationships
	universal
	focus on everyday
	not about the relationship between God and humanity
	human independence, ability to comprehend the world
Zimmerli, W.	measures everything on the basis of utility

The different items listed above can be ordered into six groups as I have indicated by the underlining:

1. universal, not nationalistic;
2. human autonomy;
3. focusing on the everyday, ordinary side of life;
4. human-centred;
5. not about the relationship between God and humanity;
6. rational, as opposed to cultic/mythic thinking.

Items 2–5 seem to be contractible for me. This way we get three broad definitions of secular:

א. Secular = universalistic, not national and particularistic thinking (item 1);
ב. Secular = human centred thinking with an emphasis on human autonomy (items 2–5);
ג. Secular = rational, non-sacral, disenchanted thinking (item 6)

There are some parallels between this classification of the definitions of 'secular' and the classification of social scientific definitions delineated earlier.[22]

TABLE 10: Definitions of 'secular' in social scientific and biblical scholarship

Definitions in Biblical Scholarship	Social Scientific Definitions
א: universalistic, not national and particularistic thinking	A: the decline of reference to the divine in public space
ב: human centred thinking with an emphasis on human autonomy	B: the decline of attention to the divine in private life
ג: rational, non-sacral, disenchanted thinking	C: the decline of "mythical," "enchanted," "sacral" human thinking

Category ג is parallel with C and category ב is at least partially parallel with B. The parallel between category א and A might be less obvious at first sight, nevertheless it will be argued shortly that the parallels are not less significant than in the other two cases.

Turning from the classification of definitions to the evaluation of them, category א seems to be the most fitting for describing Proverbs' 'secularity.' After all, such national institutions like 'temple,' 'law,' or 'covenant' are hardly mentioned in it, which gives it a universalistic flavour despite the use of the Tetragrammaton. However, I am not arguing that the authors of Proverbs had 'universalistic' thinking or that Proverbs was originally interpreted in a 'universalistic' way. I am simply claiming that it can appear as such. It is another question if this appearance is historically misleading or not (which I think it is). My questions are, however, not about the historical reality behind the text but about possible theological utilisations of this apparent feature of the text.

I argue in this IV. part of the book that the universalistic, 'secular' appearance does not mean that Proverbs stands in opposition to the rest of the Old Testament. It can easily be read 'canonically' because it fits well into the context of the more national, more 'Jewishly religious' parts of the Old Testament. Read this way it can provide important theological insights for the 'secularised' Christian and Jewish reader in the twenty-first century.

Categories ב and ג seem to be a bit more problematic as descriptions of Proverbs. Can we really call Proverbs 'disenchanted' when it contains such 'enchanted' verses as Prov 3:7-8 which propose a connection between ethics and health: 'Do not be wise in your own eyes, fear the Lord, and depart from evil. It will be healing to your navel and refreshment to your bones';[23] or consider 26:2 which allows for the effectiveness of 'right' curses: 'As a sparrow for wandering

---

22. See page 163.
23. See Whybray's comment: 'Nowhere in the book of Proverbs are health, sickness and longevity attributed to what we should call "natural causes", nor is there any suggestion of medical skill that can give relief to the sick: only God can give life and only God can heal.' Whybray 2002: 170.

and a swallow for flying, so a gratuitous curse will not alight'? Or, to foreshadow a little bit the later discussion, can we really speak about 'human autonomy' when one of the key teachings of Proverbs is about having a humble, obedient, listening heart?

Of course, the refutation or modification of categories ב and ג would require much more than a few dismissive sentences.[24] However, as these interpretations are not as fashionable nowadays, I am going to concentrate instead on a more recent theological reading of Proverbs which, in many ways, is the offspring of these 'old-fashioned' secular interpretations. This theological reading is Walter Brueggemann's treatment of Proverbs in his *Theology of the Old Testament*.

Thus, in the following two chapters I discuss whether Proverbs really offers a secular language in the non-Yahwistic, universalistic sense (category א). Then I look more closely at Brueggemann's more recent interpretation of Proverbs that has developed from his earlier 'secular interpretation' which emphasised mainly the human-centred and disenchanted nature of Proverbs (definitions ב and ג).

---

24. Such a discussion, besides providing a careful reading of some biblical texts, should also include thoroughgoing interaction with influential scholars representing these different views of a 'secular wisdom,' like, for example, Zimmerli for ב (human autonomy) or R. E. Clements for category ג (non-sacral thinking).

11

Secular (Universal) vs. National (Particular) I

11.1 Proverbs and the Common Language of Humanity

The definition that describes the secular as the separation of religious and non-religious institutions, like the separation between church and state, is one of the most influential sociological definitions of the secular.[1] Although it seems to be inapplicable to an ancient Near Eastern society at first sight, there is an aspect of this classic definition which is parallel with the Proverbs-interpretation of some biblical scholars.

Sociologists, politicians, and philosophers often emphasise the importance of the separation between religious and non-religious institutions because it provides a 'common space,' a 'neutral ground' on which non-religious and all sorts of religious people can meet each other. Even if one wants to avoid the controversial word 'neutral,'[2] they can argue that secularity provides a language which is at least understandable to everyone (like the language of the Universal Declaration of Human Rights) and can be a medium through which the negotiation between competing values and interests can happen.[3]

---

1. Taylor 2007: 779 n. 1.
2. See Adams 2009: 154–155; Higton 2009: 147–154; Madeley 2003: 1–22.
3. Clayton 2004: 36–41; see also Charles Taylor's opinion in the debate between him and Jürgen Habermas during a symposium called 'Rethinking Secularism: the Power of Religion in the Public Sphere,' organised by the Institute for Public Knowledge of New York University on 22 October 2009 (Taylor and Habermas 2009). For a discussion of this 'neutral' (i.e. not anti-religious) definition of the 'secular' by biblical scholars, see

Similarly, some biblical scholars emphasise the willingness of the Hebrew sages to listen to other cultures and the universal nature of their language, which is, in its biggest part, applicable, or at least understandable to everyone regardless of his or her worldview. As Crenshaw writes, 'none can deny the universality of wisdom's language and concerns, the timeless problems of human existence and general observations about life.'[4] Claus Westermann concludes his investigation of biblical proverbs by encouraging the reader to follow the impetus of those proverbs and have an understanding and open conversation with other (religious) cultures:

> One manifestation of the universal character of proverbial wisdom is that one can observe a far-reaching agreement among the exhortations and warnings. For example, proverbs found all over the world contain warnings against people who are unable to govern themselves.... The question is whether or not a common understanding of commendable behaviour ... lies at the root of these many common sayings—that is to say, a general 'knowledge of good and evil.' If our awareness of this state of affairs is for the most part lost, then conscious recognition of the possibility that this 'common knowledge' has more in common than not possesses considerable significance for drawing humanity closer together.... The manner in which God is depicted, both as the human and material Creator and as the one who determines the limitations placed on humans, is common to most religions. This is not a phenomenon that separates religions; rather, it unifies them.... Proverbial wisdom retains a certain significance that, in terms of its effects, is accessible to all people. The notion of humanity as a whole is indeed an ingredient of the proverbs of Israel in their universal function. Thus L. Naré: 'Biblical wisdom seems to have been built on the ground of a common human wisdom.'[5]

Westermann certainly has a point here. Even if one doubts that this was the intention of Proverbs' authors, the apparent universal nature of the book could encourage the ancient as well as the modern reader to be engaged in mutual, appreciative conversation with other cultures. However, this is not the only potential impact of the book on the reader. The consequent usage of the Tetragrammaton, the many canonical allusions and the Yahwistic connotations of certain structurally key passages make a different understanding in a canonical interpretation of the book possible, if not more likely. According to this, Proverbs is more about the 'sanctification' of the secular space and language than simply the presentation of it.

Brett 2010: 60 and Davies 2010: 204–205. For the origins of both 'anti-religious' and 'neutral' secularisms, see Turner 2010: XXII.

4. Crenshaw 1976b: 5.

5. Westermann 1995: 132–133; see also von Rad 1972: 57–58 and Lelievre's opinion in Whybray 1995: 132.

In the following sections I investigate two, interrelated reading strategies. The first sees Proverbs in the light of the theological vision offered by Proverbs 8; the second sees Proverbs in the light of the vision of the Jerusalem temple offered by the canonical context of the book. Rather than creating a 'neutral space,' both of these readings encourage the reader to 'sanctify' the 'neutral space' of everyday life.

11.2 Proverbs 8 as Theological Vision

11.2.1 Theories about the Figure of Lady Wisdom

Proverbs 8 provides such a vivid description of Wisdom that I would find it unlikely that it would not influence most readers' interpretation of the following chapters. However, as soon as one tries to go beyond this general statement, problems abound. Who is this Wisdom in chapter 8? What is the nature of her description? What is its theological significance? How does it change the reading of chapters 10–31?

Several ancient goddesses have been suspected of influencing the picture of woman Wisdom in Proverbs 8: unnamed Assyrian and West Semitic goddesses, Inanna, Ishtar, Ashtart or Asherah, *Ma'at*, a divine patroness of scribal education like the Sumerian Nisaba, the Persian Asha Vahishta, Hellenistic Isis, a pregnostic divinity, etc. However, a consensus has not been reached, neither about which of these goddesses influenced the biblical image nor about the measure and nature of this influence. Furthermore, these religio-historical considerations, very interesting though they are from a historical point of view, are usually an end in themselves and do not shed very much light on the role of Wisdom in our received text.[6]

Unfortunately, if we turn to the question of her role and identity in the present form of the text we find an even more confusingly high number of scholarly suggestions. What is she? A 'universal' like a Platonic idea?[7] The aphorisms and sayings of the book?[8] The Torah?[9] A literary figure standing for human/divine

---

6. Baumann 1996: 13–25; Day 2000: 66–67; Fox 2000: 334–338; Handley 1995: 234–243; Murphy 1995: 222–223; Perdue 1994: 88–89; Perdue 2007: 54; Perdue 2008: 108–109, 111–112; Weeks 2007: 89–90; a fuller bibliography can be found in Sinnott 2005: 11–13, 34–51. Not unrelated is the similar debate about the mythological background of Wisdom in Job 28: Coogan 1999: 203–209; Lang 1997: 400–423; Perdue 1991: 245.

7. Fox 2000: 352–356.

8. Murphy 1995: 225.

9. Philip R. Davies tentatively writes that 'Here [Proverbs 1–9] the address given by Dame Wisdom (chap. 8) identifies the secular belief in the rational order of the universe with the divine plan, potentially equating empirically derived knowledge with obedience to the torah.' (Davies 1998: 137). Weeks argues more forcefully that wisdom in Proverbs

wisdom?[10] Yahweh himself?[11] The world order?[12] A Hypostasis of God?[13] Instead of evaluating these theories at this point, I am going to focus first on a problem which is related to all possible hypotheses about Lady Wisdom's identity: the question of her relationship to Yahweh.

11.2.2 Lady Wisdom's Relation to Yahweh

On the one hand, she is described in terms used elsewhere of Yahweh:
- Life and death depend on one's relationship to her (Prov 8:35-36, compare with Exod 33:11; Jer 21:8; 38:16; 1 Kgs 10:8; Prov 14:27; Isa 56:1-2; etc.).[14]
- She is the source of legitimate government (Prov 8:15-16, compare with Num 11:16-17; 1 Sam 2:11; 10:1; 1 Kgs 3:4-15; 10:9; Ps 2:7).
- She is the giver of wealth (Prov 8:18-21, compare with Deut 28:8; 1 Kgs 3:13; 1 Chr 29:12; 2 Chr 1:12; 17:5).
- She is the one who loves and is to be loved (Prov 8:17, compare with Deut 6:5; 1 Sam 2:30; 2 Sam 12:23; 1 Kgs 3:3; Neh 13:26; Isa 48:14)—interestingly, Yahweh is nowhere mentioned as the direct object of love in Proverbs though that is a quite common topic elsewhere in the Old Testament (see Deut 5:10; 7:9; 10:12; 11:13, 22; 19:9; 30:20; Ps 97:10; 145:20).[15]
- The seeking and finding motif (Prov 8:17) is also very emphatic elsewhere in connection with Yahweh (Deut 4:29; Hos 5:6; Amos 5:4-6).[16] Similarly, when שחר II. (Prov 8:17) refers to searching for a transcendent

---

1–9 represents the internalised Law (Weeks 2007: 109–113; similarly Marcus 1950–1951: 157–171, 166–167). This is close to how many devout Jews understood it in the second temple period, see Deut 4:5-7, Sirach (especially chapter 24), Wisdom of Solomon.

10. This option covers several possibilities not only because she can refer to divine or human wisdom, but also because 'literary figure' can be defined in many ways, like 'personification,' 'metaphor,' or 'symbol.' See Camp 1985: 57–60, 72–77.

11. Longman 2006: 222; Schroer 2000: 18–30; Stallman 2000: 126.

12. Von Rad 1972: 190–191, 307.

13. Marcus 1950–1951: 157–171; Ringgren 1947; Whybray 1965b: 80–82. For an almost comprehensive list of twentieth century scholars supporting the hypostasis theory, see Baumann 1996: 4–12.

14. Baumann 1996: 156–157.

15. For Wisdom as a direct object of love compared to Yahweh as the direct object of love elsewhere in the Old Testament, see Baumann 1996: 99–100 and Treier 2011a: 68. The parallels between Yahweh and Wisdom and most of the biblical places mentioned so far in the list and also other parallels based on the figure of Wisdom in previous chapters of Proverbs are also listed in Camp 1985: 28. See also her discussion of the topic on p. 104 in the same work.

16. Schroer 2000: 27–28.

object, outside of Proverbs it always refers to Yahweh (Job 8:5; Ps 63:2 [English 63:1]; 78:34; Isa 26:9; Hos 5:15).[17]

- Wisdom is more precious than riches (Prov 8:10-11) and the same might be said about Yahweh in Prov 18:10-11 where 18:10 says in an unqualified way that 'the Lord's name is a fortified tower' whereas 18:11 qualifies the similar 'A rich man's wealth is his fortified city—in his imagination' (במשכיתו).
- Her words are described with terms in Prov 8:6-9 (בצדק, מישרים) which, when used in connection with speech, only describe Yahweh's words elsewhere (Neh 9:13; Ps 19:9; 33:4; 119:137; Isa 45:19).[18]
- Her old age is described with expressions (מאז קדם, מעולם) that are also used to describe Yahweh (Ps 93:2; Hab 1:12).[19]
- 'Her lips loath wickedness,' (תועבת שפתי; Prov 8:7), which might also bring to mind the תועבת יהוה expression which is characteristic only for Deuteronomy and Proverbs (Prov 3:32; 11:1, 20; 12:22; 15:8-9, 26; 16:5; 17:15; 20:10, 23; Deut 7:25; 12:31; 17:1; 18:12; 22:5; 23:19; 25:16; 27:15).[20]
- Her role at the time of creation might be comparable to that of רוח אלהים in Gen 1:2.[21]
- Some even propose that the double use of אהיה in Prov 8:30 echoes the אהיה אשר אהיה of Exod 3:14.[22]

It is also noteworthy that Psalm 104, which seems to be the closest to Prov 8:22-29 in its language and concepts among all biblical creation texts (though probably not close enough to suspect direct dependence between the two texts), uses this language for praising God and not wisdom.[23]

On the other hand, Proverbs 8 clearly differentiates Lady Wisdom from Yahweh. She might be understood as a creature of Yahweh, if we translate קנני

---

17. Baumann 1996: 101.
18. Baumann 1996: 78–79.
19. Treier 2011a: 62.
20. Baumann 1996: 80.
21. Bauks and Baumann 1994: 49–50.
22. Lenzi 2006: 711–712.
23. If we do not only consider vocabulary but also some structural elements then Gen. 1 might be a relatively close parallel, too (Bauks and Baumann 1994). Nonetheless, no other biblical creation story has so many common words with Prov 8:22-29 as Psalm 104: תהום, הר, שמים, ארץ, מעין, חכמה, עפר, תבל, מים, ים, etc. Interestingly the parallels between Psalm 104 and Proverbs 8 have not been investigated so far by scholarship. Baumann does not even mention it when she delineates the similarities and dissimilarities between Prov 8:22-31 and other biblical creation texts (Baumann 1996: 144–151). Similarly, Whybray did not mention Psalm 104 in his article on some alleged (though by him refuted) close parallels to Prov 8:22-31 (Whybray 1965a). Saebø at least mentions the psalm occasionally as an important parallel to Proverbs 8 in his recent commentary (Saebø 2012: 129, 133), but he does not offer a thoroughgoing comparison either.

in 8:22 as 'created me,'[24] or as a being who is co- or even pre-existent with Yahweh, if we translate קנני as 'acquired me.'[25] She might also be understood as the daughter of Yahweh, as the verb חיל in verses 24-25 refers more often to giving birth than to creation activity.[26] But however ambiguous the description is, all of the possibilities speak about a separate being from Yahweh and this separateness is maintained throughout the whole description: she is *beside* (אצלו) and *in front of* (לפניו) Yahweh (8:30).

It seems that Proverbs 8 does two different things at the same time. It associates Wisdom with Yahweh so closely that she appears as a divine being with Yahweh's characteristics; at the same time it differentiates her from Yahweh.

11.2.3 A 'Mistake' or Sophisticated Theological Discourse?

Stuart Weeks realises the same ambiguity in his work on Proverbs 1–9.[27] He proposes that Wisdom's separation from Yahweh (i.e., her personification) is only a byproduct of the author's intention to parallel wisdom with Lady Folly. The 'poor' writer was simply not aware of what huge theological debates and speculations his rather unfortunate literary move would initiate in the following centuries:

> The personification of wisdom is . . . creating an issue that does not exist in the underlying thought. . . .[28]
> Judging by the vagueness of 8:22, indeed, the author has little interest in trying to specify just how such a figure might have come into existence, or in creating an explanatory cosmological framework within which his characters may be understood. We are on our own, then, if

---

24. On the basis of Gen. 4:1; Deut 32:6; Ps 139:13. See Fox 2000: 279–280; Van Leeuwen 1997: 92; Whybray 1995: 94. I would also mention the praiseful exclamation of Ps 104:24, where God's creatures are called his קנין.

25. See Weeks 2007: 219–220. For a balanced discussion of the word's translation which argues that the word can be deliberately ambiguous and might contain both the 'created' and the 'acquired' meanings, see Baumann 1996: 116–118.

26. If we accept the repunctuation of נְסַכְתִּי to נָסַכְתִּי proposed by many and so derive it from סכך (wave together) instead of נסך (pour out), then it is noteworthy that קנה and סכך are used together in Ps 139:13 describing the formation of the embryo. No wonder, קנני is translated by some as 'begot me' in Prov 8:22. See Longman 2006: 203–205; McKane 1970: 352–354; Murphy 1998: 47; Perdue 1994: 90; Perdue 2007: 55; Toy 1899: 174; Waltke 2004: 408–409. Baumann provides one of the most detailed and clearest lists of the possible translations of נסכתי (Baumann 1996: 120–122—she also opts for the translation 'woven' or 'formed').

27. Weeks 2007: 119–125. Strictly speaking he writes about a slightly different ambiguity. I have been writing about the dichotomy of 'Wisdom as Yahweh' vs. 'Wisdom as separate from Yahweh'; he speaks about 'Wisdom as Yahweh's attribute' vs. 'Wisdom as separate from Yahweh. Nevertheless, the basic issue is the same: is Wisdom separate from Yahweh or not?

28. Weeks 2007: 124.

we wish to understand just how wisdom in Proverbs 1–9 can at once be a divine attribute or possession, and at the same time have a personality distinct from God. . . .[29]

In particular, I am not convinced that the writer is trying to establish wisdom as something that has an active intermediary role between humans and God. Viewed as a concept, wisdom is essentially a spiritual or intellectual attainment which gives one automatic insight into the divine will, not a messenger service from God. . . .[30]

Since the most obvious role of the character is as a counterpart to the foreign woman, it is tempting to suppose, therefore, that the idea of that woman came first. . . . Whether that is the case or not, the author's decision not only to use a character to represent wisdom, but also to use a personification of the concept, rather than a type like the woman or the sinners, has left him with problems both in correlating their roles, and in dealing with the implications of Wisdom (the person) for wisdom (the concept). . . .[31]

While fully acknowledging the powerful influence of the personification on subsequent literature and thought, I am wary of attributing an authorial intention to many of the implications that have been identified. Gerlinde Baumann, for instance, . . . lists a wide range of consequences, and describes the personification in terms of filtering and unifying a previously diverse phenomenon: even if it does all these things, I suspect that many were incidental, or even contrary to the author's intentions. . . .[32]

Thus, according to Weeks, the author's aim was to depict wisdom as belonging to Yahweh and at the same time he (I just presume we are speaking about a male author)[33] wanted to parallel this wisdom with Lady Folly.[34] He simply did not think through that this would result in contradictory pictures. He wanted to speak about a wisdom in which we can participate and thereby have *direct* access to Yahweh's mind. The picture of a separate, personified wisdom in an intermediary role between Yahweh and humanity is only a mistake, or to put it more positively, a literary tool, ornamentation, to which we should not pay serious theological attention. Or, if we do, then we need to be aware that what we find in the text was not intended by the author and might even go against his intentions.

---

29. Weeks 2007: 123.
30. Weeks 2007: 124 n. 50.
31. Weeks 2007: 125.
32. Weeks 2007: 125–126 n. 54.
33. For the probability of male authorship, see Camp 1997: 99.
34. In this Weeks is tentatively following Boström's old suggestion according to which the figure of Lady Folly was the primary one and Lady Wisdom was only created subsequently as an antithesis for it. (G. Boström, *Proverbiastudien. Die Weisheit und die fremde Weib in Spr. 1–9*, LUÅ 1/30, Nr 3 (Lund: Gleerup, 1935); referred to in Whybray 1995: 72.)

Maybe Weeks is right in his conjecture about the author's intention. However, I see another possible explanation for the semantic tensions in Proverbs 8 (and Proverbs 1–9 in general). One of the things Lady Wisdom does is mediate God's presence, as I will argue shortly. Now, speaking about God's presence in the world is a complicated issue, so complicated that it almost inevitably leads to stammering and to (apparent?) contradictions. How can we point at a well circumscribed space, time, or human experience and say 'there is God' without making God into one item of the world, a creature, so to speak—without falling into idolatry, in other words? Nicholas Lash provides a 'post-biblical' conceptualisation of 'idolatry,' in which he emphasises that it is crucial to maintain a dialectic while speaking about the presence of God in the world. As Lash puts it,

> Alerted to God's presence by some person, some occurrence, fact or thing; some dream or project, institution or idea, we take off our shoes, bow down and offer sacrifice. Here, we recognise, is God. At once, however, *our first lesson has to be: where God is, is not God; this sanctuary of God's presence is, however holy, not divine.*[35]

My argument can be summarised like this: Proverbs 8, or more precisely Proverbs read in the light of chapter 8, depicts wisdom in/through which human beings can experience God's presence. But speaking about God's presence, or about the 'things' through which God is present, requires the dialectic language of 'where God is, is not God.' Through this theological principle it is possible to make sense of the ambiguous language of Proverbs 8.

11.2.4 Is Lady Wisdom a Mediator?

One of the main questions of Proverbs 8 seems to be 'Where can we find wisdom'?[36] It speaks a lot about finding her (verses 17, 35, and also verse 9 though, strictly speaking, the latter is about finding דעת and not חכמה) and also about the places where she can be found.[37] She is 'on the top of the heights' (בראש מרומים; verse 2), 'at the crossroads' (or 'between the paths,' בית נתיבות; verse 2), 'next to the gates at the entrance of the city' (ליד שערים לפי קרת; verse 3), 'at the doors' (מבוא פתחים; verse 3), 'on the path of righteousness' (בארך צדקה; verse 20), 'amongst the paths of justice' (בתוך נתיבות משפט; verse 20), 'in the beginning of Yahweh's way' (ראשית דרכו; verse 22). When God ordered the elements of the world, she 'was there' (שם אני; verse 27). Now she is playing in

---

35. Lash 1996: 61, emphasis mine.
36. It is not dissimilar in this respect to Job 28, though the question in Proverbs 8 is not as explicit as there.
37. It is noteworthy that the 'find' (מצא) verb occurs with the third highest frequency proportionately in Proverbs 8 of all of the chapters of the Old Testament: 1. Song of Songs 3 (4 occurrences/191 words in the chapter); 2. Ecclesiastes 7 (9/440); 3. Proverbs 8 (6/337).

God's habitable world (בתבל ארצו; verse 31), and, as we have already noted earlier, she is 'besides' Yahweh (אצלו; verse 30) and 'in front of him' (לפניו; verse 30). To summarise all these, we can say that Proverbs 8 has two fundamental things to say about Wisdom's whereabouts: 1. she has been constantly with Yahweh; 2. she is amongst us, in the world.

Of course, some of these expressions can only be understood in a metaphorical way, especially the ones speaking about her relationship to Yahweh. As Fox reminds us:

> Wisdom is unlocalized, unbound by space. Being everywhere, she is, in a sense, nowhere. She says, 'When he established the heavens, there was I' (8:27). Where? It cannot be the heavens, for God did not carry out the creation of the heavens in the heavens. 'There' is nonspatial.[38]
>
> Since the creation of wisdom was the first deed of God's 'way' and prior to his other 'works,' the implication is that before he created wisdom, he had no 'ways' or works. Though the author may not realize it, the underlying assumption is that prior to creation God was in stasis, his power only potential. He brought his power to actuality by acquiring wisdom. He acquired wisdom by creating it, drawing it from within, from the infinite potential for being that is inherent in Godhead. There is nowhere else he could have gotten it. That is why God's acquiring . . . wisdom is figured in terms of giving birth.[39]

Fox's logical delineations of Wisdom's 'place' highlight how undividable Wisdom is from Yahweh: she is where Yahweh is in a 'nonspatial' sense, and she appears whenever Yahweh acts. If Yahweh is eternal, she is also. However, according to our chapter, this very same Wisdom lives among human beings. She is with God *and* playing on the inhabited world (verses 30-31). It seems that 'in the city gates' (verses 2-3) is compatible with 'next to God' (verses 22-31).

Fox conceptualises this Wisdom as a 'universal,' a transcendent entity (like a Platonic idea), of which human wisdom and Yahweh's wisdom are different realisations.[40] I have two problems with this understanding of Wisdom. First, I am not sure that it is in accordance with my last quotation from Fox himself about Yahweh giving birth, so to speak, to Wisdom. Second, Fox is able to maintain this understanding of Wisdom for the 'interludes' (1:20-33; 3:13-20; 6:1-19; 8:1-36; 9:1-18). Elsewhere in Proverbs 1–9, however, according to Fox, 'Wisdom is a power. . . . The function of this power is explicitly defined in sentences dependent on the exhortations: protection from sinful men and women. . . . Wisdom is a configuration of soul; it is *moral character*.'[41] However, as Weeks comments, such a differentiation between the two wisdoms in Proverbs

---

38. Fox 2000: 355.
39. Fox 2000: 294.
40. Fox 2000: 352–356.
41. Fox 2000: 347–348, Fox's emphasis.

1–9 (a universal vs. a protective power which is moral character) is unlikely given the 'substantial overlap of language and attitude':[42]

> It is difficult to see how the exhortation to 'love her and she will guard you', in 6: 6 (lecture), is very different from Wisdom's declaration in 8: 17 (interlude), that she loves those who love her.[43]

In my view, if we understand Wisdom in chapter 8 as the personification of a divine attribute and take seriously the intermediary position of Wisdom, that she is with God and at the same time in the world, then it is easy to construe a unified picture of wisdom in Proverbs 1–9: being wise (which is a protective power indeed, expressed in human character, as Fox suggests about the 'lectures') is participating in God's wisdom. It is experiencing the presence of the 'nonspatial' God himself in the world. This seems to me to be the theological vision of Proverbs 8, which is supposed to make the reader enthusiastic about wisdom and eager to continue reading the wise sayings of Proverbs 10–31.

This understanding of Wisdom explains another feature of the text, recognised by Fox: Wisdom is in an intermediate position but she is not a mediator.[44] As he writes,

> In Prov 8, Wisdom is portrayed as an entity proceeding from God (according to 2:6, from his *mouth*) and intermediate between him and the world....[45]
>
> It is true that Wisdom exists on an intermediate plane: below God as his creation and 'child' and above humanity as their superior and patroness. But she does not *mediate*. God never speaks to her, and she does not quote him....[46]
>
> There is no suggestion that individuals can pray to her or that she can intercede.[47]

As has already become clear, in my view Wisdom is, in a sense, not below God but represents God. She is intermediate between God and the world because it is through her that humans can access and experience God's presence. But she is not mediating like a prophet does, as meeting her means such a direct, unmediated meeting with God as it is possible for human beings. She is simply

---

42. Weeks 2007: 92.
43. Weeks 2007: 92. Weeks' first biblical reference is incorrect, instead of 6:6 it should be Prov 4:6.
44. The majority of twentieth century interpreters saw Wisdom as a mediator, see Baumann 1996: 28, 41–43, 57, who lists Meinhold, Heinisch, Kraus, Tournay, Aletti, Bonnard, and Camp, but her list is far from comprehensive. Miura 2004: 138–149 lists von Rad, McCreesh, Perdue, Murphy. Baumann, similarly to Fox, also emphasises that although Wisdom seems to be a mediator in some ways, she actually does not *do* mediatory activities (Baumann 1996: 291–294).
45. Fox 2000: 293, Fox's emphasis.
46. Fox 2000: 334, Fox's emphasis.
47. Fox 2000: 345.

in the world and can be met in all worldly phenomena, from power (Prov 8:14-16) through wealth (Prov 8:18-21) to love (especially if the picture of the good wife in Prov 31:10-31 is an echo of Wisdom herself).[48] However, she does not simply equal these phenomena: she is also God, present in the world.

Understanding Wisdom this way is not entirely dissimilar to what Gese wrote about Wisdom's mediating role: 'Sophia appears as a *mediatrix dei*. Every realisation [*Erkenntnis*] of Sophia on the side of humans leads to a partaking in God.'[49] However, Gese understood wisdom mainly as a cognitive phenomenon: realising wisdom, according to him, is mainly a mental activity; it is an understanding of the order of creation.[50] In contrast, though I do not wish to deny the mental aspect of being wise, the latter part of Proverbs depicts wisdom at least as much as wise living as wise thinking. This means that in order to experience God's presence in one's life it is inevitable not only to think the right things but also to do them, according to Proverbs.

This understanding of wisdom echoes (again) what Lash—building on Karl Rahner—says about experiencing God in the world:

> *All* human experience is, in varying degrees of 'latency' or 'actuality,' experience in relation to the mystery of God, and may be accepted as such 'even if the word "God" is never heard and is never used as the term for the direction and goal of the transcendental experience known in this way.'[51]

We can find the same idea in several writings of Rahner. One example: 'The experience of God constitutes, rather . . . the ultimate depths and the radical essence of every spiritual and personal experience (of love, faithfulness, hope and so on).'[52]

The main difference between Proverbs and the just quoted theologians seems to be that whereas Lash and Rahner would probably happily include wisdom as one of the basic spiritual experiences of humanity, they would say that experiencing God is even one step further—it is even more basic; it is a sort of common denominator of all these spiritual experiences—whereas Proverbs, as I

---

48. Camp 1985: 179–206; Hausmann 1992: 261–266; McCreesh 1985: 25–46; Yoder 2003: 427–447. Regardless of the significance of Prov 31:10-31, the search for and blessing of a good wife is not an infrequent topic in Proverbs, see Prov 5:15-20; 12:4; 18:22; 19:14.

49. Gese 1979: 87.

50. 'God reveals himself in her [Wisdom] to the cognizant and thinking people.' (Gese 1979: 87.)

51. Lash 1988: 246, Lash's emphasis; quoting Karl Rahner, 'Religious Feeling Inside and Outside the Church', in Karl Rahner, *Theological Investigations,* vol. 17, trans. Margaret Kohl (London: Darton, Longman & Todd, 1981) 228–242.

52. Rahner 1974: 154. It should be noted here that in one of his numerous works Murphy draws a parallel between his interpretation of Proverbs and Rahner's theology, too. Murphy also argues that, according to Proverbs, it is God who can be experienced through the world (Murphy 2002: 120, 124).

understand it, does not go further than wisdom. However, the difference between Lash and Rahner, on the one hand, and Proverbs, on the other, might not be as big as it appears if we consider how complex a category the wisdom of Proverbs is. As we have seen, it can be found in all sorts of human activities and it incorporates moral character. It includes a right vision of reality, too (see previous discussion of Proverbs 2). So, just like Lash's and Rahner's 'experience of God,' it can be present in all human experiences.

11.2.5 Is Lady Wisdom a Hypostasis of Yahweh?

I described wisdom in the previous section as 'God present in the world.' However, maybe I should have been more careful in my language, since 'where God is, is not God.' As Lash would no doubt warn us, even if it is true in a sense that wisdom is 'God present in the world,' we should

> ... keep the word 'God' holy by using it only for that unfathomable mystery with which no individual, no image, person, power, fact or thing, neither the world nor all the wonders of the world, may simply be identified.[53]

If Wisdom mediates God's presence in the world but we are better not to call her God, then what kind of being is she? Again, the theological discussion of Lash can help us. Writing about the Trinity, he explains,

> that the Christian doctrine of God, declared in the threefold structure of the single creed, protects the reference to God of Christian action and speech by simultaneously serving as a set of what I have come to call 'protocols against idolatry.'
> The creed performs this single twofold service (the technical correlates of which, in theological grammar, are three 'hypostases' and one 'nature') by indicating, at each point, where God is truly to be found and then, at each point, by denying that what we find there is simply to be identified with God. ... It enables us to make true mention of God and, by denying that the forms of our address (our confession of God as 'gift', as '*verbum*' and as 'Father', for example) furnish us with some hold upon the 'nature' of God, it sustains our recognition of the absolute otherness or non-identity of the world and God.[54]

It is tempting to understand Lady Wisdom in Proverbs 8 as a hypostasis of God in the light of Lash's clarifying thoughts about the Christian theological usage of the word: it is 'where God is truly to be found,' but we should deny 'that what we find there is simply to be identified with God.'

---

53. Lash 1996: 52.
54. Lash 1996: 89–90; see also Lash 1988: 275–280.

Hypostasis is a much debated concept in biblical studies. It was often used as a category fitting for Wisdom in the nineteenth century and also in the first half of the twentieth century, but it has been somewhat out of fashion for the last few decades.⁵⁵ Fox and von Rad, for example, dismiss it rather easily, saying that Wisdom cannot be a hypostasis of God since she is created and as such she is outside of the divine realm.⁵⁶ However, as we have seen, the קנני of Prov 8:22 and the whole description of Wisdom's existence in Prov 8:22-31 is ambiguous enough to do justice to the dialectic nature of a hypostasis: she is, in a certain sense, part of creation indeed, but as the daughter of God begotten in the 'atemporal' moment God became active, she is always where the nonspatial God is.

Claudia V. Camp expressed another critique of understanding Wisdom as hypostasis. The main thrust of her sophisticated criticism seems to be rather technical: defining and using hypostasis is a complicated and not a clear-cut manoeuver at all.⁵⁷ It is hard not to agree with her, but if I am right that Proverbs 8 is at least partly about meeting/experiencing/participating in God in the world then the subject matter of the book is complicated enough to validate the usage of similarly complicated theological terms in the interpretation of it.

The biblical scholar G. Pfeifer provides a definition of 'hypostasis' which matches rather nicely Lash's understanding of the word's function:⁵⁸ a Hypostasis is 'a divine being that participates in the essence of a deity who, acting through it, intervenes in the world, without exhausting its essence in the work of the hypostasis.'⁵⁹ Whether we use 'hypostasis' or not for describing Wisdom in Proverbs 8—and as it is a loaded and debated word, its usage requires special care and clarity indeed—this understanding of it expresses what I have been trying to argue on the previous pages.

---

55. Baumann 1996: 12; see also the discussion and literature in Sinnott 2005: 18, 22.
56. Fox 2000: 353; von Rad 1972: 153.
57. Camp 1985: 34–36,209–214; she simply recommends 'personification' instead, admitting, that it 'neither excludes the possibility of hypostasis nor demands it.' (Camp 1985: 213.)
58. Which is no wonder since he takes its usage in the Christian Trinitarian language as his basis for the definition. He admits that it can be used and defined in many ways and, furthermore, though it might seem unfortunate to use a so clearly Christian term for describing a pre-Christian phenomenon, nevertheless, he recommends this usage which is rooted in Christian theological language since this is how it was embedded into the theoretical language of the Academia. ('Da aber der Begriff im wissenschaftlichen Sprachgebrauch eingebürgert ist.') Pfeifer 1967: 15.
59. Pfeifer 1967: 15.

11.3 Summary

I have argued in this section that the theological vision provided by Proverbs 8 depicts a wisdom who mediates, or more precisely displays the presence of Yahweh in the world. When one sees wisdom, one sees Yahweh, so to speak.

However, speaking about Yahweh's presence in the world requires dialectic language, which is well represented by the personification of wisdom in Proverbs 8: it distances wisdom from Yahweh, whereas the chapter uses language for describing her as if she were Yahweh. Weeks has suggested that this language is rather problematic and only accidental, stemming from the carelessness of the author. In contrast, I do not see the language as problematic. I rather see it fitting for the discussion of a problematic issue: Yahweh's presence in the world.

It has to be admitted that the primary aim of the author of Proverbs 8 was probably not the writing of an analytical theological treatise about the nature of Yahweh and his relationship to the world. His basic intention was to recommend wisdom, as Fox emphasises, and Weeks might very well be right, too, that the parallel with the strange woman influenced significantly the creation of the literary figure of Lady Wisdom. Nevertheless, the well-defined exhortatory and literary purposes of the text do not necessarily mean that it is confused or irrelevant on a theological level. To adjust Fox's observation slightly to this discussion,

> ... granted this rhetorical thrust [and literary function], the poem still conveys an unusual conception of wisdom and makes powerful claims for this entity, and these may also be read from a theoretical or philosophical [or theological] perspective.[60]

The theological interpretation I have provided is mainly about the function of wisdom ('mediating' Yahweh's presence) and not about her precise identity. Is she a literary figure or a hypostasis? Is she Yahweh or part of the world? Is she the Torah or the rest of Proverbs? In my view, a definitive decision on the answers to these questions is not only impossible but also unwarranted as these options are not necessarily mutually exclusive. In a sense any of them can be true to Wisdom. Relatedly, I do not see significant difference between Wisdom (with a capital 'W') and wisdom. Reading the received form of the book, the reader inevitably brings the vivid picture of Lady Wisdom to the rest of the book: as a consequence, wise human behaviour and also the wisdom of Proverbs 10-31 (i.e., the manifestations of Lady Wisdom) appear as 'channels' to him or her through which he or she can experience Yahweh.

This leads us back to our initial question. If I am right that wisdom is about being with Yahweh and this comprises the background for the reading of the whole book of Proverbs, then we can hardly call this book, or the world and behaviour which it is about, 'secular.' Quite the opposite. The thrust of the book seems to be to encourage the reader to experience Yahweh *in the*

---

60. Fox 2000: 293, the [bracketed] words are my additions.

world. In this sense, it is more about the 'sanctification' of the 'secular' world than about worldliness.

This interpretation of Proverbs is in a sense parallel with the interpretation I offered earlier in connection with the question of self-interest. Both here and there the emphasis is on a relational interpretation of the book. What might appear as 'selfishness' for some, can be looked at from another angle and can be seen as participating in divine providence: that is, one can experience properly self-interested wisdom as being in the presence of God. In a similar way, what might appear as simply affirming the secular world, can be looked at from another angle and can be seen as being in the presence of God by being wise in everyday life.

As we will see shortly, these conclusions about the 'sanctification' of the secular and about the 'relational' understanding of Proverbs are also reinforced by another reading strategy which interprets the book in the light of the vision of the Jerusalem temple as it is offered by the canonical context.

12

Secular (Universal) vs. National (Particular) II

12.1 The Temple as Theological Vision

In the following I argue that a fruitful theological interpretation of the book of Proverbs can be done along the lines of temple theology. This interpretation understands wise living as living in a temple. I am agnostic about whether this is an intended meaning by some of the authors and editors of the book. Rather, my proposal is that this should be a possible reading strategy of the book in a canonical context.

The picture of everyday wise living as entering into a temple matches nicely what I wrote in the previous chapter about wisdom mediating the presence of God. In ancient societies, and Israel was not an exception, it was, first of all, the temple where one could experience God's presence.[1] Everyday life lived in wisdom provides such a temple setting.

The inspiration for my thoughts have come mainly from two sources: the insights of Raymond C. Van Leeuwen and Claudia V. Camp.[2] Van Leeuwen argues that the activity of building (a house or a temple) and wisdom were closely connected in ancient Near Eastern thinking. Camp offers an imaginative reading of the Solomon narrative in 1 Kings and the book of Proverbs in the light of each other.[3]

---

1. Keel 1997: 111–176.
2. Van Leeuwen 2007: 67–90; Camp 2000: 144–186. See also Zabán 2012: *passim*.
3. Miles (Miles 2004) also offers an interesting reading of Proverbs 1–9 in the light of 1 Kings 1–11 but his method of relating almost every detail of Proverbs 1–9 to King Solomon does not always sound persuasive to me.

The main difference between the interpretation of Camp and that of myself is that whereas she sees the book of Proverbs as the image of the temple,[4] I am rather inclined to see Proverbs as a book *about* the image of the temple: that is, about everyday life. The book teaches that the reader experiences God's presence when he or she actively follows the book's instructions and not when he or she only reads them. Entering the temple is living wisely and not just reading about wisdom.

The main difference between my interpretation and that of Van Leeuwen is mainly one of emphasis. I agree with him that the conceptual background of the book of Proverbs is comprised partly by a connection of wisdom with house-building. However, I would like to emphasise that, in the light of Camp's arguments, in the case of Proverbs we should rather speak about the building of a particular kind of house, namely, the (Solomonic) temple.

In order to delineate my thoughts it will be necessary to describe the close association between temple, wisdom, and universe in ancient Near Eastern thinking and literature. As the major part of this task has been accomplished several times by very able writers, I am going to list the main arguments as succinctly as possible, only providing a few brief examples.[5]

12.2 Temple, Universe, and Wisdom in the Ancient Near East

Temple, universe, and wisdom were closely related to each other in ancient Near Eastern thinking. Temple and universe were often identified with each other; they comprised a 'homology,' to use Levenson's expression.[6]

In Egypt, the temple represented heaven on earth, but this did not prevent Egyptians from perceiving it as the representation of the whole universe at the same time. This was expressed not only in inscriptions but also in the decoration of many temples: the floor represented the earth, the blue ceiling decorated with stars or constellations stood for the heavens, and the vegetation was not only represented by the plant-rooms but also by the decoration of the walls which often contained many different types of plants.[7]

In Mesopotamia, they also often described temples in cosmic imagery. For example, in Sumerian Lagash king Gudea described his temple building project with these words:

---

4. For a very similar, though more tentative, suggestion, see Baumann 1996: 202–209.
5. The literature is vast, for example Beale 2004: 29–167; Hurowitz 1992; Levenson 1988: 78–99; Smith 2001: 167–172; Smith 2010; Stordalen 2000; Walton 2011.
6. Levenson 1988: 88. Levenson might be following Mircea Eliade's usage of the word, who used it often in connection with religious and mythical ideas.
7. Janowski 2001: 229–260, especially 242–251.

The building of the temple [was done] according to its holy star(s) [and the builders] were making the temple grow (high) like a mountain range making it float in mid-heaven like a cloud . . . [it was like] brilliant moonlight . . . shining. It illuminated the land.[8]

Enuma Elish, the Babylonian creation myth speaks about the establishment of *Esagila* (Marduk's temple) and indeed the whole temple district as part of the creation process. In an inscription of Esarhaddon the temple of Assur is described with the words:

I raised the top of Esharra to heaven,
above, to heaven I elevated its top.
Below in the netherworld
I made firm its foundation.[9]

These and other Mesopotamian texts show the close association between the universe and temple, though they are not as unambiguous evidence for the 'homology' of the universe and temple as the Egyptian temple-decoration. Depending on context, they may not only express an identification between temple and world but that building a temple is part of the gods' creation activity, or that the temple is the centre of the universe, or that the temple fills the whole universe.[10] Nevertheless, the temple–universe parallel was frequently expressed in temple names, like *Esharra* (house of the cosmos), *Etemenanki* (house of the foundation platform between heaven and earth), *Ekunankuga* (house, pure stairway of heaven), etc.[11] Furthermore, even if a direct identification between the universe and the temple is not clearly stated, Mesopotamian creation texts do follow the model of temple-building texts, and, as John H. Walton concludes, 'in this way, at least, they imply that the cosmos is conceived to be a temple.'[12]

It seems that the temple (microcosm)–universe (macrocosm) topos was typical for much of the ancient Near East. However, as I have mentioned above, the topos was more complex than this. Creating the universe and building a temple were equally connected to wisdom. To name a famous example, Marduk, the world-creator god in *Enuma Elish*, was not only the son of Ea, the god of wisdom, but the very first thing we learn about him is how wise he was:

Bel, cleverest of the clever, sage of the gods, was begotten.
And inside Apsu, Marduk was created;
Inside pure Apsu, Marduk was born.
Ea his father created him.[13]

---

8. Quoted in Beale 2004: 52.
9. Quoted in Hurowitz 1992: 336.
10. Sheriffs 1988: 24; Beale 2004: 51–52; Hurowitz 1992: 337.
11. Levenson 1984: 295; Walton 2009: 80; Walton 2011: 103.
12. Walton 2011: 110.
13. Dalley 1989: 235.

Enki, the Sumerian equivalent of Ea is another good example. He was responsible for ordering the world and thereby bringing prosperity.[14] It is noteworthy that in connection with his ordering and temple building activity he praises himself in a similar fashion as Lady Wisdom does in Proverbs 8:

> I am the first born of An ... I am the principal among rulers ... I bring prosperity to perfection ... I am the wisdom and understanding of all the foreign lands. With An the king, on An's dais, I oversee Justice.... I was born as the firstborn son of holy An.[15]

This is a collection of those elements from lines 61–80 of *Enki and the World Order*, which especially resemble the language of Proverbs 8. However, the similarities should not be overemphasised. There is clearly a huge spatial, temporal, and conceptual gap between the two texts, which is disguised by this collection of similarities. Nevertheless, the parallels exemplify well the similar role and depiction of divine figures responsible for wisdom throughout the ancient Near East. It is worth quoting the following lines, too:

> In a state of high delight[16] Enki, the king of the Abzu, rejoicing in great splendour, again justly praises himself: 'I am the lord, I am one whose word is reliable,[17] I am one who excels in everything. ... I have built my house,[18] a shrine, in a pure place, and named it with a good name.[19]

Similarly, human builders were supposed to be wise, just like their heavenly counterparts. As Esarhaddon prays in connection with a temple-building:

> Oh ye creators of gods and goddesses, build the structure with your own hands, the abode of your exalted divinity. Whatever is in your hearts, so let it be done, without any deviations from the command of your lips. The skilled (lit. wise) artificers whom you called to carry out this commission,—like Ea, their creator, grant unto them the high(est) wisdom, so that their strength and skill, at your exalted command, may accomplish, through the craftsmanship of Nin-igi-kug [=Ea], what their hands undertake.[20]

Many more examples could be listed but those given above are enough to demonstrate the close connection in the ancient Near East between the universe (macrocosm) and the temple (microcosm) on the one hand, and between wisdom and the building of the universe and earthly temples on the other hand.

---

14. Cf. wisdom as providing prosperity in Proverbs.
15. Cunningham 2003.
16. Cf. Prov 8:30.
17. Cf. Prov 8:6-9.
18. Cf. Prov 9:1.
19. Cunningham 2003.
20. Daniel David Luckenbill, *Ancient Records of Assyria and Babylonia*, vol. 2 (Chicago: The University of Chicago Press, 1927) 670; quoted in Van Leeuwen 2007: 74.

12.3 Temple, Universe, and Wisdom in the Old Testament

Biblical literature presents a similar temple–universe–wisdom topos to what we have just observed in the wider ancient Near Eastern context. Wisdom was closely related both to creating the world and to building the temple.

As for the wisdom–world-creation relationship, we are told several times that God created the universe by wisdom and knowledge (Ps 104:24; 136:5; Jer 10:12; 51:15; Prov 3:19-20). The fact that we can find this statement in different parts of the Hebrew canon, often expressed in very similar vocabulary, shows that this was a well acknowledged, maybe even proverb-like idea in ancient Hebrew thinking.

Eden narratives might also play on wisdom motifs. This Eden–wisdom connection fits the temple–universe–wisdom topos well since Eden-narratives are not unrelated to the creation, and, as we will see shortly, there is also an Eden–temple connection. A high number of wisdom motifs is observable for example in Genesis 2–3. The knowledge (of good and evil) is an important topic in it just like in wisdom texts; the serpent was shrewd (Gen 3:1; cf. Prov 1:4; 8:12; 12:16; 27:12); the tree of life appears at crucial points (Gen 2:9; 3:22; cf. Prov 3:18; 11:30; 13:12; 15:4); and it was even suggested that Adam is depicted as the first sage (mainly based on the texts of Job 15:6-7 and Ezekiel 28, especially verses 12b-15).[21]

Thus, wisdom seems to play an important role at the primordial times of creating the world and human beings. It is, however, more surprising to the modern reader that wisdom was also closely related to building the tabernacle/temple. Not only was Solomon, the builder of the temple, the wise king *par excellence* (1 Kings 3–11), but Hiram, the craftsman working on the furnishing of the temple, and Bezalel, who worked on the tabernacle, were also especially wise people. Hiram was filled with wisdom, understanding, and knowledge (1 Kgs 7:14: וימלא את החכמה ואת התבונה ואת הדעת) just like Bezalel who even had the Spirit of God (Exod 31:3: ואמלא אתו רוח אלהים בחכמה ובתבונה ובדעת), which recalls Gen 1:2. Indeed, it is noteworthy that 16 occurrences of the word חכמה in Exodus are connected to the making of the tabernacle or its holy equipment.[22]

People in the twenty-first century tend to connect wisdom to the existential decisions of everyday life. It is also understandable that creating the world requires some wisdom. We would, furthermore, understand that the decision of whether to build a temple or not might require wisdom, but that the actual building activity itself requires wisdom could sound a bit unusual for modern readers. It seems that in the ancient Near East, and the Old Testament is not an exception, wisdom was connected to everyday life, creation, and (especially temple-)

---

21. LaCocque and Ricoeur 1998: 3–29, especially pages 11–13; Alonso-Schökel 1976: 468–480, especially pages 472–474.

22. Van Leeuwen 2007: 88.

building.²³ This becomes more understandable if we consider the close connection between temple-building and creating the world in biblical thinking.

In Israel the same macrocosm–microcosm relationship can be observed between the universe and the temple as throughout the ancient Near East. The tabernacle and the temple were decorated with motifs of the cosmos (bronze sea as sea, blue curtains as sky, altar as earth, seven branched lamp-stand as five planets plus moon and sun, etc.). As Josephus remarked, writing about the tabernacle, 'every one of these objects is intended to recall and represent the universe,' and in this case modern scholarship agrees with him.²⁴

The major biblical creation stories are told in a way that they echo the tabernacle/temple texts. There are many resemblances between Gen 1:1–2:4a and the tabernacle narratives.²⁵ The two most striking ones are probably the sentences about finishing the work and the usage of number seven.²⁶ As for the work-finishing formula, in Exod 39:43 we read about how Moses inspected the work on the tabernacle:

וירא משה את כל המלאכה והנה עשו אתה כאשר צוה יהוה

And Moses saw all the work, and behold, they had done it as the Lord had commanded.

In Gen 1:31 we read similarly about God:

וירא אלהים את כל אשר עשה והנה טוב מאד

And God saw everything that he had made, and behold, it was very good.²⁷

A similar parallel can be found between 1 Kgs 7:40b (cf. 7:51) and Gen 2:2:

ויכל חירם לעשות את כל המלאכה אשר עשה למלך שלמה בית יהוה

And Hiram finished all the work he was doing, what he did for king Solomon on the house of the Lord.

ויכל אלהים ביום השביעי מלאכתו אשר עשה

And God finished [all] the work he had been doing on the seventh day.

Hurowitz argues that it was the creation language which borrowed these and similar formulas and expressions from the building language and not vice versa.

---

23. This does not necessarily mean that creation theology is *the* theology of wisdom (see discussion in the first part and also in the conclusions of this work). Even if it could be described as 'creation theology,' it is at least as much 'temple theology.' In a sense the temple is even more substantial than creation. See following discussion.

24. Josephus 1930: 403; Levenson 1988: 95–99.

25. Cf. Sommer 2009: 111.

26. Van Leeuwen 2000: 206; Hurowitz 1992: 242. For these and other parallels, like the occurrence of the motifs of light and Sabbath in Gen. 1:1–2:4a and temple related texts, see also Smith 2010: 14–17; 104–109.

27. For the extended verbal parallels between Gen. 1:31–2:3 and Exod 39:32–40:11, see Levenson 1988: 85–86 and Blenkinsopp 1976: 276–278.

This might be so, but for our purpose it is more important to recognise that whatever direction the influence was between creation language and temple-building language, this close relationship between the two types of texts in the Bible mirrors the same homology between world and temple that we have observed in the non-biblical ancient Near Eastern literature.

As for the number seven, just as creation was accomplished in seven days and many other details of the story are organised around the same number (for example the first verse contains 7 words, the second contains 14, key expressions like חיה, כי טוב, ברא occur seven times, etc.) so the temple was built for seven years. It was dedicated during tabernacles, the seven-day feast of the seventh month (1 Kgs 8:2), and Solomon's temple-dedication speech is structured in seven specific petitions (1 Kgs 8:31-32, 33-34, 35-37a, 37b-40, 41-43, 44-45, 46-53).[28]

At this point we should also note that although Psalm 104, which might have influenced the first creation story,[29] does not parallel the temple texts so nicely, it also uses the language of building: the heaven is stretched out like a tent (verse 2), the beams of the upper chambers are laid in waters (verse 3), the earth is set on its foundation (verse 5), a boundary was put to the waters (verse 9); furthermore, cedars were planted (verse 16) just as in ancient Near Eastern temple districts and probably in the Jerusalem temple (cf. Ps 92:13-14).[30]

The second creation story has even more parallels with the temple than the first one. The cherubim, gold, trees, tree of life, Gihon, precious stones and many more motifs have their cultic equivalents in the temple.[31] It is interesting that the language of Lev 26:9-12 echoes both creation stories of Genesis at the same time when, in connection with God's tabernacle we read: 'I will ... make you fruitful and multiply you (והפריתי אתכם והרביתי אתכם cf. Gen 1:28: פרו ורבו).... I will place my dwelling among you.... I will walk among you (והתהלכתי, cf. Gen 3:8: אלהים מתהלך בגן).'[32]

The world–temple connection not only characterises the first two creation stories of Genesis, Psalm 104, and the temple texts but, as several studies argue,

---

28. For the significance of number seven in Gen. 1:1–2:4a and the tabernacle and temple texts, see especially Levenson 1988: 78–99.

29. Day 2000: 101.

30. For the planting of trees and cedars in the Jerusalem temple, see Levenson 2006: 85–87. For the building language of Psalm 104, see Keel 2001: 35; Schmid 2012: 101.

31. Stordalen 2000: 409–437; Wenham 1987: 55–86; Wenham 1994: 399–404. In my view Sommer downplays the role of such Eden–temple linkages too much when he writes that 'in JE, they are absent or at best implied' (Sommer 2009: 118). Sommer does not refer to the work of Stordalen and mentions the arguments of Levenson and Wenham only selectively (Sommer 2009: 118, 121, and related endnotes).

32. Cf. Beale 2004: 110–111; Wenham 1987: 76.

it permeates the whole Bible.[33] As Levenson delineates, writing about two (not yet mentioned) examples,

> If the double directionality of the homology of temple and world sometimes yields texts such as Psalm 78:69, in which the Temple is described as a world, it also yields texts in which the world is described as a temple:
> Thus said the Lord:
> The heaven is My throne
> And the earth is My footstool:
> Where could you build a house for Me,
> What place could serve as My abode?
> All this was made by My hand,
> And thus it all came into being
> —declares the Lord.
> Yet to such a one I look:
> To the poor and broken-hearted,
> Who is concerned about My word. (Isa 66:1-2)[34]

Or as he writes in an earlier article:

> YHWH is building a new Temple, therefore creating a new world, and vice versa.... Perhaps it is not coincidence that the Hebrew Bible begins with an account of the creation of heaven and earth by the command of God (Gen 1:1) and ends with the command of the God of heaven 'to build him a Temple in Jerusalem' (2 Chron. 35:23). It goes from creation (Temple) to Temple (creation) in twenty-four books.[35]

We can conclude that in the Bible we see the temple–universe–wisdom topos familiar from other ancient Near Eastern literature. Wisdom is closely connected to the construction of both the temple and the world, which is understandable since the temple and the world form a homology.

It has to be realised, however, that the relationship between the temple and the world is more complex than this brief summary would so far suggest. In particular, the temple represents the world in two different senses. On the one hand, it stands for the whole universe. On the other hand, it represents the original, idyllic state of the creation, the Edenic garden, and as such it is radically different from the 'profane' or 'secular' world, the world outside the sanctuary. The temple is the world but not simply the world. It is the world where the tree

---

33. See, for example, Psalm 29 (Van Leeuwen 2000: 206); Isaiah 60 (Beale 2004: 42–43); Jeremiah 17 (Beale 2004: 73); Ezekiel 28 (Smith 2001: 171–172). For the ongoing significance of the temple–universe homology in Jubilees, Josephus, Philo, Aristeas, etc., see Hayward 1996.

34. Levenson 1988: 88, the biblical quotation is from *Tanakh*, as quoted by Levenson.

35. Levenson 1984: 295.

of life flourishes and where the Lord is present. This is the world/temple which one can enter by following the directions of Proverbs, as I argue in what follows.

12.4 Temple, Universe, and Wisdom in Proverbs

It was Patrick Skehan who argued most extensively not only for the unity of the book of Proverbs but that its structure represents the architecture of Solomon's temple.[36] He claimed that the number of columns into which the book was organised on the 'original' scroll and the number of lines in those columns reflect the measurements and proportions of the temple. However, there are two interrelated problems concerning Skehan's thoughts. First, enough questions have come up about his theory to justify not taking it for granted.[37] For example, he had to do some re-organisation of the text, even if not too much, to fit it to his theory. Also, we do not know about any examples of Jewish manuscripts from the Persian or Hellenistic periods which displayed those picture-like organisational characteristics which Skehan suspected for Proverbs. The second problem is connected to the first one. Despite these general doubts, no one has yet undertaken a thoroughgoing evaluation of his arguments, no doubt partly because of the enormous work this would require, since 'Skehan's argument is detailed to the point of esotericism,' as Camp writes. Camp herself seems to have adopted the approach that 'Skehan's theory sounds too good to be true; if it was true it would support my arguments immensely but it sounds suspicious enough not to build too much on it.'[38] I accept this approach and so, in what follows, I will avoid any appeal to Skehan's arguments despite their alluring attractiveness.

Let us start with Prov 9:1, which has fascinated the imagination of the interpreters (not least that of Skehan) for a long time:

חכמות בנתה ביתה חצבה עמודיה שבעה
Wisdom has built her house, hewn out her seven pillars.[39]

What pillars and what house is this verse about? The *Midrash Mishle*, from the (probably) 9th century, understood Wisdom's house in Prov 9:1 as referring to the universe:

> *Wisdom has built her house, she has hewn her seven pillars* (Prov. 9:1): This refers to the Torah, which built the entire universe through her wisdom. *She has hewn her seven pillars*—she was hewn from the seven firmaments and was given to humanity. Another interpretation:

---

36. Skehan 1947: 190–198; Skehan 1948: 115–130; Skehan 1967: 468–486.
37. Baumann 1996: 205–206; Fox 2000: 323; Hatton 2008: 54–57; Zabán: 39–45.
38. Camp 2000: 182 n. 28. Here I am not quoting Camp but paraphrasing her approach.
39. Vulg., α', σ' have 'set up' (הצבה from נצב); MT, LXX, Syr., Targ. have 'hewn out' (חצבה from חצב). The MT does make sense and there is a rabbinic parallel for the expression in Exodus Rabba 15 (Baumann 1996: 204–205), so there is no need to change the MT.

Wisdom has built her house—God said: If one has earned the merit of teaching Torah to others, [I will account it to him] as though he had erected the entire universe. *She has hewn her seven pillars*—these refer to the seven lands. If one has earned the merit of upholding the Torah, he will inherit the seven lands; if not, he will be expelled from the seven lands.[40]

These medieval Jewish interpretations presumably follow from the assumption that Proverbs 9 is connected with Proverbs 8, and they understand the creation of the universe in Proverbs 8 as referring to building the house of Wisdom in Prov 9:1. This medieval understanding is in harmony with the opinion of many contemporary scholars. Proverbs 8 uses architectural language (כון, מוסד, דלתת, מזוזת, פתח), thus, its universe is like a building. As Van Leeuwen writes,

> ... the pillars are most likely a reference to the 'pillars of the earth' (Ps 75:3; cf. 1 Sam 2:8; Job 9:6; 26:11). ... But the seven pillars may also be a case of inner-biblical allusion to Gen 1:1–2:3. ... The text of Proverbs 8–9 appears to be playing with the pattern six plus one. ... In [9:]1-6, the preparation of the house and its feast takes six actions (past tense verbs), and the invitation to celebrate in the completed house takes one action, 'she calls.' ... In the preceding chapter, the account of creation falls into two connected sections. The first (8:22-26) has six verbs of creation; the second (8:27-29) has six infinitives of creation. These sections are followed by two identical verbs ('I was', 8:30). ... In 9:7-12, the root for 'wisdom' ... appears six times, in addition to the reference to Wisdom in the phrase 'by me'.[41]

Building activity was a source of delight throughout the ancient Near East and usually was followed by a banquet. For example, Solomon and the people celebrated 'before Yahweh' (לפני יהוה) for seven and seven days and went home joy-fully after finishing the temple in 1 Kgs 8:62-66. In a similar fashion Wisdom delights in front of Yahweh (8:30b: משחקת לפניו) and organises a banquet in Prov 9:1-6.[42]

That Prov 9:1, through its picture of house-building, refers back to the creation of the universe in the previous chapter is supported by other observations, too. It is possible to understand אמון in 8:30 as 'artisan,'[43] emending it to אָמָּן on the basis of Cant 7:2 and Akkadian *ummanu*, which means 'sage' with the connotations of scholar, scribe, royal counselor (cf. 8:15-16) and also craftsman.[44]

---

40. Visotzky 1992: 49.
41. Van Leeuwen 1997: 102.
42. Van Leeuwen lists several ancient Near Eastern parallels for the building–delight–banquet pattern (Van Leeuwen 1997: 95). See also Baumann 1996: 214–221; Van Leeuwen 2007: 71–72.
43. As it was done by Syr., Vulg., Wis 7:21; 8:6, and maybe the LXX.
44. Cazelles 1995: 45–55; Clifford 1999: 99–101; Greenfield 1985: 17; Saebø 2012: 131–135; Van Leeuwen 2007: 85.

In Prov 3:19-20 God built the universe (see the building vocabulary, יסד and כון in 3:19) using wisdom (חכמה), knowledge (תבונה), and understanding (דעת), the very same 'tools' used by Bezalel and Hiram for building the tabernacle and the temple. Here, in chapter 8, the same three words are used seven times all together (חכמה—verses 1, 11, 12; תבונה—verse 1; דעת—verses 9, 10, 12), and Wisdom herself helps God to build the universe, that is, her house, as a sage/masterworker.

The motif of building a house and providing for it appears several times in the whole book of Proverbs.[45] Some of these occurrences might refer back to the house of Wisdom in 9:1. In 14:1 we read,

חכמות נשים בנתה ביתה ואולת בידיה תהרסנו
The wise among women (each one) builds her house but a foolish one tears it down with her own hands.

If נשים is deleted from the text then 14:1a is identical with 9:1a: 'Wisdom has built her house.' Whether נשים was part of the original text,[46] or it is a corruption which should be deleted,[47] or we should understand it as an editorial addition,[48] the verse in its present context echoes both the house building of Lady Wisdom from chapters 1–9 and that of flesh and blood women from later chapters, thereby building a bridge between the two parts of the book. 24:3-4 can fulfill a similar bridge-building role with its similarities to 3:19-20:

בחכמה יבנה בית ובתבונה יתכונן
ובדעת חדרים ימלאו כל הון יקר ונעים
By wisdom a house is built by knowledge it is established,
by understanding its rooms are filled with all precious and pleasant treasures.

Again, we can see here the typical house-building 'tools' (wisdom [חכמה], knowledge [תבונה], and understanding [דעת]) in the same order as in 3:19-20.[49] Finally, at the end of Proverbs we meet the valiant woman whose figure echoes Lady Wisdom and who provides for her house abundantly (31:15, 21, 27), just as Wisdom fills the treasure-houses of her lovers (8:21).[50] Thus, Lady Wisdom's building activity in Prov 9 is not only connected to the creation of the world in

---

45. Building a house and providing for it comprise one topos in the ancient Near East according to Van Leeuwen 2007: 67–72.

46. Longman 2006: 296–297; Plöger 1984: 168–169; Waltke 2004: 576.

47. Fox 2009: 572; McKane 1970: 472; Murphy 1998: 101–103. Toy 1899: 280–281 cannot decide between keeping or deleting it.

48. Van Leeuwen 1997: 138.

49. Van Leeuwen 2007: 77–79. The text of Prov 3:19-20:
יהוה ב**חכמה** יסד ארץ כונן שמים ב**תבונה**
ב**דעתו** תהומות נבקעו ושחקים ירעפו טל

50. Camp 1985: 200–201.

Prov 8, but there are subsequent echoes of it in the later chapters. These echoes suggest that human beings can join in her house-building activities.

Certain verses modulate this house-building motif and suggest that the picture is not only of an ordinary house but of the temple itself. As we have noted, besides the creation stories, the wisdom–knowledge–understanding triad of 24:3-4 occurs only in the context of the temple/tabernacle building. There might also be a direct hint at the temple in Prov 8:34, which speaks about the doors, doorposts, and doorways (פתח, מזוזה, דלת) of Wisdom. These three words occur together only twice outside Proverbs (1 Kgs 6:31; Ezek 46:2-3), both times referring to the doors of the temple.[51] As Baumann writes, 'in an analogous way to the temple doors of Yahweh's house, Wisdom would possess an—imaginative—temple in 8:34.'[52] Furthermore, Lady Wisdom seems to have built her house on a high point of the city (cf. 9:1 in parallel with 9:3 and 14) just as temples used to be built on high points of cities in the ancient Near East.[53] We have also seen that the temple, just like creation, was associated with number seven in the biblical tradition which might be the background for the seven pillars of 9:1. Finally, in 31:21-22 we read that the valiant woman makes scarlet (שני), linen (שש), and purple (ארגמן) clothes and coverings for her house. These three expressions occur together only in connection with making the tabernacle and the clothes of the high priest, but there they occur often.[54]

Thus, we can conclude that the house-building motif goes through the whole book of Proverbs hand in hand with allusions to the tabernacle/temple. The interpretation towards which all these point is that the whole universe is Wisdom's house (בית חכמות) and this house is at the same time God's temple (בית יהוה). Human beings can join Wisdom in her house (i.e., the Lord in his temple) by being wise in the world. Building one's own earthly household and human relationships through being wise equals building the temple of the Lord, so to speak.

This interpretation can be translated into theological language by saying that living wisely is the way to the presence of God. As Lundquist writes,

> One must not be dealing with an actual building in order to be in what I would call a 'temple' setting in the ancient Near East.... Basic to temple ideology is the act of appearing 'before the Lord.' As Menahem Haran states it: 'In general, any cultic activity to which the biblical text applies the formula 'before the Lord' can be considered an indication of a temple at the site, since this expression stems from

---

51. Baumann 1996: 161; Zabán 2012: 176.
52. Baumann 1996: 162.
53. Baumann 1996: 211; Longman 2006: 58–59, 217, 222.
54. Fischer 2005: 237–253; see Exod 25:4; 26:1, 31, 36; 27:16; 28:5, 6, 8, 15; 35:6, 23, 25, 35; 36:8, 35, 37; 38:18, 23; 39:2, 3, 5, 8, 29.

the basic conception of the temple as a divine dwelling-place and actually belongs to the temple's technical terminology.[55]

Lady Wisdom is 'before the Lord' (לפניו) in 8:30, a phrase most often used to describe the priests' place and role in the temple, especially in Leviticus,[56] but also in other parts of the Old Testament.[57] Thus, those who come to her, come into the presence of the Lord, i.e., come to the temple.

12.5 Proverbs' 'Temple-Interpretation' in Canonical Context

However, not everything is as neat and clear as I have implied so far. The above understanding is an *arguable* interpretation of the text but not one explicitly stated by it. It is far from being an irrefutable interpretation. Some of the arguments I have listed are hotly debated. The prime example is, of course, the אמון in 8:30. It is a *crux interpretatum*, and there are many rival theories about its meaning. Besides the 'craftsman/sage' understanding, other possible translations include 'growing up,' 'child,' 'faithfully.'[58] Similarly, though it is indeed possible that the seven pillars of 9:1 allude to the temple, the number seven is so widely used that it can allude to many other things, too.[59] Also, though the language of construction is clearly there in chapter 8, it is not emphasised very much, so it might be only a 'dead' literary convention, the way people wrote about creation in the ancient Near East anyway, without giving much thought to the picture of building behind some words. All in all, although I find the 'temple-building interpretation' of Proverbs 8–9 theologically promising and defendable, it is not necessarily more compelling than some other possible construals of the text's meaning and theological significance, at least not on the basis of the arguments delineated so far.

However, this interpretation becomes more persuasive if we read Proverbs in its canonical context. The idea of the temple as a hermeneutical key for the book of Proverbs becomes especially attractive if we read the text together with the Solomon narrative (1 Kings 3–11) and some psalms.

---

55. Lundquist 1983: 207.
56. 1:11; 4:6-7, 17; 6:7; 14:11-12, 16, 18, 23-24, 27, 29, 31; 15:14-15, 30; 19:22; 23:11, 20.
57. For example Num 3:4; 5:16; 6:16; 15:25; Deut 19:17; 26:4; Josh 6:8; 1 Sam 21:6; Jer 33:18; Ezek 43:24; 44:15.
58. For these and other solutions, see Baumann 1996: 131–138; Fox 2000: 285–287; Hurowitz 1999: 391–400; Waltke 2004: 417–420; Weeks 2006: 433–442.
59. See the wide array of explanations that has been offered for the number seven in Prov 9:1 throughout the history of its interpretation in Fuhs 2001: 164–165. The explanation that I find at least as persuasive as the one which understands the seven pillared building to refer to 'creation' is the one that understands it as referring to the book of Proverbs, which contains seven major units (Baumann 1996: 205–207; Hurowitz 2001: 209–218).

12.5.1 The Canonical Context: 1 Kings 3–11

It is a long-established fact that Prov 10:1–22:16 contains 375 single-line proverbs, the numerical value of the name Solomon.[60] Of course, we do not have to rely only on such 'secret hints' if we search for Solomon in the book. He is explicitly mentioned in some headings (1:1; 10:1; 25:1). If one is willing to follow this Solomonic connection and read Proverbs together with 1 Kings 3–11, he or she can find numerous parallels between the two texts. Just to list some of them briefly:

- As we have noted above, the wisdom (חכמה), knowledge (תבונה), and understanding (דעת) triad appears in both texts in the same order (1 Kgs 7:14 cf. Prov 3:19-20; 24:3-4).
- Solomon, of course, was the wise king *par excellence* in Hebrew tradition (1 Kgs 3:4-15; 5:9-14).
- Nothing could be compared to wise Solomon (1 Kgs 3:12-13)—as nothing compares to wisdom in Proverbs (Prov 3:15).[61]
- Together with the gift of wisdom Solomon also gains the promise of riches and long life (1 Kgs 3:12-14)—the most typical gifts of wisdom in Proverbs (Prov 3:2, 16; 8:18; 22:4; 28:16).
- As the queen of Sheba remarked, happy was the one who listened to Solomon (1 Kgs 10:8)—just like the one who listens to Wisdom (Prov 8:34).[62]
- Solomon had an interesting story with foreign women (daughter of pharaoh, queen of Sheba, foreign wives; 1 Kgs 3:1; 10:1-13; 11:1-13)—the relationship with foreign women is a major topic in Proverbs, especially, though not exclusively, in the first nine chapters (2:16; 5:20; 6:24; 7:5; 23:27). The 'foreign woman' (אשה נכריה) as an important type appears only in Proverbs, 1 Kings, Nehemiah, and Ezra, so the parallel is probably more significant than it might appear at first sight.[63]
- The strange woman has a house in both of the texts (1 Kgs 9:24—Prov 2:16; 5:8; 7:27; 9:14).[64]
- At the beginning of his royal career Solomon had to choose between two women (1 Kings 3)—just like the reader has to choose between woman Wisdom and woman Folly in Proverbs 9.[65]
- Right after choosing between the women, Solomon's wisdom is demonstrated through effective governance (1 Kgs 4:1-19)—which is one of Wisdom's main territories, too, in Proverbs (Prov 8:15-21).[66]

---

60. Skehan 1948: 117.
61. Camp 2000: 177.
62. Camp 2000: 177.
63. Camp 2000: 168.
64. Camp 2000: 183.
65. Camp 2000: 166.
66. Camp 2000: 169.

- Solomon established (כון) David's throne (כסא) (1 Kgs 2:45)—establishing the throne is also an important topic in Proverbs (cf. Prov 16:12; 25:5; 29:14).[67]
- In his government Solomon maintained justice (משפט) and righteousness (צדקה) (1 Kgs 10:9)—the social categories in which Wisdom moves (Prov 8:20).[68]
- Solomon provides food for Hiram (1 Kgs 5:23, 26)—just like the valiant woman (personified Wisdom?) provides food for her house in Proverbs (Prov 31:14-15, 27).[69]
- As Solomon's words make Hiram rejoice (שמח) (1Kgs 5:7)—so the good son (and good words) make a father rejoice (שמח) in Proverbs (10:1; 12:25; 15:20; 22:11).[70]

Not all of these parallels are equally persuasive and significant but they have a strong cumulative effect. If one allows for their influence, they create a 'Solomonic atmosphere' for the reading of Proverbs. Indeed, 'it is hard to imagine ancient readers interpreting these two texts independently of each other,' as Claudia V. Camp remarked.[71] This must have been true at least for those who were aware of both texts, and this should be true for those modern readers, too, who wish to read Proverbs in a canonical context.

The major topic of 1 Kings 1–11, which I did not mention explicitly in the above list is, of course, the building of the temple. This topic is presented in close connection with the other themes of the Solomon narrative. Solomon's wisdom, which made Hiram rejoice (1 Kgs 5:21; the last point in the above list), was in fact his intention to build the temple (1 Kgs 5:15-20). Wisdom and temple-building are woven together from the beginning: we read a eulogy about Solomon's wisdom (1 Kgs 5:9-14), then we learn about his intention to build the temple (1 Kgs 5:15-20), then Hiram rejoices over Solomon's wisdom (1 Kgs 5:21), then the two of them agree about some details of the work of temple-building and payment (1 Kgs 5:22-25), then we read again that God gave wisdom to Solomon and about his treaty with Hiram (1 Kgs 5:26).

If someone reads Proverbs in the context of the Solomon-narrative then the question 'How does the wisdom of Proverbs relate to the temple?' does not seem artificial. One can even suggest, based on the intermingling of the themes of temple and wisdom, that the answer 'living wisely is like building a temple' also receives affirmation from 1 Kings 1–11.

---

67. Camp 2000: 177.
68. Camp 2000: 175.
69. Van Leeuwen 2000: 206.
70. Van Leeuwen 2000: 206.
71. Camp 2000: 150.

12.5.2 The Canonical Context: Psalms

Besides 1 Kings 3–11, my other suggestion for providing a canonical context for the interpretation of Proverbs would be to read the book in the light of some psalms. My prime example is Psalm 15. The table below contains the NRSV translation of the psalm and its semantic and lexical parallels with Proverbs.

TABLE 11: Psalm 15 and Proverbs

Psalm 15	Comments
¹ (A Psalm of David.) Oh Lord, who sojourns (מי יגור) in your tent? Who dwells on your holy hill?	
² The one who walks blamelessly (הולך תמים),	The expression הולך תמים occurs twice in the Bible, here and in Prov 28:18. The word תמים/תם is proportionately the most common in Proverbs among the biblical books.
does what is right (פעל צדק),	The expression פעל צדק is unique but in its present form and place the psalm seems to be a deliberate contrast with Psalm 14,[72] which speaks about פעלי און in verse 4; פעל און is rare outside Psalms (it occurs 16 times in Psalms, 10 times outside of it) but it does occur three times in Proverbs (10:29; 21:15; 30:20).
and speaks the truth from their heart;	Speaking is the most common topic in Proverbs.[73]
³ no slander on his lips,	The topic of slander is also one of the main themes of Proverbs.[74]
and does no evil to his friend (רעהו רעה),	The 'רע רעה' sequence of words occurs only here and in Prov 3:29.
nor shames (חרפה) his neighbour;	Although the exact word חרפה occurs only twice in Proverbs (6:33; 18:3), the topic of shame is quite common in it.[75]

---

72. Hossfeld and Zenger 1993a: 166–182.
73. 2:12; 4:24; 6:12; 8:13; 10:8, 10, 11, 13, 14, 18, 19, 20, 21, 31, 32; 11:9, 11, 12, 13; 12:6, 13, 14, 16, 17, 18, 19, 22, 23, 25; 13:2, 3, 5; 14:3, 5, 23, 25; 15:1, 2, 4, 7, 14, 23, 26, 28; 16:1, 13, 23, 24, 27; 17:4, 7, 15, 20, 27, 28; 18:4, 6, 7, 8, 13, 20, 21; 19:1, 5, 9, 22, 28; 20:15, 17, 19; 21:6, 23; 24:2, 7, 28; 25:11, 12, 15, 20, 23; 26:4, 5, 22, 23, 24, 25, 28; 29:20; etc.
74. 1:22; 3:34; 14:6; 18:8; 19:29; 20:19; 21:24; 22:10; 29:8; etc.
75. 3:35; 6:33; 9:7; 11:2; 12:16; 13:18; 18:3; 22:10; etc.

Psalm 15	Comments
⁴ in whose eyes the despising (נבזה) is rejected (נמאס), but who honours those who fear the Lord;	Despising is also condemned in Proverbs (14:2; 15:20; 19:16). A similar cluster of words is used in Prov 15:32-33: the fear of the Lord and honour are mentioned together in Prov 15:33 and the previous verse uses the word מאס.
who stands by his oath even to his hurt;⁷⁶	
⁵ who does not lend money at interest, and does not take a bribe against the innocent.	For lending money at interest and bribing, see the parallels in Prov 28:8 and 6:35.
The one who does these things shall never be moved (לא ימוט לעולם).	Verse 5b is parallel to Prov 10:30 (צדיק לעולם בל ימוט; see also Prov 12:3).

Despite its similarities to Proverbs' world of thought, Psalm 15 is usually not listed among the wisdom psalms.⁷⁷ Even where its similarity to Proverbs is mentioned, it is not utilised for a theological discussion. Most commentaries only highlight that ethical behaviour is indeed very important, even in cultic contexts.⁷⁸ The reason for the reluctance to emphasise too strongly its resemblance to Proverbs may be the psalm's close connection to the cult as it speaks about the requirements for dwelling in the temple. Consequently, most commentators try to explain it in a cultic and not in a wisdom context. Some argue that it is an 'entrance liturgy,' which formed a part of ceremonies in which priests at the entrance of the temple questioned those who wished to enter, in order to establish prerequisites for admission.⁷⁹ However, as Terrien observes,

> Psalm 15 is not merely a request for entrance: the double question does not ask, 'Who is permitted to come in?' The two verbs, 'to sojourn' and 'to dwell,' clearly ask the conditions for residence in the sanctuary side chambers (1 Kgs 6:5), or the subsidiary edifices erected on the holy hill.⁸⁰

Others argue that it might have been carved on the doorposts of the temple as similar texts were carved on pillars next to the doors of Egyptian sanctuaries.⁸¹ Hossfeld cuts the Gordian knot bound by 'wisdom-' and 'cultic ropes' by

---

76. The sense and interpretation of the last line of Ps 15:4 is not clear. See Craigie 2004: 150; Hossfeld and Zenger 1993b: 106.

77. It is not listed in Dell's quite comprehensive list of wisdom psalms. She lists the following psalms: 1, 14, 19, 25, 32, 33, 34, 36, 37, 39, 49, 51, 53, 62, 73, 78, 90, 92, 94, 104, 105, 106, 111, 112, 119, 127, 128 (Dell 2000: 64). However, occasionally it was included among the wisdom psalms by scholars who defined this category very broadly (Murphy 1976: 461 n. 4).

78. Like Craigie 2004: 150; Dahood 1965: 83; Goldingay 2006b: 218–225.

79. Gunkel 1998: 72; Kraus 1988: 227.

80. Terrien 2003: 170.

81. Levenson 2006: 93; Weinfeld 1982: 224–250.

understanding the psalm as an entrance liturgy which was modified (especially in verses 4 and 5) later on by wisdom circles.[82]

At this point, I should clarify that I am not arguing that this psalm should be understood as a wisdom psalm. I am rather arguing that whatever label we attach to the psalm, its similarities to Proverbs can be utilised in our interpretation. It is precisely the cultic connection of the psalm which can be fertile to our reading of Proverbs. Can we not understand the book of Proverbs in the light of this psalm as presenting ethical life as the representation of the temple? After all, according to the psalm, those who 'walk blamelessly,' dwell in the temple.

Psalm 15 is the first one in a series of psalms which probably forms a sub-collection in the first book of Psalms.[83] The last psalm in this series is Psalm 24, which is parallel with Psalm 15 in its content. It also says that it is the blameless person (though does not use the actual word 'blameless') who ascends the hill of the Lord and stands in his holy place (Ps 24:3-6). Just before saying this, however, it proclaims that

ליהוה הארץ ומלואה תבל וישבי בה
כי הוא על ימים יסדה ועל נהרות יכוננה

The earth and everything in it, the world and whoever lives in it are the Lord's,
since he founded it on waters and established it on rivers.

(Ps 24:1-2)

The sequence of themes (the world is the Lord's, and those who behave ethically [in the world] stand in the temple) seems to express the same idea that we have already discussed: speaking about the world and speaking about the temple flows into each other seamlessly. World and temple form a 'homology.' However, Psalm 24 is not only an expression of the homology of the world and temple but also of the homology of the 'worldly behaviour' and the 'temple worship' of the believer, just like Psalm 15. This is the same homology that is visible in Proverbs if it is interpreted in the context of the Jerusalem temple.

There are other psalms outside of Psalms 15–24 which might support an interpretation of Proverbs that tries to understand the book's teaching in the light of the temple. Ps 84:11-12 [10-11] also speaks side by side about walking blamelessly and being in the temple. Ps 92:13-14 [12-13] says too that the righteous are in the Lord's house: 'the righteous flourish like the palm tree, and grow like a cedar in Lebanon. They are planted in the house of the Lord; they flourish in the court of our God.' Only when he entered the temple did the psalmist of Psalm 73 understand that evil people will have a bad end even if they seem to flourish now.[84] This is exactly what Proverbs wants the reader to understand, too

---

82. Hossfeld and Zenger 1993b: 103–105.
83. Hossfeld and Zenger 1993b: 157–158; for further literature, see Brown 2010: 259.
84. At least if we understand עד אבוא אל מקדשי אל in Ps 73:17a as 'till I enter the sanctuary.' This is a plausible understanding in the light of Jer 51:51 and Lev 21:23,

(cf. Prov 1:8-19; 2:22; 10:25, 27; 13:9; 14:32; 24:20; etc.), so again, being in the temple (Psalm 73) and being wise (Proverbs) have the same effects.

The parallels between Psalms and Proverbs deserve a more thorough and systematic investigation but that is beyond the scope of this work. Nevertheless, the examples given above provide enough basis for the conclusion that at least some psalms, just as 1 Kings 1–11, provide canonical support for reading the wise, ethical behaviour of Proverbs as tantamount to entering and residing in the temple, that is, in the presence of Yahweh.

12.6 Summary: The Solomonic Temple and Proverbs

Jon Levenson writes about biblical temple-oriented devotion as follows:

> The familiar Christian use of Genesis 3 is temporal: the opportunity for immortality lay in the past and is unavailable now. Psalm 133 and its kindred literature offer a paradigm that is spatial: death is the norm outside Zion and cannot be reversed, but within the temple city, death is unknown, for there God has ordained the blessing of eternal life. To journey to the Temple is to move toward redemption, to leave the parched land of wasting and death for the fountain of life and the revival and rejuvenation it dispenses. This conception of the Temple as paradise, the place rendered inviolable by the pervasive presence of God, explains one of the more striking features of Temple-oriented devotion in the Hebrew Bible. [85]

Though Levenson wrote about the temple, his lines make sense just as well if we refer them to Proverbs. It is probably not accidental that the word חיים occurs most frequently in Proverbs (34 times) among the biblical books. If one follows the instructions of Proverbs she enters the realm of life here and now. It is like entering into the temple.

The concept of 'wisdom' was closely connected to the Solomonic temple, and, as I have argued above, Proverbs, like the temple, offers the presence of God, life, and abundance to those who listen to its instructions. It often does this through language used elsewhere for describing temple-oriented devotion or temple-building activity.

Based on these observations I suggest that seeing wise life as tantamount to being in the temple and experiencing the presence of God, eternal life, and abun-

---

where מקדשים probably refers to the temple. Some understand it, however, as referring to synagogues, or undefined 'holy things,' or sanctuaries but not the Jerusalem temple. Nevertheless, most of these understandings would not alter my conclusion since they also express the same point which is relevant to my argument: something is understood as a result of being in the holy presence of the Lord.

85. Levenson 2006: 92; for the special relationship between the temple and life, see also Keel 1997: 186.

dance is a fitting theological vision for interpreting Proverbs. This interpretation does justice to the text and provides a theological perspective for its practical admonitions. There are enough hints in the text of Proverbs itself to suggest that it presents acting wisely as akin to being in the temple. However, these are only hints, and not a clear and explicit teaching of the text. The main impetus for this reading, in my opinion, rather comes from outside of Proverbs. It comes from its canonical context, mainly 1 Kings 3–11, some psalms, and some creation and Eden narratives. I cautiously conclude, therefore, that the temple as a 'theological key' for Proverbs is provided mainly by the canonical context and that the language and conceptuality of Proverbs resonates with this canonical context.[86]

12.7 Conclusions

Let us go back to the original question at the beginning of Part IV. Is Proverbs secular in the sense of presenting a common ground which is experienced and understood by everyone regardless of race, nationality, gender, and religion?

My answer to this question is 'yes and no.' Yes, it speaks about everyday life and utilises international wisdom language. Nevertheless, something more is going on than simply presenting a universal common ground: Proverbs not only *presents* the secular but at the same time *sanctifies* it.

In the last two chapters I have offered two parallel, canonical readings of Proverbs. The first one was canonical in the sense that it was seeking to understand the book as a whole, paying attention to the theological framework provided in the first nine chapters, especially in chapter 8. The second was canoni-

---

86. Seeing Proverbs in the light of temple devotion is in accordance with some strands of the later tradition, too. In Sirach 24 the role of Wisdom is explained through the language of the temple and the garden of Eden (Beale 2004: 160; Hayward 1996: 7, 71, 98, 123; Winston 1979: 204). Hayward argues that Sirach deduced that Wisdom lives in the temple mainly from a close reading of Proverbs 8 (Hayward 1999: 33–35). Philo writes: 'When God willed to send down the image of divine excellence from heaven to earth in pity for our race, that it should not lose its share in the better lot, he constructs as a symbol of the truth the holy tabernacle and its contents to be a representation and copy of wisdom.' (*De Congressu Eruditionis Gratia*, the translation is taken from Philo 1932b: 336–339.) And again: 'And further on he [Moses] will speak of God's dwelling-place, the tabernacle, as being 'ten curtains' (Ex. xxvi. 1), for to the structure which includes the whole of wisdom the perfect number ten belongs, and wisdom is the court and palace of the All-ruler, the sole Monarch, the Sovereign Lord. This dwelling is a house perceived by the mind, yet it is also the world of our senses, since he makes the curtains to be woven from such materials as are symbolical of the four elements; for they are wrought of fine linen, of dark red, of purple and of scarlet, four in number as I said. The linen is a symbol of earth, since it grows out of earth; the dark red of air, which is naturally black; the purple of water, since the means by which the dye is produced, the shell-fish which bears the same name comes from the sea; and the scarlet of fire, since it closely resembles flame.' (*Quis Rerum Divinarum Heres Sit?*, the translation is taken from Philo 1932a: 516–519.)

cal in the sense that it was seeking to understand the book in its canonical context. In the first one I argued that Proverbs 8 depicts Wisdom as mediating the presence of Yahweh, suggesting that through listening to the rest of the book and through acting wisely one can experience Yahweh. My second canonical reading led to a similar conclusion: allusions to the Jerusalem temple provide a parallel between temple worship and everyday behaviour.

Comparing these readings with a quotation from José Casanova, a sociologist and an expert in the secularisation process, might help to clarify my statement that Proverbs seeks to 'sanctify' the secular. In a recent article Casanova explains that secularisation can follow two different dynamics:

> One is the dynamic of internal Christian secularization that aims to spiritualize the temporal and to bring the religious life of perfection out of the monasteries into the secular world, so that everybody may become 'a secular ascetic monk,' a perfect Christian in the *saeculum*. Such a dynamic tends to transcend the dualism by blurring the boundaries between the religious and the secular, by making the religious secular and the secular religious through mutual reciprocal infusion. . . . The other different, indeed almost opposite, dynamic of secularization takes the form of laicization. It aims to emancipate all secular spheres from clerical-ecclesiastical control, and in this respect, it is marked by a laic/clerical antagonism. . . . Here the boundaries between the religious and the secular are rigidly maintained. . . . With many variations, these are the two main dynamics of secularization that culminate in our secular age. In different ways, both paths lead to an overcoming of the medieval Christian dualism through a positive affirmation and revaluation of the *saeculum*, that is, of the secular age and the secular world, imbuing the immanent secular world with a quasi-transcendent meaning as the place for human flourishing. In this broad sense of the term 'secular,' that of 'living in the secular world and within the secular age,' we are all secular, and all modern societies are secular and are likely to remain so for the foreseeable future, one could almost say *per saecula saeculorum*.[87]

I have argued that Proverbs fits the first dynamic of secularisation better. That is, it heightens the significance of the secular everyday life, not by emancipating it *from* the sacred but by blurring the boundary between sacred and secular, not by pushing the boundaries of the secular as far as possible but by seeing the secular in the light of the *regular*. This understanding of 'secularisation' is actually closer to the word's original meaning. Originally 'religious (*regular*) clergy' referred to ecclesiastical personnel who lived in the monasteries, whereas 'secular clergy' referred to ecclesiastical personnel who chose to serve outside the walls of a monastery (i.e., in the present time instead of in eternity) for a period of time or for the whole of their lives. Nevertheless, they still belonged to the religious institution; they simply performed their religious service in the context

---

87. Casanova 2011: 56–57.

of everyday life. In many senses they lived the life of the monastery—outside of its walls. Similarly, the vision of Proverbs is the vision of the sacred in the secular, the vision of living the life of the temple worship but outside the temple.

Contrasting my interpretation of Proverbs with the views of another sociologist-philosopher expert in the secular, Jürgen Habermas, might shed some further light on my usage of the expression 'sanctifying the secular.' Habermas is arguing that the history of secularisation can be usefully understood as the increasing level of self-reflexion of humankind:

> The progress in morality and law ... [is] the decentering of our ego- or group-centered perspectives, when the point is to non-violently end conflicts of action. These social-cognitive kinds of progress already refer to the further dimension of the increase in reflection, that is, the ability to step back behind oneself. This is what Max Weber meant when he spoke of 'disenchantment.' ...
> In early modernity, the instrumental attitude of state bureaucracy toward a political power largely free of moral norms signifies such a reflexive step ...
> It is also in connection with this widespread push toward reflection that we have to view the progressive disintegration of traditional, popular piety. Two specifically modern forms of religious consciousness emerged from this: on the one hand, a fundamentalism that either withdraws from the modern world or turns aggressively toward it; on the other, a reflective faith that relates itself to other religions and respects the fallible insights of the institutionalized sciences as well as human rights.[88]

If I understand Habermas correctly, he argues that the morally (and religiously) free secular space which has developed in the last few hundred years has enabled us 'to step behind ourselves,' to look at ourselves as if from outside, and realise that there are other players on the field. This space potentially enables us to view our motives and actions in a less biased way and those of others in a more understanding way.

These are certainly developments which must be welcomed in many respects. However, my claim is that Proverbs is not so much about 'stepping behind ourselves' as about realising that it is impossible to step behind God. It is not so much about reflection on the self with the help of the neutral secular horizon but about reflection on the secular in the light of the temple, that is, in the light of the ever-present God. It is a second step of reflection, if you like: first one might step behind oneself through the 'secular space' but then she might also step behind the 'secular space' itself and reflect on it in the light of the divine. This 'second step' enables one to realise that though the 'neutral space' might seem to be outside of the temple, in reality this 'neutral space' is the sacred temple itself where God can be met.

---

88. Mendieta 2010.

All of these mean that 'everyday life is understood as a liturgy.' I am borrowing this sentence (altering some words) from Charles Mathewes' *A Theology of Public Life*. It is worth quoting a bit more from the wider context of Mathewes' statement:

> [I attempt] to offer a theological interpretation of the world as a form of participation in the divine *perichōrēsis*. . . . It is a participation necessarily mediated through the world, through our condition as existing in God's Creation. Creation is not the 'background' to our redemption, it plays an essential role within it. . . . Given this, citizenship is usefully understood as a liturgy, . . . because, by engaging in apparently political activities, we are participating in properly theological activities as well.[89]

Mathewes' text contains two ideas I have tried to delineate through my two canonical readings: participation and liturgy. The vision of Proverbs 8 can be understood to be about participating in the divine through wise living. The temple parallel envisions life in the world as liturgy in the Jerusalem temple. In other words, by 'sanctification' I mean that Proverbs provides a vision for everyday life, in which mundane 'worldly' acts gain a new significance. They become the means for glorifying God, being in contact with him and enjoying his presence. Making wise decisions becomes worship of Yahweh.

---

89. Mathewes 2007: 26.

13

A 'Post-Secular' Interpretation of Proverbs: The Hidden God[1]

So far I have discussed the understanding of 'secular' in terms of 'universalistic, neutral language' (my earlier category א). Space does not allow a thorough discussion of the other two secular interpretations (human autonomy [category ב], disenchanted thinking [category ג]). This, however, is not a serious problem in itself as they are less popular nowadays. Instead of discussing them directly in detail, I am going to investigate an interpretation which I consider their contemporary offspring. Thus, the following discussion is an evaluation of the recent theological fruits of these two, once popular secular interpretations of Proverbs.

13.1 Walter Brueggemann's Interpretation of Proverbs

Walter Brueggemann in his *Theology of the Old Testament* describes two different accounts of Yahweh in Israel's testimony. The 'core testimony' speaks about a reliable, benevolent God, who acts out of righteousness and steadfast love. However, there is a 'countertestimony,' claims Brueggemann, which depicts Yahweh as a God who can be quite difficult to live with, and whose acts

---

[1]. Some parts of this chapter have been published in an abbreviated form in Hungarian as Schwáb Zoltán, 'Hogyan rejtőzködik Isten a Példabeszédek könyvében—Walter Brueggemann értelmezésének kritikája' [How Is God Hiding in the Book of Proverbs—A Critique of Walter Brueggemann's Interpretation], in Szávai László (ed.), *Vidimus enim stellam eius... Konferenciakötet* (Budapest: Károli Gáspár Református Egyetem, L'Harmattan Kiadó, 2011) 360–366.

are rather arbitrary if not deliberately abusive. Brueggemann builds his argument mainly on texts like Ecclesiastes, Job, lament psalms and some passages from the prophets.[2]

There is one other biblical book which plays a key role in Brueggemann's argument for the existence of 'Israel's countertestimony': the book of Proverbs. In fact, Proverbs is the key text with which Brueggemann starts his discussion of the 'countertestimony.'[3] This might be somewhat surprising since Proverbs does seem to affirm the positive characteristics of Yahweh. Why does Brueggemann consider it to be a part of the 'countertestimony'?

First, he thinks that Proverbs is quite different from the majority of biblical books. He builds on von Rad's evaluation:

> In his *Old Testament Theology 1*, von Rad presented wisdom, along with the Psalms, as response to Israel's credo theology....
> Von Rad, in his final book, revised this assessment to argue that wisdom is simply an alternative way of doing theology, one that represents a different context of faith and offers very different intellectual, cultural, and sociological options.... I advance the notion of wisdom as alternative in order to suggest that wisdom is not simply an unrelated, second effort, but is an attempt to speak of Yahweh in all of those contexts of Israel's lived experience wherein the main claims of the core testimony are not persuasive.[4]

Second, this alternative theology speaks about a hidden God as opposed to the God who is visible through his dramatic interventions in history: 'a Yahweh who is not direct and not visible.'[5] Israel's core testimony about the deliverance from Egypt, the Sinai covenant, about God who performs 'mighty acts'[6] was simply not applicable in the intricacies of everyday struggles.

> In Israel's primary testimony, as we have seen, Yahweh is known by Israel to be the subject of active verbs of transformation, whereby Yahweh dramatically and identifiably intervenes and intrudes into the life of Israel in order to work Yahweh's righteousness, which is marked by justice, equity, and reliability....[7]
> Israel had to learn to live (and testify) in contexts where the intense engagement of Yahweh, as given in the great transformative verbs of the core testimony, simply was not available.[8]

---

2. Brueggemann 1997: 315–403.
3. Brueggemann 1997: 333–358.
4. Brueggemann 1997: 335.
5. Brueggemann 1997: 335.
6. For the theological significance of the terms, see Brueggemann 1997: 335 n. 8.
7. Brueggemann 1997: 333.
8. Brueggemann 1997: 357.

A 'Post-Secular' Interpretation of Proverbs: The Hidden God   215

Besides mentioning the above two points, Brueggemann also emphasises, right at the beginning of his discussion, that the theology of hiddenness of God has a venerable history. It is well attested in the Hebrew Bible:

> The core testimony of active verbs speaks of Yahweh with the claim that Yahweh was known and seen directly in the ongoing life of Israel. A strong and crucial counterclaim, however, maintains that the God of Israel is hidden: 'Truly, you are a God who hides himself, O God of Israel, the Savior' (Isa 45:15).[9]

Furthermore, hiddenness theology is also part of the spiritual heritage of the Christian Church and other religions. Besides other works he refers to Luther's use of the term 'hidden God' and Buber's discussion of the topic from a Jewish perspective.[10]

In this alternative theology Yahweh does not act directly in the world. He just sustains the order of the universe.

> Yahweh is the hidden guarantor of an order that makes life in the world possible.[11]
> Human deeds have automatic and inescapable consequences.... The deed carries within it the seed of its own consequence, punishment or reward, which is not imposed by an outside agent (Yahweh)....[12]
> This articulation of the hidden God permits Israel to affirm about Yahweh what the dominant 'mighty deeds' testimony did not permit, or at least what scholarly attention did not entertain. The wisdom tradition is able to affirm that blessing, Yahweh's power and will for life, is intrinsic in the life process itself.[13]

This alternative theology required a new mode of speech.

> Israel learned, living in the absence of Yahweh's great interventions, to speak of Yahweh in yet another way. This way of speaking assigns very few active verbs of transformation to Yahweh.... Rather, as Israel pondered the regularities of its daily life, Yahweh is assigned functions that concern especially governance, order, maintenance, and sustenance.[14]

This new way of speaking is striking where Israel speaks about the freedom of Yahweh. As Brueggemann argues, the fact that Israel emphasised the deed–consequence relation does not mean that she abandoned her faith in Yahweh's freedom. There are verses (16:1-2, 9; 19:14, 21; 20:24; 21:30-31) in which the authors of Proverbs reasserted this freedom. But even in these verses,

---

9. Brueggemann 1997: 333.
10. Brueggemann 1997: 333 n. 1.
11. Brueggemann 1997: 336.
12. Brueggemann 1997: 338.
13. Brueggemann 1997: 341.
14. Brueggemann 1997: 334.

...the way in which this ultimate affirmation of Yahweh is articulated... is odd. These sayings seem reluctant to grant to Yahweh any active verbs. Of the eight verses from Proverbs noted above, five assign Yahweh no verb at all, but only a preposition. Thus in 16:1, 19:14, and 20:24, what is decisive is 'from Yahweh.' In 21:30-31, the two prepositions are 'against' (*ngd*) and 'to' (*l*). In 19:21, moreover, the verb is passive, 'will be established' (*taqûm*). Only in two of these passages is a direct, active verb assigned to Yahweh. In 16:9, the verb translated 'direct' is *kûn*; this, as we shall see, is a preferred word with which to speak about Yahweh's hidden, long-term providential care. The other verb, in 16:2, rendered 'weigh,' is *tōkēn*, which may be linked to *kûn*. This word is used in Job 28:25, Isa 40:12, and Ps 75:3, in order to assert Yahweh's majestic power as the orderer and governor of all of creation. But it is not a verb that witnesses to any direct, visible act on Yahweh's part.[15]

To summarise Brueggemann's account of the theology of the book of Proverbs, we can say that this biblical book stemmed from the negative experience of Yahweh's perceived absence in everyday life, from his hiddenness behind the ordinary processes, rules, and regularities of daily happenings. More positively, the authors of Proverbs celebrated the order of creation and its hidden sustenance by Yahweh.

God's hiddenness had been mentioned occasionally in connection with Proverbs already before Brueggemann's utilisation of the notion.[16] Maybe he got the inspiration from one of these earlier applications of the term. However, it is Brueggemann's distinctive contribution that he put such a strong emphasis on the 'hiddenness' of God and built his Proverbs interpretation around this suggestive theological theme.

13.1.1 The Place of *Theology of the Old Testament* among Brueggemann's Interpretations of Proverbs

It has to be noted that the discussion of Proverbs in the *Theology of the Old Testament* is not Brueggemann's last word on the subject. One of the main differences between this and his later interpretations is that the category of 'hiddenness' ceases to play such a significant role in them.[17] It is not always clear whether he wishes to modify, downplay, or even contradict his hiddenness theology in these more recent writings, or if he still maintains its main statements, and just wants to emphasise other, complementary aspects of Proverbs. This last option seems to be the more likely as he does occasionally refer to God's hidden

---

15. Brueggemann 1997: 350.
16. E.g., Bryce 1979: 158–161; Crenshaw 1976b: 17; von Rad 1972: 299.
17. Brueggemann 2003: 305–317; Brueggemann 2008: 178–193; Brueggemann 2011: 247–260.

A 'Post-Secular' Interpretation of Proverbs: The Hidden God   217

work in his later writings.[18] Whatever the case might be, the focus of the following investigation will be Brueggemann's treatment of God's hiddenness in Proverbs in his *Theology of the Old Testament* and not a comprehensive study of his changing (or not changing) views on Proverbs.

It might be worthwhile, however, to note some similarities and differences between his hiddenness-interpretation in the *Theology of the Old Testament* and his earlier discussion of Proverbs. In his *In Man we Trust* (1972) one of Brueggemann's main interpretative categories was the 'secular.' He understood Proverbs' secularity both as non-sacral thinking and as emphasis on human autonomy. Consider, for example, the following quotation:

> I believe it is ... plausible to suggest that in the wisdom traditions of Israel we have a visible expression of secularization as it has been characterised in the current discussions. Wisdom teaching is profoundly secular in that it presents life and history as a human enterprise. ... Retribution theology as found in the wisdom teachings is a warning that one cannot flee to the sacral for escape from the result of foolish actions and choices.[19]

In the *Theology of the Old Testament* Brueggemann continues speaking about human freedom and autonomy in Proverbs:[20]

> Israel's imagination is shaped in this venue by an awareness of givens, limits, and payouts authorized by Yahweh, which create large zones of human choice, freedom, responsibility. ...[21]
> Human life is lived in a well-ordered, reliable world ... from that wisdom tradition may derive a large zone of human freedom and responsibility (as in Proverbs).[22]

Concerning the sacral/secular dichotomy, Brueggemann abandoned this vocabulary already before his *Theology of the Old Testament*. He suggests instead the usage of sociological categories like 'priestly' and 'bureaucratic groups' or 'religious' and 'ideological legitimation.'[23] Despite the changes in vocabulary, however, he keeps the dichotomy, and his description of the 'bureaucratic,' 'ideological' wisdom circles still keeps many characteristics of his earlier description

---

18. 'The God of Proverbs is the Creator God who in hidden ways has ordered the world and presides over that order.' (Brueggemann 2003: 308.) 'The wisdom traditions keep the way of the purpose of Yahweh mostly hidden.' (Brueggemann 2008: 182.) 'God is working out God's purposes in steady, faithful, reliable but hidden ways.' (Brueggemann 2011: 259–260.) See also his contrast between the God of miracles (history) and the God of order (wisdom) in Brueggemann 2008: 157–193.

19. Brueggemann 1972: 82.

20. Though, as it is obvious from these quotations too, he did not speak of a limitless autonomy, see Brueggemann 1997: 337–338.

21. Brueggemann 1997: 338.

22. Brueggemann 1997: 350.

23. Brueggemann 1990: 121, 124–126.

of secular wisdom.[24] In his earlier *In Man We Trust* he contrasted secular thinking with the 'sacral view of reality in which the *intrusion* ... of the holy ... causes the decisive turn.'[25] This is a very similar statement to the one in his later *Theology of the Old Testament* in which he says that Yahweh in Proverbs does not 'intervene[s] and intrude[s] into the life of Israel.'[26]

One of the main developments that can be noted in Brueggemann's discussion in *Theology of the Old Testament* is that there he does not replace the category of 'secular' with sociological categories but with the theological category of 'hiddenness.' Nevertheless, given the similarities to his earlier interpretation of Proverbs, the overlap between these two categories is clear. Therefore, in Brueggemann's later treatment of Proverbs Yahweh's 'hiddenness' is in a way a theological outworking of his earlier 'secular' interpretation.

I suspect that one of Brueggemann's motivations in his more recent (1997) interpretation is the same as in his earlier one (1972): to offer, with the help of a 'secular-looking' Proverbs, a useful model of theological thinking for modern people in a disenchanted world. The 'Yahweh who is not direct and not visible, but who in fact is hidden in the ongoing daily processes of life'[27] seems to be more in line with the modern, 'secular' people's experience and thinking than the God of the *Heilsgeschichte*.

13.2 Preliminary Evaluation of Brueggemann's Interpretation

There is much that is of value in Brueggemann's discussion. The important place he gives to wisdom in his account of Old Testament theology and the imaginative introduction of the theological category of 'hiddenness' into the discussion of 'wisdom theology' are innovations for which scholars working on wisdom literature should be grateful. His emphasis on the importance of everyday life in wisdom can hardly be contested. Furthermore, though the above short introduction cannot do justice to this, his discussion is characterised by theological richness: he touches on issues of ethics and aesthetics, follows wisdom trajectories into the New Testament, and investigates important topics like liberation and providence.

However, there are two interrelated issues where, in my judgement, his account deserves nuancing. The first is his understanding of wisdom (and

---

24. For instance, he referred to divine wisdom as Yahweh's 'rationality' (Brueggemann 1997: 345) which is built 'into the very fabric of creation' (Brueggemann 1997: 338). He also referred to Israel's wisdom as investigating the world's 'predictability that is almost scientific in its precision' (Brueggemann 1997: 349), and referred to the valuing of the 'ordinariness of daily life' (Brueggemann 1997: 341) instead of relying on the narrative of Yahweh's 'intrusive' mighty acts (Brueggemann 1997: 338).
25. Brueggemann 1972: 81, original emphasis.
26. Brueggemann 1997: 333–334.
27. Brueggemann 1997: 335.

Proverbs) as 'countertestimony.' There is obviously much in Proverbs that differs from other parts of the Bible, not least its special focus on everyday life. Thus, in a sense, the word 'alternative' is justified. However, I am not persuaded that Proverbs' thought does not leave space for God's dramatic intrusions at all. The category 'countertestimony' surely represents an overstatement of Proverbs' 'alternativeness.'

The second issue is Brueggemann's understanding of 'hiddenness.' The words Brueggemann most often uses together with the word 'hiddenness' are 'indirect' and 'invisible': 'Yahweh ... is, on many occasions, hidden—indirect and not visible,' '... Yahweh who is not direct and not visible, but who in fact is hidden ... ,' '... Yahweh's indirection and hiddenness,' '... hidden, indirect way of its [Yahweh's governance] working,' '... Yahweh's hidden, inscrutable, indirect, invisible ways ...' 'Yahweh was "taken underground" into hiddenness ... in indirectness and invisibility ... ,' etc.[28] This vocabulary seems to represent Brueggemann's understanding of God's hiddenness, namely that God's activity (and, consequently, God himself) is not visible in everyday life, not least because he does not intervene into history in direct, dramatic, miraculous ways.

God's 'hiddenness' has been understood in many ways in the last few thousand years of theological discussion. Brueggemann's understanding of 'hiddenness' as 'invisibility in everyday life' sounds most natural to contemporary, 'secular' readers, and it certainly has some pedigree during the rich history of hiddenness theology.[29] However, in Christian theology there is another, more dominant understanding of this concept which differs from Brueggemann's usage in at least two aspects. First, it takes as the subject of hiddenness not simply 'God' but 'God's essence'; second, it explains hiddenness mainly as incomprehensibility and not primarily as invisibility.

The Eastern Orthodox Christian tradition differentiates between God's 'energies' and God's essence.[30] The Western tradition speaks about God's 'effects' and God's essence. As Thomas says, 'God's effects, therefore, can serve to demonstrate that God exists, even though they cannot help us to know him comprehensively for what he is (*suam essentiam*).'[31] God's energies/effects are visible, well perceivable. These energies/effects can include dramatic and non-dramatic, supernatural and non-supernatural things equally. It does not really

---

28. Brueggemann 1997: 333, 335, 349, 350, 354, 357.
29. Just two years before the publication of the *Theology of the Old Testament* Friedman wrote about God's hiddenness in a very similar way (Friedman 1995). Von Rad, whose influence Brueggemann acknowledged several times in his writings, also used the concept of hiddenness in a similar fashion occasionally (see von Rad 1966a: 203–204; von Rad 1966c: 68–74).
30. Clément 1993: 237–240; Louth 2007: 88.
31. *ST* I, 2, 2, ad. 3; cf. Turner 2004: *passim*. For an insightful discussion of Thomas's understanding of God's incomprehensibility, see Rahner 1978: 107–125.

matter if the visible energy/effect is dramatic or not. It can be the growth of grass, the love between two persons, turning water into wine, or the cross of Christ. The invisible God is completely visible through the (extraordinary and ordinary) visible phenomena of the world. Yet, God's *essence* is incomprehensible. It is a dark abyss, vastness, otherness which is completely beyond human perception. This is what is called God's hiddenness in many patristic, medieval, and even modern theological discussions and not that God and his activity are not visible in mundane everyday reality.

I am going to argue in the following that although Brueggemann's understanding of hiddenness offers itself most readily to modern, 'disenchanted' readers and although it can be easily seen in the text of Proverbs, it is actually not something which is claimed explicitly by the text. I will also suggest that the other, 'classical' understanding of hiddenness not only fits the explicit statements of the text better but also that it is at least as useful a category for a theological interpretation of Proverbs as Brueggemann's understanding of hiddenness.

13.3 Evaluation of Brueggemann's Interpretation

13.3.1 Hiddenness in Proverbs

Nowhere does Proverbs explicitly claim that God is hidden. The vocabulary of hiddenness (verbs such as כחד, סתר, חבא/חבה, צפן, טמן, עלם) is almost entirely missing from the book.[32] This in itself does not prove anything, since the idea can be present in the text without using the specific vocabulary, but as we are speaking about a supposed implicit meaning and not about an explicit statement, we need extra care in circumscribing its existence and role in Proverbs' thought.

In order to establish his understanding of hiddenness in relation to Proverbs, Brueggemann refers to Yahweh's governing role in the book as a fairly passive one. According to Brueggemann, 'human deeds have automatic and inescapable consequences.... The deed carries within it the seed of its own consequence, punishment or reward, which is not imposed by an outside agent (Yahweh).'[33] Here Brueggemann follows the argument of Klaus Koch.[34] However, as was noted in Part I, Koch's theory is debatable.[35] Furthermore, besides the numerous linguistic and historical problems, the theological problem that such a mechanistic order would restrict the freedom of God was also recognised by some.[36]

---

32. We do read occasionally that God hides things, but we never read that God or characteristics of God are hidden (Balentine 1983: 9).
33. Brueggemann 1997: 338.
34. Koch 1955: 1–42.
35. See discussion on pages 58–59.
36. Perdue 1994: 46–47.

A 'Post-Secular' Interpretation of Proverbs: The Hidden God 221

Brueggemann has recognised this theological problem, too. We have seen above that he tries to evade it by saying that although Israel did recognise the freedom of Yahweh, in those verses in which she spoke about his omnipotent governance she either did not use verbs at all, or used verbs which referred to a passive kind of governance rather than to active 'intrusions' into the world.[37]

At this point Brueggemann explicitly builds on von Rad's work, but also goes beyond it. The eight verses which Brueggemann refers to (16:1-2, 9; 19:14, 21; 20:24; 21:30-31) were mentioned together by von Rad in his book about Israelite wisdom.[38] He referred to them as examples of the 'remarkable dialectic' of the book of Proverbs: a considerable part of the book seems to teach that it is possible to understand the 'automatic' rules of life; however, there are a lot of verses (like these eight) which teach Yahweh's sovereignty and freedom:

> Reduced to its bare essentials, these regulations of theirs [the sages'] for a fruitful life seem determined by a remarkable dialectic. Do not hesitate to summon up all your powers in order to familiarize yourself with all the rules which might somehow be effective in life. Ignorance in any form will be detrimental to you; only the 'fool' thinks he can shut his eyes to this. Experience, on the other hand, teaches that you can never be certain. You must always remain open for a completely new experience. You will never become really wise, for, in the last resort, this life of yours is determined not by rules but by God.[39]

Unlike Brueggemann, however, von Rad did not say that these verses depict a rather passive Yahweh. He speaks about the '*intervention* of the divine mystery' or, giving an example for this activity of Yahweh from the historical books, he says that 'Yahweh had "broken", in dramatic fashion, the counsel of the wise man Ahithophel' in Absalom's council of war (2 Samuel 17).[40] Thus, from his vocabulary, it seems to me that von Rad understood Yahweh's interaction with the world—at least in the case of these particular verses—as fairly active. Even if his activity is not 'miraculous,' nonetheless it is an activity which at least can be described with active words. At this point Brueggemann goes beyond von Rad.

According to von Rad, the appeal and pedagogical usability of Proverbs' take on the issue is precisely that it does not try to dilute the dialectic between 'automatic' rules and divine freedom with a sophisticated theological synthesis:

> The statements of the teachers move in a dialectic which is fundamentally incapable of resolution, speaking on the one hand of valid rules and, on the other, of *ad hoc* divine actions....

---

37. 'Intrusive acts,' 'intrude,' 'intervention' are words often used by Brueggemann throughout Brueggemann 1997: 333–358.
38. Von Rad 1972: 99–101.
39. Von Rad 1972: 106.
40. Von Rad 1972: 100, 103, my emphasis.

Their [the sages'] task was a predominantly practical one; they endeavoured to place their pupils within the sphere of influence of varied and partly contradictory experiences of life.... By means of their teachings, derived from experience, they set the pupil in the midst of the constant oscillation between grasp of meaning and loss of meaning, and in this way they induced him to make his own contribution in this exciting arena of knowledge of life. In this way they probably achieved more than if they had trained their pupils to find a better solution for theological problems.[41]

It seems to me that Brueggemann tries to do what, according to von Rad, the sages tried to avoid: he tries to construe a theological synthesis and the means for this is to downplay to some extent one side of the tension, namely Yahweh's free activity.

Does this mean that Brueggemann's description of those eight verses is incorrect? Not necessarily. They do not refer unambiguously to divine activity. However, many of these verses are in close proximity to verses with very similar content, which do use active verbs, and this weakens Brueggemann's argument. Verses 16:1-2 and 16:9 are at both ends of a verse chain in which almost all of the verses, except verse 8, mention the Tetragrammaton. Not all of these verses use passive verbs for describing Yahweh's activity. Verse 7 says that 'when the Lord likes someone's way he makes even his enemies peaceful (יַשְׁלִם) towards him.' Brueggemann mentions 19:14 as a verse which does not use a verb at all and 19:21 as using a passive verb in connection with Yahweh. However, between these verses we read 19:17, which uses an active verb (יְשַׁלֶּם), and which asserts in accordance with these verses that '[Yahweh] will reward him.'[42] He also mentions 20:24 as a verse speaking about Yahweh without a verb, but again, two verses earlier we can read 'wait for the Lord and he will save you' (or 'he will give you victory'—יֹשַׁע).[43]

In general we can say that it is not rare that Proverbs uses active verbs in connection with Yahweh. There are 87 verses which mention the Tetragrammaton, in which we can read 36 different active verbs altogether 40 times in connection with Yahweh.[44] This means that only four verbs occur twice (כון, אהב,

---

41. Von Rad 1972: 107 and 106 respectively.
42. Theoretically it would be possible to repoint שלם into a Pual form. Indeed, Murphy (Murphy 1998: 140) and NRSV translate it as passive: 'and will be repaid in full.' However, the LXX also gives an active translation. I am not aware of a compelling reason for repointing the MT (unless to bring the text into line with Brueggemann's theory).
43. For arguments for the 'victory' translation, see Fox 2009: 673–674.
44. Verses using active verbs: 2:6; 3:12, 19, 26, 33; 5:21; 6:16; 10:3, 22, 12:2; 15:3, 9, 25, 29; 16:2, 4, 7, 9; 17:3; 19:17; 20:12, 22; 21:1, 2; 22:2, 12, 23; 24:18; 25:22; 29:13. 'Active verb' is the terminology of Brueggemann which is somewhat imprecise. These verses contain 22 Qal, 5 Piel, 1 Polel, and 12 Hiphil forms. However, the differences between the factitive and causative meanings of Piel and Hiphil and the difference between them and Qal does not seem to have a direct relevance for my argument. (For the

תכן, שלם). Yahweh gives wisdom: 'For the Lord gives (יתן) wisdom, knowledge and understanding are from his mouth' (2:6); thwarts the desires of the wicked: 'The Lord does not let the righteous hunger (לא ירעיב), but thwarts (יהדף) the desire of the wicked' (10:3); tears down the house of the proud: 'The Lord tears down (יסח) the house of proud people, but protects (יצב) the boundary of the widow' (15:25); etc.

Brueggemann could argue that all of these verbs refer to the invisible governing activity of Yahweh (as he does in the case of כון and תכן) and these verbs just prove his case. This might be so. However, it is not easier to defend this claim than to prove the opposite of it. The fact is that Proverbs does not specify *how* Yahweh saves, tears down houses, rewards, etc. Usually the book just does not make it clear if these activities are visible or not, 'supernatural' or not, dramatic or not—hence the impression of some scholars that Proverbs is 'secular' in the sense of 'disenchanted,' i.e., does not count on the active presence of transcendent powers in the world. However, what really happens in these verses is that they only express the general rule without giving concrete examples. We are simply not told how 'intrusive' or 'miraculous' the concrete manifestations of these general rules are. The book speaks about a quite active Yahweh; it just does not specify his activity. If we recognise that Brueggemann's argument is one based on silence, it does not look so persuasive anymore.

However, regardless of whether Yahweh 'intervenes' or not, is not the concept of 'hiddenness' still a fruitful interpretative category? It can be, but it is also not without its question marks. A large percentage of those verses which speak about Yahweh's activity refer to his seeing, perceiving, examining, paying attention, as in 15:3 ('The eyes of the Lord are in every place, keeping watch on the evil and the good') or 24:18 (' . . . or the Lord will see it and it will be bad in his eyes and he will turn away his anger from them').[45] This group of verses is significant because, as Perlitt—a scholar to whom Brueggemann refers as one who investigated God's hiddenness in the Bible from an exegetical point of view—argues, in Psalms and in other ancient Near Eastern texts God's seeing or not seeing, listening or not listening express his presence or hiddenness.[46] Proverbs consistently speaks about God as the one who is close, who listens and watches. In Proverbs, God gives what some psalmists seem to miss: his close attention. So, if Proverbs speaks about God's 'hiddenness' then this is accompanied by a strong emphasis on his closeness—an issue which would deserve a closer investigation than it receives in Brueggemann's discussion. At any rate, Psalms' and Perlitt's understanding of hiddenness is different from how Brueggemann understands it in relation to Proverbs.

---

different and somewhat debated nuances of these 'active' meanings, see Blau 2010: 216–224, 229, 234; Jenni 1968: *passim*.)

45. See also 5:21; 15:29; 16:2; 17:3; 21:2; 22:12.
46. Perlitt 1971: 369.

Another issue that could be relevant for Brueggemann's subject, yet he fails to address it, is that the main question of Proverbs is not 'How to see God?' but rather 'How to find Wisdom?' The latter question seems to be neglected almost completely in Brueggemann's treatment.[47] Similarly, he does not write about the 'fear of the Lord,' which is a key concept in Proverbs that teaches that the 'fear of the Lord is the beginning of wisdom' (9:10). One wonders whether it would have led to a more persuasive account of God's 'hiddenness' in Proverbs if Brueggemann had been able to incorporate these key proverbial themes into his argument.

One can sum up this brief evaluation of Brueggemann's exegesis in four points. First, Brueggemann's insistence on the automatic relationship between deed and reward does not pay attention to the severe criticism of Koch's theory. Second, although his statement that Proverbs does not refer to big, dramatic interventions of Yahweh seems to be true, after a closer look it turns out to be an argument based on silence. The 'tension' between Proverbs and the 'core testimony' is that when Proverbs speaks about God's activity in the world it does not specify whether it is a dramatic, visible activity (as it often is in the 'core testimony') or a less visible one (for which we also find several examples in the 'core testimony').[48] This silence is hardly enough ground for speaking about a 'counter testimony.'[49] Third, the understanding of hiddenness which Brueggemann uses for interpreting Proverbs seems to differ from how other parts of the Old Testament understand God's hiddenness. At least, when Proverbs speaks about God's activity, its language is different from when the Psalms speaks about the hiding God. Fourth, Brueggemann fails to interact with some key themes of Proverbs which might be important for the theological interpretation of hiddenness in the book.

Despite this critical evaluation of Brueggemann's discussion, I still find 'hiddenness' a potentially useful category for interpreting Proverbs, even if its definition and the argument for finding it in the book requires some modifications. For clarifying how I would like to modify Brueggemann's understanding of hiddenness, it will be useful to interact not only with what he writes about it

---

47. At least in his *Theology of the Old Testament*, in which he most extensively discusses divine hiddenness in Proverbs.

48. A classic example could be when someone draws his bow 'at random' and hits the king of Israel (1 Kgs 22:34-36). And was it just a pure accident that Moses killed an Egyptian and as a result had to flee and live in the wilderness for many years, changing from the man of initiative of Exodus 2 into the man of reluctance (or 'humility,' Num 12:3) of Exodus 3? Or was it only the good mood of Artaxerxes that made him react positively to Nehemiah's request (Neh 2:1-8)? The 'core testimony' is full of examples which explicitly teach or implicitly suggest Yahweh's invisible governance. It is however not evident, whether the implied reader of the biblical books sees such a huge difference between God's 'dramatic intrusions' and his 'invisible governance' as Brueggemann does.

49. For the danger of constructing a special wisdom-worldview on the basis of wisdom's silence about certain themes, see Sneed 2011: 50–71.

13.3.2 Hiddenness in the Old Testament

Brueggemann introduces his discussion of the hidden God in Proverbs by quoting Isa 45:15: 'Truly, you are a God who hides himself, O God of Israel, the Savior.'[50] However, a look at the verse in its context puts question marks behind Brueggemann's use of it.

[14] Thus says the Lord: the product of Egypt and the profit of Ethiopia, and Sabeans, tall men, will come to you and will be yours. They will walk behind you, in chains they will come, to you they will bow down, you they will beg: God is only with you, and there is no other, there is no [other] God.	כה אמר יהוה יגיע מצרים וסחר כוש וסבאים אנשי מדה עליך יעברו ולך יהיו אחריך ילכו בזקים יעברו ואליך ישתחוו אליך יתפללו אך בך אל ואין עוד אפס אלהים
[15] Indeed, you are a God who hides himself,[51] God of Israel, Saviour.	אכן אתה אל מסתתר אלהי ישראל מושיע
[16] All of them are ashamed and humiliated at once,[52] the makers of idols walk in disgrace.	בושו וגם נכלמו כלם יחדו הלכו בכלמה חרשי צירים
[17] Israel will be saved by the Lord, everlasting deliverance. You will not be ashamed and humiliated to everlasting ages.	ישראל נושע ביהוה תשועת עולמים לא תבשו ולא תכלמו עד עולמי עד
[18] For thus says the Lord, the creator of heavens, he is the God, the shaper of earth and its maker, he is its establisher. He did not create it chaotic,[53] he shaped it to be inhabited; I am the Lord, there is no other.	כי כה אמר יהוה בורא השמים הוא האלהים יצר הארץ ועשה הוא כוננה לא תהו בראה לשבת יצרה אני יהוה ואין עוד
[19] I did not speak in hiddenness, somewhere in a dark land; I did not say to the seed of Jacob 'seek me in chaos.' I am the Lord, speaking right, declaring equity.	לא בסתר דברתי במקום ארץ חשך לא אמרתי לזרע יעקב תהו בקשוני אני יהוה דבר צדק מגיד מישרים

---

50. NRSV translation, as used by Brueggemann.
51. For the reflexive meaning, see the comment of Goldingay and Payne: 'The literal occurrences of *sātar* (hit), in 1 Sam 23.19; 26.1 and the heading to Psalm 54, underline that the hitpael by its nature is reflexive ("to hide oneself") not passive ("to be hidden").' (Goldingay and Payne 2006: 46.)
52. It is not entirely clear whether יחדו modifies the first colon or the second one. See Goldingay and Payne 2006: 47.
53. Whatever the precise meaning and wider intertextual resonances of תהו are, it is the opposite of 'habitable' in this text. The meaning seems to be that the end result of the tumultuous historical events initiated by Cyrus will be favourable to the people. See Koole 1997: 477–478.

It is debated how Isa 45:15 relates to its context: is verse 15 the nations' confession of a God who was not visible to them but was visible to Israel,[54] or is it Israel's confession?[55] Some argue that it is a speech of Cyrus.[56] Maybe it is an interjected speech or prayer of the prophet himself.[57] Or shall we 'only' see it as a gloss in the text, a theological comment by the author or a later scribe?[58] Speaking about the cause of this hiddenness, is it caused by sin,[59] or does it belong to the character of Yahweh?[60] Does God's 'hiding' in 45:15a refer to the exile and 'savior' in 45:15b to the deliverance of Israel from the exile?[61] Or does it mean rather that the God of Israel cannot be seen in cult images?[62]

Whatever the answers to some of the above questions may be, the wider context suggests that the reason for God's hiddenness lies not in the hidden nature of God but in the lack of human perception.[63] After all, just a few verses later God reminds Israel that he spoke clearly and openly, so no one can blame him that he hid himself: 'I did not speak in hiddenness (בסתר), somewhere in a dark land' (Isa 45:19a).[64]

Indeed, some have argued that seeing a reference to God's hidden nature in Isa 45:15 or in any other Old Testament passage is probably a misreading of the text influenced by a post-biblical theological tradition of *deus absconditus*:

> The 'hidden God'... has little to do with the phrase's meaning in the context [of Isa. 45:15], nor with any broader First Testament theme. 'The prophets do not speak of the *hidden God* but of the *hiding God*. His hiding is... an act not a permanent state.' It is not the case that 'for Israel's faith, God is essentially hidden,' though it is no doubt the case that God would be hidden were it not for the fact that God wills to be known, as is the case with any person.... The acknowledgment of Yhwh as one who hides recognizes that God sometimes hides from Israel but then returns.[65]

---

54. Goldingay 2005: 285–288; Herbert 1975: 68–71; Knight 1965: 141; McKenzie 1968: 82–83; Torrey 1928: 361.
55. Childs 2001: 355; Merendino 1981: 435.
56. Watts 2005: 705–706.
57. Hanson 1995: 108–109; Smart 1965: 130–131.
58. Blenkinsopp 2000: 258.
59. Goldingay 2005: 285–288; it is worth noting that Isa 54:8; 59:2; and 64:6 [English 64:7] speak about God hiding his face because of Israel's sins.
60. Brueggemann 1998: 81; North 1964: 158–159.
61. For literature, see Koole 1997: 469.
62. Koole 1997: 469–470.
63. *Pace* Brueggemann 1998: 81 and North 1964: 158–159.
64. In its present form Isa 45:14-19 can be easily perceived as a literary unit, using characteristic deuteronomistic language throughout. Sommer 1998: 136–137; see also Tiemeyer 2011: 234–237.
65. Goldingay 2006a: 137–138; quoting Heschel 1951: 153 and Wolfhart Pannenberg, *Basic Questions in Theology*, vol. 2 (London: SCM Press, 1971) 154 respectively.

What exegetical foundation is Brueggemann building on then, except Isa 45:15, when he refers to the idea of 'hidden God' in the Old Testament? He mentions Samuel E. Balentine's *The Hidden God* as a work which lays the 'exegetical ground' for his discussion.[66] However, Balentine's understanding of hiddenness is in fact more in line with Goldingay's opinion.

Balentine differentiates between two distinct lines in the Old Testament: first, in the majority of the OT, especially in the prophets, God's hiddenness is caused by human guilt; second, in Psalms (and in Job) it is often not specified why God withdrew and the psalmist protests and asks God to reveal himself.[67] At first sight, the second point is parallel with Brueggemann's notion of the hidden God, since Balentine also argues that it is not always human sin that causes God's hiddenness. However, we do not read about protest in the book of Proverbs comparable to that of the Psalms. Brueggemann, in fact, does not write about the 'withdrawal' of God. The God of Proverbs, according to Brueggemann, did not withdraw, he is simply not visible and this invisibility is a key characteristic of his being: 'The countertestimony of wisdom is that in much of life, if Yahweh is to be spoken of meaningfully, it must be a Yahweh who is not direct and not visible, but who in fact is hidden in the ongoing daily processes of life.'[68]

This invisibility of the deity is different from what we can read about in Psalms, according to Balentine. According to Brueggemann, Proverbs speaks about the (sometimes) frustrating invisibility of God, but not about his terrifying and devastating withdrawal. As Perlitt, in accordance with Balentine but in contrast with Brueggemann's hiddenness definition, put it, in the Psalms we never read 'about the in principle unknowability of Yahweh but about the existential misery which stems from his temporary concealment.'[69]

To summarise my argument so far, though Brueggemann refers to Balentine and Perlitt, their understanding of 'hiddenness,' together with that of Goldingay, is different from his understanding. They see it as a response to human sin, or an inexplicable but painful withdrawal, but not as something which belongs to God's existence, or which is in any way connected to the everyday, mundane human experience.

At this point we should note that neither Brueggemann nor Balentine mentions all of the biblical passages which could have some bearing on the theme of God's hiddenness. For example in Exod 33:20 the Lord tells Moses that 'you cannot see my face, for no one [can] see me and live.' Then Moses, from the shelter of a rock, is allowed to see God's glory passing by (Exod 33:21-23; 34:6-

---

66. Brueggemann 1997: 333 n. 1. He mentions it together with Perlitt 1971: 367–382. Balentine is aware of Perlitt's essay, and he is basically in agreement with Perlitt's opinion, only he gives a more detailed exegetical argument for it.
67. Balentine 1983: 166.
68. Brueggemann 1997: 335.
69. Perlitt 1971: 372; see also Doyle 2010: 377–390.

7). Another unmentioned, but potentially related text on hiddenness is 2 Kgs 6:17, in which Elisha prays for his servant boy that he may see, and then 'the Lord opened the boy's eyes and he saw and behold the mountain was full of horses and chariots of fire surrounding Elisha.'[70]

In some respects these texts provide better support for Brueggemann's understanding of hiddenness than Balentine's discussion of the topic. They do suggest that a perfect vision of God is inaccessible for human beings (Exod 33:20) and that even seeing the divine presence is not always an easy matter (2 Kgs 6:16-17). Nevertheless, their understanding of divine hiddenness still does not match perfectly the concept of 'hiddenness' applied by Brueggemann for interpreting Proverbs. Their hiddenness is not connected to a differentiation between the mundane and ordinary life versus dramatic divine interaction. Furthermore, they suggest that different human beings have different capacities to perceive divine presence, and at least implicitly they suggest that divine visibility or invisibility is not solely dependent on the hidden nature of God but also on human capacity to see and on human readiness to receive divine revelation.[71]

Turning back to Brueggemann's discussion of the topic in his *Theology of the Old Testament*, he refers to one more theologian, whose thoughts about God's hiddenness in biblical wisdom literature do seem to be more in line with those of Brueggemann than with the 'hiddenness' definitions of Balentine, Perlitt, or the just mentioned biblical passages. The scholar in question is Samuel Terrien. Brueggemann refers to his *The Elusive Presence* as a book which 'has made much of the notion of the hiddenness of God.'[72] My impression is that, besides von Rad's work, Terrien's book may have been the most influential for Brueggemann's views. Terrien writes about biblical wisdom, that

> There were no *Magnalia Dei* at the Babylonian seizure of Zion in 587 B.C., but the first Jews saw a new form of the *Opus Dei* in their own lives. God was absent from history although he had been present for the fathers at the Sea of Reeds. The sages espoused the theological rigor of the prophets, but they went further. Although Amos and his successors had hailed Yahweh as the creator of heaven and earth, the sages shifted their attention from history—a stage now empty of God—to the theater of the universe, where they detected his presence.[73]

One should note, however, that the prophetic view and the view of many post-exilic writings was not that history was empty of the *magnalia dei*. Quite the opposite, for Jeremiah and Isaiah 40–66, for Ezra and Nehemiah, it was precisely the exile and the return from exile that represented *magnalia dei*. God

---

70. I am grateful to Prof. Walter Moberly for drawing my attention to these passages.

71. These statements about the human preconditions of seeing are in general agreement with Brueggemann's discussion of seeing and discernment which he provides in connection with 2 Kgs 6:8-23 in Brueggemann 2000:348–351.

72. Brueggemann 1997: 333 n. 1.

73. Terrien 1978: 380.

was not hidden; he was revealed and present in judgement and deliverance. Thus, if the sages did not mention history because they thought that it was empty of God's deeds, then it is not that they 'went further' than the prophets, as Terrien writes, but that they went against them. We have seen, however, that the fact that history is not mentioned in wisdom writings could be explained in many other ways,[74] and, unfortunately, Terrien did not back up his claims with extensive exegetical and theological investigations of many wisdom texts.

However, regardless of the above reservations about Terrien's interpretation, one has to see the similarities between Terrien's thoughts about biblical wisdom and those of Brueggemann: the God of wisdom is not a God who intervenes in dramatic ways but a *deus absconditus*.

One has to recognise, however, that although Terrien used 'elusive' in the sense of 'not visible,'[75] he also offered many alternative understandings of God's 'elusiveness,' if not in connection with Proverbs but in connection with the rest of the Old Testament. He defined it as referring to a God who is surprising and unpredictable,[76] whose self-disclosure is limited to short instants of visitations,[77] who is constantly on the move and whose absence and presence alternate,[78] who is completely free from human manipulation,[79] who is known as unknown,[80] whose essence is not graspable and can be hidden either behind blinding light or darkness,[81] who sometimes abases himself,[82] who is untamable,[83] who is inaccessible to empirical verification.[84] Some of these can be clearly understood not only as elusiveness but also as 'hiddenness,' and in fact Terrien uses the word 'hiddenness' rather often. To foreshadow my later discussion, some of these definitions of 'elusiveness' seem to me better descriptions of Proverbs' vision of God than the one used by Brueggemann (and Terrien himself) to describe it.

As a conclusion to this brief investigation into the notion of God's hiddenness in the Bible, we should say that Brueggemann's references to Isa 45:15 and to the works of Balentine and Perlitt do not provide clear biblical basis for his definition of 'hiddenness.' They do use the word 'hiddenness' but in a different

---

74. For example, it could be the result of stylistic characteristics of sentence literature; it could be because these writings were written on a different (philosophical) level than the rest of the Old Testament, nevertheless presupposing the rest; it could be because they concentrate on the individual. See Part I about the history of interpretation.
75. Terrien 1978: 202.
76. Terrien 1978: 28, 119, 234–235.
77. Terrien 1978: 76, 180.
78. Terrien 1978: 234.
79. Terrien 1978: 94, 170, 186, 202, 264, 371.
80. Terrien 1978: 119, 326.
81. Terrien 1978: 259.
82. Terrien 1978: 265.
83. Terrien 1978: 457.
84. Terrien 1978: 457.

sense: mainly as divine withdrawal from humans because of human sin or because of unknown reasons, but not in the sense of invisibility in everyday life. This definition does not fit other relevant biblical texts either, like Exod 33:20-23 and 2 Kgs 6:8-23. Terrien did use 'elusive' in the sense of a 'not visible' God, but he did not offer exegetical proofs for why one should understand God this way in Proverbs. He also offered many alternative understandings of God's 'elusiveness,' some of which might be more fitting to Proverbs.

As some of Terrien's descriptions of 'elusiveness' are widely discussed in philosophical theology, it is worth having a brief look at those discussions before I move on. This might help to clarify 'hiddenness' more precisely.

13.3.3 Hiddenness in Theology

Brueggemann refers to Buber as the one who investigated God's hiddenness from a Jewish perspective.[85] However, Buber in his *Eclipse of God* places the main responsibility of this eclipse on humans and not on God's invisible nature. Discussing the philosophical tradition (mainly from Kant and Hegel) he describes how we made an idol out of the notion of God and terminated the real relationship with him. Or, using the language of his famous book, *I and Thou*, the thought of which he clearly follows in the *Eclipse of God*, we made an 'it' out of the 'Thou.' Here are two typical quotations from *I and Thou* and the *Eclipse of God* respectively:

> Man desires to possess God; he desires a continuity in space and time of possession of God. He is not content with the inexpressible confirmation of meaning, but wants to see this confirmation stretched out as something that can be continually taken up and handled, a continuum unbroken in space and time that insures his life at every point and every moment. Man's thirst for continuity is unsatisfied by the life-rhythm of pure relation, the interchange of actual being and of a potential being in which only our power to enter into relation, as hence the presentness (but not the primal Presence) decreases. He longs for extension in time, for duration. Thus God becomes an object of faith. At first faith, set in time, completes the acts of relation; but gradually it replaces them.[86]

> Understandably, the thinking of the era, in its effort to make God unreal, has not contented itself with reducing Him to a moral principle. The philosophers who followed Kant have tried essentially to reinstate the absolute, conceived of as existing not 'within us,' or at least not only within us. The traditional term 'God' is to be preserved for the sake of its profound overtones, but in such a way that any connection it may have with our concrete life, as a life exposed to the mani-

---

85. Brueggemann 1997: 333.
86. Buber 1958: 113.

festations of God, must become meaningless. The reality of a vision or a contact that directly determines our existence, which was a fundamental certainty to thinkers such as Plato and Plotinus, Descartes and Leibniz, is no longer found in the world of Hegel. . . . The radical abstraction, with which philosophizing begins for Hegel, ignores the existential reality of the I and of the Thou, together with that of everything else.[87]

It is worth comparing Buber's thought with that of Heschel, another Jewish thinker:

> The prophets do not speak of the *hidden God* but of the *hiding God*. His hiding is a function not His essence, an act not a permanent state. It is when the people forsake Him, breaking the Covenant which He has made with them, that He forsakes them and hides His face from them. It is not God who is obscure. It is man who conceals Him. His hiding from us is not in His essence: 'Verily Thou art a God that hidest Thyself, O God of Israel, the Saviour!' (Isaiah 45:15). A hiding God, not a hidden God. He is waiting to be disclosed, to be admitted into our lives.[88]

Both Heschel and Buber place the main responsibility of God's hiddenness on humans and not on God. However, Heschel speaks about the guilt of humans, whereas the guilt dimension is less clear in Buber. It is probably a matter of definition whether we should call mistaken (philosophical) thinking, stemming from obsession with security and possession, 'sin.' Be that as it may, the cause of God's hiddenness in Buber is not God's character but human blindness.

Turning from Jewish to Christian philosophical theology, Brueggemann refers the reader to John Dillenberger's *God Hidden and Revealed* as an introduction to Luther's understanding of the hiddenness of God. Dillenberger analyses the notion of the hidden God of several commentators of Luther and that of Luther himself. It would go beyond our interests to list all the different views delineated in Dillenberger's book, but it is worth mentioning one of the main questions along which the various opinions can be classified: how the revelation and hiddenness of God relate to each other. The two main options seem to be:
1. God has a revealed and a hidden side
2. God reveals himself through hiding himself (and vice versa).

The former view can be exemplified by the words of Luther himself:

> While a differentiation must be made between the revealed and the hidden will of God, God in the latter sense does not concern us. . . . God does much which he does not make known to us in his Word. He also desires many things which he does not in his Word reveal to us that he wants. . . . We must let ourselves be led by the Word of God

---

87. Buber 1979: 18–19.
88. Heschel 1951: 153–154.

and not by his unsearchable will. It is sufficient just to know that in God there is an unsearchable will.[89]

As a later interpreter explains it,

> The implication of hiddenness is that that which lies behind revelation is not caprice or arbitrariness, but can be trusted to the same extent as revelation even though one does not understand it.... The hidden God, though one is not able to understand him, is not different from the revealed God.[90]

The second view is based on a different line of Luther's thought in which he does not differentiate revelation from hiddenness but equates the two. This is clearly more sympathetic to Dillenberger himself. As he writes, 'God is not simply apparent in the cross as other things are apparent to human beings.... God gives himself but the content of that gift is still surrounded by mystery.... God is most hidden at the moment of fullest disclosure.'[91]

Dillenberger introduces several theologians who understood Luther's thoughts along similar lines. One of them is Ferdinand Kattenbusch:

> Revelation introduces mysteries and depths too great for man's comprehension. This, Kattenbusch believes, was the most distinctive meaning of the hidden God for Luther.... God's revelation overwhelms man and appears so differently than expected that a new riddle or enigma of its own emerges.... What Luther had in mind, suggests Kattenbusch, is that love cannot be measured by human findings, standards, or thoughts. The mystery of God is that in him person and love are so closely connected.[92]

Similarly, Karl Barth believed that it is revelation itself that defines God as hidden.[93] That God revealed himself and his power through the weakness of the cross means that he unveiled himself in veiling.[94] Furthermore, the fact that we only know God through Christ and that we do not have access to him without his revelation in Christ (that is, he is completely hidden from us), and the fact that revelation (unveiling) is hiding (veiling) at the same time, also means that his revelation comes from divine freedom; we cannot possess him. Let us note here that, despite Dillenberger's and Barth's seeming neglect of the Old Testament and Jewish perspectives, there is significant overlap in their and Buber's discussion of God's hiddenness, not least an emphasis on the fact that one cannot possess God:

---

89. Luther, *Bondage of the Will*, quoted in Dillenberger 1953: 3.
90. Dillenberger on the notions of Karl Holl. Dillenberger 1953: 21.
91. Dillenberger 1953: xvi.
92. Dillenberger 1953: 29–30.
93. Dillenberger 1953: 119.
94. Dillenberger 1953: 124–127.

A 'Post-Secular' Interpretation of Proverbs: The Hidden God   233

> It is . . . this freedom which constitutes the hiddenness of God in the sense of his inconceivability and mystery. In his revelation, God does not give himself to man to possess. In his operation he reveals what he actually is, but one cannot get hold of his essence.[95]

Although Brueggemann notes Dillenberger's work, he seems to utilise it little. He does not speak about a hidden characteristic of God, or the hidden will of God as opposed to the revealed one (as the first, though for Dillenberger less attractive, option of interpreting the notion of *deus absconditus*), he rather speaks about the wholeness of God as hidden and invisible. Neither does he connect revelation with hiddenness. He sees Proverbs as the wrestling with the invisibility of God in the 'ordinary,' or at maximum as the proclamation of the invisible presence of God, but does not see God's invisibility in Proverbs as intrinsically connected to God's self-revelation the way Kattenbusch, Barth, or Dillenberger understood it.

This is a good place to take notice of the work of Karl Rahner, who wrote about the hidden God extensively from a Catholic perspective and whose idea of God's hiddenness is not dissimilar to that of Barth and Dillenberger. The most characteristic point of Rahner's opinion is that we should not really speak about God's 'hiddenness' but about God's 'incomprehensibility.' God is not someone who tries to hide some characteristics of himself. No, quite the opposite, he reveals himself. However, we are not able to comprehend his being; he always remains 'hidden,' but not because we cannot see him. In a sense we are able to see him in his fullness:

> The concept 'hiddenness' is less frequently used in Catholic theology than that of 'incomprehensibility.' . . . This does not mean, however, that in God some things are known . . . , while others simply remain unknown. Rather one and the same God is known and is at the same time fundamentally incomprehensible. . . . It is not true that the 'deus absconditus' is the sort of God who desires that we should not recognize him at all. He does not share one part of himself with us and conceal the other; rather he bestows his whole being upon us. In communicating himself as 'deus revelatus' he becomes radically open to man *as* the 'deus absconditus.'[96]

Rahner was not an inventor. Rahner, Luther, and Dillenberger only follow the patristic tradition of connecting the *deus revelatus* with the *deus absconditus*. As the Orthodox theologian Olivier Clément summarises the teaching of numerous

---

95. Dillenberger 1953: 135.
96. Rahner 1979: 228, 229, 243. Other significant contemporary Catholic theologians with a similar understanding of God's hidden presence (and partly building on Rahner's thought) are Nicholas Lash and Hans Urs von Balthasar. See Lash 1988: 231–242; about Balthasar's thought, see Kerr 2002: 90–91.

patristic texts about human beings' experience of God: 'the more it is hidden the more it is given; the more it is given the more hidden it is.'[97]

One important difference between this approach to the hidden God (represented by the Catholic Rahner, the Protestant Dillenberger, and the Orthodox Clément) and the approach of Brueggemann is that whereas Brueggemann defined the hiddenness of God as a lack of supernatural interventions, they do not differentiate between 'ordinary' and 'non-ordinary,' between 'natural' and 'supernatural'—just as, it seems to me, such a differentiation is missing from Proverbs. According to this 'classical' understanding of hiddenness, God's revelation can take 'ordinary' and 'supernatural' forms, but whatever form revelation takes, it, besides revealing him, also hides the inexpressible, incomprehensible Being of God because that Being is beyond every being, whether those beings are extraordinary or ordinary.

In other words, God's hiddenness can be interpreted in two different ways:
- The existence and activity of God is not detectable by human beings;
- The nature of God is incomprehensible for human beings.

Classically the emphasis was on the second understanding of divine hiddenness.[98] Brueggemann, however, in contrast to the theologians to whom he refers (but in accordance with many modern thinkers since the enlightenment), builds his understanding of hiddenness on the first aspect.

13.4 Wisdom Is Ungraspable in its Fullness

We have seen so far that although Brueggemann's application of the category 'hiddenness' in the interpretation of Proverbs is creative and theologically promising, there are problems with his actual exposition of Proverbs. His exegesis depends on Koch's debated theory of deed–consequence relationship and his argument is mainly built on the silence of the text about *how* God acts. We have also seen that although he refers to numerous theologians, his description of God's hiddenness usually differs from their description of it.

Maybe Brueggemann's understanding of 'hiddenness' was influenced by his earlier 'secular' interpretation of Proverbs. 'Hiddenness' to him meant God's indirect governance (compare the understanding of 'secular' as leaving [some] autonomy to human beings) and God's 'invisible' governance (compare the understanding of 'secular' as disenchantment and lack of 'intrusion' of the sacred).

---

97. Clément 1993: 26–34, 31.
98. Here I am following Schellenberg's classification (Schellenberg 1993: 4–5), but I am merging his first two categories as he originally spoke about three versions of hiddenness: hiddenness of existence, hiddenness of activity, and hiddenness of essence. Schellenberg's classification was rightly criticised by some as too simplistic, because these three understandings of divine hiddenness are not as neatly differentiable as he suggests (Ross 2002: 189). Nevertheless, the classification describes well the difference in emphasis between different theologians.

However, I want to suggest that even if Brueggemann's concept of 'hiddenness' sprouted from the soil of an unpersuasive secular understanding of wisdom, it might be used fruitfully for interpreting Proverbs if one goes back to its classical understanding. In the following I argue briefly that some features of Proverbs can be correlated with an understanding of 'hiddenness' as 'incomprehensibility.'

One of the paradoxes about wisdom is that she is crying out at the most frequented, most visible places of the world (1:20-21; 8:1-2; 9:1-6), yet Proverbs speaks as if it were not the easiest task to find her: 'If to insight you call out, to understanding you raise your voice, if you seek it like silver, and like treasure you search for it, then you will understand . . . ' (2:3-5a). The task obviously requires determination from the student and many fail in their search. (On the determination required for the search for wisdom and the possibility of failure see also 1:28; 3:13; 4:1-8; 8:9, 17, 35; 24:14; 31:10.) Why is it so difficult to find something which is so visibly there? Maybe one can see in this phenomenon a parallel to the hiddenness of God, not to the hiddenness in the sense of not being visible, but to the hiddenness in the sense of being fully visible yet somehow hard to grasp.

Another, related paradox about wisdom is that she is there, visible, graspable—indeed Proverbs constantly urges the student to grasp her—yet, one should not consider oneself wise. That it is possible to find her is suggested by the fact that Proverbs constantly speaks about wise people. However, it also teaches that there is more hope for fools than for those who think they are wise: 'Have you seen a man wise in his own eyes? There is more hope for a fool than for him' (26:12; see also 3:5, 7; 27:1; 28:11). Does this mean that wise people have to lie to themselves and that they have to claim, contrary to the fact of their wisdom, that they are not wise? I argue in the following that there is a more natural interpretation that is actually very much in line with a classical understanding of hiddenness: not the hiddenness in the sense of not being visible in everyday life, but the hiddenness described by Buber and Dillenberger, which teaches that although the hidden God is in relationship with human beings, he resists complete comprehension and possession by them.

Let us have a closer look at these issues: why is it so difficult to find wisdom, when she is so close and visible; and why cannot one consider him- or herself wise when finding wisdom is not only possible but the aim of the whole enterprise? In fact, Proverbs does provide explanation for how one can miss Lady Wisdom even when she is clearly visible. Possible causes for failure are the tempting presence of Lady Folly (Proverbs 9) or the alluring prospect of gaining riches through unwise means (Prov 1:11-14). However, there is a further difficulty which is especially relevant for our questions: pride and unwillingness to listen to advice and instruction prevent people from becoming wise.

The idea seems to be that one should always remain open for correction, for the wisdom of others, and no one should think that he or she possesses wisdom in its entirety. This attitude is not only appropriate for the 'not yet wise' but also for the wise: 'Give [instruction] to a wise person (חכם) and he will become even wiser' (9:9a);[99] 'The wise of heart (חכם לב) takes in precepts (מצות) while a babbling fool will go astray (ילבט)' (10:8; see also 1:5; 13:1; 18:15).[100]

It is apparently one of the key characteristics of wise people that they can listen to instruction. This explains why listening to instruction is one of the most emphasised topics in Proverbs. מוסר (instruction) occurs 30 times in the book out of the 50 occurrences in the whole Old Testament.[101] The meaning of 'instruction' (מוסר) is broad and its content is diverse. It can mean punishment (16:22), even physical punishment (13:24), but usually it would be hard to decide whether it refers to teaching or reproach. Fox suggests that in most cases the best translation is 'correction.'[102] However diverse though its semantic range was or whatever development its meaning undertook during the time of Proverbs' birth, it was always used to emphasise the importance of being open towards some kind of correction.

One should note, however, that it is not so much the *content* of the instruction which interests the authors of Proverbs. As Stuart Weeks writes,

> When an instructional work lays as much emphasis as does Proverbs 1–9 on the importance of instruction, we might expect it to tell us what that instruction is. Instead . . . most of the work is devoted to asserting the need for the uneducated to receive teaching, and not to providing teaching itself.[103]

This neglect of giving precise instructions can support Weeks' thesis that instruction in Proverbs 1–9 was closely associated with the Law. However, if one interprets Proverbs 1–9 as an introduction to the rest of Proverbs (as I do) and not as an independent work (as Weeks does), then it is also a logical possibility that Proverbs 1–9 does not specify the content of the 'instruction' because it is given in the following chapters.

There is, however, something interesting here: 'instruction' is not only never identified explicitly with the law or with the teaching of the following chapters in Proverbs 1–9, but even the following chapters fail to specify what exactly they mean whenever they use the word 'instruction.' Those verses which mention the word 'instruction' almost always speak about the required attitude (that is, they urge the reader to 'listen to instruction') and not about its content.[104]

---

99. 'Give' lacks a direct object in Hebrew but תוכחת or מוסר can be inferred from the previous verses (Fox 2000: 307).

100. The meaning of ילבט in this verse is uncertain. Fox concludes at the end of a thorough lexical note on the word that 'In Prov 10:8, either "go astray" (in sin) or "be cast aside" (in punishment) seems possible.' (Fox 2009: 516).

101. Merrill 1997: 479–482.

102. Fox 2000: 34–35.

103. Weeks 2007: 96.

104. Like 10:17; 12:1; 13:1, 18; 15:5, 10, 32; 19:20, 27; 23:12.

This surprising phenomenon of not specifying instruction in Proverbs can not only be understood as suggesting that the content is given somewhere else (law, or some other parts of Proverbs), but also as suggesting that the *attitude* of humble listening is not less important than the content of the instruction itself. Maybe, if they had met, the different authors of Proverbs would have had a debate about what the best source of correction is but they would have definitely agreed that the way towards wisdom is being open for correction.[105]

Opposed to the wise, the scoffers are not willing to listen: 'The scoffer you strike but the simple will learn prudence; but rebuke the discerning person (נבון) and he will understand (יבין) knowledge' (19:25; see also 1:5; 9:7-9; 10:8; 13:1; 15:12; 21:11).[106] The characteristics of humility and pride are probably partly responsible for this difference in teachability. No wonder, the categories of 'wise' and 'scoffer' are closely associated with these characteristics: 'The proud (זד), arrogant (יהיר) person: scoffer (לץ) is his name' (21:24a); 'He [the Lord] scoffs (יליץ) at scoffers (לצים); but to the humble he shows favour' (3:34).

The humility–wisdom–listening cluster is also expressed by the fact that the fear of the Lord, which is the beginning of wisdom (1:7; 9:10), is not only associated with the ability to listen to instruction,[107] but it is also associated with humility: 'The fear of the Lord [is?] the instruction (מוסר) of wisdom, and before honour, humility (ענוה)' (15:33).[108] There are many uncertainties about the precise meaning of this verse. However, we can at least state with relative certainty that it is 'humility' which is in parallel with 'fear of the Lord.'[109] This parallelism is reinforced by 22:4: 'The reward of humility (ענוה) is fear of the Lord; riches, and honour, and life.'[110] It is also reinforced by 8:13 where fear of the

---

105. We have to note, however, that not all parts of Proverbs put the same emphasis on the topic. The word מוסר does not occur after chapter 24 and the whole topic of attentive listening seems to be less significant in the last few chapters. These chapters, however, do not deny the significance of attentive listening explicitly, they only deal with other issues. An exception might be Prov 30:1-9, which emphasises careful listening to God's words but the text is full of lexical and interpretative difficulties, for which see Crenshaw 1989: 51–64; Franklyn 1983: 238–252; Moore 1994: 96–107; Sauer 1963; Yoder 2009: 254–263.

106. The נבון, which is often co-referential with the חכם, has the connotation of someone who is docile (see 14:6b: 'knowledge comes easily to the נבון'), argues Fox 2000: 30.

107. See discussion on pages 142–143.

108. Felix Perles suggested that we should read מוסד instead of מוסר, simply on the basis that the text does not make sense otherwise (Perles 1895: 60). This emendation is noted by the apparatus of *BHS*, too. However, this alteration loses the catchword connection with the previous verses (Plöger 1984: 185; Waltke 2005: 3). The other suggestion that one should read מקור (based on 14:27; see Chajes 1899: 23) faces the same problem.

109. See Fox 2009: 604–605; McKane 1970: 487.

110. Waltke suggests the translation 'the wage for humility—the fear-of-the-Lord sort—is riches, honour, and life.' (Waltke 2005: 193.) This or a very similar understanding of the verse is also supported by Fox 2009: 697; Jones 1961: 183; McKane 1970:

Lord is contrasted with pride: 'Fear of the Lord [is] to hate evil: pride, and arrogance, and an evil way and a mouth of perversion [that] I [i.e., חכמה] hate.'

To summarise the foregoing discussion, one of the key characteristics which enables one to become and remain wise is the ability to listen attentively to instruction and advice.[111] This ability is supported by fear of the Lord and humility, whereas it is hindered if one is proud and has a mocking attitude.

After this brief investigation of the theme of listening to instruction it is more understandable why it is perceived to be so dangerous in Proverbs if someone considers him or herself wise. Wisdom is not something one can possess forever without the possibility of losing it. No one can say that 'I am wise' in the sense of having comprehended and possessed wisdom. Being wise is at least as much a character trait as possessing a sharp mind and having vast experience. Being wise is being humble, 'denying our knowledge' in the sense of leaving behind our knowledge constantly and listening to instruction, being ready to change. It is more about having an attentive relationship with wisdom than having wisdom herself. In other words, it is accepting and being open to the incomprehensibility of wisdom.

If this reconstruction of Proverbs' thought-world is correct, then 'hiddenness' in it is not so much about being invisible but about human inability to see and comprehend wisdom fully. This inability can be caused by false (i.e., proud) thinking and by human limitations, not being able to comprehend and possess wisdom in its fullness. As a consequence, Proverbs is not so much about human autonomy as about being attentive, listening humbly, and constantly being willing to change and leave behind one's own 'precious' wisdom. We can see the same dynamic here that we have already seen in Proverbs several times. One has to let go his or her wisdom if he or she wants to remain wise. As Lash writes,

> The self-acceptance to which basic experience invites us is always a matter of 'decentring,' of surrendering what we took to be autonomy; a matter of that *conversion* which entails the surrender of the 'false

---

570; Meinhold, 1991b: 365; Murphy 1998: 164; Oesterley 1929: 184; Perdue 2000: 188; Plöger 1984: 251; Saebø 2012: 264; Toy 1899: 414–415. Though, see Whybray, who takes fear of the Lord as the fruit of humility (Whybray 1972: 123). Some suggest that we should read 'humility *and* fear of the Lord,' like Gemser 1937: 64, Kidner 1964: 147; Ringgren and Zimmerli 1962: 86, Ross 2008: 187. The suggestion is also mentioned in the apparatus of *BHS*. Fritsch and Schloerb 1955: 907, despite accepting the suggestion, think that humility and fear of the Lord are practically identical. The insertion of 'and' is not supported by any ancient version; it is not mentioned in the apparatus of *BHQ*, either.

111. Though our primary concern has been 'instruction' and not 'advice,' much of what was said about 'instruction' applies to 'advice,' too. Fox observes that מוסר denotes instruction which usually comes from a superior whereas עצה (advice) usually comes from equals or from inferiors, though this is not always the case, as sometimes God gives the advice (Fox 2000: 32, 34–35). However, this slight difference in connotation does not affect the fact that the wise is eager to listen to advice no less than to instruction (1:25, 30; 12:15; 13:10; 15:22; 19:20; 24:6).

drive for self-affirmation which impels man to flee from the unreliable, unsolid, unlasting, unpredictable, dangerous world of relation into the having of things.'[112]

13.5 Summary

By introducing the category 'hiddenness,' Brueggemann developed his earlier 'secular' interpretation of Proverbs in which 'secular' meant an emphasis on human autonomy and a lack of sacral thinking. I appreciated his initiative to interpret Proverbs in the light of the theologically fertile category of the hidden God. However, I have argued that contrary to Brueggemann's claim, Proverbs does not depict a passive deity. It is true that it usually does not specify whether his activity is done through grand, intrusive deeds or through invisible work in the background, but basing a whole theory on this silence is risky. Furthermore, Brueggemann fails to address topics which are key issues in Proverbs, like 'how to find wisdom,' and 'fear of the Lord.'

Turning from his exegesis to his theological category, 'hiddenness,' we had to recognise that Brueggemann's understanding of 'hiddenness' was probably influenced by his earlier 'secular' interpretation of Proverbs, and it does not agree with the most decisive thoughts of those theologians to whom he is referring. This, actually, gives us the opportunity to 'save' his idea of interpreting Proverbs in the light of the theological tradition of the hidden God. I have suggested that we should utilise the 'classical' concept of divine hiddenness, as defined by Rahner, Buber, and others. This 'classical hiddenness' describes God as incomprehensible and as someone who cannot be possessed.[113]

Finally, I have noted that Proverbs teaches about a radical openness towards instruction. One's character plays a crucial role in enabling one to have an (at least partial) vision of Wisdom. Being wise, in this sense, is not a conceptual mastery, possession of knowledge and sharp mind, but the state of being open towards wisdom. Though wisdom fully presents herself to us, still, one cannot grasp her fully.

Understood this way, 'hiddenness' is not so much about the invisibility of the other but, to use Buber's expression, it is 'the life-rhythm of pure relation' with the absolute Being, experiencing his freedom, uncontrollability and incom-

---

112. Lash 1988: 246, quoting Buber 1958: 126.
113. To be fair, in one of his more recent works Brueggemann also contrasts divine hiddenness with human manoeuvring to possess God: ' ... [divine] hiddenness has not been handed over to any interpretive community, nor does that hiddenness serve any particular community or interest.' (Brueggemann 2011: 260.) However, his emphasis is slightly different from that of the above investigations. He seems to write here mainly on exploiting God in defending ideological positions in earthly power struggles and not on the incomprehensibility of God in a Human—God relationship (though, admittedly, the two topics are not unrelated).

prehensible depth. This way hiddenness theology becomes a theology of relation instead of a theology of autonomy.

One could make, however, a serious objection to the above argument: it is unfair to compare Proverbs' understanding of wisdom with the interpretation of Brueggemann since he wrote about the hiddenness of God and not that of wisdom. This criticism is partly valid, of course. However, as we have seen in the previous chapters, one can argue that in Proverbs, especially in its framework (i.e., Proverbs 1–9), and most clearly in Proverbs 8, Wisdom and God are so closely associated that one's relationship to one of them is intrinsically related to one's relationship to the other.

14

Conclusions

14.1 Lessons from the History of Interpretation

Nineteenth century interpreters saw almost all of those special features of wisdom writings that were recognised by their twentieth century colleagues. However, their theological interpretation differed in some important points. Most of them saw more continuity with the rest of the Bible than many twentieth century scholars. Instead of seeing its universal character as theologically challenging, they saw its 'self-interest' as more problematic. Instead of explaining Proverbs in the framework of creation theology, they taught that its peculiarity is simply the result of being written on a different, 'philosophical' level.

Some features of my argument can be seen as parallel to nineteenth century interpretation. Similarly to many nineteenth century scholars, I have also seen the continuities between Proverbs and the rest of the Bible as more significant than wisdom's 'alternativeness.' I have also considered it important to try to handle the emphasis on self-interest in the book from a theological point of view. Furthermore, I have not used the category of 'creation theology' for explaining Proverbs' 'universalism' and silence about national history. Instead, I have explained these features of the book by different factors: by the special literary form of (some parts of) Proverbs (i.e., sentence literature); by its interest in everyday life; and by it being written on a 'more abstract, theoretical level'—an understanding which has some parallels with the nineteenth century understanding of wisdom as 'philosophical.'

The idea of creation is, of course, present. However, it is just as much present in other parts of the Bible. I argued that it should be classified as a 'worldview' instead of presenting it as a characteristic theology which can be opposed to *Heilsgeschichte*. I suspect that its status is rather similar to the modern European 'scientific worldview.' According to this analogy, saying that the theology of Proverbs is 'creation theology' which is an alternative to *Heilsgeschichte* is a similar statement to 'I am not religious because I rather accept the scientific worldview.' Such a statement would rightly provoke the disapproval of many theologians as these categories function on different levels, and they are not alternatives to each other. Of course, just like science, the theme of creation becomes theologically significant sometimes. It happens in Proverbs 8, for example, and I have also made use of it in my interpretation. However, in my utilisation of this theme I have understood it as connecting Proverbs with the rest of the Bible (through the picture of the temple) and not as presenting an alternative theology. I have not seen it as a teaching about a world order which is in any sense independent from God. Furthermore, instead of seeing the creation-theme as *the* theology of Proverbs I have seen it as only one of the many important themes in Proverbs which can be utilised theologically.

From these many themes I chose two as the foci of my theological investigation, both of them once popular but less extensively discussed nowadays. The first one is the seemingly self-interested nature of Proverbs, which was a major problem for nineteenth century scholarship. The second one is the seemingly secular nature of Proverbs, which was popular for a few decades in the second half of the twentieth century.

14.2 Self-Interest and the Secular

As for self-interest, some recent commentators try to explain it by a reference to creation order. According to this explanation, Proverbs does not recommend self-interest, it only describes the good order of the world. I have not found this explanation satisfying. The reasons for my dissatisfaction are twofold. First, seeing an automatic act–consequence relationship in Proverbs is not persuasive. Second, Proverbs not only states that because of the good order of creation a righteous act is also beneficial for the actor, but it explicitly motivates the reader through appealing to his or her self-interest. For handling such a strong emphasis on self-interest I have found a *eudaemonistic* frame of reference the most promising because that gives a central role to human, individual flourishing.

A comparison with the Thomistic version of *eudaemonism* has shown that, despite the differences, Proverbs can be interpreted along Thomistic lines. Thomas both accepts self-interest as good and valuable and differentiates between selfishness and legitimate self-interest. I have found most of his criteria for a legitimate self-interest present in Proverbs to a greater or lesser extent. These criteria comprise a stronger emphasis on self-preservation than on success; an emphasis on justice and community; a greater emphasis on spiritual than on material success; and a hierarchy of human ends with 'knowledge of God' being the highest end.

Thomas taught that care for oneself in a proper, wise way means participation in divine providence, that is, participation in the divine mind. I have argued that some sections of Proverbs which provide a theological context for the whole book can be understood in this way. In discussing this question, my concrete example was Proverbs 2, but my later discussion of Proverbs 8 could also support the same argument. According to this argument, Proverbs is not only *eudaemonistic* but it is *relationally eudaemonistic*: it puts an emphasis on the relationship with the divine. That relationship is what it considers as the greatest human good, or at least its teaching can be read like this.[1] According to this reading, Proverbs attracts the reader to self-interested wise behaviour not only because it is beneficial for him or her but also because it connects him or her to divine care and activity in the world.

Turning from the problem of self-interest to the question of the 'secular' made the emphasis on 'relational/participational theology' even stronger. I have ordered the different understandings of 'secular' into three major groups. The one that seemed to be most applicable to Proverbs is the one which sees the secular as a neutral space in which people from different backgrounds can meet, communicate, and negotiate. This understanding of secular fits Proverbs because the book does not mention typical Israelite religious institutions and therefore most of it would probably be understandable and acceptable for many readers coming from outside a Jewish or Christian context. However, I argued that reading it canonically, i.e., taking its literary framework and biblical context seriously, Proverbs is more about the 'sanctification' of the secular space than simply a description of it. Placing side by side the divine Wisdom of the first nine chapters and the practical wisdom of the later chapters suggests continuity between the two. This, in turn, suggests that one can participate in the divine presence through wise action. Reading Proverbs in the context of some psalms and 1 Kings 3–11 has the same effect: it suggests that wisdom leads one into the presence of the Lord rather as if it led one into the temple. Thus, this canonical reading has led to a very similar conclusion to the one I have reached in connection with self-interest: being wise connects one to God, makes one participate in divine presence.

Other definitions of 'secular,' like disenchantment or human-centredness, seemed to be less applicable to Proverbs because the support for them is mainly based on an argument from silence; and, in fact, there are verses in Proverbs which do not fit these categories so smoothly. However, I have found a more recent offspring of these secular interpretations imaginative and worth further consideration. This is Brueggemann's reading of Proverbs, which promotes hiddenness theology. I suggested that if we alter Brueggemann's 'hiddenness' definition (i.e., non-visible) to another definition which is more represented in

---

1. Few interpreters put such a strong emphasis on the divine–human relationship in Proverbs. There are, however, notable exceptions, e.g., Eaton 1989: 79–90; Longman 2008: 539, 549; Murphy 2002: 114, 121–126.

classical theological discussions (i.e., incomprehensible, something that cannot be ultimately possessed by human beings) then we might find some support for it in Proverbs. Wisdom in Proverbs is easily accessible in one sense yet not that easy to gain in another. No one can claim that he or she grasped her fully, but everyone has to be constantly open towards her. To revise slightly one of the important statements of Proverbs: wisdom only has a beginning (the fear of the Lord) but not an end. As there is a certain continuity between the Lord and wisdom, maybe it is arguable that these characteristics of wisdom in Proverbs tell something of Proverbs' view of God, too. This understanding of divine hiddenness is not so much connected to a feeling of divine passivity or invisibility in the (secular) life, but, to an ever deepening relationship, even to participation in (but not possession of) the divine. Thus, again, my interpretation has put a strong emphasis on the relationship with the divine through wisdom.

14.3 A Non-Kantian Reading

It may not be just an accident that the discussion of both self-interest and the secular in Proverbs has led to very similar conclusions. This can signal the not immediately obvious, yet intrinsic connection between these two subjects. This intrinsic connection is visible in the writings of one of the most influential enlightenment philosophers, Immanuel Kant.

In *Religion within the boundaries of mere reason* Kant argues that the true and pure rational religion does not justify any action based on self-interest.[2] Human beings have to do their duty not because it brings happiness but simply because it is their duty, because they rationally perceive what the moral law is and this perception prompts them to choose moral behaviour. Therefore, argues Kant, the true believers do not do good because God ordains them to do so, especially not because God rewards them for doing so, but because they see that it is good. As he says,

> So far as morality is based on the conception of the human being as one who is free but who also, just because of that, binds himself through his reason to unconditional laws, it is in need neither of the idea of another being above him in order that he recognize his duty, nor, that he observe it, of an incentive other than the law itself.[3]

The only true worship of God is the rational, free, independent, morally

---

2. Different English translations render the German title (*Die Religion innerhalb der Grenzen der blossen Vernunft*) slightly differently. Quotations are always taken from the translation of George di Giovanni (Kant 1996b). Besides the page numbers of this particular translation I also provide in my footnotes the volume and pagination of the standard German edition of Kant's works: *Kants gesammelte Schriften*, 1. Abteilung: Werke (Berlin: Georg Reimer, 1902–1923).

3. Kant 1996b: 57 (6: 4).

good conduct, which is dependent not on learned faith but on rational perception of universal moral laws and free choice of behaving according to these laws:

> The one and true religion contains nothing but laws, i.e., practical principles, of whose unconditional necessity we can become conscious and which we therefore recognize as revealed through pure reason (not empirically).[4]

However, Kant also saw that the human striving for happiness is a natural inclination and that it is not easy for human beings to put it behind their inclination to do the moral duty.[5] Furthermore, many human beings are not prepared to perceive clearly the abstract, rational idea of moral good, and therefore, at least in the beginning, humanity needs some help in this. The historical faiths can serve this end.[6] But these historical faiths that are not universally binding, as is the rational moral law, can only be means to the 'promotion and propagation' of the rational religion, and nothing more.[7] Even the best of these faiths can only help to introduce people to the rational religion but its function terminates there:

> [I]n the end religion will gradually be freed of all empirical grounds of determination, of all statutes that rest on history and unite human beings provisionally for the promotion of the good through the intermediary of an ecclesiastical faith. Thus at last the pure faith of religion will rule over all, 'so that God may be all in all.'—The integuments within which the embryo is first formed into a human being must be laid aside if the latter is to see the light of day. The leading-string of holy tradition, with its appendages, its statutes and observances, which in its time did good service, become bit by bit dispensable, yea, finally, when a human being enters upon his adolescence, turn into a fetter. So long as he (the human species) 'was a child, he was as clever as a child' and knew how to combine learning too, and even a philosophy helpful to the church, with propositions imposed upon him without any of his doing: 'But when he becomes a man, he puts away the childish things.'[8]

Several observations offer themselves. Let us take first the theme of secularisation. It is true that Kant himself did not use the expression 'secularisation.' Furthermore, he explicitly counted on the idea of God. He thought that the existence of a universal law-giver can be hypothesised on the basis of the existence

---

4. Kant 1996b: 188 (6: 167–168). This tenet is expressed in several forms by Kant, see especially Kant 1996b: 175–215 (6: 151–202).
5. Kant 1996a: 26 (8: 257).
6. Kant differentiates these historical 'faiths,' like Hinduism, Judaism, Christianity, etc. from the true rational 'religion' which consists in recognising the moral law as revelation.
7. Kant 1996b: 138 (6: 104).
8. Kant 1996b: 151 (6: 121–122); see also Kant 1996b: 137 (6: 103), 142 (6: 109), 178 (6: 155–156).

of universal moral law.⁹ Nevertheless, his argument, even if only in an indirect way, often influenced later secularisation theories. One could rephrase Kant's thoughts by saying that historical faiths are self-defeating: they are only here to educate humanity; when they have successfully accomplished this education, they are not needed anymore, and they will gradually disappear. According to Kant, Christianity is one of the most 'developed' religions which is particularly close to rational religion; therefore, it is also particularly close to self-defeat. This understanding of religion as a self-defeating system, and especially that of Christianity, often appears in later secularisation theories in one form or another.[10]

As for self-interest, Kant contrasted it with independence and autonomy. According to him, human beings do not need a divine motivation to do the good in the form of rewards and punishments; they do not even need God to tell them what is right and what is not. They are capable of knowing what is right, and they are capable of doing it on the basis of their own rational powers, regardless of whether it is beneficial for them or not. This opposition of self-interest with autonomy is revealing because it highlights the often overlooked connection between self-interest and dependence. If I await rewards from someone then this longing, besides my 'selfish' motivations, also reveals the fact that I am not able to satisfy my needs completely on my own. Ultimately it is precisely this self-interested act that can lead towards real community. As Charles Taylor writes, when he discusses the seemingly superior ethical ideal of self-giving without the slightest traces of self-interest:

> Is this the ultimate measure of excellence? If we think of ethical virtue as the realization of lone individuals, this may seem to be the case. But suppose the highest good consists in communion, mutual giving and receiving.... The heroism of gratuitous giving has no place for reciprocity. If you return anything to me, then my gift was not totally gratuitous; and besides, in the extreme case, I disappear with my gift and no communion between us is possible. This unilateral heroism is self-enclosed. It touches the outermost limit of what we can attain to when moved by a sense of our own dignity. But is that what life is about?[11]

In Kant's system the connection between self-interest and secularisation is straightforward. Religions (or faiths, to use Kant's terminology) are here to bring people closer to disinterested obedience to the universal moral law. The more they achieve their mission, the less they are needed. The less self-interested people are, the further the secularisation process can progress. This close connection between self-interest and secularisation in Kant's thought high-

---

9. Kant 1996b: 177 (6: 154).
10. See, for example, the very diverse discussion of related topics in Casanova 2011: 60; Gauchet 1997; Taylor 2007: 90–145, 261; Turner 2011: 4–5.
11. Taylor 2007: 702.

lights the intrinsic relationship between the two: both are connected to the question of human autonomy.

My interpretation of Proverbs goes against most of Kant's thoughts about the role of self-interest and religion. According to the interpretation I have offered, Proverbs accepts human needs as legitimate motivations for behaviour (if the appropriate *eudaemonistic* checks are applied). The attunement to the moral law is not the result of an autonomous rational human choice but that of the dependent listening to divine teaching. This teaching does not reach humans through the autonomous rational perception of universal moral law but through humble listening to 'empirical' tradition (the teaching of the father and mother). The emphasis of the book, both in relation to self-interest and the secular, is not on human autonomy but on human dependence.

This interpretation of Proverbs is, however, not in direct conflict with Immanuel Kant himself. He would probably have gladly accepted this understanding of Proverbs since he considered Judaism to be a faith that is far from pure rational religion. Kant had a rather negative opinion of Judaism, and he would not have a problem with finding several of its supposedly negative features (like emphasis on self-interest) in Proverbs.[12] My interpretation challenges scholars who have evaluated Proverbs positively even though they accept some or all of the Kantian criteria for evaluation. Those who have been arguing that self-interest does not feature in Proverbs or those who have seen the book as emphasising human autonomy and advocating a secular space in which humans, without dependence on divine guidance, can decide what is right on the basis of universal, rational laws. I do not claim that those who argue along these lines are directly influenced by Kant or that they would accept the whole Kantian philosophical framework. Nonetheless, Kant's long-term, often indirect, influence on modern thinking seems to be at least a partial explanation for the popularity of such thoughts.

14.4 Methodological Considerations: A Canonical Reading

Finally, it might be useful to reiterate some of the methodological assumptions of the above investigations as my results are often explicitly related to the methods used for reaching them.

I have argued in Part II that it is a legitimate reading strategy to pay serious attention to the book's canonical context. Besides utilising intertextual resonances, my canonical approach also pays attention to the book as a whole. In the case of Proverbs, this involves interpreting the framework of the book as framework and not as an (originally) independent work. As understanding the theological vision of the framework is crucial for understanding Proverbs as a book, I have been focusing mainly on this theological/literary framework of

---

12. See Kant 1996b: 118–119 (6: 79–80).

Proverbs, though I have tried not to neglect the sentence literature completely. Regrettably, even this limited task could not be accomplished entirely within the limits of this work. Important sections would deserve much further discussion. For example, how does Prov 1:20-33, through resonances with prophetic material, emphasise that Wisdom speaks with the authority of Yahweh? How does Prov 16:1-9, a structurally crucial part of Proverbs, emphasise humble listening and reliance on Yahweh instead of human autonomy? How does Prov 31:10-31, through the picture of a marriage to a wise woman/Wisdom combine self-interest and being in a true, mutual, loving relationship in a real *eudaemonistic* way? Nevertheless, I hope that even the selective discussion of the literary/theological framework offered here has shown that taking the framework of the book seriously and reading it in its canonical context opens up interesting theological possibilities for understanding the book.

The canonical reading I have advocated not only pays attention to the literary framework of the book and to its biblical context, but also to the theological tradition of the community (or communities) which is (are) connected to the canon. This does not necessarily mean that reading Proverbs canonically should follow ecclesiastical readings in every detail (see, for example, the differences between my reading and that of Thomas Aquinas despite the appreciative utilisation of Thomas's categories and thoughts). Nevertheless, the reading(s) of the canonical community (or communities) can inspire the modern interpreter through being a conversation partner, and, occasionally, it can provide vocabulary for contemporary theological interpretation (like the language of divine hiddenness).

The relationship between old and modern interpretations is reciprocal. Sometimes old theological readings gain confirmation from modern scholarly ones. For example, recognition of the idea of participation in the divine through wisdom can be understood as a confirmation of ancient readings of the Bible. It was a typical understanding of the patristic age. Origen, for example, taught that 'each of the sages, in proportion as he embraces wisdom, partakes to that extent of Christ.'[13] Evagrius also taught that through *paideia* the divine wisdom of God comes to dwell in man and incorporates him into the life of God.[14] Maximus the Confessor taught too that 'there is nothing interposed between wisdom and God.'[15]

However, the fact that this understanding of wisdom is ancient does not necessarily mean that interpreting Proverbs along these lines is not relevant to modern people anymore. This is another disagreement between my reading of Proverbs and some who emphatically support a non-canonical reading. McKane

---

13. Origen, *In Johannem* 1.34, translation is from Plested 2009: 242.
14. Plested 2009: 242–243.
15. Maximus Confessor, *Quaestiones ad Thalassium* 63, translation from Plested 2009: 244. For a discussion of these and other patristic authors' similar views about wisdom, see Plested 2009: 239–248.

and Westermann, for example, not only claimed that one has to make a distinction between an earlier secular and a later 'pietistic' layer in Proverbs, but they also claimed that the later layer is conceptually shallower and that it exhibits 'extreme tidiness' and 'sterility';[16] it is 'only morality' which is characterised by 'abstract, didactic discourse' and has 'lost its connection to real life.'[17]

In contrast, I have found, in my canonical reading of Proverbs, a fascinating vision of God in everyday life, and a vision of life in God through everyday activities. It is morality, yes, but a morality that stems from the incomprehensible mystery of God.

---

16. McKane 1970: 19.
17. Westermann 1995: 67.

Bibliography

Primary Sources
(For biblical texts see the Abbreviations in the beginning of the book.)

Aquinas, St. Thomas
    1928   *The Summa Contra Gentiles*, trans. the English Dominican Fathers. London: Burns Oates & Washbourne Ltd.

    1963   *Commentary on Aristotle's Physics*, trans. Richard J. Blackwell, Richard J. Spath, and W. Edmund Thirlkel. London: Routledge & Kegan Paul.

    1974   *Compendium of Theology*, trans. Cyril Vollert, S.F., S.T.D. Binghamton: B. Herder Book Co.

    1963–1981 *Summa Theologiae, Latin text and English translation, Introductions, Notes, Appendices and Glossaries.* London–New York: Blackfriars.

Charlton, William
    1970   *Aristotle's Physics.* CAS. Oxford: Clarendon Press.

Cunningham, Graham, ed.
    2003   Enki and the World Order. *ETCSL.* http://etcsl.orinst.ox.ac.uk/cgi-bin/etcsl.cgi?text=t.1.1.3#

Dalley, Stephanie
    1989   *Myths from Mesopotamia.* Oxford: Oxford University Press.

Josephus
    1930   *Jewish Antiquities*, trans. H. St. J. Thackery. LCL Josephus vol. 4. Cambridge, Mass.: Harvard Univerity Press.

Philo
    1932a   *Preliminary Studies (De Congressu Eruditionis Gratia)*, trans. F. H. Colson and Rev. G. H. Whitaker. LCL Philo vol. 4. London: William Heinemann Ltd.

    1932b   *Who is the heir of divine things (Quis rerum divinarum heres sit)*, trans. F. H. Colson and Rev. G. H. Whitaker. LCL Philo vol. 4. London: William Heinemann Ltd.

Visotzky, Burton L.
    1992   *The Midrash on Proverbs.* YJS. New Haven: Yale University Press.

Winston, David
    1979   *The Wisdom of Solomon.* AB 43. New York: Doubleday.

Secondary Sources

Achtemeier, Elizabeth
    1996   *Minor Prophets I*. NIBC. Peabody: Hendrickson.

Adams, Marilyn McCord
    2010   *Some Later Medieval Theories of the Eucharist, Thomas Aquinas, Giles of Rome, Duns Scotus, and William Ockham*. Oxford: Oxford University Press.

Adams, Nicholas
    2009   Author Response. *CRT* 7/2: 154–155.

Adams, Samuel L.
    2008   *Wisdom in Transition, Act and Consequence in Second Temple Instructions*. SJSJ 125. Leiden: Brill.

Albertz, Rainer
    1994   *A History of Israelite Religion in the Old Testament Period*, trans. John Bowden. London: SCM Press.

Albertz, Rainer and Schmitt, Rüdiger
    2012   *Family and Household Religion in Ancient Israel and the Levant*. Winona Lake: Eisenbrauns.

Aldridge, Alan
    2000   *Religion in the Contemporary World*. Cambridge: Polity Press.

Allen, Leslie C.
    2002   *Psalms 101–150*. WBC 21. Revised edition. Nashville: Thomas Nelson.

Alonso-Schökel, Luis
    1976   Sapiential and Covenant Themes in Genesis 2–3. Pp. 468–480 in *Studies in Ancient Israelite Wisdom*, ed. James L. Crenshaw. New York: KTAV Publishing House.

Andersen, Francis I., and Freedman, David Noel
    1980   *Hosea*. AB 24. New York: Doubleday.

Anderson, Albert Arnold
    1972   *The Book of Psalms*. NCBC. London: Oliphants.

Anderson, Bernhard W.
    1967   *Creation versus Chaos*. New York: Association Press.
    1984   Mythopoeic and Theological Dimensions of Biblical Creation Faith. Pp. 1–24 in *Creation in the Old Testament*, ed. Bernhard W. Anderson. London: SPCK.

Anderson, Bernhard W., with the assistance of Bishop, Steven
    1999   *Contours of Old Testament Theology*. Minneapolis: Fortress Press.

Ansberry, Christopher B.
    2011   *Be Wise, My Son, and Make My Heart Glad—An Exploration of the Courtly Nature of the Book of Proverbs*. BZAW 422. Berlin: De Gruyter.

Assmann, Jan
  1995   *Maat, Gerechtigkeit und Unsterblichkeit im Alten Ägypten.* 2nd ed. (1st ed. 1990). München: C. H. Beck.

Balentine, Samuel E.
  1983   *The Hidden God.* Oxford: Oxford University Press.

Barr, James
  1993   *Biblical Faith and Natural Theology.* Oxford: Clarendon Press.
  1999   *The Concept of Biblical Theology.* London: SCM Press.

Barth, Karl
  1960   The Fear of the Lord Is the Beginning of Wisdom. *Interpretation* 14/4: 433–439.

Bartholomew, Craig G. and O'Dowd, Ryan P.
  2011   *Old Testament Wisdom Literature—A Theological Introduction.* Downers Grove, Nottingham: IVP Academic, Apollos.

Barton, John
  1979   Natural Law and Poetic Justice in the Old Testament. *JTS* 30: 1–14.
  1984   Gerhard von Rad on the World-view of Early Israel. *JTS* 35: 301–323.
  2003   *Understanding Old Testament Ethics.* Louisville: Westminster John Knox.

Bauer, Gerhard Lorenz
  1801   *Beylagen zur Theologie des Alten Testaments.* Leipzig: Weygand.
  1838   *The Theology of the Old Testament.* London: Charles Fox.

Bauks, Michael, and Baumann, Gerlinde
  1994   Im Anfang war . . . ? Gen 1,1ff und Prov 8,22-31 im Vergleich. *BN* 71: 24–52.

Baumann, Gerlinde
  1996   *Die Weisheitsgestalt in Proverbien 1–9.* FAT 16. Tübingen: Mohr Siebeck.
  1998   A Figure with Many Facets: The Literary and Theological Functions of Personified Wisdom in Proverbs 1–9. Pp. 44–78 in vol. 2 of *The Feminist Companion to the Bible* (Second Series), eds. Athalya Brenner and Carole R. Fontaine. Sheffield: Sheffield Academic Press.

Baumgarten-Crusius, Ludwig Friedrich Otto
  1828   *Grundzüge der biblischen Theologie.* Jena: Frommann.

Baumgartner, Walter
  1933   *Israelitische und altorientalische Weisheit.* SVSGTR 166. Tübingen: Mohr Siebeck.

Beale, Gregory K.
  2004   *The Temple and the Church's Mission—A biblical theology of the dwelling place of God.* NSBT 17. Downers Grove: Apollos.

Becker, Joachim
  1965   *Gottesfurcht im Alten Testament.* Rome: Papstliches Bibelinstitut.

Bibliography

Bellah, Robert N.
- 2011 *Religion in Human Evolution, From the Paleolithic to the Axial Age.* Cambridge, Mass.: The Belknap Press of Harvard University Press.
- 2012 *Axial Age and Its Consequences.* Cambridge, Mass.: Harvard University Press.

Bennett, W. H. and Adeney, Walter F.
- 1899 *Biblical Introduction.* London: Mehuen & Co.

Bertheau, Ernst
- 1847 *Die Sprüche Salomo's.* KEHAT 7. Leipzig: Weidmann'sche Buchhandlung.

Bertholet, D. Alfred
- 1911 *Biblische Theologie des Alten Testaments*, vol. 2. Tübingen: Mohr Siebeck.

Bewer, Julius A.
- 1933 *The Literature of the Old Testament.* 2nd ed. New York: Columbia University Press.

Birch, Bruce C.
- 1997 *Hosea, Joel, and Amos.* WeBC. Louisville: Westminster John Knox Press.

Black, Jeremy
- 1998 *Reading Sumerian Poetry.* London: The Athlone Press.

Blau, Joshua
- 2010 *Phonology and Morphology of Biblical Hebrew.* LSAWS 2. Winona Lake: Eisenbrauns.

Bleek, Friedrich
- 1869 *An Introduction to the Old Testament*, vol. 2, trans. G. H. Venables. London: Bell and Daldy.

Blenkinsopp, Joseph
- 1976 The Structure of P. *CBQ* 38: 275–292.
- 1995 *Wisdom and Law in the Old Testament.* Oxford: Oxford University Press.
- 2000 *Isaiah 40–55.* New York: Doubleday.

Boer, Roland
- 2010 Introduction: Secularism and the Bible. Pp. 1–12 in *Secularism and Biblical Studies*, ed. Roland Boer. London: Equinox.

Bossman, David M.
- 2001 Biblical Theology for a Secular Society. *BTB* 31: 2–3.

Boström, Lennart
- 1990 *The God of the Sages.* CBOTS 29. Stockholm: Almqvist & Wiksell.

Brett, Mark G.
- 2010 Theological Secularity: A Response to Roland Boer. Pp. 59–66 in *Secularism and Biblical Studies*, ed. Roland Boer. London: Equinox.

Briggs, Richard S.
2010   *The Virtuous Reader.* Grand Rapids: Baker Academic.

Brown, William P.
1996   *Character in Crisis—A Fresh Approach to the Wisdom Literature of the Old Testament.* Grand Rapids: Eerdmans.
1999   *The Ethos of the Cosmos.* Grand Rapids: Eerdmans.
2010   "Here Comes the Sun", The Metaphorical Theology of Psalms 15–24. Pp. 259–277 in *The Composition of the Book of Psalms*, ed. Erich Zenger. BETL 238. Leuven: Uitgeverij Peeters.

Bruch, Johann Friedrich
1851   *Weisheitslehre der Hebräer—ein Beitrag zur Geschichte der Philosophie.* Strassbourg.

Brueggemann, Walter
1972   *In Man We Trust.* Atlanta: John Knox Press.
1990   The Social Significance of Solomon as a Patron of Wisdom. Pp. 117–132 in *The Sage in Israel and the Ancient Near East*, eds. John G. Gammie and Leo G. Perdue. Winona Lake: Eisenbrauns.
1996   The Loss and Recovery of Creation in Old Testament Theology. *TT* 53: 177–190.
1997   *Theology of the Old Testament.* Minneapolis: Fortress Press.
1998   *Isaiah 40–66.* WeBC. Louisville: Westminster John Knox Press.
2000   *1&2 Kings.* SHBC. Macon: Smyth & Helwys.
2003   *An Introduction to the Old Testament—The Canon and Christian Imagination.* Louisville: Westminster John Knox Press.
2008   *Old Testament Theology—An Introduction.* Nashville: Abingdon Press.
2011   *Disruptive Grace—Reflections on God, Scripture, and the Church*, ed. Carolyn J. Sharp. Minneapolis: Fortress Press.

Bryce, Glendon E.
1979   *A Legacy of Wisdom.* Lewisburg: Bucknell University Press.

Buber, Martin
1958   *I and Thou.* Edinburgh: T. & T. Clark.
1979   *Eclipse of God.* New Jersey: Humanities Press.
1997   Imitatio Dei. Pp. 66–75 in *Israel and the World*, Martin Buber. Syracuse: Syracuse University Press.

Bühlmann, Walter
1976   *Vom rechten Reden und Schweigen, Studien zu Proverbien 10–31.* OBO 12. Göttingen: Vandenhoeck & Ruprecht.

Camp, Claudia V.
  1985   *Wisdom and the Feminine in the Book of Proverbs*. Sheffield: Almond.
  1988   Wise and Strange: An Interpretation of the Female Imagery in Proverbs in Light of Trickster Mythology. *Semeia* 42: 14–36.
  1997   Woman Wisdom and the Strange Woman. Pp. 85–112 in *Reading Bibles, Writing Bodies, Identity and the Book*, eds. Timothy K. Beal and David M. Gunn. BL. London: Routledge.
  2000   *Wise, Strange and Holy: The Strange Woman and the Making of the Bible*. JSOTSS 320. Sheffield: Sheffield Academic Press.

Casanova, José
  2011   The Secular, Secularizations, Secularisms. Pp. 54–74 in *Rethinking Secularism*, eds. Craig Calhoun, Mark Juergensmeyer, Jonathan VanAntwerpen. Oxford: Oxford University Press.

Casanova, José and Steinfels, Peter
  2007   *Secularization—The Myths and the Realities*. Fordham University. http://www.fordham.edu/images/undergraduate/centeronreligionculture/dec_5_secular_%20transcript.pdf

Cazelles, Henri
  1995   Aḥiqar, *Ummân* and *Amun*, and Biblical Wisdom Texts. Pp. 45–55 in *Solving Riddles and Untying Knots*, eds. Ziony Zevit, Saymour Gitin, Michael Sokoloff. Winona Lake: Eisenbrauns.

Ceresko, Anthony R., O.S.F.S.
  1982   The Function of *Antanaclasis* (mṣ' "to find" // mṣ' "to reach, overtake, grasp") in Hebrew Poetry, Especially in the Book of Qoheleth. CBQ 44: 551–569.
  2002   The Function of "Order" (ṣedek) and "Creation" in the Book of Proverbs, with Some Implications for Today. Pp. 23–46 in *Prophets and Proverbs —More Studies in Old Testament Poetry and Biblical Religion*, Anthony R. Ceresko, O.S.F.S. Quezon City: Claretion.

Cessario, Romanus O.P.
  2002   *The Virtues, or the Examined Life*. AMATECA Handbooks of Catholic Theology. London: Continuum.

Chajes, Hirsch Perez
  1899   *Proverbia-Studien zu der Sog. Salomonischen Sammlung C. X–XXII, 16*. Berlin: C. A. Schwetschke.

Chapman, Stephen B.
  2000   *The Law and the Prophets*. Tübingen: Mohr Siebeck.

Cheyne, Thomas Kelly
  1887   *Job and Solomon*. London: Kegan Paul, Trench, & Co.

Cheyne, Thomas Kelly and Black, J. Sutherland, eds.
2003   *Encyclopaedia Biblica*. The reprint of the 1899–1903 edition. Bristol, Uchikanda: Thaemes Press and Edition Synapse.

Childs, Brevard S.
1986   *Old Testament Theology in a Canonical Context*. Philadelphia: Fortress.
1992   *Biblical Theology of the Old and New Testaments*. London: SCM Press.
2001   *Isaiah*. OTL. Louisville: Westminster John Knox Press.

Chirichigno, Greg
1981   A Theological Investigation of Motivation in Old Testament Law. *JETS* 24/4: 303–313.

Christensen, Duane L.
2001   *Deuteronomy 1:1–21:9*. WBC 6A. 2nd ed. Nashville: Thomas Nelson.

Clayton, John
2004   Universal Human Rights and Traditional Religious Values. *Society* 41/2: 36–41.

Clements, Ronald E.
1992   *Wisdom in Theology*. Carlisle: Paternoster Press.
1995   Wisdom and Old Testament theology. Pp. 269–286 in *Wisdom in Ancient Israel*, eds. John Day, Robert P. Gordon and H. G. M. Williamson. Cambridge: Cambridge University Press.
2003   Proverbs. Pp. 437–466 in *Eerdmans Commentary on the Bible*, eds. James D. G. Dunn and John W. Rogerson. Grand Rapids: Eerdmans.

Clément, Olivier
1993   *The Roots of Christian Mysticism*, trans. Theodore Berkeley, O.C.S.O. London: New City.

Clifford, Richard J.
1985   The Hebrew Scriptures and the Theology of Creation. *TS* 46: 507–523.
1988   Creation in the Hebrew Bible. Pp. 151–170 in *Physics, Philosophy, and Theology: A Common Quest for Understanding*, eds. Robert J. Russell, William R. Stoeger, S.J., and George V. Coyne, S.J. Vatican City State: Vatican Observatory.
1999   *Proverbs*. OTL. Louisville: Westminster John Knox Press.
2003   *Psalms 73–150*. AOTC. Nashville: Abingdon Press.
2009   Reading Proverbs 10–22. *Interpretation* 63/3: 242–253.

Clifford, Richard J. and Collins, John J.
1992   Introduction: The Theology of Creation Tradition. Pp. 1–15 in *Creation in the Biblical Traditions*, eds. Richard J. Clifford and John J. Collins. CBQMS 24. Washington: The Catholic Biblical Association of America.

Clines, David J. A.
  2003   "The Fear of the Lord is Wisdom" (Job 28:28), A Semantic and Contextual Study. Pp. 57–92 in *Job 28, Cognition in Context*, ed. Ellen van Wolde. BIS 64. Leiden: Brill.

Clines, David J. A., ed.
  1995   בין. Pp. 142–146 in *TDCH*, vol. 2. Sheffield: Sheffield Academic Press.
  2001   נעם. Pp. 705–706 in *TDCH*, vol. 5. Sheffield: Sheffield Academic Press.

Collins, John J.
  1977   The Biblical Precedent for Natural Theology. *JAAR* Supplement XLV/1: 25–67.
  1980   Proverbial Wisdom and the Yahwist Vision. *Semeia* 17: 1–17.

Coogan, Michael D.
  1999   The Goddess Wisdom—"Where Can She Be Found", Literary Reflexes on Popular Religion. Pp. 203–209 in *Ki Baruch Hu*, eds. Robert Chazan, William W. Hallo and Lawrence H. Schiffman. Winona Lake: Eisenbrauns.

Cook, Johann
  1997   *The Septuagint of Proverbs*. Leiden: Brill.

Cornill, Carl
  1907   *Introduction to the Canonical Books of the Old Testament*. London: Williams and Norgate.

Cox, Dermot
  1982   Fear or Conscience. Yirat YHWH in Proverbs 1–9. *SH* 3: 83–90

Cölln, Daniel G. C. Von
  1836   *Die biblische Theologie des Alten Testaments*. Leipzig: Barth.

Craigie, Peter C. (with 2004 supplement by Tate, Marvin E.)
  2004   *Psalms 1–50*. WBC 19. Nashville: Nelson Reference & Electronic.

Creelman, Harlan
  1927   *An Introduction to the Old Testament*. New York: The Macmillan Company.

Crenshaw, James L.
  1969   Method in Determining Wisdom Influence upon "Historical" Literature. *JBL* 88: 129–142.
  1976a Popular Questioning of the Justice of God in Ancient Israel. Pp. 289–304 in *Studies in Ancient Israelite Wisdom*, ed. J. L. Crenshaw. New York: KTAV.
  1976b Prolegomenon. Pp. 1–60 in *Studies in Ancient Israelite Wisdom*, ed. J. L. Crenshaw. New York: KTAV.
  1977   In Search of Divine Presence. *RE* 74: 353–369.
  1989   Clanging Symbols. Pp. 51–64 in *Justice and the Holy*, eds. Douglas A. Knight and Peter J. Paris. Atlanta: Scholars Press.

- 1995 Murphy's Axiom: Every Gnomic Saying Needs a Balancing Corrective. Pp. 344-354 in *Urgent Advice and Probing Questions, Collected Writings on Old Testament Wisdom*, ed. James L. Crenshaw. Macon: Mercer.
- 1998 *Education in Ancient Israel*. New York: Doubleday.
- 2010 *Old Testament Wisdom*. 3rd ed. Louisville: Westminster John Knox.

Crüsemann, Frank
- 1996 *The Torah, Theology and Social History of Old Testament Law*, trans. Allan W. Mahnke. Edinburgh: T. & T. Clark.

Curtis, Adrian
- 2004 *Psalms*. EC. Peterborough: Epworth.

Dahood, Mitchell
- 1965 *Psalms I, 1–50*. AB 16. New York: Doubleday.

Daniels, Dwight R.
- 1990 *Hosea and Salvation History*. BZAW 191. Berlin: Walter de Gruyter.

Daube, David
- 2010 *Law and Wisdom in the Bible*. David Daube's Gifford Lectures, vol. 2, ed. Calum Carmichael. West Conshohocken: Templeton Press.

Davenport, John J.
- 2001 Towards an Existential Virtue Ethics: Kierkegaard and MacIntyre. Pp. 265–323 in *Kierkegaard After MacIntyre*, eds. John J. Davenport and Anthony Rudd. Chicago: Open Court.

Davidson, A. Bruce
- 1904 *The Theology of the Old Testament*. ITL. Edinburgh: T. & T. Clark.

Davidson, Samuel
- 1862 *An Introduction to the Old Testament*, vol. 2. Hertford: Williams and Norgate.

Davies, Graham I.
- 1992 *Hosea*. NCBC. Grand Rapids: Eerdmans.
- 1993 *Hosea*. OTG. Sheffield: JSOT Press.
- 2010 The Ethics of Friendship in Wisdom Literature. Pp. 135–150 in *Ethical and Unethical in the Old Testament—God and Humans in Dialogue*, ed. Katharine J. Dell. London: T. & T. Clark.

Davies, Philip R.
- 1998 *Scribes and Schools—The Canonization of the Hebrew Scriptures*. London: SPCK.
- 2010 The Biblical Roots of Secularism. Pp. 204–215 in *Secularism and Biblical Studies*, ed. Roland Boer. London: Equinox.

Davis, Ellen F.
- 2000 *Proverbs, Ecclesiastes, and the Song of Songs*. WeBC. Louisville: Westminster John Knox Press.

2007 The Soil That Is Scripture. Pp. in *Engaging Biblical Authority: Perspectives on the Bible as Scripture*, ed. William P. Brown. Louisville: Westeminster John Knox Press.

Day, John
1990 *Psalms*. OTG. Sheffield: Sheffield Academic Press.
2000 *Yahweh and the Gods and Goddesses of Canaan*. JSOTSS 265. Sheffield: Sheffield Academic Press.

De Wette, Wilhelm M. L.
1831 *Biblische Dogmatik Alten und Neuen Testaments*. 3rd ed. Berlin: Reimer.
1840 *Lehrbuch der historisch-kritischen Einleitung in die Bibel Alten und Neuen Testamentes*. 5th ed. Berlin: G. Reimer.

Delitzsch, Franz
1874 *Biblical Commentary on the Proverbs of Solomon*, trans. M. G. Easton. CFTL. Edinburgh: T. & T. Clark.

Dell, Katharine J.
1994 "Green" Ideas in the Wisdom Tradition. *SJT* 47: 423–451.
1998 The King in the Wisdom Literature. Pp. 163–186 in *King and Messiah in Israel and the Ancient Near East*, ed. John Day. JSOTSS 270. Sheffield: Sheffield Academic Press.
2000 *Get Wisdom, Get Insight*. London: Darton, Longman and Todd Ltd.
2003 Covenant and Creation in Relationship. Pp. 111–133 in *Covenant as Context*, eds. A. D. H. Mayes and R. B. Salters. Oxford: Oxford University Press.
2004 How much Wisdom Literature has its Roots in the Pre-Exilic Period? Pp. 251–271 in *In Search of Pre-Exilic Israel*, ed. John Day. JSOTSS 406. London: T. & T. Clark.
2006 *The Book of Proverbs in Social and Theological Context*. Cambridge: Cambridge University Press.
2007 God, Creation and the Contribution of Wisdom. Pp. 60–72 in *The God of Israel*, ed. Robert P. Gordon. Cambridge: Cambridge University Press.
2009 Proverbs 1–9: Issues of Social and Theological Context. *Interpretation* 63/3: 229–240.
2010 The Significance of the Wisdom Tradition in the Ecological Debate. Pp. 56–69 in *Ecological Hermeneutics*, eds. D. Horrell et al. London: T. & T. Clark.
2013 Interpretation of Proverbs in the 19th Century. Pp. 603–624 in *Hebrew Bible Old Testament, The History of its Interpretation*, ed. M. Saebø. Göttingen: Vandenhoeck & Ruprecht.

Derksen, Mario
2011 Causality and the Metaphysics of Change in Aristotle and St. Thomas Aquinas. http://www.catholicapologetics.info/catholicteaching/philosophy/cause.htm

DeYoung, Rebecca Konyndyk; McCluskey, Colleen; and Van Dyke, Christina
2009 *Aquinas's Ethics—Metaphysical Foundations, Moral Theory, and Theological Context*. Notre Dame: University of Notre Dame Press.

Dillenberger, John
1953 *God Hidden and Revealed*. Philadelphia: Muhlenberg Press.

Doll, Peter
1985 *Menschenschöpfung und Weltschöpfung in der alttestamentlichen Weisheit*. SB 117. Stuttgart: Verlag Katholisches Bibelwerk GmbH.

Doyle, Brian
2010 Where Is God When You Need Him Most? The Divine Metaphor of Absence and Presence as a Binding Element in the Composition of the Book of Psalms. Pp. 377–390 in *The Composition of the Book of Psalms*, ed. Erich Zenger. BETL 238. Leuven: Uitgeverij Peeters.

Driver, Daniel R.
2010 *Brevard Childs, Biblical Theologian*. FAT II 46. Tübingen: Mohr Siebeck.

Driver, Samuel Rolles
1891 *An Introduction to the Literature of the Old Testament*. ITL. Edinburgh: T. & T. Clark.

Duhm, Bernhard
1875 *Die Theologie der Propheten*. Bonn: Adolph Marcus.

Dyk, Janet W. and Talstra, Eep
1999 Paradigmatic and Syntagmatic Features in Identifying Subject and Predicate in Nominal Clauses. Pp. 133–185 in *The Verbless Clause in Biblical Hebrew*, ed. Cynthia L. Miller. LSAWS 1. Winona Lake: Eisenbrauns.

Eaton, John
1989 *The Contemplative Face of Old Testament Wisdom in the Context of World Religions*. Philadelphia: Trinity Press International.

Ehrlich, Arnold B.
1968 *Randglossen zur Hebräischen Bibel*, vol. 6. Hildesheim: Georg Olms Verlagsbuchhandlung.

Eichhorn, Johann Gottfried
1824 *Einleitung in das Alte Testament*, vol. 5. 4th ed. Göttingen: Carl Eduard Rosenbusch.

Eichrodt, Walther
1935 *Theologie des Alten Testaments*, vol. 2. Leipzig: Hinrichs.

1951	*Man in the Old Testament*, trans. K. and R. Gregor Smith (first German edition: 1944). SBT. London: SCM Press.
1967	*Theology of the Old Testament*, vol. 2, trans. J. A. Baker. London: SCM Press.

Eissfeldt, Otto
1913   *Der Maschal im Alten Testament*. BZAW 24. Giessen: Alfred Töpelmann.

Emmerson, Grace I.
1984   *Hosea, An Israelite Prophet in Judean Perspective*. JSOTSS 28. Sheffield: JSOT Press.

Estes, Daniel J.
1997   *Hear, My Son—Teaching and Learning in Proverbs 1–9*. NSBT. Leicester: Apollos.
2008   Wisdom and Biblical Theology. Pp. 853–858 in *Dictionary of the Old Testament, Wisdom, Poetry & Writings*, eds. Tremper Longman III and Peter Enns. Downers Grove: IVP Academic.
2010   What Makes the Strange Woman of Proverbs 1–9 Strange? Pp. 151–169 in *Ethical and Unethical in the Old Testament—God and Humans in Dialogue*, ed. Katharine J. Dell. London: T. & T. Clark.

Ewald, Heinrich
1867   *Die Dichter des Alten Bundes*. 2nd ed. Göttingen: Vandenhoeck & Ruprecht.

Falcon, Andrea
2011   Aristotle on Causality. In *The Stanford Encyclopedia of Philosophy*, ed. Edward N. Zalta. http:// plato.stanford.edu/entries/aristotle-causality/

Farmer, Kathleen A.
1991   *Proverbs & Ecclesiastes*. ITC. Grand Rapids: Eerdmans.

Fichtner, Johannes
1933   *Die Altorientalische Weisheit in Ihrer Israelitisch–Jüdischen Ausprägung*. BZAW 62. Giessen: Alfred Töpelmann.

Finnis, John
1998   *Aquinas*. Oxford: Oxford University Press.

Fischer, Irmtraud
2005   Gotteslehrerin, Ein Streifzug durch Spr 31,10–31 auf den Pfaden unterschiedlicher Methodik. *BZ* 49: 237–253.

Fohrer, Georg
1955   Umkehr und Erlösung beim Propheten Hosea. *TZ* 11/3: 161–185.

Fontaine, Carole R.
1982   *Traditional Sayings in the Old Testaments*. BLS. Sheffield: The Almond Press.
1988   Proverbs. Pp. 447–465 in *The Harper Collins Bible Commentary*, ed. James L. Mays. New York: Harper San Francisco.

Fox, Michael V.
- 1968 Aspects of the Religion of the Book of Proverbs. *HUCA* 39: 55–69.
- 1989 *Qohelet and his Contradictions*. JSOTSS 71. Sheffield: The Almond Press.
- 1994 The Pedagogy of Proverbs 2. *JBL* 113/2: 233–243.
- 1995 World Order and Ma'at: A Crooked Parallel. *JANESCU* 23: 31–48.
- 2000 *Proverbs 1–9*. AB 18a. New York: Doubleday.
- 2007 The Epistemology of the Book of Proverbs. *JBL* 126/4: 669–684.
- 2009 *Proverbs 10–31*. AB 18b. New Haven: Yale University Press.

Frankenberg, Wilhelm
- 1895 Ueber Abfassungs-Ort und -Zeit, sowie Art und Inhalt von Prov. I–IX. *ZAW* 15: 104–132.
- 1898 *Die Sprüche, Prediger und Hoheslied*. HAT 3. Göttingen: Vandenhoeck and Ruprecht.

Franklyn, Paul
- 1983 The Sayings of Agur in Proverbs 30: Piety or Scepticism? *ZAW* 95: 238–252.

Fretheim, Terence E.
- 2005 *God and World in the Old Testament*. Nashville: Abingdon Press.

Freuling, Georg
- 2004 *"Wer eine Grube gräbt ..." Der Tun–Ergehen–Zusammenhang und sein Wandel in der alttestamentlichen Weisheitsliteratur*. WMANT 102. Neukirchen-Vluyn: Neukirchener.

Friedman, Richard Elliott
- 1995 *The Disappearance of God—A Divine Mystery*. Boston: Little, Brown and Company.

Fritsch, Charles T. and Schloerb, Rolland W.
- 1955 *The Book of Proverbs*, vol. 4: *IB*. New York: Abingdon Press.

Frydrych, Tomáš
- 2002 *Living Under the Sun—Examination of Proverbs and Qoheleth*. Leiden: Brill.

Fuhs, Hans F.
- 2001 *Das Buch der Sprichwörter*. FB 95. Würzburg: Echter.

Gabler, Johann P.
- 2004 An Oration on the Proper Distinction between Biblical and Dogmatic Theology and the Specific Objectives of Each, trans. John Sandys-Wunsch and Laurence Eldredge. Pp. 497–506 in *Old Testament Theology: Flowering and Future*, ed. Ben C. Ollenburger. Winona Lake: Eisenbrauns.

Gammie, John G.
- 1970 The Theology of Retribution in the Book of Deuteronomy. *CBQ* 32: 1–12.

Garrett, Duane A.
  2008   Proverbs: History of Interpretation. Pp. 566–578 in *Dictionary of the Old Testament, Wisdom, Poetry & Writings*, eds. Tremper Longman III and Peter Enns. Downers Grove: IVP Academic.

Gauchet, Marcel
  1997   *The Disenchantment of the World—A Political History of Religion*, trans. Oscar Burge. NFT. Princeton: Princeton University Press.

Gemser, Berend
  1937   *Sprüche Salomos*. Tübingen: Mohr Siebeck.
  1953   The Importance of the Motive Clause in Old Testament Law. Pp. 96–115 in *Congress Volume in Memoriam Aage Bentzen*. SVT 1. Leiden: Brill.
  1976   The Spiritual Structure of Biblical Aphoristic Wisdom. Pp. 208–219 in *Studies in Ancient Israelite Wisdom*, ed. J. L. Crenshaw. New York: KTAV.

Gerstenberger, Erhard
  1965a   Covenant and Commandment. *JBL* 84: 38–51.
  1965b   *Wesen und Herkunft des apodiktischen Rechts*. Neukirchen-Vluyn: Neukirchener Verlag.
  2001   *Psalms Part 2 and Lamentations*. FOTL 15. Grand Rapids: Eerdmans.
  2002   *Theologies in the Old Testament*, trans. John Bowden. London: T. & T. Clark.

Gese, Hartmut
  1958   *Lehre und Wirklichkeit in der alten Weisheit*. Tübingen: Mohr Siebeck.
  1979   Die Weisheit, der Menschensohn und die Ursprünge der Christologie als konsequente Entfaltung der biblischen Theologie. *SEÅ* 44: 77–114.

Goldingay, John
  1977   Proverbs V and IX. *RB* 84: 80–93.
  2005   *The Message of Isaiah 40–55*. London: T. & T. Clark.
  2006a   *Israel's Faith, Old Testament Theology*, vol. 2. Downers Grove: Inter Varsity Press.
  2006b   *Psalms I, 1–41*. Grand Rapids: Baker Academic.

Goldingay, John, and Payne, David
  2006   *Isaiah 40–55*, vol. 2. ICC. Edinburgh: T. & T. Clark.

Golka, Friedemann W.
  1993   *The Leopard's Spots—Biblical and African Wisdom in Proverbs*. Edinburgh: T. & T. Clark.

Goyette, John; Latkovic, Mark S.; and Myers, Richard S., eds.
  2004   *St. Thomas Aquinas & the Natural Law Tradition*. Washington: The Catholic University of America Press.

Gramberg, Carl Peter Wilhelm
  1828   *Das Buch der Sprüche Salomo's*. Leipzig: Joh. Aug. Gottl. Weigel.
  1829   *Kritische Geschichte der Religionsideen des alten Testaments, Erster Theil, Hierarchie und Cultus*. Berlin: Verlag von Duncker und Humblot.

Grant, Robert M.
  1952   *Miracle and Natural Law in Graeco-Roman and Early Christian Thought*. Amsterdam: North-Holland Publishing Company.

Gray, George Buchanan
  1919   *A Critical Introduction to the Old Testament*. London: Duckworth & Co.

Greenfield, Jonas C.
  1985   The Seven Pillars of Wisdom (Prov. 9:1): A Mistranslation. *JQR* 76/1: 13–20.

Gressmann, Hugo
  1925   *Israels Spruchweisheit im Zusammenhang der Weltliteratur*. Berlin: Karl Curtius.

Gunkel, Hermann
  1913   Weisheitsdichtung im AT. Pp. 1869–1874 in *Die Religion in Geschichte und Gegenwart*, vol. 5, eds. F. M. Schiele, H. Gunkel, O. Scheel. Tübingen: Mohr Siebeck.
  1928   What is left of the Old Testament. Pp. 13–56 in *What Remains of the Old Testament—and Other Essays*, ed. H. Gunkel, trans. A. K. Dallas. London: George Allen & Unwin Ltd.

Gunkel, Hermann (completed by Joachim Begrich)
  1998   *Introduction to Psalms*, trans. James D. Nogalski. Macon: Mercer University Press

Habel, Norman C. with the Earth Bible Team
  2001   Where Is the Voice of Earth in Wisdom Literature? Pp. 23–34 in *The Earth Story in Wisdom Traditions*, eds. Norman C. Habel & Shirley Wurst. Sheffield: Sheffield Academic Press.

Handley, Judith
  1995   Wisdom and the Goddess. Pp. 234–243 in *Wisdom in Ancient Israel*, eds. John Day, Robert P. Gordon, and H. G. M. Williamson. Cambridge: Cambridge University Press.

Hanson, Paul D.
  1995   *Isaiah 40–66*. Louisville: John Knox Press.

Hastings, James, ed.
  1898–1904 *A Dictionary of the Bible*. Edinburgh: T. & T. Clark.

Hatton, Peter T. H.
  2008   *Contradiction in the Book of Proverbs*. SOTSM. Aldershot: Ashgate.
  2011   A Cautionary Tale: The Acts-Consequence "Construct". *JSOT* 35/3: 375-384.

Hausmann, Jutta
- 1992 Beobachtungen zu Spr 31:10–31. Pp. 261–266 in *Alttestamentliche Glaube und Biblische Theologie*, eds. J. Hausmann and H.-J. Zobel. Stuttgart: Kohlhammer.
- 1995 *Studien zum Menschenbild der älteren Weisheit*. FAT 7. Tübingen: Mohr Siebeck.

Hayward, T. Robert
- 1996 *The Jewish Temple*. London: Routledge.
- 1999 Sirach and Wisdom's Dwelling Place. Pp. 31–46 in *Where Shall Wisdom Be Found?*, ed. Stephen C. Barton. Edinburgh: T. & T. Clark.

Heaton, Eric William
- 1974 *Solomon's New Men*. London: Thames and Hudson.

Heim, Knut Martin
- 2001 *Like Grapes of Gold Set in Silver*. Berlin: Walter de Gruyter.

Heinisch, Paul
- 1923 *Die persönliche Weisheit des Alten Testaments in religionsgeschichtlicher Beleuchtung*. Biblische Zeitfragen 1/2. Münster: Verlag der Aschendorffschen Verlagsbuchhandlung.

Herbert, Arthur S.
- 1975 *The Book of the Prophet Isaiah, Chapters 40–66*. Cambridge: Cambridge University Press.

Hermisson, Hans-Jürgen
- 1978 Observations on the Creation Theology in Wisdom. Pp. 43–57 in *Israelite Wisdom*, eds. J. G. Gammie et al. Missoula: Scholars Press.

Heschel, Abraham J.
- 1951 *Man Is Not Alone*. New York: Farrar.

Heschel, Susannah
- 2008 *The Aryan Jesus—Christian Theologians and the Bible in Nazi Germany*. Princeton: Princeton Universtiy Press.

Hesselgrave, Charles Everett
- 1910 *The Hebrew Personification of Wisdom*. New York: G. E. Stechert & Co.

Higton, Mike
- 2009 Review of "Habermas and Theology". *CRT* 7/2: 147–154.

Hittinger, Russell
- 1997 Natural Law and Catholic Moral Theology. Pp. 1–30 in *A Preserving Grace—Protestants, Catholics, and Natural Law*, ed. Michael Cromartie. Grand Rapids: Eerdmans.

Hitzig, Ferdinand
- 1858 *Die Sprüche Salomo's*. Zürich: Verlag von Orell, Füssli und comp.

Hobgood-Oster, Laure
- 2001 Wisdom Literature and Ecofeminism. Pp. 35–47 in *The Earth Story in Wisdom Traditions*, eds. Norman C. Habel & Shirley Wurst. Sheffield: Sheffield Academic Press.

Hossfeld, Frank Lothar and Zenger, Erich
- 1993a "Wer darf hinaufziehen zum Berg JHWHs?"—Zur Redaktionsgeschichte und Theologie der Psalmgruppe 15–24. Pp. 166–182 in *Biblische Theologie und gesellschaftlicher Wandel*, eds. Norbert Lohfink et al. Freiburg: Herder.
- 1993b *Die Psalmen I, Psalm 1–50*. Würzburg: Echter Verlag.

Høgenhaven, Jesper
- 1988 *Problems and Prospects of Old Testament Theology*. The Biblical Seminar. Sheffield: JSOT Press.

Hubbard, David Allan
- 1966 The Wisdom Movement and Israel's Covenant Faith. *TB* 17: 3–33.
- 1989 *Hosea*. TOTC. Leicester: Inter Varsity Press.

Hudal, Alois
- 1914 *Die religiösen und sittlichen Ideen des Spruchbuches*. Rome: Verlag des Päpstl. Bibel-Instituts.

Humphreys, W. Lee
- 1978 The Motif of the Wise Courtier in the Book of Proverbs. Pp. 177–190 in *Israelite Wisdom*, ed. J. G. Gammie. Missoula: Scholars Press.

Hurowitz, Victor (Avigdor)
- 1992 *I Have Built you an Exalted House—Temple Building in the Bible in Light of Mesopotamian and Northwest Semitic Writings*. JSOTSS 115. Sheffield: Sheffield Academic Press.
- 1999 Nursling, Advisor, Architect? אמון and the Role of Wisdom in Proverbs 8,22–31. *Biblica* 80/3: 391–400.
- 2001 The Seventh Pillar—Reconsidering the Literary Structure and Unity of Proverbs 31. *ZAW* 113: 209–218.

Inglehart, Ronald
- 2011 Inglehart–Welzel Cultural Map of the World. In *World Value Survey*. http://www.worldvaluessurvey.org/wvs/articles/folder_published/article_base_54

Insole, Christopher J.
- 2008 Two Conceptions of Liberalism—Theology, Creation, and Politics in the Thought of Immanuel Kant and Edmund Burke. *JRE* 36: 447–489.

Jamieson-Drake, David W.
- 1991 *Scribes and Schools in Monarchic Judah*. SWBAS 9, JSOTSS 109. Sheffield: Almond Press.

Janowski, Bernd
- 1994 Die Tat kehrt zum Täter zurück. *ZTK* 91: 247–271.

2001　　Der Himmel auf Erden. Pp. 229–260 in *Das biblische Weltbild und seine altorientalischen Kontexte*, eds. Bernd Janowski and Beate Ego. Tübingen: Mohr Siebeck.

Jenks, Alan W.
1985　　Theological Presuppositions of Israel's Wisdom Literature. *HBT* 7: 43–75.

Jenni, Ernst
1968　　*Das hebräische Pi^{c}el*. Zürich: EVZ-Verlag.

Johnston, Robert K.
1987　　Wisdom Literature and Its Contribution to a Biblical Environmental Ethic. Pp. 66–82 in *Tending the Garden*, ed. W. Granberg-Michaelson. Michigan: Eerdmans.

Jones, Edgar
1961　　*Proverbs and Ecclesiastes*. London: SCM Press Ltd.

Kant, Immanuel
1996a　　On the miscarriage of all philosophical trials in theodicy. Pp. 24–37 in *Religion and Rational Theology*, The Cambridge Edition of the Works of Immanuel Kant, trans. George Di Giovanni, eds. Allen W. Wood, George Di Giovanni. Cambridge: Cambridge University Press.

1996b　　Religion within the boundaries of mere reason. Pp. 57–215 in *Religion and Rational Theology*, The Cambridge Edition of the Works of Immanuel Kant, trans. George Di Giovanni, eds. Allen W. Wood, George Di Giovanni. Cambridge: Cambridge University Press.

Kassis, Riad Aziz
1999　　*The Book of Proverbs and Arabic Proverbial Works*. SVT 74. Leiden: Brill.

Kayatz, Christa
1966　　*Studien zu Proverbien 1–9*. WMANT 22. Neukirchen-Vluyn: Neukirchener Verlag.

Keel, Othmar
1997　　*The Symbolism of the Biblical World*, trans. Timothy J. Hallett. Winona Lake: Eisenbrauns.

2001　　Altägyptische und biblische Weltbilder, die Anfänge der vorsokratischen Philosophie und das Ἀρχή-Problem in späten biblischen Schriften. Pp. 27–47 in *Das biblische Weltbild und seine altorientalischen Kontexte*, eds. Bernd Janowski and Beate Ego. Tübingen: Mohr Siebeck.

Kent, Charles Foster
1926　　*The Growth and Contents of the Old Testament*. London: John Murray.

Kerr, Fergus
2002　　*After Aquinas—Versions of Thomism*. Malden: Blackwell.

Kidner, Derek
1964　　*The Proverbs*. London: The Tyndale Press.

King, Peter
    1999   Aquinas on the Passions. Pp. 101–132 in *Aquinas's Moral Theory*, eds. Scott MacDonald and Eleonore Stump. Ithaca: Cornell University Press.

Kittel, Rudolf
    1925   *The Religion of the People of Israel*, trans. R. Caryl Micklem. London: George Allen & Unwin Ltd.

Kline, Meredith G.
    1972   *The Structure of Biblical Authority*. 2nd ed. Grand Rapids: Eerdmans.

Knierim, Rolf
    1981   Cosmos and History in Israel's Theology. *HBT* 3: 59–123.

Knight, George A. F.
    1965   *Deutero-Isaiah—A Theological Commentary on Isaiah 40–55*. New York: Abingdon Press.

Koch, Klaus
    1955   Gibt es ein Vergeltungsdogma im Alten Testament? *ZTK* 52: 1–42.
    1983   Is There a Doctrine of Retribution in the Old Testament?, trans. Thomas H. Trapp. Pp. 57–87 in *Theodicy in the Old Testament*, ed. James L. Crenshaw. London: SPCK.

Koole, Jan L.
    1997   *Isaiah III*, vol. 1/Isaiah 40–48. HCOT 3. Kampen: Kok Pharos Publishing House.

Krašovec, Jože
    1999   *Reward, Punishment, and Forgiveness*. SVT 78. Leiden: Brill.

Kraus, Hans-Joachim
    1988   *Psalms 1–59*, trans. Hilton C. Oswald. Minneapolis: Augsburg Publishing House.

Kronholm, Tryggve
    1998   נָעַם. Pp. 467–474 in *TDOT*, eds. G. Johannes Botterweck, Helmer Ringgren, and Heinz-Josef Fabry. Grand Rapids: Eerdmans.

Kugel, James
    1997   Wisdom and the Anthological Temper. *Prooftexts* 17: 9–32.

Kuhn, Gottfried
    1931   *Beiträge zur Erklärung des Salomonischen Spruchbuches*. Stuttgart: Kohlhammer.

LaCocque, André and Ricoeur, Paul
    1998   *Thinking Biblically*, trans. David Pellauer. Chicago: The University of Chicago Press.

Landes, George M.
    1984   Creation and Liberation. Pp. 135–151 in *Creation in the Old Testament*, ed. Bernhard W. Anderson. IRT 6. London: SPCK.

Lang, Bernhard
　1972　　*Die weisheitliche Lehrrede*. Stuttgart: KBW Verlag.
　1997　　Lady Wisdom: A Polytheistic and Psychological Interpretation of a Biblical Goddess. Pp. 400–423 in *A Feminist Companion to Reading the Bible*, eds. Athalya Brenner, Carole Fontaine. Sheffield: Sheffield Academic Press.

Lash, Nicholas
　1988　　*Easter in Ordinary*. London: SCM Press.
　1996　　*The Beginning and the End of 'Religion'*. Cambridge: Cambridge University Press.

Legaspi, Michael C.
　2010　　*The Death of Scripture and the Rise of Biblical Studies*. OSHT. Oxford: Oxford University Press.

Lemaire, André
　1990　　The Sage in the School. Pp. 165–181 in *The Sage in Israel and the Ancient Near East*, eds. John G. Gammie and Leo G. Perdue. Winona Lake: Eisenbrauns.

Lenzi, Alan
　2006　　Proverbs 8:22–31: Three Perspectives on its Composition. *JBL* 125/4: 687–714.

Levenson, Jon D.
　1984　　The Temple and the World. *JR* 64/3: 275–298.
　1988　　*Creation and the Persistence of Evil*. San Francisco: Harper & Row.
　2006　　*Resurrection and the Restoration of Israel*. New Haven: Yale University Press.

Lewis, Clive Staples
　1941　　The Weight of Glory. *Theology* 43: 263–274.

Limburg, James
　1988　　*Hosea–Micah*. Interpretation. Atlanta: John Knox Press.

Lindeskog, Gösta
　1953　　The Theology of Creation in the Old and New Testaments. Pp. 1–22 in *The Root of the Vine*, eds. Anton Fridrichsen et al. Westminster: Cacre Press.

Long, Steven A.
　2004　　Natural Law or Autonomous Practical Reason: Problems for the New Natural Law Theory. Pp. 165–193 in *St. Thomas Aquinas & the Natural Law Tradition*, eds. John Goyette, Mark S. Latkovic, and Richard S. Myers. Washington: The Catholic University of America Press.

Longman, Tremper III
　2006　　*Proverbs*. Grand Rapids: Baker Academic.

2008 Proverbs, Book of. Pp. 539–552 in *Dictionary of the Old Testament, Wisdom, Poetry & Writings*, eds. Tremper Longman III and Peter Enns. Downers Grove: IVP Academic.

Louth, Andrew
2007 *The Origins of the Christian Mystical Tradition, From Plato to Denys*. 2nd ed. Oxford: Oxford University Press.

Löhr, Max
1906 *Alttestamentliche Religions-Geschichte*. Leipzig: Göschen'sche Verlagshandlung.

Lucas, Ernest. C.
2008 Wisdom Theology. Pp. 901–912 in *Dictionary of the Old Testament, Wisdom, Poetry & Writings*, eds. Tremper Longman III and Peter Enns. Downers Grove: IVP Academic.

Lundquist, John M.
1983 What is a Temple? A Preliminary Typology. Pp. 205–219 in *The Quest For the Kingdom of God*, eds. H. B. Huffmon, F. A. Spina, and A. R. W. Green. Winona Lake: Eisenbrauns.

Lütgert, Wilhelm
1984 *Schöpfung und Offenbarung*. Reprint of the 1934 first edition. Biessen: Brunnen Verlag.

Lyu, Sun Myung
2012 *Righteousness in the Book of Proverbs*. FAT II 55. Tübingen: Mohr Siebeck.

Macintosh, Andrew A.
1997 *Hosea*. ICC. Edinburgh: T. & T. Clark.

MacIntyre, Alasdair
1984 *After Virtue*. 2nd ed. Notre Dame, Indiana: University of Notre Dame Press.

1988 *Whose Justice? Which Rationality?* Notre Dame, Indiana: University of Notre Dame Press.

2009 From Answers to Questions: A Response to the Responses. Pp. 313–351 in *Intractable Disputes about the Natural Law—Alasdair MacIntyre and Critics*, ed. Lawrence S. Cunningham. Notre Dame: University of Notre Dame Press.

Madeley, John
2003 European liberal democracy and the principle of state religious neutrality. *WEP* 26/1: 1-22.

Malan, Solomon Caesar
1889–1893 *Original Notes on the Book of Proverbs*, vol. 1–3. London: Williams and Norgate.

Marcus, Ralph
1950–1951 On Biblical Hypostases of Wisdom. *HUCA* 25: 157–171.

Marti, D. Karl
1906   *Die Religion des Alten Testaments unter den Religionen des Vorderen Orients.* Tübingen: Mohr Siebeck.

Martin, James D.
1995   *Proverbs.* OTG. Sheffield: Sheffield Academic Press.

Mathewes, Charles
2007   *A Theology of Public Life.* Cambridge: Cambridge University Press.

May, William E.
2004   Contemporary Perspectives on Thomistic Natural Law. Pp. 113–156 in *St. Thomas Aquinas & the Natural Law Tradition*, eds. John Goyette, Mark S. Latkovic, and Richard S. Myers. Washington: The Catholic University of America Press.

Mays, James Luther
1994   *Psalms.* Interpretation. Louisville: John Knox Press.

McConville, J. Gordon
2002   *Deuteronomy.* ApOTC 5. Leicester: Apollos.

McCreesh, Thomas P.
1985   Wisdom as Wife: Proverbs 31:10–31. *RB* 92/1: 25–46.
1990   Proverbs. Pp. 453–461 in *The New Jerome Biblical Commentary*, eds. Raymond E. Brown, S.S., Joseph A. Fitzmeyer, S.J. (emeritus), Roland E. Murphy, O. Carm (emeritus). Upper Saddle River: A Pearson Education Company.

McCurdy, J. Frederic
1889   Proportion and Method in Old Testament Study. *OTS* 8: 325–331.

McKane, William
1970   *Proverbs.* London: SCM Press.

McKeating, Henry
1971   *Amos, Hosea, Micah.* CBC. Cambridge: Cambridge University Press.

McKenzie, John L., S.J.
1968   *Second Isaiah.* AB. New York: Doubleday.

Meinhold, Arndt
1987   Gott und Mensch in Proverbien III. *VT* 27/4: 468–477.
1991a *Die Sprüche, Teil 1: Kapitel 1–15.* ZB. Zürich: Theologischer Verlag.
1991b *Die Sprüche, Teil 2: Kapitel 16–31.* ZB. Zürich: Theologischer Verlag.

Meinhold, Hans
1908   *Die Weisheit Israels.* Leipzig: Quelle & Meier.

Mendieta, Eduardo
  2010 *A Postsecular World Society?—An Interview with Jürgen Habermas*, trans. Matthias Fritsch. http://blogs.ssrc.org/tif/2010/02/03/A-Postsecular-World-Society/

Merendino, Rosario Pius
  1981 *Der Erste und der Letzte—Eine Untersuchung von Jes 40–48*. SVT 31. Leiden: Brill.

Merrill, Eugene H.
  1997 יסר. Pp. 479–482 in *NIDOTTE*, vol. 2, ed. Willem A. VanGemeren. Carlisle: Paternoster Press.

Merwe, Christo van der; Naudé, H. J. Jackie A.; and Kroeze, Jan H. A.
  1999 *Biblical Hebrew Reference Grammar*. BLH 3. Sheffield: Sheffield Academic Press.

Michel, Diethelm
  1992 Proverbia 2—ein Dokument der Geschichte der Weisheit. Pp. 233–243 in *Alttestamentlicher Glaube und Biblische Theologie*, eds. Jutta Hausmann und Hans-Jürgen Zobel. Stuttgart: Kohlhammer.

Middleton, J. Richard
  1994 Is Creation Theology Inherently Conservative? A Dialogue with Walter Brueggemann. *HTR* 87: 257–277.

Mieder, Wolfgang
  1974 The Essence of Literary Proverb Studies. *Proverbium* 23: 888–894.

Miles, Johnny E.
  2004 *Wise King—Royal Fool*. JSOTSS 399. London: T. & T. Clark.

Miller, J. Maxwell
  1997 Separating the Solomon of History. Pp. 1-24 in *The Age of Solomon—Scholarship at the Turn of the Millennium*, ed. Lowell K. Handy. Leiden: Brill.

Miller, Patrick D.
  1982 *Sin and Judgment in the Prophets*. SBLMS 27. Chico: Scholars Press.
  1995 Creation and Covenant. Pp. 155–168 in *Biblical Theology, Problems and Perspectives*, eds. Steven J. Kraftchick, Charles D. Myers, Jr., and Ben C. Ollenburger. Nashville: Abingdon Press.

Miura, Nozomi
  2004 A Typology of Personified Wisdom Hymns. *BTB* 34/4: 138–149.

Moberly, R. W. L.
  1999 Solomon and Job: Divine Wisdom in Human Life. Pp. 3–17 in *Where Shall Wisdom Be Found?*, ed. Stephen C. Barton. Edinburgh: T. & T. Clark.
  2000 *The Bible, Theology, and Faith*. Cambridge: Cambridge University Press.

2006 *Prophecy and Discernment*. Cambridge: Cambridge University Press.

Montefiore, Claude G.
1890 Notes upon the Date and Religious Value of the Book of Proverbs. *JQR* 2: 430–453.

Moore, Rick D.
1994 A Home for the Alien: Worldly Wisdom and Covenantal Confession in Proverbs. *ZAW* 106: 96–107.

Morgan, Donn F.
1981 Wisdom in the Old Testament Traditions. Atlanta: John Knox Press.

Morris, Gerald
1996 *Prophecy, Poetry and Hosea*. JSOTSS 219. Sheffield: Sheffield Academic Press.

Moshavi, Adina
2010 *Word Order in the Biblical Hebrew Finite Clause*. LSAWS 4. Winona Lake: Eisenbrauns.

Mowinckel, Sigmund
1962 *The Psalms in Israel's Worship*, vol. 2, trans. D. R. Ap-Thomas. Oxford: Basil Blackwell.

Mowley, Harry
1991 *The Books of Amos & Hosea*. EC. London: Epworth Press.

Murphy, Roland E.
1975 Wisdom and Yahwism. Pp. 117–126 in *No Famine in the Land*, eds. James W. Flanagan & Anita Weisbrod Robinson. Claremont: Scholars Press.

1976 A Consideration of the Classification, "Wisdom Psalms". Pp. 456–467 in *Studies in Ancient Israelite Wisdom*, ed. James L. Crenshaw. New York: KTAV.

1978 Wisdom: Theses and Hypotheses. Pp. 35–42 in *Israelite Wisdom*, ed. J. G. Gammie. Missoula: Scholars Press.

1985 Wisdom and Creation. *JBL* 104: 3–11.

1986 Proverbs and Theological Exegesis. Pp. 87–95 in *The Hermeneutical Quest*, ed. Donald G. Miller. Allison Park: Pickwick Publications.

1987 Religious dimensions of Israelite wisdom. Pp. 449–458 in *Ancient Israelite Religion*, eds. P. D. Miller Jr., P. D. Hanson, and S. D. McBridge. Philadeplhia: Fortress Press.

1995 The Personification of Wisdom. Pp. 222–233 in *Wisdom in Ancient Israel*, eds. John Day, Robert P. Gordon and H. G. M. Williamson. Cambridge: Cambridge University Press.

1998 *Proverbs*. WBC 22. Nashville: Thomas Nelson.

2000   Wisdom and Yahwism Revisited. Pp. 191–200 in *Shall Not the Judge of all the Earth Do What is Right?*, eds. D. Penchansky and P. L. Reddit. Winona Lake: Eisenbrauns.

2001   Can the Book of Proverbs Be a Player in "Biblical Theology"? *BTB* 31: 4–9.

2002   *The Tree of Life, An Exploration of Biblical Wisdom Literature*. 3rd ed. Grand Rapids: Eerdmans.

Napier, B. Davie
1962   On Creation-Faith in the Old Testament. *Interpretation* 16: 21–42.

Naumann, Thomas
1991   *Hoseas Erben, Strukturen der Nachinterpretation im Buch Hosea*. BWANT 131. Stuttgart: Kohlhammer.

Nel, Philip Johannes
1982   *The Structure and Ethos of the Wisdom Admonitions in Proverbs*. BZAW 158. Berlin: Walter de Gruyter.

Newsom, Carol A.
1989   Woman and the Discourse of Patriarchal Wisdom: A Study of Proverbs 1–9. Pp. 142–160 in *Gender and Difference in Ancient Israel*, ed. Peggy L. Day. Philadelphia: Fortress.

2012   Positive Psychology and Ancient Israelite Wisdom. Pp. 117–135 in *The Bible and the Pursuit of Happiness—What the Old and New Testaments Teach Us about the Good Life*, ed. Brent A. Strawn. Oxford: Oxford University Press.

Nicholson, Ernest W.
1986   *God and his People*. Oxford: Clarendon Press.

Noack, Ludwig
1853   *Die Biblische Theologie*. Halle: Pfeffer.

Nöldecke, Theodor
1868   *Die Alttestamentliche Literatur*. Leipzig: Quandt & Händel.

Norris, Pippa, and Inglehart, Ronald
2004   *Sacred and Secular—Religion and Politics Worldwide*. Cambridge: Cambridge University Press.

North, Christopher R.
1964   *The Second Isaiah*. Oxford: Clarendon Press.

Nowack, Wilhelm
1883   *Die Sprüche Salomo's*. KEHAT 7. Leipzig: Verlag von S. Hirzel.

Oesterley, William O. E.
1929   *The Book of Proverbs*. London: Methuen & Co. Ltd.

Ollenburger, Ben C.
2004   Old Testament Theology before 1933. Pp. 3–11 in *Old Testament Theology: Flowering and Future*, ed. Ben C. Ollenburger. Winona Lake: Eisenbrauns.

Otto, Eckart
1983   Schöpfung als Kategorie der Vermittlung von Gott und Welt in Biblischer Theologie. Pp. 53–68 in *"Wenn nicht jetzt, wann dann?"*, eds. Hans-Georg Geyer et al. Neukirchen-Vluyn: Neukirchener Verlag.

Paine, Thomas
1852   *Age of Reason*. Boston: Josiah P. Mendum.

Paley, William
1860   *Natural Theology*. Boston: Gould and Lincoln.

Pardee, Dennis
1988   *Ugaritic and Hebrew Poetic Parallelism*. Leiden: Brill.

Perdue, Leo G.
1977   *Wisdom and Cult*. SBLDS 30. Missoula: Scholars Press.
1991   *Wisdom in Revolt—Metaphoric Theology in the Book of Job*. BLS 29. Sheffield: The Almond Press.
1994   *Wisdom & Creation—The Theology of Wisdom Literature*. Nashville: Abingdon Press.
1997a   The Household, Old Testament Theology, and Contemporary Hermeneutics. Pp. 223–257 in *Families in Ancient Israel*, eds. Leo G. Perdue, et al. Lousiville: Westminster John Knox.
1997b   Wisdom Theology and Social History in Proverbs 1–9. Pp. 78–101 in *Wisdom, You Are My Sister*, ed. Michael L. Barré, S.S. CBQMS 29. Washington: Catholic Biblical Association of America.
2000   *Proverbs*. Interpretation. Lousiville: John Knox Press.
2007   *Wisdom Literature—A Theological History*. Louisville: Westminster John Knox Press.
2008   *The Sword and the Stylus—An Introduction to Wisdom in the Age of Empires*. Grand Rapids: Eerdmans.

Perles, Felix
1895   *Analekten zur Textkritik des Alten Testaments*. München: Theodor Ackermann.

Perlitt, Lothar
1971   Die Verborgenheit Gottes. Pp. 367–382 in *Probleme biblischer Theologie*, ed. Hans Walter Wolff. München: Chr. Kaiser Verlag.

Perowne, Thomas Thomason
1899   *The Proverbs*. Cambridge: Cambridge University Press.

Perry, T. Anthony
  1993 *Wisdom Literature and the Structure of Proverbs*. University Park, Pennsylvania: The Pennsylvania State University Press.
  2008 *God's Twilight Zone—Wisdom in the Hebrew Bible*. Peabody: Hendrickson.

Pfeifer, Gerhard
  1967 *Ursprung und Wesen der Hypostasenvorstellung im Judentum*. AT I/31. Stuttgart: Calwer.

Pfeiffer, Robert H.
  1976 Wisdom and Vision in the Old Testament—the opening address at the Harvard Divinity School, 26 Sept. 1933. Pp. 305–313 in *Studies in Ancient Israelite Wisdom*, ed. J. L. Crenshaw. New York: KTAV.

Pieper, Josef
  1959 *Prudence*, trans. Richard and Clara Winston. London: Faber and Faber.

Plath, Siegfried
  1962 *Furcht Gottes*. Stuttgart: Calwer Verlag.

Plested, Marcus
  2009 Wisdom in the Fathers: An (Eastern) Orthodox Perspective. Pp. 239–248 in *Encounter Between Eastern Orthodoxy and Radical Orthodoxy*, eds. Adrian Pabst and Christoph Schneider. Farnham: Ashgate.

Plöger, Otto
  1984 *Sprüche Salomos*. Neukirchen: Neukirchener Verlag.

Porter, Jean
  1994 *The Recovery of Virtue*. London: SPCK.
  1999 *Natural & Divine Law*. Grand Rapids: Eerdmans.
  2002 Natural Law as a Scriptural Concept. *TT* 59/2: 226–243.
  2005 *Nature as Reason—A Thomistic Theory of the Natural Law*. Grand Rapids: Eerdmans.
  2009 Does the Natural Law Provide a Universally Valid Morality? Pp. 53–95 in *Intractable Disputes about the Natural Law—Alasdair MacIntyre and Critics*, ed. Lawrence S. Cunningham. Notre Dame: University of Notre Dame Press.

Preuss, Horst Dietrich
  1970 Erwägungen zum theologischen Ort alttestamentlicher Weisheitsliteratur. *ET* 30: 393–417.
  1989 Alttestamentliche Weisheit in Christlicher Theologie? Pp. 165–181 in *Questions Disputées D'Ancien Testament*, eds. C. Brekelmans, V. Vervenne. 2nd ed. Leeuven: Leuven University Press.

Priest, John F.
    1976   Where Is Wisdom to be Placed? Pp. 281–288 in *Studies in Ancient Israelite Wisdom*, ed. J. L. Crenshaw. New York: KTAV.

Rad, Gerhard von
    1952   *Das erste Buch Mose, Genesis Kapitel 12,10–25,18*. ATD 3. Göttingen: Vandenhoeck & Ruprecht.
    1961   *Genesis*, trans. John H. Marks. London: SCM Press.
    1962   *Old Testament Theology*, vol. 1, trans. D. M. G. Stalker (first German edition: 1957). Edinburgh: Oliver and Boyd.
    1966a   The Beginnings of Historical Writing in Ancient Israel. Pp. 166–204 in *The Problem of the Hexateuch and Other Essays*, trans. Rev. E. W. Trueman Dicken. (First German edition: 1944.) Edinburgh: Oliver & Boyd.
    1966b   The Joseph Narrative and Ancient Wisdom. Pp. 292–300 in *The Problem of the Hexateuch and Other Essays*, trans. Rev. E. W. Trueman Dicken. (First German edition: 1938.) Edinburgh: Oliver & Boyd.
    1966c   The Problem of the Hexateuch. Pp. 1–78 in *The Problem of the Hexateuch and Other Essays*, trans. Rev. E. W. Trueman Dicken. (First German edition: 1953.) Edingurgh: Oliver & Boyd.
    1972   *Wisdom in Israel*, trans. James D. Martin. Harrisburg: Trinity Press International.
    1984   The Theological Problem of the Old Testament Doctrine of Creation. Pp. 53–64 in *Creation in the Old Testament*, ed. Bernhard W. Anderson. IRT 6. (First German edition: 1936.) London: SPCK.

Rahner, Karl
    1974   The Experience of God Today. Pp. 149–165 in *Theological Investigations*, vol. 11, trans. David Bourke. London: Darton, Longman & Todd.
    1978   Thomas Aquinas on the Incomprehensibility of God. Pp. 107–125 in *Celebrating the Medieval Heritage: A Colloquy on the Thought of Aquinas and Bonaventure*, ed. David Tracy. JRS 58. Chicago: The University of Chicago Press.
    1979   The Hiddenness of God. Pp. 227–243 in *Theological Investigations*, vol. 16, trans. David Morland O.S.B. London: Darton, Longman & Todd.

Rankin, Oliver S.
    1936   *Israel's Wisdom Literature*. Edinburgh: T. & T. Clark.

Ranston, Harry
    1930   *The Old Testament Wisdom Books and their Teaching*. London: The Epworth Press.

Rendtorff, Rolf
- 1993 "Where Were You When I Laid the Foundation of the Earth?" Creation and Salvation History. Pp. 92–113 in *Canon and Theology*, trans. Margaret Kohl. Edinburgh: T. & T. Clark.
- 2005 *The Canonical Hebrew Bible—A Theology of the Old Testament*, trans. David E. Orton. TBS 7. Leiden: Deo Publishing.

Reuss, Eduard
- 1890 *Geschichte des Alten Testaments*. Braunschweig: C. A. Schwetschke und Sohn.

Reventlow, Henning Graf
- 1960 Sein Blut komme über sein Haupt. *VT* 10: 311–327.
- 1985 *Problems of Old Testament Theology in the Twentieth Century*, trans. John Bowden. London: SCM Press.
- 2010 *History of Biblical Interpretation*, vol. 4, trans. Leo G. Perdue. SBLRBS 63. Atlanta: Society of Biblical Literature.

Ringgren, Helmer
- 1947 *Word and Wisdom*. Lund: Hakan Ohlssons Boktryckeri.
- 1977 בִּין *bîn*; בִּינָה *bînāh*; תְּבוּנָה *tᵉbhûnāh*. Pp. 99–107 in *TDOT*, vol. 2, eds. G. Johannes Botterweck and Helmer Ringgren, trans. John T. Willis. 2nd ed. Grand Rapids: Eerdmans.

Ringgren, Helmer and Zimmerli, Walther
- 1962 *Sprüche, Prediger*. Göttingen: Vandenhoeck & Ruprecht.

Rodd, Cyril S.
- 2001 *Glimpses of a Strange Land—Studies in Old Testament Ethics*. Edinburgh: T. & T. Clark.

Rofé, Alexander
- 2002 *Deuteronomy, Issues and Interpretation*. OTSt. London: T. & T. Clark.

Rogerson, John W.
- 1984 *Old Testament Criticism in the Nineteenth Century England and Germany*. London: SPCK.
- 2009 *A Theology of the Old Testament—Cultural memory, communication and being human*. London: SPCK.

Rogerson, John W. and McKay, J. W.
- 1977 *Psalms 101–150*. CBC. Cambridge: Cambridge University Press.

Rosenzweig, Franz
- 1994 The Unity of the Bible: A Position Paper vis-à-vis Orthodoxy and Liberalism. Pp. 22–26 in *Scripture and Translation*, Martin Buber and Franz Rosenzweig, trans. Lawrence Rosenwald with Everett Fox. Bloomington: Indiana University Press.

Ross, Allen P.
2008   Proverbs. Pp. 22–252 in *EBC*, vol. 6, eds. Tremper Longman III and David E. Garland. Grand Rapids: Zondervan.

Ross, Jacob Joshua
2002   The Hiddenness of God—A Puzzle or a real Problem? Pp. 181–196 in *Divine Hiddenness, New Essays*, eds. Daniel Howard-Snyder, Paul K. Moser. Cambridge: Cambridge University Press.

Rudnig-Zelt, Susanne
2006   *Hoseastudien, Redaktionskritsche Untersuchungen zur Genese des Hoseabuches*. FRLANT 213. Göttingen: Vandenhoeck & Ruprecht.

Rudolph, Wilhelm
1966   *Hosea*. KAT 13. Gütersloh: Gütersloher Velagshaus Gerd Mohn.

Ruether, Rosemary Radford
1983   *Sexism and God-Talk—Toward a Feminist Theology*. Boston: Beacon Press.
2005   *Goddesses and the Divine Feminine*. Berkeley: University of California Press.

Rylaarsdam, J. Coert
1946   *Revelation in Jewish Wisdom Literature*. Chicago: The University of Chicago Press.

Sacks, Jonathan
1995   *Faith in the Future*. London: Darton, Longman and Todd.

Saebø, Magne
2012   *Sprüche*. ATD 16,1. Göttingen: Vandenhoeck & Ruprecht.

Safra, Jacob E. (chairman of the board)
2010   Eudaemonism. In *The New Encyclopaedia Britannica*, vol. 4, Micropaedia. 15th ed. Chicago/London: Encyclopaedia Britannica, Inc.

Sandoval, Timothy J.
2006   *The Discourse of Wealth and Poverty in the Book of Proverbs*. BIS 77. Leiden: Brill.

Sauer, Georg
1963   *Die Sprüche Agurs*. BWANT. Stuttgart: W. Kohlhammer Verlag.

Schäfer, Rolf
1999   *Die Poesie der Weisen*. WMANT 77. Neukirchen-Vluyn: Neukirchener.

Schellenberg, John L.
1993   *Divine Hiddenness and Human Reason*. CSPR. Ithaca and London: Cornell University Press.

Schencke, Wilhelm
1913   *Die Chokma (Sophia) in der jüdischen Hypostasenspekulation*. Kristiania: Jacob Dybwad.

Schleiermacher, Friedrich
 1969   *On Religion*, trans. Terrence N. Tice. Richmond: John Knox Press.
Schmid, Hans Heinrich
 1966   *Wesen und Geschichte der Weisheit*. BZAW 101. Berlin: Verlag Alfred Töpelmann.
 1968   *Gerechtigkeit als Weltordnung*. BHT 40. Tübingen: Mohr Siebeck.
 1974a Altorientalisch- alttestamentliche Weisheit und ihr Verhältnis zur Geschichte. Pp. 64–90 in *Altorientalische Welt in der alttestamentlichen Theologie*, H. H. Schmid. Zürich: Theologischer Verlag.
 1974b Jahweglaube und altorientalisches Weltordnungsdenken. Pp. 31–63 in *Altorientalische Welt in der alttestamentlichen Theologie*, H. H. Schmid. Zürich: Theologischer Verlag.
 1984   Creation, Righteousness, and Salvation: "Creation Theology" as the Broad Horizon of Biblical Theology. Pp. 102–117 in *Creation in the Old Testament*, ed. Bernhard W. Anderson, trans. B. W. Anderson and Dan G. Johnson. (First German edition: 1973.) London: SPCK.
 1997   בין *bîn* to understand. Pp. 230–232 in *TLOT*, vol. 1, eds. Ernst Jenni, Claus Westermann, trans. Mark E. Biddle. Peabody: Hendrickson.

Schmid, Konrad
 2012   *Schöpfung*. Themen der Theologie 4. Tübingen: Mohr Siebeck.
Schroer, Silvia
 2000   *Wisdom Has Built Her House*. Collegeville: The Liturgical Press.
Schultz, Hermann
 1892   *Old Testament Theology*, vol. 2. Edinburgh: T. & T. Clark.
Scott, Robert Balgarnie Young
 1955   Solomon and the Beginnings of Wisdom in Israel. Pp. 262–279 in *Wisdom in Israel and in the Ancient Near East*, eds. M. Noth and Winton Thomas. Leiden: Brill.
 1965   *Proverbs, Ecclesiastes*. AB. New York: Doubleday.
 1972   Wise and Foolish, Righteous and Wicked. Pp. 146–165 in *Studies in the Religion of Ancient Israel*, eds. G. W. Anderson, et al. SVT 23. Leiden: Brill.
Sellin, Ernst
 1923   *Introduction to the Old Testament*, trans. W. Montgomery. London: Hodder and Stoughton.
Shapiro, David
 1987   Proverbs. Pp. 313–330 in *Congregation—Contemporary Writers Read the Jewish Bible*, ed. David Rosenberg. San Diego: Harcourt Brace Jovanovich.

Sheppard, Gerald T.
- 1980 *Wisdom as a Hermeneutical Construct: A Study in the Sapientalizing of the Old Testament*. BZAW 151. Berlin: Walter de Gruyter.

Sheriffs, Deryck C. T.
- 1988 "A Tale of Two Cities"—Nationalism in Zion and Babylon. *TB* 39: 19–57.

Sherry, Patrick
- 2009 Disenchantment, Re-enchantment, and Enchantment. *MT* 25: 369–386.

Simundson, Daniel J.
- 2005 *Hosea, Joel, Amos, Obadiah, Jonah, Micah*. AOTC. Nashville: Abingdon Press.

Sinnott, Alice M.
- 2005 *The Personification of Wisdom*. SOTSM. Aldershot: Ashgate.

Skehan, Patrick
- 1947 The Seven Columns of Wisdom's House in Proverbs 1–9. *CBQ* 9: 190–198.
- 1948 A Single Editor for the Whole Book of Proverbs. *CBQ* 10: 115–130.
- 1967 Wisdom's House. *CBQ* 29: 468–486.

Smart, James D.
- 1965 *History and Theology in Second Isaiah*. Philadelphia: Westminster Press.

Smend, Rudolf
- 1995 The interpretation of wisdom in nineteenth-century scholarship. Pp. 257–268 in *Wisdom in Ancient Israel*, eds. John Day, Robert P. Gordon, H. G. M. Williamson, trans. Henrike Lahnemann. Cambridge: Cambridge University Press.
- 2007 *From Astruc to Zimmerli*, trans. Margaret Kohl. Tübingen: Mohr Siebeck.

Smith, Mark S.
- 2001 *The Origins of Biblical Monotheism*. Oxford: Oxford University Press.
- 2010 *The Priestly Vision of Genesis 1*. Minneapolis: Fortress Press.

Sneed, Mark
- 2011 Is the "Wisdom Tradition" a Tradition? *CBQ* 73/1: 50–71.

Snell, Daniel C.
- 1993 *Twice-Told Proverbs and the Composition of the Book of Proverbs*. Winona Lake: Eisenbrauns.

Sommer, Benjamin D.
- 1998 *A Prophet Reads Scripture*. Stanford: Stanford University Press.
- 2009 *The Bodies of God and the World of Ancient Israel*. Cambridge: Cambridge University Press.

2011 Dating Pentateuchal Texts and the Perils of Pseudo-Historicism. Pp. 85–110 in *The Pentateuch: International Perspectives on Current Research*, eds. Tom Dozeman, Konrad Schmid, and Baruch Schwartz. Tübingen: Mohr Siebeck.

Stallman, Robert C.
 2000 Divine Hospitality and Wisdom's Banquet. Pp. 117–133 in *The Way of Wisdom*, eds. J. I. Packer and Sven K. Soderlund. Grand Rapids: Zondervan.

Stordalen, Terje
 2000 *Echoes of Eden*. CBET. Leuven: Peeters.

Strack, Hermann L.
 1888 *Die Sprüche Salomos*. KKANT 5. Nördlingen: C. H. Beck'sche Buchhandlung.
 1898 *Einleitung in das Alte Testament*. München: C. H. Beck'sche Verlagsbuchhandlung.

Stuart, Douglas
 1987 *Hosea–Jonah*. WBC 31. Waco: Word Books Publisher.

Stump, Eleonore
 1999 Wisdom: Will, Belief, and Moral Goodness. Pp. 28–62 in *Aquinas's Moral Theory*, eds. Scott MacDonald and Eleonore Stump. Ithaca: Cornell University Press.
 2003 *Aquinas*. London: Routledge.

Taylor, Charles
 2007 *A Secular Age*. Cambridge, Mass.: The Belknap Press of Harvard University Press.

Taylor, Charles and Habermas, Jürgen
 2009 Rethinking Secularism: the Power of Religion in the Public Sphere. http://blogs.ssrc.org/tif/2009/11/20/rethinking-secularism-jurgen-habermas-and-charles-taylor-in-conversation

Terrien, Samuel
 1978 *The Elusive Presence*. San Francisco: Harper & Row Publishers.
 1981 The Play of Wisdom: Turning Point in Biblical Theology. *HBT* 3: 125–153.
 2003 *The Psalms*. Grand Rapids: Eerdmans.

Tiemeyer, Lena-Sofia
 2011 *For the Comfort of Zion—The Geographical and Theological Location of Isaiah 40–55*. SVT 139. Leiden: Brill.

Toombs, Lawrence E.
 1955 O.T. theology and the Wisdom Literature. *JBR* 23: 193–196.

Torrey, Charles Cutler
 1928 *The Second Isaiah*. Edinburgh: T. & T. Clark.

Towner, Wayne Sibley
  1977 The Renewed Authority of Old Testament Wisdom for Contemporary Faith. Pp. 132–147 in *Canon and Authority*, eds. George W. Coats and Burke O. Long. Philadelphia: Fortress Press.

Toy, Crawford H.
  1899 *The Book of Proverbs*. ICC. Edinburgh: T. & T. Clark.

Treier, Daniel J.
  2006 *Virtue and the Voice of God—Toward Theology as Wisdom*. Grand Rapids: Eerdmans.
  2011a Proverbs 8: Hearing Lady Wisdom's Offer Again. Pp. 57–72 in *Theological Commentary: Evangelical Perspectives*, ed. R. Michael Allen. Edinburgh: T. & T. Clark International.
  2011b *Proverbs & Ecclesiastes*. BTCB. Grand Rapids: Brazos Press.

Turner, Bryan S.
  2010 Introduction. Pp. XXI–XXV in *Secularization, Volume I: Defining Secularization—The Secular in Historical and Comparative Perspective*, ed. Bryan S. Turner. Los Angeles: SAGE.
  2011 *Religion and Modern Society—Citizenship, Secularisation and the State*. Cambridge: Cambridge University Press.

Turner, Denys
  2004 *Faith, Reason and the Existence of God*. Cambridge: Cambridge University Press.

Umbreit, Friedrich Wilhelm Carl
  1826 *Philologisch-kritischer und philosophischer Commentar über die Sprüche Salomos*. Heidelberg: Mohr Siebeck.

Vaihinger, Johann Georg
  1857 *Die dichterischen Schriften des Alten Bundes*, vol. 3. Stuttgart: Chr. Belser'sche Buchhandlung.

Van Leeuwen, Raymond C.
  1988 *Context and Meaning in Proverbs 25-27*. SBLDS 96. Atlanta: Scholars Press.
  1992 Wealth and Poverty: System and Contradiction in Proverbs. *HS* 33: 25–36.
  1997 Proverbs. Pp. 17–264 in *NIB*, vol. 5, eds. Leander E. Keck et al. Nashville: Abingdon.
  2000 Building God's House: An Exploration in Wisdom. Pp. 204–211 in *The Way of Wisdom*, eds. J. I. Packer and Sven K. Soderlund. Grand Rapids: Zondervan.
  2007 Cosmos, Temple, House: Building and Wisdom in Mesopotamia and Israel. Pp. 67–90 in *Wisdom Literature in Mesopotamia and Israel*, ed. Richard J. Clifford. SBLSS 36. Leiden: Brill.

Vatke, Johann K. W.
1835   *Die Biblische Theologie Büchern entwickelt*. Berlin: Bethge.

Waltke, Bruce K.
1979   The Book of Proverbs and Old Testament Theology. *BS* 136: 302–317.
2004   *The Book of Proverbs, Chapters 1–15*. NICOT. Grand Rapids: Eerdmans.
2005   *The Book of Proverbs, Chapters 15–31*. NICOT. Grand Rapids: Eerdmans.

Waltke, Bruce K. and O'Connor, Michael Patrick
1990   *Introduction to Biblical Hebrew Syntax*. Winona Lake: Eisenbrauns.

Walton, John H.
2009   *The Lost World of Genesis One—Ancient Cosmology and the Origins Debate*. Downer Grove: IVP.
2011   *Genesis 1 as Ancient Cosmology*. Winona Lake: Eisenbrauns.

Watts, John D. W.
2005   *Isaiah 34–66*. 2nd ed. WBC 25. Nashville: Thomas Nelson.

Weber, Max
1976   *The Protestant Ethic and the Spirit of Capitalism*, trans. Anthony Giddens. London: George Allen & Unwin Ltd.
1989   Science as a Vocation. Pp. 3–31 in *Max Weber's 'Science as a Vocation*, eds. Peter Lassman and Irving Velody, trans. Michael John. London: Unwin Hyman.

Weeks, Stuart
1994   *Early Israelite Wisdom*. Oxford: Oxford University Press.
1999   Wisdom in the Old Testament. Pp. 19–30 in *Where Shall Wisdom Be Found?*, ed. Stephen C. Barton. Edinburgh: T. & T. Clark.
2005   Wisdom Psalms. Pp. 292–307 in *Temple and Worship in Biblical Israel*, ed. John Day. London: T. & T. Clark.
2006   The Context and Meaning of Proverbs 8:30a. *JBL* 125/3: 433–442.
2007   *Instruction & Imagery in Proverbs 1–9*. Oxford: Oxford University Press.
2010   *An Introduction to the Study of Wisdom Literature*. London: T. & T. Clark.

Wehrle, Josef
1993   *Sprichwort und Weisheit, Studien zur Syntax und Semantik der ṭōb…min-Sprüche im Buch der Sprichwörter*. ATSAT 38. München: EOS Verlag Erzabtei St. Ottilien.

Weinandy, Thomas G., O.F.M., Cap.
2000   *Does God Suffer?* Edinburgh: T. & T. Clark.

Weinfeld, Moshe
1972   *Deuteronomy and the Deuteronomic School*. Oxford: Clarendon Press.

1982	Instructions for Temple visitors in the Bible and in Ancient Egypt. Pp. 224–250 in *Egyptological Studies*, ed. Sarah Israelit-Groll. SH 28. Jerusalem: The Magnes Press.

Wellhausen, Julius
- 1885   *Prolegomena to the history of Israel*, trans. J. Sutherland Black and Allan Menzies. Edinburgh : A. & C. Black.
- 1958   *Israelitische und jüdische Geschichte.* 9th ed. Berlin: Verlag Walter de Gruyter & Co.

Wenham, Gordon J.
- 1987   *Genesis 1–15.* WBC 1. Nashville: Nelson Reference & Electronic.
- 1994   Sanctuary Symbolism in the Garden of Eden Story. Pp. 399–404 in *I studied Inscriptions from Before the Flood*, eds. R. S. Hess and D. Toshio Tsumura. Winona Lake: Eisenbrauns.

Westermann, Claus
- 1974   *Creation*, trans. John J. Scullion, S.J. London: SPCK.
- 1978   *Blessing in the Bible and the Life of the Church*, trans. Keith Crim. (First German edition: 1968.) Philadelphia: Fortress.
- 1984   Biblical Reflection on Creator–Creation. Pp. 90–101 in *Creation in the Old Testament*, ed. Bernhard W. Anderson. IRT 6. London: SPCK.
- 1995   *Roots of Wisdom.* Edinburgh: T. & T. Clark.
- 1998   *Elements of Old Testament Theology*, trans. Douglas W. Stott. (First German edition: 1978.) Atlanta: John Knox Press.

Whybray, R. Norman
- 1965a   Proverbs VIII 22-31 and its Supposed Prototypes. *VT* 15/4: 504-514.
- 1965b   *Wisdom in Proverbs.* SBT. London: SCM Press.
- 1966   Some Literary Problems in Proverbs I–IX. *VT* 16: 482–496.
- 1968   *The Succession Narrative.* SBT 9. London: SCM.
- 1972   *The Book of Proverbs.* CBC. Cambridge: Cambridge University Press.
- 1974   *The Intellectual Tradition in the Old Testament.* BZAW 135. Berlin: Walter de Gruyter.
- 1979   Yahweh-Sayings and their Contexts in Proverbs 10:1–22:16. Pp. 153–165 in *La Sagesse de l'Ancien Testament*, ed. M. Gilbert. Leuven: Leuven University Press.
- 1982   Wisdom Literature in the Reigns of David and Solomon. Pp. 13–26 in *Studies in the Period of David and Solomon and Other Essays*, ed. T. Ishida. Winona Lake: Eisenbrauns.
- 1990   *Wealth and Poverty in the Book of Proverbs.* JSOTSS 99. Sheffield: Sheffield Academic Press.

- 1995 *The Book of Proverbs—A Survey of Modern Study*. Leiden: Brill.
- 1996 *Reading the Psalms as a Book*. JSOTSS 222. Sheffield: Sheffield Academic Press.
- 2002 *The Good Life in the Old Testament*. London: T. & T. Clark.

Wildeboer, D. Gerrit
- 1897 *Die Sprüche*. Freiburg: Mohr Siebeck.

Williams, James G.
- 1981 *Those Who Ponder Proverbs*. BLS. Sheffield: The Almond Press.

Wilson, Lindsay
- 2004 *Joseph Wise and Otherwise*. Carlisle: Paternoster.

Wolff, Hans Walter
- 1953 "Wissen um Gott" bei Hosea als Urform von Theologie. *ET* 12: 533–554.
- 1974a *Anthropology of the Old Testament*, trans. Margaret Kohl. London: SCM Press.
- 1974b *Hosea*, trans. Gary Stansell. Hermeneia. Philadelphia: Fortress Press.

Wright, Christopher J. H.
- 2004 *Old Testament Ethics for the People of God*. Leicester: IVP.

Wright, G. Ernest
- 1952 *God Who Acts*. London: SCM Press.

Wright, J. Robert
- 2005 *Proverbs, Ecclesiastes, Song of Solomon*. ACCS/OT IX. Downers Grove: IVP.

Wurst, Shirley
- 2001 Woman Wisdom's Way: Ecokinship. Pp. 48–64 in *The Earth Story in Wisdom Traditions*, eds. Norman C. Habel & Shirley Wurst. Sheffield: Sheffield Academic Press.

Yee, Gale A.
- 1985 *Composition and Tradition in the Book of Hosea*. SBLDS 102. Atlanta: Scholars Press.
- 1992 The Theology of Creation in Proverbs 8:22–31. Pp. 85–96 in *Creation in the Biblical Traditions*, eds. Richard J. Clifford and John J. Collins. CBQMS 24. Washington: The Catholic Biblical Association of America.

Yoder, Christine Roy
- 2003 The Woman of Substance (אשת־חיל): A Socioeconomic Reading of Proverbs 31:10–31. *JBL* 122/3: 427–447.
- 2009 On the Threshold of Kingship: A Study of Agur (Proverbs 30). *Interpretation* 63: 254–263.

Zabán, Bálint Károly
    2012   *The Pillar Function of the Speeches of Wisdom—Proverbs 1:20-33, 8:1-36 and 9:1-6 in the Structural Framework of Proverbs 1–9.* BZAW 429. Berlin: De Gruyter.

Zimmerli, Walther
    1964   The Place and Limit of the Wisdom in the Framework of the Old Testament Theology. *SJT* 17: 146–158.

    1976a   Concerning the Structure of Old Testament Wisdom. Pp. 177–204 in *Studies in Ancient Israelite Wisdom*, ed. J. L. Crenshaw, trans. Brian W. Kovacs. (First German edition: 1933.) New York: KTAV.

    1976b   *The Old Testament and the World*, trans. John J. Scullion, S.J. London: SPCK.

Zöckler, Otto
    1867   *Die Sprüche Salomonis*. THB 12. Bielefeld: Velhagen und Klasing.

Index of Subjects and Authors

abomination, 50, 166
Abraham, 156
Absalom, 221
absence, 5–6, 50, 166, 169, 215–216, 229
abundance, 208, 209
accountability, 49, 165
Achtemeier, E., 138
acts-consequence relationship (Tun-Ergehen Zusammenhang), 45–46, 57–59, 61, 69, 215, 220, 235, 242
Adams, M.M., 151
Adams, N., 175
Adams, S.L., 39, 50–51, 58–59, 80
Adeney, W.F., 8, 14
admonitions, 44, 56, 90, 97, 148, 209
adultery, 140
advice, 89, 101, 105, 235, 238
agape, 89
age, 1, 14, 17, 26–27, 32, 51, 89, 163–164, 179, 210, 248
agnostic, 190
agrarian, agricultural, 89, 118, 167, 172
Agur, 262, 279, 286
Ahithophel, 221
Akkadian, 120, 199
Albertz, R., 17, 38, 64
Aldridge, A., 163
Aletti, J.N., 184
allegory, 90
Allen, L.C., 144
Alonso-Schökel, L., 194
Amenemope, 10, 79
ancient Near East, 34, 46, 51–52, 65, 67, 107, 163–164, 168, 175, 190–197, 199–202, 223
Andersen, F.I., 137–138
Anderson, A.A., 144
Anderson, B.W., 33, 35–36
anger, 113–114, 118–119, 223
Ansberry, C.B., 39

anthropocentrism, 43–44, 46, 49, 53, 57, 62, 64, 105
anthropology, 57, 75, 107
anti-Judaism, 43
antisemitism, 43
Aquinas, Thomas, 2, 92–99, 109–110, 115–116, 126–129, 139, 145–159, 219, 242–243, 248
Arabic, 10–11
Aristeas, 197
Aristotle, 91–93, 151–153
art, 110, 117, 231
Artaxerxes, 224
Asha, 177
Asherah, 177
Ashtart, 177
Assmann, J., 59–61, 63
Assur, 192
Assyria, 177, 193
authority, 5, 23, 44, 49, 143, 165, 248
authorship, 8–9, 181
autonomy, 44–45, 47, 52, 64, 117, 169, 172–174, 213, 217, 234, 238–240, 246–248
axial age, 89
Babylon, 32, 67, 192–193, 228
Baeck, L., 68
Balentine, S.E., 220, 227–229
Balthasar, H.U. von, 233
banquet, 199
Barr, J., 55, 63–64
Barth, K., 31, 33, 63, 110, 232–233
Bartholomew, C.G., 7, 40, 58, 61, 63, 82
Barton, J., 39, 45, 50, 55, 58, 65, 91, 143
Bauer, G.L., 11, 21–24, 26–27
Bauer, J.B., 33
Bauks, M., 179

Index of Subjects and Authors 289

Baumann, G., 46, 52, 54, 64, 82, 177–181, 184, 187, 191, 198–199, 201–202
Baumgarten-Crusius, L.F.O., 24, 27
Baumgartner, W., 43, 66
Beale, G.K., 191–192, 196–197, 209
beatitudes, 96
Beaucamp, E., 33
beauty, 25, 31, 56
Becker, J., 141
Bede, 154
beginning, 5, 11, 14, 21–23, 42–43, 50–51, 62, 142, 148, 150, 154, 168, 182, 203–204, 209, 215, 224, 237, 244–245
begotten, 187, 192
behaviour, 1, 15, 58, 69, 89, 92, 96, 103–105, 107–108, 134, 136–137, 139–141, 144–146, 150–151, 157, 176, 188, 206–208, 210, 243–245, 247
Bel, 192
belief, 17, 33, 35, 53, 64–65, 79, 177
Bellah, R.N., 89
benefits, 1, 16, 92, 99, 107, 111, 115, 125–126, 128–129, 139, 148, 151, 156–158, 242–243, 246
Bennett, W.H., 8, 14
Bernhardt, K.H., 33
Bertheau, E., 11, 26
Bertholet, D.A., 8, 11, 13–17
Bewer, J.A., 11, 14–15, 17
Bezalel, 194, 200
Birch, B.C., 138
Black, J., 81–82
Black, J.S., 7, 13
Blau, J., 223
Bleek, F., 8
Blenkinsopp, J., 38, 46, 105, 195, 226
blessing, 41–42, 54, 56, 105, 156, 185, 208, 215
boasting, 150
body, 98, 110, 127, 166
Boer, R., 163
Boman, T., 33
Bonnard, P.-E., 184
Bossman, D.M., 164–165, 171
Boström, L., 41, 57–60, 63, 181
bread, 153
Brett, M.G., 176

bribe, 144, 206
bridge, 54–55, 74, 200
Briggs, R.S., 57, 115
Brown, W.P., 32, 56–57, 64, 108, 207
Bruch, J.F., 13, 19
Brueggemann, W., 2, 32, 37–38, 41–42, 48–49, 52–56, 60–61, 64, 165, 171, 174, 213–231, 233–234, 239–240, 243
Brunner, E., 63
Bryce, G.E., 216
Buber, M., 48, 81, 143, 168, 215, 230–232, 235, 239
Buddhism, 67, 88
Bühlmann, W., 121
building, 12, 21, 38, 41, 45, 48–49, 55, 57, 73, 75, 90, 107–109, 112–113, 151, 176, 185, 190–202, 204, 208, 214, 216, 218, 221, 227, 233–234
Camp, C.V., 50–51, 54, 68, 80, 84, 178, 181, 184–185, 187, 190–191, 198, 200, 203–204
canon, canonical, 2, 5, 22, 28, 40–41, 49, 67, 71–79, 81–82, 85, 139, 141, 143, 173, 176–177, 189–190, 194, 202–205, 208–209, 212, 243, 247–249
cardinal virtues, 96–98
Casanova, J., 88–90, 156, 210, 246
Catholic, 67, 74, 233–234
causality, 48, 60, 137, 151–152, 223
cause, 22, 28, 46, 59, 97, 101, 108, 111, 136, 151–153, 226–227, 231, 238
Cazelles, H., 199
Ceresko, A.R., 61, 136
certainty, 56, 58, 77–78, 231, 237
Cessario, R., 94, 98
Chajes, H.P., 237
chaos, 35–36, 225
Chapman, S.B., 99, 150
character, 6, 9, 11–12, 15, 24, 31, 44, 55–56, 60, 69, 81–82, 104, 108, 117, 124–126, 140, 142, 150, 154, 158, 170, 176, 181, 183–184, 186, 226, 231, 238–239, 241
charity, 96–98, 126, 154
Charlton, W., 151–152
Cheyne, T.K., 7–8, 11, 13–16, 18, 27
child, childishness, 16–17, 23, 96, 105, 151, 184, 202, 245

Index of Subjects and Authors

Childs, B.S., 39, 73, 75–76, 226
Chirichigno, G., 102
Christ, 74, 94, 155–156, 220, 232, 248
Christensen, D.L., 106
Christianity, Christians, 11, 17, 19, 23, 32, 37, 74, 77–78, 81, 88–89, 91–93, 107, 140, 169, 173, 186, 187, 208, 210, 215, 219, 231, 243, 245–246
Chronicles, 7, 21, 24
church, 16, 33, 73–75, 77, 163–164, 175, 185, 215, 245
city, 108, 119, 179, 182–183, 201, 208
Clayton, J., 175
Clements, R.E., 40, 55–57, 65, 132, 165–166, 171, 174
Clément, O., 219, 234
clergy, 163, 210
Clifford, R.J., 64, 82, 84, 120–122, 130–132, 135, 140, 144–145, 199
Clines, D.J.A., 102, 136, 140
closeness, 123, 223
clothing, 12, 128, 144, 201
cluster, 206, 237
cognitive, 135–136, 139, 141, 185, 211
Collins, J.J., 53, 55, 64
comfort, 120–121
command, commandment, 101, 105, 115, 129
communion, 54, 156, 246
community, 49, 74–75, 77, 84, 95, 98–100, 107–109, 127, 157–158, 239, 242, 246, 248
comprehension, 48, 101, 232, 235
comprehensiveness, 46, 219
conduct, 44, 56, 144, 245
confidence, 52, 77, 125
conflict, 48, 95, 169, 211, 247
Confucius, 89
conscience, 55, 140
contemplation, 96, 145–146, 153
contentment, 67, 126–127, 230
Coogan, M.D., 177
Cook, J., 73, 129–131
Cornill, C., 7, 8, 13–14
cosmic, 43, 191
cosmology, 57, 64, 180
cosmos, 59, 192, 195
council, 101, 221
counsel, 15, 44, 96, 130, 221
counselor, 199

countertestimony, 213–214, 219, 227
courage, 96, 149
court, 32, 35, 38–39, 135, 207, 209
covenant, 5–6, 9–10, 32, 35–37, 40–41, 43, 60, 100, 105, 129, 137–139, 141, 166, 170–171, 173, 214, 231
Cox, D., 141
Cölln, D.G.C., 25, 27
craftsman, 194, 199, 202
Craigie, P.C., 206
creating, 31–32, 34, 40, 56, 58–60, 65, 68, 141, 143, 148, 167, 177, 180–181, 183, 187, 192, 194, 197, 204, 217, 225
creation, 1, 4–5, 9, 19–21, 29–38, 40–49, 52–57, 60–68, 72, 85, 91–92, 116, 149, 157, 162, 165, 170, 179–180, 183–185, 187–188, 192, 194–197, 199–202, 209, 212, 216, 218, 241–242
creator, 20–22, 32, 35, 53–54, 65, 68, 149, 168–170, 176, 193, 217, 225, 228
creature, 68, 94, 147, 169, 179–180, 182
credo, 214
creed, 186
Creelman, H., 8, 11, 14, 16–17
Crenshaw, J.L., 5, 7–9, 12, 27–28, 30, 39–40, 45–46, 49–50, 52–53, 55, 57, 60, 68–69, 79, 92, 166–167, 171, 176, 216, 237
crooked, 120, 122, 124, 129
cross, 220, 232
Crüsemann, F., 106
culture, 18–19, 34, 40, 51–52, 65, 76, 79, 81, 85, 116, 168, 172, 176, 214
cultus, 9–11, 14, 33–34, 36, 38, 40, 47, 54, 66, 141, 165–166, 168, 170–172, 196, 201, 206–207, 226
Cunningham, G., 193
curse, 90, 105, 173
Curtis, A., 144
Cyrus, 225–226
Dahood, M., 206
Dalley, S., 192
Dame Wisdom (see Lady Wisdom), 68, 177
danger, 23, 65–66, 114, 149–150, 166, 224

Index of Subjects and Authors 291

dangerous, 54, 110, 114, 238–239
Daniel, 7, 24, 93, 137–138, 193
Daniels, D.R., 137–138
dating, 8–10, 26, 51, 75, 141
Daube, D., 100, 105
daughter, 180, 187, 203
Davenport, J.J., 95–96
Davidson, A.B., 8
Davidson, S., 13
Davies, G.I., 122, 138
Davies, P.R., 52, 176–177
Davis, E.F., 77
Day, J., 144, 177, 196
dead, 84, 129, 202
death, 9, 17, 83, 101–102, 112, 114, 125, 129, 178, 208
Decalogue, 140
deed, 5, 45–46, 92, 105, 107, 127, 136–137, 144, 166, 215, 220, 229, 239
deity, 13, 17, 79, 187, 227, 239
delight, 85, 113, 129, 193, 199
Delitzsch, F., 8, 12, 19
deliverance, 41–42, 125, 138, 214, 225–226, 229
Dell, K.J., 4, 19, 26, 36, 39–40, 42, 50–52, 54, 61, 65, 68, 79–83, 100, 141, 162, 167–168, 172, 206
de-mystifying, 166, 171
Derksen, M., 152
Descartes, 231
desire, 22, 66, 89–91, 98, 116, 120, 122, 127, 148, 223, 230–231, 233
despising, 17, 31, 142, 206
deus absconditus, 55, 226, 229, 233
deuteronomic, 137, 140, 143
deuteronomistic, 100, 143, 226
Deuteronomy, 7, 14, 42, 79, 90, 100–109, 114, 137, 143, 179
development, 10–11, 21–27, 51, 75, 82, 116, 141, 236
devotion, 140, 163, 208–209
DeYoung, R.K., 147
diachronic, 75, 77, 79
dichotomy, 98, 180, 217
didactic, 60, 80, 249
Dillenberger, J., 231–235
disaster, 101–102, 111, 125
discernment, 228
disciplining, 17
discourse, 37–38, 66–67, 163, 170, 249

disenchantment, 163, 172–174, 211, 213, 218, 220, 223, 234, 243
dishonest, 125
disordered, 99
disposition, 151, 153
divine, 5, 8, 11–12, 16, 20, 23, 25, 31–33, 36, 42, 45, 47, 51, 53–54, 60, 68–69, 89, 96–97, 101, 128, 132–133, 135, 139, 143–148, 150–151, 163, 167, 172–173, 177–178, 180–182, 184, 187, 189, 193, 202, 209, 212, 218, 221–222, 224, 228, 230, 232, 234, 239, 243–244, 246–248
divinity, 68, 177, 193
doctrine, 22–23, 28, 31–33, 74, 168, 172, 186
dogma, 23, 25, 77, 79
Doll, P., 49, 55, 57, 64
domestic, 167, 172
doubt, 46–47, 103, 150, 186, 198, 226
Doyle, B., 227
Driver, D.R., 74
Driver, S.R., 8, 13–14, 16
dualism, 210
Duhm, B., 20
dwelling, 123, 196, 202, 206–207, 209, 248
Dyk, J.W., 149
Ea, 192–193
earth, earthly 32, 85, 146, 154, 157, 191–193, 195–197, 199, 201, 207, 209, 225, 228, 239
Eaton, J., 243
Ecclesiastes, 6–7, 24–25, 27, 39, 182, 214
ecofeminism, 54
ecology, 9, 19, 54, 65, 72
Eden, 194, 196–197, 209
education, 9, 13, 16, 21, 23, 28, 56, 69, 88, 154, 162, 169, 177, 246
effectiveness, 26, 105, 173
efficient, 151–152
ego, 211
egoism (see also selfishness and self-interest), 89–91
Egypt, 10, 31–32, 34, 36, 38, 45–47, 58–59, 67, 79, 138, 170, 191–192, 206, 214, 224–225
Ehrlich, A.B., 104, 118, 120, 135–137, 145

Eichhorn, J.G., 11
Eichrodt, W., 32, 43, 45, 49
Eissfeldt, O., 9
election, 5–6, 166
Eliade, M., 191
elusiveness, 143, 228–230
Emmerson, G.I., 137
empirical, 114, 177, 229, 245, 247
enchantment, 163, 173
encouragement, 38, 41, 76, 89, 127, 143, 149, 151, 176–177, 188
Enki, 193
enlightened, 21, 48
enlightenment, 32, 39, 50, 163, 234, 244
Enuma Elish, 192
Ephraim, 138
equity, 108, 129, 139, 142, 214, 225
Esarhaddon, 192–193
Esharra, 192
essence, 11, 18, 41, 89, 171, 185, 187, 219, 229, 231, 233–234
Estes, D.J., 57, 65, 132, 145
Esther, 7
eternal, 12, 28, 146–147, 163, 183, 208
eternity, 163, 210
ethics, 1–2, 6, 15–16, 22, 54–55, 91–92, 94, 101–102, 104, 134, 141, 147, 162, 169, 172–173, 206–208, 218, 246
eudaemonism, 2, 15, 26, 30, 46–47, 91–93, 96, 157, 159, 242–243, 247–248
Evagrius, 248
everyday, 14, 38, 54, 66, 69, 98, 140, 159, 164, 170, 172, 177, 189–190, 191, 194, 209–210, 212, 214, 216, 218–220, 227, 230, 235, 241, 249
evil, 17, 83, 112, 129, 131, 149, 166, 173, 176, 194, 205, 207, 223, 238
Ewald, H., 13, 19, 26
exile, 8, 16, 18, 25–26, 53, 226, 228
existence, 38, 41, 50, 52, 59, 64, 66, 75, 82, 92, 129, 152, 165, 176, 180, 184, 187, 214, 219–220, 227, 231, 234, 245
existential, 88–89, 136, 156, 194, 227, 231
exodus, 6, 35, 42, 49, 165, 194, 198, 224

experience, 17, 38, 48, 55–56, 63, 68, 81, 136, 167, 182, 184–186, 188–190, 210, 214, 216, 218, 221–222, 227, 234, 238
experiencing, 54, 64, 67, 184–185, 187, 191, 208–209, 222, 239
eye, 1, 18, 26, 103, 121, 136, 169, 173, 206, 221, 223, 228, 235
Ezekiel, 7–8, 24, 194, 197
faith, 30–31, 33–35, 47, 56, 65, 74, 84, 96, 140, 148–149, 153, 165, 211, 214–215, 226, 230, 245–247
faithfulness, 12, 75–76, 110, 129, 185, 217
Falcon, A., 151
family, 32, 38, 114, 138
Farmer, K.A., 132
father, 112–113, 115–116, 122, 142–143, 148, 151, 154, 192, 204, 247
fear, 11, 52, 63, 90, 96, 98, 103, 105, 111, 115, 118–119, 122, 124, 126–127, 129, 133, 135–137, 139–145, 147, 150, 154–157, 173, 206, 224, 237–239, 244
female, 53, 80
feminine, 53–54, 131
feminism, 9, 19, 29, 53–54, 72
Festorazzi, F., 33
Fichtner, J., 32, 43, 45, 49
finding, 12, 46, 52, 56, 64, 111, 130, 133–134, 169, 178, 182, 224, 235, 247
Finnis, J., 94, 98
Fischer, I., 201
flourishing, 25, 32, 75, 89–90, 164, 198, 207, 210, 242
Foerster, W., 33
Fohrer, G., 140, 261
folk-religion, 20–21
folly, 83, 180–181, 203, 235
Fontaine, C.R., 84, 132
food, 83, 102, 111, 114, 118, 123–124, 126, 128, 144, 154, 156, 204
fool, 44, 112, 120, 221, 235–236
foolish, 83, 200, 217
foreign, 5, 10–11, 13, 28, 32, 38–39, 46, 66, 79, 129, 131, 143, 167, 172, 181, 193, 203
Fox, M.V., 13, 46, 49–50, 59–60, 63, 82, 84–85, 89, 92–93, 118–120,

Index of Subjects and Authors

122–125, 130–136, 140–141, 145, 154, 177, 180, 183–184, 187–188, 198, 200, 202, 222, 236–238
framework, 20–21, 42–43, 47, 60, 72, 79, 84–85, 106, 108, 139, 146, 155, 159, 170, 180, 209, 240–241, 243, 247–248
Frankenberg, W., 11, 13
Franklyn, P., 237
Freedman, D.N., 137–138
freedom, 46, 49, 165, 171, 215, 217, 221, 232–233, 239
Fretheim, T.E., 35, 52, 55
Freuling, G., 58
Friedman, R.E., 219
friendship, 122
Fritsch, C.T., 84, 135, 145, 238
fruitful, 190, 196, 221, 223
Frydrych, T., 141
Fuhs, H.F., 82, 131–132, 202
Gabler, J.P., 23
gain, 4, 27, 53, 76, 107, 116, 117, 126, 212, 244, 248
gaining, 47, 125, 134, 235
Gammie, J.G., 105
garden, 197, 209
Garrett, D.A., 50
Gauchet, M., 246
Gautama, 89
Gemser, B., 47, 84, 90, 102, 120–121, 238
Genesis, 42, 55, 65, 156, 194, 196, 208
genre, 10, 40, 82–83, 106, 141
Gerstenberger, E., 33, 38–39, 114, 144
Gese, H., 45–47, 51, 57, 59, 69, 92, 116, 166–167, 185
gift, 47, 56, 97, 126, 154, 169, 186, 203, 232, 246
Gihon, 196
Di Giovanni, G., 244
glory, 14–15, 54, 68, 212, 227
God, gods, 5–6, 13–17, 19–24, 28, 31–38, 41–42, 44–47, 49–60, 64, 66–68, 75, 80, 85, 89–90, 92, 94–99, 101–105, 107, 110–111, 115, 117–118, 127–129, 132–159, 166–168, 170–173, 176, 178–187, 189–197, 199–201, 204, 207–209, 211–221, 223–235, 237–240, 242–246, 248–249

God-centred, 129, 132–133, 138–139, 147, 149–150, 158
goddess, 46, 177, 193
gold, 118–119, 121, 196
Goldingay, J., 84, 206, 225–227
Golka, F.W., 38–39
Gospel, 128
governance, 203, 215, 219, 221, 224, 234
governing, 59, 98, 107, 149, 176, 220, 223
government, 17, 178, 204
governor, 22, 216
Goyette, J., 148
grace, 36, 145, 153
Gramberg, C.P.W., 15, 17, 26–27, 66
Grant, R.M., 151–152
Gray, G.B., 8, 11
Greenfield, J.C., 199
Gressmann, H., 16
guarding, 92, 112, 114, 129, 184
Gudea, 191
guilt, 104, 227, 231
Gunkel, H., 14, 17, 23, 48–49, 206
Habakkuk, 7, 24
Habel, N.C., 54
Habermas, J., 175, 211
habit, 94, 96
Hades, 169
de Haes, P., 33
Haggai, 7
Hame'iri, 120
Handley, J., 177
Hanson, P.D., 226
happiness, 15, 44, 46, 91–92, 94, 96, 98, 126–127, 145–147, 153, 157–158, 244–245
happy, 15, 91, 101–102, 203
Haran, M., 201
harmony, 2, 43, 64, 98, 100, 130, 139, 151, 158, 199
Hastings, J., 7
hatred, 119, 124, 126
Hatton, P.T.H., 7, 58, 83, 198
Hausmann, J., 58, 185
Hayward, T.R., 197, 209
health, 92, 111, 151, 173
hearing, 73–74, 136–137, 185
heart, 41, 46, 55, 96, 129, 132–133, 144, 173, 193, 205, 236

Heaton, E.W., 32
heaven, 135, 145–146, 155, 157, 163, 183, 191–193, 196–197, 209, 225, 228
Hebraism, 17, 25
Hegel, G.W.F., 22, 25, 230–231
Heilsgeschichte (see salvation-history), 6, 30–31, 33, 35, 37–38, 42–43, 72, 218, 242
Heim, K.M., 84, 107, 125, 145
Heinisch, P., 13, 184
Herbert, A.S., 226
hermeneutics, 72, 141, 202, 259
Hermisson, H.-J., 46, 56
Heschel, A.J., 226, 231
Heschel, S., 32
Hesselgrave, C.E., 13
Hezekiah, 38
hidden, 27, 55, 121–122, 213–220, 225–229, 231–235, 239
hiddenness, 55, 122, 124, 215–220, 223–235, 238–240, 243, 248
hiding, 76, 129–130, 213, 215, 220, 224–226, 231–234
higher ends, 95, 98, 128
higher religion, 30, 90, 156
Higton, M., 175
Hiram, 194–195, 200, 204
history, 2, 4–6, 8–11, 14, 16–18, 20–22, 24–26, 28–30, 32, 34–36, 38–43, 47–49, 52, 55, 66–69, 72–73, 75–77, 80–85, 92, 100, 104–106, 130, 133, 137–139, 141, 143, 165–166, 170–173, 177, 202, 211, 214–215, 217, 219, 221, 225, 228–229, 241, 245–246
Hittinger, R., 94, 146–147
Hitzig, F., 13
Hobgood-Oster, L., 54
Hoguth, A., 33
Holl, K., 232
holy, holiness, 13, 23, 49, 68, 96, 104–106, 135, 149, 165, 182, 186, 192–194, 205–209, 218, 245
home, 137, 170, 199
homology, 191–192, 196–197, 207
honesty, 107, 120–121, 124
honour, 47–48, 92, 104, 111–113, 115–117, 121, 125–127, 142, 150, 156–157, 206, 237

hope, 2, 69, 96, 113, 128–129, 139, 147, 149, 152–153, 158, 164, 185, 235, 248
Hosea, 7, 137–139
Hossfeld, F.L., 205–207
house, household, 5, 75, 112–113, 119–124, 126, 190–193, 195, 197–201, 203–204, 207, 209, 223
Høgenhaven, J., 35
Hubbard, D.A., 39, 51, 55, 66, 68, 138
Hudal, A., 15
human, 11–12, 18, 20, 22, 34, 36, 39, 44–45, 47–49, 51, 54–57, 59–60, 63–64, 67–68, 85, 89–91, 94–95, 97–100, 115–116, 120, 124–125, 127, 129, 133, 139–140, 145–148, 150, 153, 157, 159, 162–178, 181–186, 188, 193–194, 201, 210–211, 213, 215, 217, 220, 226–232, 234–235, 238–239, 242, 243–248
humanistic, 9–11, 101, 106
humanity, 56, 68, 77, 80, 169–170, 172, 175–176, 181, 184–185, 198, 211, 245–246
human rights, 55, 175, 211
humility, 30, 43, 47, 77, 115, 118–119, 121, 123–125, 143, 149–150, 173, 224, 237–238, 247–248
Humphreys, W.L., 33, 46
Hurowitz, V., 191–192, 195, 202
hypostasis, 13, 178, 186–188
idol, 225, 230
idolatry, 138, 182, 186
imitatio dei, imitatio Christi, 94, 143–144, 146–147, 151
immanence, 55, 68, 210
income, 88, 118–119, 124, 126
incomprehensibility, 219–220, 233–235, 238–240, 244, 249
independence, 47, 83, 151, 170, 172, 246
individual, 5, 9, 11–12, 14–16, 41, 49, 56, 60, 66–67, 69, 79, 84–85, 91, 94, 96, 98–99, 106–109, 148, 158, 163, 166, 171, 184, 186, 229, 242, 246
individualism, 6, 8, 10, 14–15, 44, 91, 100, 106–108, 158
inexplicable, 81, 227
Inglehart, R., 88–90, 114, 156
insecurity, 88, 150, 158

Insole, C.J., 98
institution, 39, 182, 211
instruction, 63, 79, 93, 142–143, 169, 191, 208, 235–239
integrity, 101, 118, 120, 122, 124–125, 127, 129, 150
intellectual, 10, 19, 36, 38–39, 48, 66, 96–97, 168, 181, 214
interdisciplinarity, 2, 73, 75, 85
international, 6, 9–12, 32, 55, 78–79, 168, 172, 209
interpretation, 1–2, 4–6, 9, 12, 20–21, 23–26, 29–31, 41, 47–49, 52, 54, 56, 58, 63–65, 69, 72–78, 82–84, 92–94, 117–119, 124–126, 130–131, 135, 146, 149, 151, 154–155, 157, 159, 174, 176–177, 185, 187–191, 198, 201–202, 205–207, 209, 211–213, 216, 218, 220, 224, 229, 234–235, 239–242, 244, 247–248
intervention, 54, 101–102, 187, 214–215, 218–219, 221, 223–224, 229, 234
intrusion, 49, 55, 133, 165, 214, 218–219, 221, 223–224, 234, 239
invisibility, 219–220, 223–224, 227–228, 230, 233–234, 238–239, 244
Isaiah, 7, 24, 41, 75, 136, 197, 228, 231
Ishtar, 177
Isis, 177
Israel, 5–6, 8, 10–13, 17, 22–23, 25, 31–32, 34–39, 41–42, 47–49, 55, 68, 100, 103–104, 107, 136, 138, 140, 143–144, 165–166, 176, 190, 195, 213–215, 217–218, 221, 224–226, 231
Israelite, 5–8, 10–12, 20–22, 24, 26, 28, 32, 34, 37–39, 41, 45–47, 59, 64, 79, 93, 108, 117, 138, 221, 243
Jamieson-Drake, D.W., 39
Janowski, B., 58, 191
Jenks, A.W., 46
Jenni, E., 223
Jeremiah, 7, 20, 137, 197, 228
Jerusalem, 11, 32, 36, 177, 189, 196–197, 207–208, 210, 212
Jesus, 11–12, 17, 24, 27, 42
Jewish, 12, 22, 24–27, 30, 41, 68, 75, 78–79, 173, 198–199, 215, 230–232, 243

Jews, 166, 178, 228
Job, 22–25, 27, 37, 41, 156, 214, 227
Johnston, R.K., 54
Jonah, 7, 24
Jones, E., 237
Joseph, 39
Josephus, 195, 197
Joshua, 7
joy, 56, 96, 112–113, 116, 199
Jubilees, 197
Judaic, Judaistic, 27, 42
Judaism, 16–17, 24–25, 27, 42, 245, 247
judgement, 5, 26, 42, 55, 76, 91, 103, 108, 130, 219, 229
Judges, 7
justice, 4, 15, 34–35, 53–54, 56, 63, 76, 96, 98, 107–109, 119, 124, 126, 129, 135, 138–139, 142, 144, 149, 157–158, 168, 182, 187, 193, 204, 209, 214, 218, 242
justification, 4, 32, 44, 46, 67, 76, 117, 129, 198, 219, 244
Kant, I., 22, 91, 230, 244–247
Kassis, R.A., 39
Kattenbusch, F., 232–233
Kaufmann, Y., 41
Kayatz, C., 32, 46
Keel, O., 190, 196, 208
Kent, C.F., 12–14
Kerr, F., 91, 94–95, 146–148, 233
Kidner, D., 135, 238
king, 35, 39, 50–51, 80, 94, 103, 107, 111–115, 158, 190–191, 193–195, 203, 224
King, P., 94
kingdom, 35, 58, 155–156
Kings, 7, 21, 24, 75, 156, 190, 194, 202–205, 208–209, 243
kingship, 34
kinship, 122
Kittel, R., 8, 11, 15
Kline, M.G., 39, 66
Knierim, R., 34–35, 46, 64, 68
Knight, G.A.F., 226
knowing, 17, 59, 80–81, 95, 97–98, 110, 127, 132, 135–140, 145–149, 152, 156–157, 198, 219, 232, 246
knowledge, 47–48, 57, 92, 107, 110–111, 113, 129, 133, 135–141, 143,

145–149, 157, 164, 168, 176–177, 194, 200–201, 203, 222–223, 237–239, 242
Koch, K., 16, 45, 57–58, 220, 224, 234
Koole, J.L., 225–226
Krašovec, J., 45
Kraus, H.-J., 184, 206
Kroeze, J.H.A., 129
Kronholm, T., 102
Kugel, J., 46
Kuhn, G., 13, 14
LaCocque, A., 194
Lady Wisdom (see Dame Wisdom), 54, 85, 177–179, 181–182, 186, 188, 193, 200–202, 235
Lagash, 191
Lambert, G., 33
Lamentations, 7
land, 102, 104–108, 121, 123–124, 129, 138, 143, 170, 192, 208, 225, 226
Landes, G.M., 53
Lang, B., 10, 177
Lash, N., 89–90, 156, 182, 185–187, 233, 238–239
Latkovic, M.S., 148
law, 12–14, 17, 19–20, 24, 28, 34, 38, 55, 60, 63, 79, 94, 100–102, 107, 138–139, 146–147, 151, 170, 173, 178, 211, 236–237, 244–247
Lee, S., 41
Legaspi, M.C., 25
Leibniz, G.W., 231
Lelievre, A., 176
Lemaire, A., 39
Lenzi, A., 179
Levenson, J.D., 41, 64, 107, 149–150, 191–192, 195–197, 206, 208
Levitical, 24
Leviticus, 202
Lewis, C.S., 155
liberation, 53, 65, 72, 218
life, 9, 11, 14–15, 17, 26–27, 34, 36, 38–39, 46, 48–49, 54–56, 66, 69, 79, 85, 88, 92, 95, 98, 101–103, 105, 107, 110–115, 124–129, 133, 135, 140, 145–146, 155, 158–159, 163–168, 171–173, 176–178, 185, 189–191, 194, 196, 198, 203, 207–210, 212, 214–219, 221–222, 227–228, 230, 235, 237, 239, 241, 244, 246, 248–249
light, 12, 51, 69, 77, 79, 83–85, 90, 92–93, 97, 134, 136–137, 143, 151, 153, 157, 177, 182, 186, 189–191, 195, 205, 207, 209–211, 229, 239, 245
Limburg, J., 138
Lindeskog, G., 33
listening, 45, 54, 63, 77, 85, 105, 132, 136, 142–143, 148, 150, 173, 176, 203, 208, 210, 223, 235–238, 247–248
literary, 6, 10, 14, 25, 28, 51, 72, 76, 81–82, 84, 106, 108, 133–135, 138, 163, 177–178, 180–181, 188, 202, 226, 241, 243, 247–248
liturgy, 206–207, 212
living, 14–15, 27, 47–48, 56, 60, 68, 77, 85, 90, 95, 98, 107–108, 110–111, 120–121, 123, 125, 127, 138, 143, 156, 163, 183, 185, 190–191, 201, 204, 207, 209–210, 212–215, 217, 224, 227–228, 231
Long, S.A., 147
Longman, T., 82, 84, 121, 131, 145, 178, 180, 185, 200–201, 243
Louth, A., 219
love, 12, 24, 89–90, 95, 97–100, 118–119, 121–122, 124, 126, 140, 143–144, 150–153, 178, 184–185, 213, 220, 232
loving, 90, 97–98, 108, 110, 144, 151–154, 157, 178, 184, 248
Löhr, M., 8, 11, 14, 16, 18, 26
Lucas, E.C., 58
Luckenbill, D.D., 193
Lundquist, J.M., 201–202
Lütgert, W., 33
Luther, 215, 231–233
Lyu, S.M., 57, 92, 120, 124, 126
Maat, 13, 34, 45–47, 59–60, 177
Macintosh, A.A., 138
MacIntyre, A., 96, 98, 116
macrocosm, 192–193, 195
Madeley, J., 175
Malachi, 7
Malan, S.C., 11
Marcus, R., 178
Marduk, 192
marriage, 32, 137, 248

Marti, D.K., 8, 16, 26
Martin, J.D., 33
Martin-Achard, R., 33
mashal, 9
Mathewes, C., 212
Maximus Confessor, 248
May, W.E., 147
Mays, J.L., 144
McCluskey, C., 147
McConville, J.G., 106
McCreesh, T.P., 90, 132, 184–185
McCurdy, J.F., 13
McKane, W., 49, 51–52, 76–77, 84, 101, 105, 120–121, 130–132, 135, 145, 180, 200, 237, 248–249
McKay, J.W., 144
McKeating, H., 138
McKenzie, J.L., 226
meal, 119, 126
meaning, 5, 9, 44, 56, 59, 72, 74, 76, 78–81, 84, 102, 118–121, 123, 127, 129–131, 135–137, 140–141, 152, 162–164, 180, 190, 202, 210, 220, 222–223, 225–226, 230, 232, 236–237
mediating, 80, 107, 182, 184–186, 188, 190, 210
mediator, 54, 80, 182, 184–185
medieval, 2, 110, 148, 199, 210, 220
Meinhold, A., 84, 129, 132, 145
Meinhold, H., 15, 20
Menahem, H., 201
Mendieta, E., 211
Merendino, R.P., 226
Merikare, 101, 105
Merrill, E.H., 236
Merwe, C., 129
Mesopotamia, 34, 191–192
Messiah, 17
metaphor, 30–31, 50, 53, 56, 112–113, 122, 129–130, 138, 140, 143, 145, 178, 183
metaphysics, 18–19
Micah, 7
Michaelis, J.D., 25
Michel, D., 133
microcosm, 192–193, 195
Middleton, J.R., 53
Mieder, W., 84
Miles, J.E., 190

Miller, J.M., 39
Miller, P.D., 32, 41, 58
miracle, 217
miraculous, 37, 219, 221, 223
Miura, N., 184
Moberly, R.W.L. 106, 110, 140–141, 156, 228
monarchy, 48, 168
monastery, 211
money, 206
monk, 67, 210
monogamy, 9, 17
Montefiore, C.G., 26
Moore, R.D., 237
moral, moralism, morality, 6, 12, 17, 23, 56, 65, 76, 91–99, 127, 140–141, 145–146, 148, 157–158, 162, 171, 183, 186, 211, 230, 244–247, 249
Morgan, D.F., 39, 40, 51
Morris, G., 138
Moses, 7, 12, 81, 106–107, 195, 209, 224, 227
Moshavi, A., 134
mother, 112–113, 116, 142
motivation, 1, 32, 44, 54, 66, 69, 80, 82, 89–90, 92–93, 101–106, 108–109, 115, 140, 151, 154–158, 218, 242, 246–247
motive, 15–16, 22, 44, 90, 101–102, 105–106
Mowinckel, S., 144
Mowley, H., 138
Murphy, R.E., 6–7, 27–28, 38, 40–43, 45, 52, 56–58, 63, 68, 82, 84–85, 120–121, 130–133, 135, 141, 145, 162, 177, 180, 184–185, 200, 206, 222, 238, 243
Myers, R.S., 148
mystery, 19, 36, 56, 185–186, 221, 232–233, 249
myth, 165, 192
mythological, 163, 165, 171, 173, 177, 191
Nahum, 7
Napier, B.D., 33
narrative, 37, 106–107, 168, 190, 202, 204, 218
nation, 10–13, 25, 44, 53, 100, 104–108, 138, 165, 168, 226

national, 5–6, 11, 18, 20–22, 43, 60, 66, 105, 107, 138, 166, 171–173, 209, 241
nationalism, 11, 24, 172
natural, 9, 17–20, 28, 31, 34, 54–56, 60, 63–64, 72, 94, 96–98, 101, 127, 130, 134–136, 146–147, 151, 167, 172–173, 219, 234–235, 245
nature, 1–2, 5, 10, 13, 15, 19–20, 23, 25, 28, 31–32, 34–36, 38, 44, 46, 49, 54–55, 60, 76, 79, 83–85, 92–93, 95–96, 100, 106, 109, 115, 119, 145–146, 149, 152–153, 162, 169, 172, 174, 176–177, 186–188, 225–226, 228, 230, 234, 242
Naudé, H.J., 129
Naumann, T., 138, 140
nazi, 32
nearness, 68, 118, 122
need, 11, 18, 149, 152, 181, 198, 220, 236, 244, 246
Nehemiah, 7, 24, 203, 224, 228
neighbour, 90, 97–98, 107–108, 122, 124, 205
Nel, P.J., 63, 90–92
netherworld, 22, 192
Neuer, W., 33
Newsom, C.A., 54, 93
Nicholson, E.W., 37
nineteenth century, 1, 4, 6–7, 10–14, 16, 18–24, 26–29, 42, 62, 66, 91, 155, 187, 241–242
Noack, L., 25, 27
Nöldecke, T., 13
nonspatial, 183–184, 187
Norris, P., 88–90, 156
North, C.R., 226
Nowack, W., 11
Numbers, 42
Obadiah, 7, 24
obedience, 54, 77, 115, 177, 246
obedient, 105, 142, 173
obey, obeying, 45, 59, 101, 107, 140, 143
observation, 66, 83, 95, 123, 142, 152, 169, 172, 188
observe, 72, 176, 244
O'Connor, M.P., 129
O'Dowd, R.P., 7, 40, 58, 61, 63, 82

Oesterley, W.O.E., 11, 13–17, 43, 132, 145, 238
offering, 158
Ollenburger, B.C., 22–23
order, 1, 8–9, 16, 19–20, 22, 24, 29, 31–32, 34–37, 43–47, 49, 51, 53–54, 56–57, 59–69, 73–75, 92–94, 97, 101–102, 106–107, 111, 116–117, 133–135, 148–151, 154, 156–158, 163, 168, 172, 177–178, 182, 185, 191, 193, 200–201, 203, 206, 214–217, 220–221, 242–244
ordinance, 48, 105, 115
ordinary, 55, 172, 201, 216, 220, 228, 233–234
Origen, 248
Orthodox, 74, 219, 233–234
Otto, E., 55
Paine, T., 19
Paley, W., 19
Pannenberg, W., 226
pan-sacral, 48–49, 168, 172
pantheism, 19
Pardee, D., 132
participating, 89, 139, 147, 151, 181, 184, 187, 189, 212, 243
participation, 58, 145–147, 157, 212, 243–244, 248
particular, 1, 17, 22, 25, 28, 59–60, 72, 74, 76, 80, 94–95, 97–98, 107, 134, 149, 151–152, 155, 164, 172–173, 175, 181, 190–191, 197, 221, 239, 244
particularism, 21–22, 24–25
path, 17, 129, 132, 141, 143, 182, 210
patristic, 220, 233, 248
Paul, 23, 156
Payne, D., 225
peace, 96, 118–121, 124, 126, 158
peaceful, 124, 126, 222
Pentateuch, 7, 42, 81
perceiving, 29, 97, 136, 138, 145, 191, 223, 228, 244–245
perception, 8, 63, 77, 115, 135–137, 220, 226, 244–245, 247
Perdue, L.G., 38–39, 46, 53, 56–57, 61, 79, 145, 168, 172, 177, 180, 184, 221, 238
Perles, F., 237
Perlitt, L., 223, 227–229

Perowne, T.T., 12–14, 16, 19
Perry, T.A., 118, 138
Persian, 11, 25, 53, 80, 107, 177, 198
personal, 1, 15, 67, 74, 88, 91, 111, 116, 150, 156, 185
personification, 13, 54, 68, 178, 180–181, 184, 187–188, 204
Pfeifer, G., 187
Pfeiffer, R.H., 11
Philippians, 155–156
Philo, 197, 209
philosopher, 18, 93, 145, 163, 175, 230, 244
philosophy, 2, 5–6, 9, 12, 18–21, 29, 34, 66, 73, 75, 91, 94, 150, 163, 188, 229–231, 241, 245, 247
physical, 5, 98, 102, 114, 120–121, 139, 165, 236
Pieper, J., 94
piety, 76, 96, 211
pillar, 58, 82, 198–199, 201–202, 206
pious, 47, 62
Plath, S., 141
Plato, 177, 183, 231
play, 34, 36, 98, 105, 152–153, 164, 194, 216
playing, 5, 8, 32, 35, 54, 163, 182–183, 199
pleasant, 102, 121, 129, 200
pleasure, 101–102
Plested, M., 248
Plotinus, 231
Plöger, O., 84, 121, 132, 145, 200, 238
political, 16, 32, 43, 211–212
politician, 175
poor, 53, 89, 96, 101, 104–105, 108, 120, 122–125, 144, 180, 197
Porter, J., 94, 96, 98, 147–148, 154
possession, 96, 105, 145, 181, 230–231, 235, 239, 244
power, 11, 35, 53, 59, 95, 104, 116, 128, 138, 148, 165, 171, 175, 183, 184–186, 211, 215–216, 221, 223, 230, 232, 239, 246
prayer, 9, 10, 163, 170, 226
presence, 13, 20, 34, 39, 50, 54, 63, 68, 82, 84–85, 105, 159, 182, 184–186, 188–191, 201–202, 208, 210, 212, 223, 228–230, 233, 235, 243
Preuss, H.D., 37

pride, 96, 125, 150, 235, 237–238
priest, 16, 25, 37, 51, 142, 166, 170, 201–202, 206, 217
Priest, J.F., 33, 51, 66
profane, 85, 167, 197
profit, 118, 225
promise, 102, 110, 155, 203
prophecy, 11
prophet, 9, 12–15, 18–20, 25, 27–28, 30, 33, 36, 43–44, 51, 89, 136–137, 184, 214, 226–229, 231
prophetic, 18, 20, 24, 58, 228, 248
prospering, 38, 105–107
prosperity, 47, 101–102, 105–106, 114–115, 193
protection, 19, 101–102, 111–112, 114, 124–126, 132–133, 137–138, 147, 149, 183–184
Protestant, 28, 74, 234, 284
proud, 118–119, 124, 223, 237–238
providence, 28, 132–133, 139, 145–148, 151, 156–157, 189, 216, 218, 243
providing, 32, 37, 84, 93, 102, 104, 121, 129, 133–134, 138, 147, 153, 155, 174, 188, 191, 193, 200, 205, 209, 236
prudence, 15, 94, 96–99, 109, 129–130, 133, 147, 157, 237
prudent, 98, 157, 165
Psalms, 7–8, 22–23, 31, 114, 144, 205, 207–208, 214, 223–224, 227
psychology, 93
Ptahhotep, 10, 101, 105
public, 88, 163, 173, 175, 212
punishment, 16–17, 44–45, 58, 101, 140, 152–155, 215, 220, 236, 246
Qohelet, 22, 37
Rad, G. von, 31–33, 35–39, 42–43, 48–49, 52, 57, 64, 72, 81, 140, 168–169, 172, 176, 178, 184, 187, 214, 216, 219, 221–222, 228
Radaq, 120
Rahner, K., 185, 219, 233–234, 239
Ramaq, 120
Rankin, O.S., 43–44
Ranston, H., 13, 93
rational, 22, 95, 147–148, 157, 163–164, 168, 171–173, 177, 218, 244–247

reader, 2, 36, 53, 58, 63, 69, 75, 77, 84–85, 89–90, 92, 103, 105–109, 117, 120, 125–126, 134–136, 138–139, 143, 147, 149–150, 156–158, 173, 176–177, 184, 188, 191, 194, 203, 207, 224, 231, 236, 242–243
reading, 1–2, 53, 67, 69, 72–76, 78–79, 81, 85, 106, 120, 130, 132, 134–136, 141, 143, 159, 174, 177, 184, 188–191, 204, 207–210, 243, 247–249
reality, 43, 48–49, 63, 76–77, 97, 133, 137, 148–150, 157, 159, 165, 167–168, 170–173, 186, 212, 218, 220, 231
reason, 1–2, 16, 19–20, 31, 42, 52, 59–60, 66, 73–76, 78, 92, 103, 106, 125, 134, 141, 147, 149, 152, 170, 206, 222, 226, 230, 242, 244–245
rebuke, 113, 121–122, 124, 237
redaction, 137
redactor, 26, 50, 81, 131
redemption, 31, 35, 208, 212
reflection, 21, 48, 74–76, 168, 211
rejoice, 108, 129, 204
religion, 6–8, 11, 14, 16–17, 20–27, 30, 35, 41, 46, 55, 64, 79, 82, 88–91, 105, 114, 141, 156, 175–176, 209, 211, 215, 244–247
religious, 8, 13–14, 16, 21–27, 31, 48, 50–52, 57, 68–69, 73–74, 76, 78–79, 84–85, 88–89, 91, 102, 107–108, 148, 162–163, 167–168, 171, 173, 175–176, 185, 191, 210–211, 217, 242–243
Rendtorff, R., 32, 41–42, 50, 60
retribution, 8–9, 15–17, 22, 25, 27–28, 45, 58, 101–102, 105, 143, 168, 217
Reuss, E., 13–15, 26
revelation, 5, 13, 19, 23–24, 31, 36, 48, 55, 68, 151, 166, 170, 228, 231–234, 245
Reventlow, H.G., 25, 33, 45
reward, 16–17, 44–45, 58, 69, 101–102, 104, 107, 112, 115–116, 125–127, 152–155, 157–158, 215, 220, 222–224, 237, 244, 246
rhetorics, 58, 105, 133, 188
rich, 4, 18, 53, 114, 120, 122, 124–125, 135, 156, 179, 219

riches, 111–113, 115–122, 124–127, 156–157, 179, 203, 235, 237
richness, 76, 119, 141, 218
Ricoeur, P., 194
righteous, 104, 107–108, 129, 132, 135, 144, 156, 207, 223, 242
righteousness, 34–35, 59, 68, 83, 103–104, 107–108, 118–119, 124–126, 129, 132, 134–135, 139, 144, 155–156, 158, 182, 204, 213, 214,
Ringgren, H., 121, 132, 135–136, 145, 178, 238
risk, 75, 149, 239
ritual, 48, 54, 165, 168, 172
Rodd, C.S., 55, 101–103, 105–106
Rofé, A., 106
Rogerson, J.W., 25, 53, 144
Rosenzweig, F., 81
Ross, A.P., 135, 145, 238
Ross, J.J., 234
royal, 32, 36, 38–39, 199, 203
Rudnig-Zelt, S., 137–138
Rudolph, W., 140
Ruether, R.R., 53–54
rule, 10, 17, 20, 41, 74, 107, 109, 171, 223, 245
rulers, 12, 107, 193, 209
ruling, 25, 119, 120, 130, 135
Ruth, 7, 122
Rylaarsdam, J.C., 49
Sabbath, 195
Sacks, J., 148
sacral, 32, 48–49, 163, 165, 168, 171–174, 217, 239
sacred, 19, 23, 47, 210–212, 234
sacrifice, 119, 182
Saebø, M., 33, 39, 82, 121, 132–133, 179, 199, 238
saeculum, 163, 210
safety, 104, 111
Safra, J.E., 91
sage, 12–15, 18, 25, 38, 56–57, 59, 63, 100–101, 176, 192, 194, 199, 202, 221–222, 228–229, 248
salvation, 41–42, 60, 101, 105, 130, 132, 166, 170–172
salvation-history (see Heilsgeschichte), 60
Samuel, 7, 48, 80, 221, 227–228

Index of Subjects and Authors

sanctification, 176–177, 189, 210, 212, 243
sanctifying, 166, 171
sanctuary, 166, 170, 182, 197, 206–207
Sandoval, T.J., 58
satisfaction, 88–89, 91, 150
satisfy, 1–2, 92, 116, 126, 135, 139, 156, 158, 169, 242, 246
Sauer, G., 237, 279
Saul, 168
saving, 83, 222–223, 239
saying, 48, 50–51, 79, 89–90, 108, 114, 117–118, 120–127, 142, 155, 158, 162, 167, 169, 176–177, 184, 187, 201, 207, 216, 221, 242, 246
scepticism, 78
Schäfer, R., 133, 279
Schellenberg, J.L., 234
Schencke, W., 13
Schleiermacher, F., 16–17
Schloerb, R.W., 84, 135, 145, 238
Schmid, H.H., 34, 45–46, 51, 59–60, 64, 92, 136
Schmid, K., 196
Schmitt, R., 17, 38
scholastics, 148, 154
school, 23, 38–39, 43, 89
Schroer, S., 54, 178
Schultz, H., 8, 13, 19, 27
Schultz, R.L., 41
scoffer, 142, 237
Scott, R.B.Y., 38, 79, 121
scribe, 120, 177, 199, 226
Scripture, 18, 73, 94
secular, 1–2, 47–53, 56–57, 62, 67, 69, 72, 78–79, 85, 161–168, 170–177, 188–190, 197, 209–211, 213, 217–219, 223, 234, 239, 242–244, 247, 249
secularisation, 49, 88–89, 163, 165, 168, 210–211, 217, 245–246
secularising, 163, 166, 173
secularism, 175
secularity, 1, 53, 69, 159, 163–164, 173, 175, 217
security, 47, 77, 88–89, 98, 102, 111, 114, 124, 133, 139, 149–151, 155–156, 158, 231
self, 1–2, 15–16, 18, 22, 31, 36, 51, 69, 76–77, 85, 90–95, 97–102, 105–106, 109–110, 112, 114–115, 118–119, 124, 126–128, 146–147, 149–151, 155, 157–158, 189, 211, 229, 233, 238, 241–244, 246–248
self-centred, 91, 150
self-interest (see egoism), 1–2, 16, 69, 90, 92–95, 97–102, 105–106, 109, 115, 128, 146, 149–151, 155, 157–158, 189, 241–244, 246–248
selfishness (see egoism), 1–2, 15–16, 22, 26–28, 67, 69, 85, 87, 92–94, 98–100, 106, 108–109, 177, 149, 153, 157, 189, 242, 246
selfless, unselfish, 109, 153
self-love, 97–99, 150
self-preservation, 95, 97–98, 110, 115, 118, 126–127, 157–158, 242
Sellin, E., 8, 11, 13, 19
Septuagint, 73, 106, 118–120, 129–131, 137, 198–199, 222
servant, 31, 112, 118, 123–124, 126, 142–143, 145, 149, 155–156, 228
service, 11, 18, 36, 47, 129, 139, 167, 181, 186, 211, 245
servile, 154–155
serving, 128–129, 141–143, 148, 151, 156, 159, 186
shame, 84, 111, 113, 115, 205, 225
Shapiro, D., 68
Sheol, 83
Sheppard, G.T., 40
Sheriffs, D.C.T., 192
Sherry, P., 163
shield, 129, 130, 133
silence, 58, 66–67, 223–224, 234, 239, 241, 243
silver, 118–119, 121, 130, 235
Smith, G. V., 41
Simundson, D.J., 138
sin, 96–97, 99, 150, 226–227, 230–231, 236, 272
Sinai, 5–6, 9–10, 49, 165–166, 170–171, 214
sinner, 104, 181
Sinnott, A.M., 177, 187
Sirach, Ben Sira, 5, 28, 51, 178, 209
Skehan, P., 198, 203
slander, 205
Smart, J.D., 226
Smend, R., 4, 19, 25–26

Smith, M.S., 41, 191, 195, 197
snare, 111, 114
Sneed, M., 39, 40, 224
Snell, D.C., 83
social, 32, 34, 43–44, 53–54, 58, 64, 80–81, 88, 108, 116, 126, 147, 172–173, 204, 211
society, 5, 10, 15, 39, 58, 88, 90, 107–108, 114, 116, 125, 146, 148, 175
Socrates, 89, 92
Solomon, 5, 8, 21–22, 28, 32, 38–39, 48, 50, 107, 114–115, 156, 178, 190–191, 194–196, 198–199, 202–204, 208
Sommer, B.D., 82, 195–196, 226
Song of Songs, 7, 182
Sophia, 185
soul, 14, 22, 98, 110, 116, 127, 129, 183
speaking, 4, 11–12, 21, 26, 34, 37, 39–42, 46, 48, 55, 58–61, 65–66, 68, 77, 89–90, 100–103, 105–106, 114, 116, 129, 134, 139, 142, 155, 158, 168, 170, 172–173, 180–184, 188, 191–192, 201, 205–207, 209, 213–217, 219, 221, 223–227, 231, 233, 235–236, 248
speech, 111–112, 114, 179, 186, 196, 215, 226
spirit, 10–11, 14, 18, 24, 28, 75, 96, 118–119, 123–124, 194
spiritual, 11–12, 14, 22, 67, 69, 77, 98, 110, 115–117, 125–126, 145, 147, 154, 156–158, 181, 185, 215, 242
spirituality, 48, 67, 168
Stade, B., 8
Stallman, R.C., 178
Staudenmaier, F.A., 18
Steiert, F.-J., 60
Steinfels, P., 89
Stordalen, T., 191, 196
Strack, H.L., 8
strength, 35, 54, 90, 113, 130, 143, 193
strife, 119, 124, 126
structure, 2, 34, 42, 47, 50, 80, 83, 93–94, 120, 122–123, 132–133, 138, 167, 186, 193, 198, 209
Stuart, D., 138
Stump, E., 126, 148, 150
style, 50, 56, 66, 78, 81, 117

success, 47, 69, 90, 104–105, 110, 113, 116, 126, 130, 138–139, 149, 157, 242
suffering, 5, 56, 89, 96
supernatural, 96, 163, 220, 223, 234
survival, 114–115, 125, 157
sustenance, 111, 215, 216
synchronic, 72, 85
tabernacle, 194–196, 200–201, 209
Talstra, E., 149
Taylor, C., 89–90, 150, 156, 163, 175, 246
teaching, 1, 10–12, 14, 16–20, 24, 26, 28, 30, 33, 44–45, 47, 49, 53, 55–56, 63–67, 74, 77, 79, 81, 83, 91–92, 99, 101–105, 109–110, 112–113, 133, 138–139, 146, 148–149, 151, 154–155, 157–159, 165, 173, 191, 199, 207, 209, 217, 221–222, 224, 233, 235–237, 239, 242–243, 247
teacher, 12, 14, 23, 26, 31, 36–37, 81, 101, 221
temple, 11, 39, 140, 166, 173, 177–178, 189–202, 204, 206–212, 242–243
temporal, 128, 134, 163, 193, 208, 210
Terrien, S., 54–55, 144, 206, 228–230
testimony, 31, 42, 156, 213–215, 224
Tetragrammaton, 173, 176, 222
theodicy, 34, 53, 57
theologian, 8, 17, 23–25, 27, 32, 36, 40, 62, 74, 81, 93, 163, 185, 228, 232–234, 239, 242
theological, 1–2, 4–5, 8–10, 13, 16, 20–23, 25–30, 32–33, 35–37, 40–43, 46–49, 51–52, 54, 61–67, 69, 72–76, 80, 82, 84–85, 88–89, 91, 93–97, 106, 130, 135, 146, 148, 150, 155, 162, 168, 170, 173–174, 177, 180–182, 184–188, 190, 201–202, 206, 209, 212–214, 216, 218–222, 224, 226, 228–229, 234, 239, 241–244, 247–248
theology, 1–2, 5–6, 8–10, 19–21, 24, 27, 29–38, 40–44, 46–48, 52–53, 55–57, 60, 62–67, 72–73, 75, 80–81, 91–95, 98–99, 114, 116, 127, 146, 157–158, 162, 168, 170, 172, 174, 185, 190, 195, 212–219, 224, 226, 228, 230–231, 233, 240–241, 243
this-worldly, 26, 47, 69, 164, 171

Index of Subjects and Authors 303

Thomistic, 88, 91, 93–94, 96, 100, 109, 127, 129, 139, 147, 151–152, 154–155, 157–159, 242
Tiemeyer, L.-S., 226
time, 5, 12, 16, 19, 23–24, 32–33, 35, 42, 59, 62, 65, 69, 73–76, 80, 85, 98, 103, 105, 107, 124, 128, 134, 148, 154–155, 163, 179–182, 184, 191, 196, 198, 201, 209–210, 230, 232–233, 236, 245
tongue, 121
Toombs, L.E., 66
topos, 192, 194, 197, 200
Torah, 6, 9, 13–14, 27–28, 49, 81, 165, 177, 188, 198
Torrey, C.C., 226
Tournay, R., 184
Towner, W.S., 49
Toy, C.H., 11, 13, 15, 17, 19, 27, 84, 92, 121, 131, 135, 145, 180, 200, 238
tradition, 28, 32, 35–37, 39–40, 43, 49, 55, 64, 66–68, 73–76, 79–80, 82, 92–93, 141, 154, 165, 201, 203, 209, 215, 217, 219, 226, 230, 233, 239, 245, 247–248
transcendence, 54–55, 68, 178, 183, 210, 223
transformation, 89, 214–215
treasure, 83, 200
treatment, 20, 174, 217–218, 224
tree, 194, 196–197, 207
Treier, D.J., 57, 93, 108, 116, 178–179
Trinity, 75, 186–187
trust, 41, 64, 69, 103, 119, 124, 129, 139, 147, 149–150, 158, 217, 218
truth, 11, 15–16, 33, 40, 47, 66, 75, 92, 105, 205, 209
Tun-Ergehen Zusammenhang, see acts-consequence relationship
Turner, B.S., 176
Turner, D., 94–95, 148, 219
twentieth century, 1, 4–6, 8, 11, 14, 16, 18–21, 28–29, 49, 51, 62, 141, 178, 184, 187, 241–242
Ugaritic, 120, 122
Umbreit, F.W.C., 11, 13, 27–28
uncertain, 120, 236
uncertainty, 62, 124, 126, 131, 237

understanding, 5, 17, 19, 22, 24, 29, 35–37, 39, 42, 46–51, 57–59, 63, 67–68, 72–74, 76–77, 79–85, 89–96, 105–106, 108, 111–112, 116, 118–120, 124, 129, 131–142, 145–146, 148–152, 154–155, 159, 164–170, 176, 178–180, 183–186, 187, 189–190, 193–194, 198–203, 207, 209–213, 217, 219–221, 223–225, 227–235, 237, 239–244, 246–248
unethical, 139, 149, 158
unity, 20, 38–39, 41–42, 81, 133, 155, 198
universal, 8, 11–12, 16, 20–22, 25–28, 30, 76, 79, 165, 170–172, 175–177, 183, 190, 209, 241, 245–247
universalistic, 9–11, 172–174, 213
universe, 56, 68–69, 116, 177, 191–195, 197–199, 201, 215, 228
unknowability, 227
unknown, 208, 229–230, 233
utilitarian, 15, 98
utilitarianism, 9, 15, 26, 28, 30
utility, 171–172
Vaihinger, J.G., 11, 14
valuable, 5, 26, 55, 80, 83, 118–122, 125, 242
value, 8, 14–15, 24, 26–27, 31, 48, 54, 58, 78, 88, 91, 116, 122, 126–127, 137, 203, 218
Van Dyke, C., 147
Van Leeuwen, R.C., 49, 58, 83, 121, 145, 165, 180, 190–191, 193–195, 197, 199–200, 204
Vatke, J.K.W., 24–27
virtue, 28, 57, 92–98, 124, 126, 145, 148–149, 151, 153, 157, 166, 246
virtue-ethics, 57
virtuous, 125–127, 145, 154, 156
Vischer, W., 33
vision, 43, 57, 85, 137–138, 145, 147, 151, 156, 159, 177, 184, 186, 188–190, 209, 211–212, 228–229, 231, 239, 247, 249
Visotzky, B.L., 199
walking, 101, 115, 120, 122, 127, 129, 131–132, 138, 141, 144, 196, 205, 207, 225

Waltke, B.K., 13, 51, 84, 91, 115, 119–122, 129–132, 135, 138, 145, 180, 200, 202, 237
Walton, J.H., 191–192
waters, 196, 207
Watts, J.D.W., 226
way, 6, 12, 20–21, 24, 26–27, 34–37, 39, 48, 50, 54, 60, 62, 68, 73, 75, 78, 80–81, 91–96, 98, 100, 103–104, 115, 117, 122, 124, 126–127, 129, 131, 136–137, 139–140, 144–152, 154–155, 158–159, 169, 172–174, 178–179, 182–185, 187, 189, 192, 195, 201–202, 210–211, 214–219, 222, 227, 229–230, 233–234, 237–239, 243, 246, 248
wealth, 92, 113–114, 125, 178–179, 185
Weber, M., 163, 211
Weeks, S., 39–40, 50–51, 60, 63, 65–66, 68, 79, 82–84, 110, 129–132, 135, 140, 142–143, 177, 180–184, 188, 202, 236
Wehrle, J., 120–121
Weinandy, T.G., 94
Weinfeld, M., 100, 206
well-being, 15, 91, 107–108, 114, 158
Wellhausen, J., 19–20, 25
Wenham, G.J., 196
Westermann, C., 41–42, 54–56, 58, 64–66, 77, 80–81, 162, 169–172, 176, 249
de Wette, W.M.L., 25–27
Whybray, R.N., 6–7, 27–28, 39–40, 46, 49–51, 60, 66, 81, 110–111, 133, 135, 144–145, 173, 176, 178–181, 238
wicked, 90, 101, 113, 125, 129, 132, 136–137, 223
wife, 120–121, 123–124, 126, 185, 203
Wildeboer, D.G., 11, 14–16
Williams, J.G., 46
Wilson, L., 39–42, 50
Winston, D., 209
wisdom, 4–10, 12–22, 24–25, 28, 30–49, 51–69, 75, 79–80, 83, 85, 90, 92–93, 96–97, 101–103, 107–108, 110–112, 114–115, 117–119, 124–127, 129–130, 132–145, 147–151, 154, 156–157, 162, 164–168, 170–171, 174, 176–195, 197–204, 206–210, 214–215, 217–219, 221, 223–224, 227–229, 234–235, 237–241, 243–244, 248
wise, 12, 14–15, 17–18, 21–22, 34, 36, 38, 44–45, 59, 83, 90, 107, 110–116, 125, 134, 136, 142–144, 148, 150, 157–158, 168, 173, 184–185, 188–190, 192–194, 200–201, 203, 208, 212, 221, 235–239, 243, 248
witness, 75, 85
Wolff, H.W., 110, 137–138
woman, 12, 31, 54, 83, 101, 107, 111, 123, 129, 131–132, 143, 177, 181, 183, 188, 200–201, 203–204, 248
word, 11, 18, 20, 34, 41, 48, 53, 73–74, 78, 80, 91–92, 102–103, 111, 114, 120, 126, 130, 134–139, 152, 162–164, 167, 170, 175, 180, 185–187, 191, 193–194, 197, 205–208, 210, 216, 219, 229, 236–237
work, 1–2, 4–5, 9, 11–12, 16, 20–23, 25, 32–33, 36–37, 43, 46, 62–63, 69, 72–74, 78, 80–81, 83, 85, 89, 93, 100, 102, 118, 154, 164, 178, 180, 187, 195–196, 198, 204, 208, 214, 217, 221, 227–228, 233, 236, 239, 247
world, 1, 4, 16–18, 20–22, 25, 31, 34, 36–38, 44–49, 52–53, 55–57, 59–60, 63–69, 72–73, 77, 88, 92, 97, 106, 110–111, 114, 116–117, 133, 148–149, 163–170, 172, 176, 178, 182–189, 192–194, 196–197, 200–201, 206–207, 209–212, 215, 217–218, 220–221, 223–224, 231, 235, 238–239, 242–243
worldly, 13, 48, 59, 85, 97, 163, 169–170, 185, 189, 207, 212
worldview, 37–38, 40, 46, 51, 58–59, 65, 93, 107, 117, 138–139, 146–149, 157–158, 165–166, 171, 176, 241
worship, 21, 24, 47, 56, 170, 207, 210–212, 244
Wright, C.J.H., 145
Wright, G.E., 33
Wright, J.R., 154
Wurst, S., 54
Yahweh, 5, 11, 20, 31, 33–36, 38, 44–46, 48–52, 54, 56, 58, 68, 85, 90,

100–101, 105–107, 130, 133–135, 137–138, 140–142, 144, 147, 149, 162, 166–167, 172, 178–183, 186, 188, 197, 199, 201, 208, 210, 212–224, 226–228, 248
yahwehisation, 49–50, 167
Yahweh-sayings, 50
Yahwism, 166
Yahwist, 33
Yahwistic, 6, 31, 50, 76, 106, 108, 174, 176
Yee, G.A., 54, 61, 137

Yoder, C.R., 185, 237
youth, 9, 12–13, 16, 23, 38, 129
Zabán, B.K., 82, 190, 198, 201
Zechariah, 7
Zenger, E., 205–207
Zephaniah, 7, 24
Zimmerli, W., 33, 43–47, 49, 57, 61–62, 64, 92, 100, 121, 132, 135, 145, 171–172, 174, 238
Zion, 208, 228
Zöckler, O., 14, 19

Index of Scripture

Genesis
- 1   55, 179
- 1–3   65
- 1:1   197
- 1:1–2:3   199
- 1:1–2:4   195, 196
- 1:2   179, 194
- 1:28   196
- 1:31–2:3   195
- 1:31   195
- 2–3   194
- 2:2   195
- 2:4   33
- 2:9   194
- 3   208
- 3:1   194
- 3:8   196
- 4:1   180
- 22   156
- 22:12   156
- 22:16-18   156

Exodus
- 2   224
- 3   224
- 3:14   179
- 25:4   179
- 26:1   201
- 26:31   201
- 26:36   201
- 27:16   201
- 28:5   201
- 28:6   201
- 28:8   201
- 28:15   201
- 31:3   194
- 33:11   178
- 33:20   228
- 33:20-23   230
- 33:21-23   228
- 35:6   201
- 34:6-7   227–228
- 35:23   201
- 35:25   201
- 35:35   201
- 36:8   201
- 36:35   201
- 36:37   201
- 38:18   201
- 38:23   201
- 39:2   201
- 39:3   201
- 39:5   201
- 39:8   201
- 39:29   201
- 39:32–40:11   195
- 39:43   195

Leviticus
- 1:11   202
- 4:6-7   202
- 4:17   202
- 6:7   202
- 14:11-12   202
- 14:16   202
- 14:18   202
- 14:23-24   202
- 14:27   202
- 14:29   202
- 14:31   202
- 15:14-15   202
- 15:30   202
- 19:22   202
- 21:3   122
- 21:23   208
- 23:11   202
- 23:20   202
- 26:9-12   196

Numbers
- 3:4   202
- 5:16   202
- 6:16   202
- 11:16-17   178
- 12:3   224
- 15:25   202

Deuteronomy
- 1:17   103
- 1:30-31   103
- 2:5   104
- 2:7   103
- 2:9   104
- 2:19   104
- 2:31   104
- 3:22   103
- 4:1   102
- 4:5-7   178
- 4:24   102
- 4:10   143
- 4:29   178
- 4:31-38   104
- 4:39   137
- 4:40   102
- 5:9   102
- 5:9-10   102
- 5:10   178
- 5:11   102
- 5:14   104
- 5:15   102, 104
- 5:16   102, 143
- 5:29   102
- 5:29-33   102
- 5:33   102, 143
- 6–26   106
- 6:2   102–105
- 6:3   102
- 6:5   178
- 6:13   142–143
- 6:15   102

306

Index of Scripture

6:18   102, 143
6:24   102
7:4   102, 143
7:6   104
7:9   103, 137, 143, 178
7:10   102
7:12-15   102
7:18-19   104
7:25   179
7:26   102
8:1   102
8:1-5   103
8:1–9:6   105
8:5-10   137
8:19-20   102
9:3-6   137
10:13   102
10:12-13   105
10:12-20   143
10:12   142–143, 178
10:19   104
10:20   142–143
11:1   104
11:8-9   102
11:9   143
11:13   178
11:13-17   102
11:22   178
11:22-25   102
11:28   143
12:23-25   103
12:25   102
12:28   102
12:31   103, 179
13:2-3   104
13:5[4]   142–143
13:6[5]   143
13:17-18   102
14:1-2   104
14:21   104
14:23   103
14:29   102
15:4-5   102, 105, 143
15:9   104
15:10   102
15:11   104
15:15   104
15:18   102
15:23   104
16:1   104
16:3   104
16:12   104
16:15   102
16:19-20   102
16:20   102, 143
16:22   103
17:1   103, 179
17:16   104
17:19   103
17:20   103, 143
18:9-12   103
18:12   179
19:9   102, 178
19:13   102
19:17   202
20:5-8   104
20:16-18   103
20:19   104
21:14   104
21:17   104
21:22-23   103
21:23   104
22:1   107
22:5   103, 179
22:7   102, 107, 143
23:3-6   104
23:14   104
23:15-16   104
23:18   103
23:19   179
23:19-20   102
23:21-22   104
24:4   103–104
24:6   104
24:8-9   104
24:13   104
24:15   104
24:17-18   104
24:19   102
24:21-22   104
25:3   104
25:15   102, 107, 143
25:16   179
26:4   202
26:5-9   33
27–33   105
27:9-10   104
27:14-26   102
27:15   179
28:1-14   102
28:8   178
28:15-68   102
28:30   107
29:8   102–103, 105–106
29:16-28   106
29:20   102
30:5-6   102
30:9   102
30:15-16   102
30:17-18   102
30:19-20   102
30:20   102, 178
31:3-8   103
32:6   180
32:20-26   102
32:29   136–137
32:47   102, 143
33:29   130
34:5   155

Joshua
6:8   202
24:14   142

Judges
2:8   155

Ruth
2:20   122

1 Samuel
2:8   199
2:11   178
2:30   178
10:1   178
12:14   142
12:24   142
13   169
13–14   48
21:6   202
23:19   225
26:1   225

2 Samuel
- 12:23 178
- 17 221

1 Kings
- 1–11 75, 190, 204, 208
- 2:45 204
- 3 203
- 3–11 194, 202–203, 205, 209, 243
- 3:1 203
- 3:3 178
- 3:4-15 178, 203
- 3:9 107
- 3:10-14 156
- 3:12-13 203
- 3:12-14 203
- 3:13 178
- 3:13-14 115
- 4:1-19 203
- 5:7 204
- 5:9-14 203–204
- 5:15-20 204
- 5:21 204
- 5:22-25 204
- 5:23 204
- 5:26 204
- 6:5 206
- 6:31 201
- 7:14 194, 203
- 7:40 195
- 8:2 196
- 8:31-32 196
- 8:33-34 196
- 8:35-37 196
- 8:37-40 196
- 8:41-43 196
- 8:44-45 196
- 8:46-53 196
- 8:62-66 199
- 9:24 203
- 10:1-13 203
- 10:8 178, 203
- 10:9 178, 204
- 11:1-13 203
- 22:34-36 224

2 Kings
- 6:8-23 228, 230
- 6:16-17 228
- 6:17 228

1 Chronicles
- 29:12 178

2 Chronicles
- 1:12 178
- 17:5 178
- 35:23 197

Nehemiah
- 1:11 142
- 2:1-8 224
- 9:13 179
- 13:26 178

Job
- 1:1 156
- 1:8 142
- 1:9 156
- 2:3 142
- 5:12 130
- 6:13 130
- 8:5 179
- 9:6 199
- 11:6 130
- 15:6-7 194
- 26:3 130
- 26:11 199
- 28 177, 182
- 28:25 216
- 42:12-17 156

Psalms
- 1 206
- 2:7 178
- 3:4 130
- 14 205–206
- 14:4 205
- 15 205–207
- 15–24 208
- 15:1 205
- 15:2 205
- 15:3 206
- 15:4 206
- 15:5 206
- 18 58
- 18:1 155
- 19 31, 206
- 19:9 179
- 24 207
- 24:1-2 207
- 24:3-6 207
- 25 206
- 29 197
- 32 206
- 33 206
- 33:4 206
- 34 206
- 36 206
- 37 206
- 39 206
- 49 206
- 51 206
- 53 206
- 54 225
- 62 206
- 63:2[1] 179
- 73 206, 208
- 73:17 137, 208
- 75:3 199, 216
- 78 206
- 78:69 197
- 84:11-12 [10-11] 208
- 90 206
- 92 206
- 92:6-7 137
- 92:13-14[12-13] 196, 208
- 93:2 179
- 94 206
- 97:10 178
- 104 31, 179, 196–197, 206
- 104:2 196
- 104:3 196
- 104:5 196
- 104:9 196
- 104:16 196
- 104:24 180, 194
- 105 206
- 106 206
- 111 144–145, 206
- 111–112 144
- 111:3 144

Index of Scripture

111:4   144
111:5   144
111:7   144
111:8   144
111:10   144
112   144–145, 206
112:1   144
112:3   144
112:4   144
112:5   144
112:6   144
112:8   144
112:9   144
119   206
119:38   142
119:137   179
127   206
128   206
133   208
136:5   194
139:13   180
145:20   178
148:14   122

Proverbs
1   46, 82
1–9   11, 14, 20, 53, 55, 60, 72, 75, 78–79, 81–85, 106, 117, 129, 135, 142–143, 145, 177–178, 180–184, 190, 200, 236, 240
1:1   203
1:2   111, 134
1:3   108, 131, 136
1:4   135, 194
1:5   111, 137, 236–237
1:6   111
1:7   103, 111, 135, 142, 237
1:8-19   208
1:10-19   139
1:10-33   137
1:10–2:5   130
1:11   130
1:11-14   235
1:13   130
1:13-14   124
1:18   130
1:20   111
1:20-21   235
1:20-25   142
1:20-33   142, 183, 248
1:22   150, 205
1:25   238
1:26-27   101
1:28   130, 235
1:29   143
1:30   238
1:32   101
1:33   111, 142, 143
2   2, 129, 132, 138–139, 143–149, 151, 156, 186, 243
2:1   129, 130, 132
2:1-2   143
2:1-4   133–135
2:1-5   132
2:1-11   133
2:2   111, 129, 132
2:3   130
2:3-4   132–133
2:3-5   235
2:4   130
2:5   103, 111, 129–130, 132–137, 139–142, 145, 147, 154
2:5-6   133, 138
2:5-8   133–134, 138, 147
2:6   111, 130, 132–134, 184, 222–223
2:6-8   101, 133, 138, 144
2:6-9   132
2:7   130, 133
2:7-8   101, 111, 130, 132–133
2:8   130, 140, 144
2:9   104, 108, 131–137, 139–141, 144, 147
2:9-10   134
2:9-11   133–134, 138, 147
2:10   101, 111, 131–132, 134
2:10-11   132–133, 144
2:11   111, 131–133
2:11-12   101
2:12   131, 205
2:12-15   132
2:12-22   133
2:13   131
2:14   131
2:15   131
2:16   131, 203
2:16-19   132
2:17   131
2:18   131
2:18-19   101
2:19   131
2:20   131–132
2:21   18, 132
2:21-22   101, 132, 143
2:22   132, 208
3:1-12   50
3:2   101, 203
3:3   145
3:5   103, 139, 147, 149–150, 235
3:5-6   64
3:5-8   124
3:6   139
3:7   111, 150, 235

3:7-8 173	5:20 203	8:12 112, 135, 194, 200
3:8 111	5:21 101, 222, 223	
3:10 101		8:13 141, 150, 205, 237
3:12 101, 222	5:22-23 101	
3:13 111, 235	6:1-5 111	8:14 130, 134
3:13-18 101	6:1-19 83, 183	8:14-16 185
3:14 118, 122	6:2 111	8:15-16 103, 107, 178, 199
3:15 203	6:4 184	
3:16 111, 115, 203	6:6 111	8:15-21 203
	6:8 111	8:17 178, 182, 184, 235
3:18 101, 194	6:11 101	
3:19 111, 200, 222	6:12 111, 205	8:18 112, 115, 203
	6:15 101	
3:19-20 194, 200, 203	6:16 103, 222	8:18-21 101, 178, 185
	6:24 203	
3:21 101	6:26 101	8:19 118, 122
3:21-26 124, 139, 149	6:27-29 101	8:20 108, 182, 204
	6:32-35 101	
3:22 111	6:33 115, 205	8:21 200
3:23 101	6:35 206	8:22 8, 180, 182, 187
3:23-26 111	7:1-27 111	
3:26 101, 222	7:4 111	8:22-26 199
3:27-31 108	7:5 111, 203	8:22-29 179
3:29 205	7:26-27 101	8:22-31 179, 183, 187
3:32 101, 103, 179	7:27 203	
	8 9, 13, 19, 36, 46, 54, 65, 75, 89, 177, 179–180, 182–184, 186–188, 193, 199–201, 209–210, 212, 240, 242–243	8:22-32 53
3:33 108, 222		8:24-25 180
3:34 150, 205, 237		8:27 182–183
		8:27-29 199
3:35 111, 115, 205		8:30 179–180, 183, 193, 199, 202
4:1-8 235		
4:5 111		8:30-31 183
4:6 101, 111, 184		8:31 183
		8:33 112, 114
4:7 111	8-9 199, 202	8:33-34 101
4:8 111	8:1 111, 200	8:34 201, 203
4:10 101, 111	8:1-2 235	8:35 85, 101, 182, 235
4:11 111	8:2 111, 182	
4:12 111	8:2-3 183	8:35-36 112, 178
4:13 101, 111	8:3 182	
4:22 101	8:6-9 179, 193	8:36 101
4:23 101	8:7 179	9 84, 183, 199–200, 203, 235
4:24 111, 205	8:9 182, 200, 235	
5:1 111		9:1 112, 114, 193, 198–202
5:2-6 111	8:10 179, 200	
5:4-6 101	8:10-11 179	9:1-6 199, 235
5:8 203	8:11 118, 122, 179, 200	9:3 201
5:9-11 101		9:6 112
5:15-20 185		9:7 115, 205

Index of Scripture

9:7-8   150
9:7-9   237
9:7-12   199
9:8   112
9:9   112, 236
9:10   64, 103, 112, 129, 134–135, 142, 149, 224, 237
9:12   112
9:14   201, 203
9:17   83, 139
9:18   83, 101
10–29   89, 93
10–31   55, 60, 83–84, 177, 184, 188
10:1   83–84, 112, 203–204
10:1–22:16 50, 75, 78, 110, 117, 203
10:2   83, 90, 108
10:3   90, 108, 222–223
10:5   115
10:6   90, 108
10:7   90, 108, 125
10:8   90, 112, 205, 236–237
10:9   90
10:10   90, 205
10:11   108, 205
10:13   112, 205
10:14   112, 114, 205
10:16   108
10:17   90, 236
10:18   205
10:19   205
10:20   108, 205
10:21   90, 108, 205
10:22   58, 90, 222
10:23   112
10:24   90, 108
10:25   90, 108, 208
10:27   90, 104, 208
10:28   90, 108
10:29   90, 205
10:30   90, 108, 206
10:31   90, 112, 205
10:32   205
11:1   179
11:2   90, 112, 205
11:3   90
11:4   90, 108
11:5   90, 108
11:6   90
11:8   90, 108, 125
11:9   90, 205
11:10   90, 108
11:11   205
11:12   205
11:13   205
11:17   90, 120
11:18   108
11:19   90
11:20   90, 179
11:21   90
11:23   90, 108
11:26   90
11:27   90
11:28   90
11:29   90, 112
11:30   90, 112, 194
11:31   90, 108
12:1   236
12:2   51, 222
12:3   51, 90, 108, 206
12:4   185
12:5   108
12:6   90, 205
12:7   90, 108
12:8   90
12:9   90, 118, 122–126
12:10   104, 108
12:12   90, 108
12:13   90, 205
12:14   90, 205
12:15   112, 238
12:16   115, 194, 205
12:17   85, 205
12:18   108, 112, 205
12:19   205
12:20   90
12:21   90
12:22   103, 179, 205
12:23   205
12:24   90
12:25   204–205
12:26   90
12:28   90
13:1   112, 150, 236–237
13:2   90, 205
13:3   90, 205
13:4   90
13:5   205
13:6   90
13:8   115
13:9   90, 208
13:10   112, 238
13:12   194
13:13   90
13:14   90, 112
13:15   90
13:17   90
13:18   90, 205, 236
13:20   112
13:21   90
13:22   90
13:25   90
14:1   90, 112, 200
14:2   141–142, 150, 206
14:3   90, 112, 114, 205
14:5   85, 205
14:6   112, 150, 205, 237
14:8   112

14:11 90	15:25 90, 222–223	16:31 90
14:12 64	15:26 90, 179, 205	16:32 119, 122
14:14 90	15:27 90	16:33 103
14:16 112	15:28 205	17:1 119, 122, 124–126
14:17 90	15:29 90, 108, 222–223	17:2 90
14:19 90	15:31 90, 112	17:3 90, 104, 222–223
14:21 104, 108	15:32 90, 236	17:4 205
14:22 90	15:32-33 206	17:5 55, 90
14:23 205	15:33 103, 112, 115, 125, 142, 206, 237	17:7 205
14:24 112, 115	16:1 205, 216	17:11 90
14:25 85, 205	16:1-2 215, 221–222	17:13 90
14:26 90, 124	16:1-9 64, 248	17:15 90, 179, 205
14:27 90, 104, 178	16:2 90, 104, 216, 222–223	17:16 113
14:31 55	16:4 104, 222	17:19 90
14:32 90, 130, 208	16:5 90, 150, 179	17:20 90, 205
14:33 112	16:6 141, 145	17:24 113
14:35 90	16:7 126, 222	17:27 205
15:1 205	16:7-8 126	17:28 113, 205
15:2 108, 112, 205	16:8 108, 119, 122, 124–126	18:3 115, 205
15:3 90, 222–223	16:9 215–216, 221–222	18:4 113, 205
15:4 194, 205	16:10 107	18:6 90, 205
15:5 236	16:11 90	18:7 90, 205
15:6 90	16:12 103, 204	18:8 205
15:7 108, 112, 205	16:13 205	18:10 90, 108
15:8 90, 103	16:14 90, 112	18:12 90, 115, 125, 150
15:8-9 179	16:16 112, 119, 122, 125	18:13 90, 205
15:9 90, 108, 222	16:16-19 125	18:15 113, 236
15:9-11 58	16:17 90	18:20 90, 205
15:10 90, 236	16:18 90	18:21 90, 205
15:11 90	16:18-19 150	18:22 185
15:12 112, 150, 237	16:19 119, 122–125	19:1 120, 122, 124–125, 205
15:14 205	16:20 90, 103, 149	19:2 90
15:16 119, 122, 124, 126	16:21 90, 113	19:3 90
15:17 119, 122, 124, 126	16:22 90, 236	19:5 85, 90, 205
15:19 90	16:23 113, 205	19:8 90
15:20 112, 204, 206	16:24 102, 205	19:9 85, 90, 205
15:22 238	16:27 205	19:14 185, 215–216, 221–222
15:23 205		19:15 90
15:24 90		19:16 90, 206
		19:17 90, 222
		19:18-23 50
		19:20 113, 236, 238

19:21   215–216, 221–222
19:22   120, 122, 205
19:23   90, 104
19:25   237
19:27   90, 236
19:28   85, 205
19:29   90, 150, 205
20:1   113
20:3   115
20:4   90
20:5   90
20:7   90
20:8   107
20:10   103, 179
20:12   222
20:13   90
20:15   205
20:17   90, 205
20:19   205
20:20   90
20:21   90
20:22   58, 222
20:23   179
20:24   215–216, 221–222
20:26   90, 107, 113
21 50
21:1   222
21:2   90, 222–223
21:3   90, 104, 108
21:5   90, 108
21:6   90, 205
21:7   90
21:9   120, 123–124, 126
21:11   113, 237
21:15   205
21:16   90
21:17   90
21:18   90
21:19   120–124, 126
21:20   90, 113, 115
21:21   90
21:22   90, 113
21:23   90, 205
21:24   150, 205, 237
21:25   90
21:28   85, 90
21:30   113
21:30-31   215–216, 221
22 50
22:1   121–122
22:2   55, 222
22:3   90
22:4   90, 115, 125, 203, 237
22:5   90
22:8   90
22:9   90
22:10   205
22:11   90, 204
22:12   90, 222–223
22:16   90
22:17   113
22:17–24:22   73
22:19   103, 139, 149
22:22-23   90
22:23   101, 222
22:24-25   90
22:25   101
22:26   111
23:3   101
23:5   101
23:8   101
23:9   101
23:10-11   58, 90
23:11   101
23:12   236
23:15   113
23:17   141
23:17-18   103, 149
23:19   113
23:20-21   90
23:21   101
23:23   113
23:24   113
23:27   203
23:27-28   111
23:27-35   101
23:29-35   90, 111
24 237
24:2   205
24:3   113
24:3-4   90, 200, 203
24:5   113
24:5-6   90
24:6   238
24:7   113, 205
24:8-9   90
24:11-12   58, 90
24:12   101
24:13-14   90
24:14   113, 235
24:15-16   90
24:16   101
24:17-18   58, 101
24:18   222–223
24:19-20   90
24:20   101, 208
24:21-22   90
24:23   113
24:23-24   108
24:23-34   73
24:24   90
24:25   90
24:28   85, 205
24:30-34   90
25–29   50, 73, 110–111, 117
25:1   85, 203
25:2   115
25:5   204
25:7   121–122, 125
25:10   90
25:11   205
25:12   113, 205
25:15   205
25:20   15, 205
25:21-22   58, 90
25:22   222
25:23   205
25:24   121–124, 126

25:27 115	29:6 90	26:9 179
26:1 115	29:8 113–114, 205	28:29 130
26:2 173	29:9 104, 113	32:3-4 136
26:4 205	29:11 113	40–66 24, 228
26:5 113, 205	29:13 222	40:12 216
26:12 113, 235	29:14 90, 204	45:14 225
26:16 113	29:15 113, 115–116	45:14-19 226
26:17 90	29:16 90	45:15 215, 225–227, 229, 231
26:22 205	29:20 205	45:16 225
26:23 15, 205	29:23 125	45:17 225
26:24 205	29:24 90	45:18 225
26:24-26 90	29:25 90, 103, 149	45:19 179, 225–226
26:25 205	29:26 58, 103	48:14 178
26:27 90	29:27 90	54:8 226
26:28 205	30:1-9 237	56:1-2 178
27:1 235	30:1-14 73	57:15 124
27:2 90	30:3 111, 113, 129	59:2 226
27:5 121–124	30:5 130–131	60 197
27:6 15	30:7-9 170	64:6[7] 226
27:10 15, 122–124	30:14 104	66:1-2 197
27:11 113, 116	30:20 205	
27:12 90, 194	30:24 114	Jeremiah
27:14 15	30:25-28 114	9:12 136
27:17 15	30:26 114	10:12 194
27:20 169	30:15–31:9 73	21:8 178
28:1 125	31 83	22:15-16 140
28:2 90	31:5 104	22:16 137
28:5 64, 90	31:8-9 104	33:18 202
28:6 120, 122, 124–125	31:10 235	38:16 178
28:8 90, 206	31:10-31 73, 185, 248	51:15 194
28:9 50	31:11 115	51:51 208
28:10 90	31:14-15 204	
28:11 113, 235	31:15 200	Ezekiel
28:14 90	31:21 200	28 194
28:16 90, 203	31:21-22 201	28:12-15 194
28:18 90, 205	31:27 200, 204	43:24 202
28:20 90, 115		44:15 202
28:21 108	Song of Songs	46:2-3 201
28:22 90	3 182	
28:25 90		Hosea
28:25-26 103, 124, 149–150	Isaiah	1–3 138
28:26 90, 113, 139	5:12-13 137	2:10 137–138
28:27 90	5:17 155	2:22 137
29:1 90	6:9-10 136	4:1-2 140
29:3 113	11 76	4:1 137–138
29:4 107		4:6 137–138
		5:4 137
		5:6 178

Index of Scripture

5:15   179
6:1-3   140
6:3   137
6:6   137
6:6-7   138
8:1-2   137
8:1-3   138
8:1-6   137
8:2   137–138
10:12   137–138
11:1-4   137
11:1-11   138
11:3   137–138
13:4   137–138
13:4-8   137

Amos
 5:4-6   178

Habakkuk
 1:12   179

Malachi
 1:6   142
 2:13-16   138

6:13   142

Sirach
 19:13-17   121
 24   178, 209

Wisdom of Solomon
 7:21   199
 8:6   199

Matthew
 5:3   155
 5:4   155
 5:5   155
 5:6   155
 5:7   155
 5:10   155
 5:12   155
 5:19   155
 5:22   155
 5:25   155
 5:29-30   155
 5:46   155
 6:1   155
 6:4   155

6:6   155
6:14-15   155
6:18   155
6:19-34   155
6:33   155
7:1-2   155
7:7-12   155
7:21   155

Acts
 17:27   18

Romans
 1:19   18

Philippians
 2   155–156
 2–3   156
 2:9-11   156
 3   155
 3:21   156

Colossians
 2:8   18

www.ingramcontent.com/pod-product-compliance
Lightning Source LLC
Chambersburg PA
CBHW030304080526
44584CB00012B/433